GW00535802

YANTRA MAHIMA

॥ श्री गणेशाय: नम: ॥

YANTRA MAHIMA

(A BOOK BASED ON CLASSICS)

"YANTRAS" AS MENTIONED IN THE TANTRAS, AND OTHER CLASSICS

1. If any person on the basis of yantras as provided in this book commits any nefarious acts which causes loss etc. to anybody, then for his actions the authors (compilers), printer and publisher will not be responsible in any way whatsoever.

2. The yantras as provided in this book if are tried by any body and not crowned with success, which entirely depends on practitioner, the authors (compilers), printer and publisher will not be responsible in any way for such failures.

3. The Yantra be practised and used for the help, good cause and service of mankind. These should not be used for any nefarious means, the responsibility of such actions will be only that of the practitioner.

4. The prayoga (use) should be handled only by those who possess the deserving qualifications and after getting instructions from the preceptors of the related field.

5. By the use of the yantras provided in this book one is addressing the personification of energy of God, who controls all aspects of life. The combination of the sound vibration of the mantra and the visual Vibration of yantra will immediately communicate your most heartfelt to the universal energy source. One's desire will automatically be heard if one is sincere in his belief in this process, then ones desire will be granted.

6. Please note, however, that since the personification of the energy of the Absolute is Good and will never be granted a wish that would be bad for you. Sometimes the human beings don't know what is best for us, so do not feel too bad or disheartened if one does not get his /her every wish. Must trust in HIM or the Higher Powers, keep reciting the mantras as directed which will be rewarding with greatest happiness.

YANTRA MAHIMA

(A BOOK BASED ON CLASSICS)

COMPILED BY

Dr. M.H.K. SHASTRI, VEDANG VIDVAT
M.A. (SANSKRIT), AACHAARYA (PURAN), PH.D.

Pt. LAXMI KANT VASHISTH, JYOTISH SHREE
TRANSLATOR AUTHOR LAL KITAB, LAL KITAB GUTKA (HINDI), MANTRA MAHIMA,
REMIDIAL MANTRAS

SAGAR PUBLICATIONS
72, JANPATH, VED MANSION
NEW DELHI-110 001
TELEPHONE No. (91) 011-23320648, 23328245
e-mail:sagarpub@del3.vsnl.net.in

PUBLISHER

SAGAR PUBLICATIONS
72, Janapth, Ved Mansion
New Delhi- 110 001
Tel: (91) 011-23320648, 23328245
E-mail:sagarpub@del3.vsnl.net.in

First edition - January 13, 2006 (Lohri)

ISBN - 81-7082-061-8
Published by Saurabh Sagar for:-
SAGAR PUBLICATIONS
72, Janapth, Ved Mansion
New Delhi- 110 001
Tel: (91) 011-23320648, 23328245
email:sagarpub@del3.vsnl.net.in

Printed at:
The Artwaves, Y-56 Okhla Industrial Area,
Phase-II, New Delhi- 110 020
Tel.: 51609709 E-mail: theartwaves@rediffmail.com

In the 27th sholaka, ninth chapter of Shrimadbhagwad Gita, Lord Krishna said :-

यत्करोषि यदश्नासि यज्जुहोषि ददासियत् ।
यत्तपस्यसि कौन्तेय तत्कुरुष्व मदर्पणम् ॥

yatkarosi yadasnasi yajjuhosi dadasiyat ।
yattapasyasi kaunteya tatkurusva madarpanam ॥

O son of Kunti, all that you do, all that you eat, all that you offer and give away, as well as all austerities that you may perform, should be done as an offering unto Me.

As Lord Krishna recommends we are dedicating our work to the Supreme Lord, the great saints and the scholars who did their research in the field of yantra, mantra and tantra.

Vashisth-Shastri

ACKNOWLEDGMENTS

We are indebted to Shri Harsh Kant Vashisth for his help and assistance provided in bringing out this book. We would like to place on record our sincere thanks to Shri A. S. Sharma and Dr. H.C.Sharma for guiding us to accuracy and update the knowledge and certain facts related to the project in hand. Sh.Mukesh Dagar and Sh.Dinesh Kumar Phalaswal provided timely administrative support in the completion of this work. We would also like to take this opportunity to convey our thanks to our wives Smt. Qasar Bano and Smt. Preeti Sharma who quietly and patiently bore all the inconvenience that our preoccupation with this work caused them.

This acknowledgement would have been incomplete without Sh. P.K.Vasudev (author of books on astrology) and Sh. S.K. Duggal, Chairman, ICAS (Chandigarh-chapter) for reviewing and giving valuable suggestions. We are also thankful to Sh. Saurabh Sagar, the publisher of the book who extended total support and co-operation without which this work would not have been possible.

We would like to place on records the help made by Sh. Rajeev Sarup and Sh. Umesh Sharma (astrology point) in providing us the old classics which were of immense help to us in completion of project in hand. Sh. Narender Sagar, propriter Sagar Publications, extended full co-operation with new ideas which helped in designing the book in the present context.

SHASTRI - VASHISTH

PRONUNCIATION OF SANSKRIT ALPHABETS

Vowels:

(1) Simple vovels	अ a,	आ ä,	इ i	ई é,	
	उ u,	ऊ ü,			
(2) Diphthongs	ए å	ऐ è	ओ au		
	औ auo				

Consonants:

(1) Gutturals	क ka	ख kha	ग ga	घ gha	
	ञ ña				
(2) Palatals	च ca	छ cha	ज ja	झ jha	
	ण ña				
(3) Cerebrals	öa	öha	òa	òha	ëa
(4) Dental	त ta	थ tha	ड da	ढ dha	
	न na				
(5) Labial	प pa	फ pha	ब ba	भ bha	
	म ma				
(6) Semivowals	य ya	र ra	ल la	व va	
(7) Spirants	क्ष ça	स sa			
(8) Aspirate	ह ha				
(9) Visarge	ह h				
(10) Anusvãra	म m				

GLOSSARY

Zodiac (Raashi)

	Indian name	Western name	Rashi Lord
1.	Mesha	Aries	Mars
2.	Varishbha	Taurus	Venus
3.	Mithuna	Gemini	Mercury
4.	Karak	Cancer	Moon
5.	Simha	Leo	Sun
6.	Kanya	Virgo	Mercury
7.	Tula	Libra	Venus
8.	Varischak	Scorpio	Mars
9.	Dhanu	Sagittarius	Jupiter
10.	Makar	Capricorn	Saturn
11.	Kumbh	Aquarius	Saturn
12.	Meena	Pisces	Jupiter

Month and zodiac

	Zodiac	Indian month	Equivalent georgian calendar
1.	Aries	Vaisakha	13th April-14th May
2.	Taurus	Jestha	15th May-14th June
3.	Gemini	Asar	15th June-14th July
4.	Cancer	Sarvana	15th July-14th August
5.	Leo	Bhadra	15th August-14th September
6.	Virgo	Aswij	15th September-14th October
7.	Libra	Kartik	15th October- 14th November
8.	Scorpio	Maghsar	15th November- 14th December
9.	Sagittarius	Pause	15th December- 13th January
10.	Capricorn	Magh	14th January-12th February

11.	Aquarius	Phagun	13th February-12th March
12.	Pisces	Chitra	13th March-12th April

Asterism (Nakshatra)

	Name of	Western name Nakshatra	Ruler of Nakshatra
1.	Aswini	Artictic	Ketu
2.	Bharni	Triangalara	Venus
3.	Krittika	Pleiades	Sun
4.	Rohini	Aldebran	Moon
5.	Mrigshira	Orionis	Mars
6.	Aridra	Betelgeuse	Rahu
7.	Punarvasu	Pollux	Jupiter
8.	Pushyami	Caneri	Saturn
9.	Aslesha	Hydrae	Mercury
10.	Magha	Regulas	Ketu
11.	Poorva Phalguni	Zosma	Venus
12.	Uttraphalguni	Denebala	Sun
13.	Hast	Corvi	Moon
14.	Chitra	Spica	Mars
15.	Swati	Arcturus	Rahu
16.	Vaisakha	Librae	Jupiter
17.	Anuradha	Scorpius	Saturn
18.	Jyestha	Antares	Mercury
19.	Moola	Shaula	Ketu
20.	Poorva Shada	Kaus-Aust	Venus
21.	Uttra shada	Nunki	Sun
22.	Sarvana	Aquila	Moon
23.	Dhanishta	Delphinus	Mars
24.	Satbhisha	Aquari	Rahu
25.	Poorva Bhadra	Pegasi	Jupiter
26.	Uttra Bhadra	Pegasi	Saturn
27.	Rewati	Piscium	Mercury

Gems

	Planet	Gem	Hindi name
1.	Sun	Ruby	Manik
2.	Moon	Pearl	Moti
3.	Mars	Coral	Moonga
4.	Mercury	Emerald	Panna
5.	Jupiter	Topaz	Pukhraz
6.	Venus	Diamond	Hira
7.	Saturn	Blue Sapphire	Neelam
8.	Rahu	Hessonite	Gomed
9.	Ketu	Cat's eye	Lahasunya

Tithis

The *tithi* is the distance between the Moon and the Sun. It is the phase of Moon and is called Lunar day. Moon completes the circle round the earth i.e., the zodiac in 27 days time, as Moon remains in one sign for 2¼ days. The changes or phases are the results of the changing positions of Moon and earth in relation to Sun. There are two phases of Moon, one from dark Moon (*Amavasya*) to full Moon (*Poornima*) and these periods are known as *Krishna paksha* and *Shukla Paksha* respectively. Each period comprises of 14 tihtis besides *Amasavya* and *Poornima*. The *tithis* are as under:-

- ♣ Pratipada — First day (after *Amavasya/Poornima*)
- ♣ Dvitya — Second day (after *Amavasya/Poornima*)
- ♣ Tritya — Third day (after *Amavasya/Poornima*)
- ♣ Chaturdashi — Fourth day (after *Amavasya/Poornima*)
- ♣ Panchmi — Fifth day (after *Amavasya/Poornima*)
- ♣ Shashti — Sixth day (after *Amavasya/Poornima*)
- ♣ Saptmi — Seventh day (after *Amavasya/Poornima*)
- ♣ Ashtmi — Eighth day (after *Amavasya/Poornima*)
- ♣ Navmi — Ninth day (after *Amavasya/Poornima*)
- ♣ Dashmi — Tenth day (after *Amavasya/Poornima*)
- ♣ Ekadashi — Eleventh day (after *Amavasya/Poornima*)
- ♣ Dwadshi — Twelfth day (after *Amavasya/Poornima*)

♣ Tryodashi	Thirteenth day (after *Amavasya/Poornima*)
♣ Chaturdashi	Fourteenth (after *Amavasya/Poornima*)
♣ Fifteenth day	*Amavasya/Poornima*

Steps during the pooja

1.**Dhyaanam:-**	Think or meditate on the deity
2.**Aawaahanam:-**	Offering invitation to the deity
3.**Aasanam:-**	Seat to the deity
4.**Paadyam:-**	Water to wash the feet
5.**Arghyam:-**	Water to wash the hands
6.**Aachamaneeyam:-**	Water to drink
7.**Snaanam:-**	Bath to the deity
8.**Maha Abhishekam:-**	Main head bath
9.**Pratishtaapayaami:-**	Make him seated
10.**Vasthram:-**	Clothes to the deity
11.**Yajnopaveetham:-**	The Holy Thread to the deity
12.**Gandham:-**	Sandalwood paste/powder
13. **Akshatham:-**	Akshatha to the deity (Akshatha is uncooked rice, if possible coloured with *kumkum* , saffron powder, turmeric and a little bit of water. Can be prepared well in advance for a week and kept near the altar).
14.**Pushpam:-**	Flowers to the deity
15.**Ashthothtra Poojam:-**	Holy 108 names of the deity
16.**Dhoopam Aaghraapayaami:-**	Incensed stick
17.**DeepamDarshayaami:-**	Light
18.**Neivedyam:-**	Food to the deity
19.**Phalam:-**	Fruits the deity
20.**Taamboolam:-**	Beetle nut and leaves
21.**Dakshinam:-**	Money to the deity
22.**Prayer:-**	The main aarati
23. **Pradakshinam:-**	Taking clockwise rounds in front of the deity

24.**Namaskaram:-** Prostrations offer them
25.**Mantra Pushpam:-** Both incantations and flowers
26.**Praarthanaam:-** Offering prayers
27. **Xamaapanam:-** Apologies to deity for any mistakes

Gorochan: It is a yellow (characteristic colour in animal tissue) pigment (a scented liquid) available from the forehead of the cow progeny above 15/16 years. It is generated through the horns biodynamics under the conditions when they die natural death.It may be noted here that there is no substitute for gorochan either synthetic or from any other source.

Name of herbs/shrubs used in the book and their English / botanical equivalent

	Herbs/ Shrubs	**English name**	**Botanical name**
1.	Aak	Madar	Calotropis gigantean
2.	Adusa	————	Justicea Adhatoda
3.	Agar	Aloe wood	Aquillaria malaccencis
4.	Alsi	Linseed	Linum usitatissimum
5.	Alta	Red Lac	Morinda pubescens
6.	Anaar	Pomegranate	Punica granatum
7.	Ark	Akund swallow wart	Calotropis Procera
8.	Ashok	Mast tree	Saraca indica
9.	Baans	Bamboo	Arundinaria
10.	Badaam	Indian Almond	Terminalia catappa
11.	Baheda	Belleric Myrobalan	Terminalia Bellirica
12.	Bakula/Mollsiri	Spanish cherry	Mimusops elengi
13.	Banslochan	Thorny bamboo	Bambusa arundinacea
14.	Bar	Banyan	Ficus benghalensis
15.	Bel (Bilva)	Bael fruit (wood apple)	Aegle marmelos
16.	Ber	Indian jujube	Zizyphus mauritiana
17.	Bhang	Indian hemp	Cannabis
18.	Bhojpatra	Indian birch	Betula alnoides
19.	Caru (nilkanth)	Indian gentian root	Gentiana kurroo
20.	Chameli	Jasmine	Jasminum arborescens

21.	Champa	Champak	Michelia champaca
22.	Chandan (lal)	Red Sanders	Daphniphyllum himalayense
23.	Chandan (white)	Sandal	Santalum album
24.	Devdaroo	Mast tree	Saraca indica
25.	Dhatura	Thorn apple	Datura
26.	Dhoop	Black dammer gum	Dendranthema mutellina
27.	Durva	Bermuda grass	Cynodon dactylon
28.	Gandh (kapur kachri)	Spiked ginger lily	Hedychium spicatum
29.	Giloy	Gulancha tinospora	Tinospora sinensis
30.	Guduci	Gulanche Tinospora	Tinospora Sinensis
31.	Gugal Dhoop	Alston	Ailanthus triphysa
32.	Guggal	Bdellium	Commpihora wightii
33.	Gular	Cluster fig	Ficus racemose
34.	Haldi/Haridara	Turmeric	Curcuma longa
35.	Haritala	Yellow orpiment	Cascabella thevetia
36.	Illaaichi	Lesser cardamom	Elettaria cardamomum
37.	Indrayan	Bitter apple	Citrullus lanatus
38.	Jata mansi	Indian Nard	Nardostachys jatamansi
39.	Joo	Barley	Hordeum vulgare
40.	Juhi	Jasmine	Jasminum auriculatum
41.	Kadamba	Kadam	Anthocephalus chinensis
42.	Kamal	Indian Lotus	Nelumbo Nucifera
43.	Kaneer	Indian oleander	Nerium indicum
44.	Kapur	Camphor	Cinnamomum camphora
45.	Karavir	Indian oleander	Nerium indicum
46.	Keekar	Babul	Acacia nilotica
47.	Kesar	Saffron/Crocus	Crocus sativus
48.	Khadir	Cutch tree	Acacia catechu
49.	Khair/Kattha	Red cutch	Acacia chundra
50.	Khas khas	Poppy seeds	Papaver

51.	Kimsuka	Flame of the forest	Butea superba
52.	Kusha	Long Grass	Desmostachya bipinnata
53.	Kusth	Kuth/costus	Saussurea costus
54.	Kusum	Lac tree	Schleichera oleosa
55.	Latjira	Prickly chaff flower	Achyranthes aspera
56.	Lobhaan	Benzoin	Styrax benzoin
57.	Mahua	Butter tree	Madhuca longifolia
58.	Mehndi	Henna	Lawsonia inermis
59.	Mushak/kasturi	Musk Mallow/ambrette	Abelmoschus moschatus
60.	Naariyal	Coconut	Cocos nucifera
61.	Nag-Keesar	Alexandrian laurel	Mammea longifolia
62.	Neem	Margosa	Azadirachta indica
63.	Paan	Betel leaves	Piper betle
64.	Palas lata	Fragrant oleander	Butea suberba
65.	Palas	Bengal Kino	Butea monosperma
66.	Peepal	Bo tree	Ficus religiosa
67.	Rai	Black mustard	Brassica nigra
68.	Rudraksh	Bastard cedar	Guazuma ulmifolia
69.	Sarpgandha	Rauwolfia	Rauvolfia
70.	Sarsoon (black)	Black Mustard	Brassica napus
71.	Sarsoon (yellow)	Indian colza	Brassica campertris
72.	Sauf	Anise	Pimpinella anisum
73.	Sawa	Little Millet	Panicum sumatrense
74.	Shami	Cineraria	Prosopsis cineraria
75.	Shataver	Wild bean	Asparagus racemosus
76.	Sudhavalli	Gulanche Tinospora	Tinospora Sinensis
77.	Supari	Areca nut	Areca catechu
78.	Tagar	Indian valerian	Valeriana jatamansi
79.	Talpatra	Birch of Palmyra palm	Borassus flabellifer
80.	Til	Sesame/gingelly	Sesamum orientale
81.	Tulsi	Holy Basil	Ocimum sanctum
82.	Udumbar	Cluster fig	Ficus racemose
83.	Van-Mallika	Wild Jasmine	Jasminum angustifolium

Contents

FOREWORD

In our Hindu legacy there are two types of techniques emancipated by great preachers called *Munis* to energise and activate the inherent symbiotic energy of consciousness. We may term the synchronised energy of consciousness as *manas*. *Manas* is base of physical, vital and conscious expressions. It is not an extension only but is a means to achieve the goal par excellence.

The first technique was *Shraut yajnas* restricted for some erudite class of the society of India and the second one was open to general human beings of the world which was know as ***Tantra***. A common perception about the term tantra is that there are mysterious performances and activities performed by some superstitiously influenced people throughout the world. Those who are elementary in their thoughts and life styles go to *tantric* performances and do some avoidable activities etc. However, if one goes through the scriptures and finds any actual performer that is *Sadhak* can easily review his false perceptions about tantra.

Tantra is well thought, well atriculated technique to strengthen *manas* as well as physical and celestial body and experiences some super natural activities in the world. It has many branches first revealed by supreme *guru* Shiva and adopted by generations of traditional *sadhaks*. Shiva has five or seven heads, from each head one branch of tantric tradition flourished.

The authors of the book have tried their best efforts to collate every traditional way of tantric *sadhana* and depicted it lucidly. As I have gone through, the book is useful for devotees of any sect of traditional *samart* sadhana. The authors have compiled some least known *Yantras* and its usage. As we know, Yantra is accepted as abode of the respective deity. These are not merely geometric projections neither these are mysterious expressions of lines. Each and every line has its own relevance. The drawing techniques are traditionally designed and I can say that the authors has followed those traditionally accepted manners describing *Yantras*. I shower my best wishes to them and hope for the time they will be enlightening us more by precious research work like **Yantra Mahima.**

(Dr. Prakash Pandey)
M.A. (Vedas), Acharya (Yog Tantra)
Vidya Varidhi (Ph.D), Tantra,
Author of Seven original books in Sanskrit,
Hindi (on Tantra, Jyotish and Cultural history).
Chief Priest Vindhyachal Maha Shakti Pitha
Assistant Director (Research and Publication)
Rashtriya Sanskrit Sansthan,
Ministry of HRD, Govt. of India
New Delhi

PREFACE

In Hindu mythology everything is a projection of God and Human being is considered His best creation. It is the human who discovered the God in its form after discovering death. Now it can be said that if death is eternal, same with the omnipresent God. If He has created problems for his creations, of course, He has also devised remedy for it. It is not now that man is facing problems and finding remedies for them, but our sages also spent their lives to find solutions to different problems such as ailments, hunger, poverty, etc. During this exercise the mantras were given by Lord Shiva to saints and to get best out of it the saints ritualised ways and means in the course of actions. This whole exercise is known as Tantra (technology) of whose mantra and yantra are two pillars. Before we give you an introduction about yantras and its practical aspects it is necessary to understand what are Tantras, yantras and mantras.

Tantra is defined as a rich and diverse spiritual tradition which is found in dialogue form between Shiva and Shakti. In essence, Tantra is the art and science of receiving, conserving and transacting energy from cosmic resources; it encompasses every activity of life. Tantra is ritually systematized scientific strategy to get plugged to the cosmic pool of energy to optimize creativity.

Mantras are the spells of single syllables or short phrases which when chanted correctly as well as repeatedly produce vibrations which set the nerves in motion and stimulate them for suitable action in consonance with desired achievement.

People know very little about **Yantra** and consider them beyond their comprehensive power. They are very far from the true meaning and use of Yantras. Yantras cannot be simply discovered from imagination. Every specific mood and emotion has an associated form of energy and shape. This clearly determines the form of the Yantra associated to that mood. The traditional Yantras were discovered through revelation, by perceptiveness, not invented.

Yantra means a "talisman", or "instrument" or "Amulet" or "*Kavach*" when prepared and created by a competent person and used under specific instructions for fruitful results, will help to gain the devotee objects of desire or ambition. Although it would not be a difficult task for most of us to copy the form of a yantra, it would not have the desired effect. Furthermore, it would be all but useless if not created by a qualified person and then "infused" with the specific energy via the medium of mantra. Otherwise, it becomes just an interesting form or picture to look at, but has no real effect on time or circumstances within life.

The power of Yantras to stimulate resonance is based on the specific form of its appearance. Such a projection can be composed from one or more geometrical shapes which combine into a precise model representing and transfiguring in essence, at the level of the physical universe, the subtle sphere of force corresponding to the invoked deity. From this point it can be argued that the Yantra functions similarly to a mantra. By resonance, certain energy from the practitioner's microcosm vibrates on the same wavelength with the corresponding infinite energy present in the macrocosm which is represented in the physical plane by the Yantra. The principle of resonance with any deity, cosmic power, aspect, phenomenon or energy owes its universal applicability to the perfect correspondence existing between the human being (seen as a true microcosm) and the Creation as a whole (macrocosm). All ancient cultures had sacred geometric designs representative of their Gods, which had a mantra (or sacred sound vibration) that corresponded to it. In the Hindu culture, much power and energy is said to be held within sacred geometric symbols. Yantras are not "lucky charms" to be worn or displayed as icons of power in and of themselves. Much specific knowledge and ability must go into their preparation and much dedication and worship is required to achieve the desired effects.

Some points to remember while practicing the yantras as told in this book.

In the book we have discussed practical part of yantras and did not go into the details keeping into the length of the book. We would like to underscore here that the mantras given with the yantra are only for recital of the said deity. The worship of the Deity is done through the *Panchanga sevanam* (five subsidiaries) which are known as *Gita* (Philosophical basis of a deity), *Sahasranama* (thousand names for frequent devotional repetitions), *Stotra* (hymns for invocation), *Kavacha* (Armour of the God), *Hrdaya* (Heart) #. **Before energising any yantra it is advised to read *kavacha* of the deity along with the other *panchangas*.**

Rishi :- (Sage) All mantras have certain subsidiary attachment Rishi and are originated from Lord Siva. Certain sages have been dictated these Mantras from the Lord and practiced them for years together and had achieved success. Those sages have transmitted the Mantra to their disciples and these disciples to their disciples. This tradition 'had been kept orally for thousands of years. Consigning them to writing was supposed to deprive, them of their efficacy. The original Sage is always mentioned as the concerned Sage, before repeating a mantra for ritualistic purposes. While mentioning the name of the Sage the devotee touches his 'head or he 'performs the "Nyasa" on his head.

Chandas:- (Meter) The Mantra has to be covered and protected well. This rite is Chandas ordinarily the meter is also meant. The Nyasa of Chandas is in mouth.

Devta : - (Deity) The 'vital element 'that controls influences and manages all the activities of human 'beings, is caused by the Devta. Since this vital power is situated in the individual's heart the Nyasa of the deity is in the heart.

Bija (Seed):- Bija means the seed. The principle that generates the power of a Mantra is called by the term Bija (the seed). Hence the Nyasa of the Bija is in the privies. Each letter in the *Devanagari* script has a mystic value. The symbolic significance of each letter of the Sanskrit language is given in this book. According to the Bija-Code each letter of the Sanskrit *varnamala* (alphabet) represents certain instincts. Since each letter has a different acoustic root, each one of them creates a different vibration which often corresponds to the psyche of the persons being addressed. For the persons practicing Yantras it is important to know the sound root and the power of all the letters used in Sanskrit.

a	अ	Death destroying (It is in the image of the all-pervading Lord)
aa	आ	Attracts (feminine gender)
i	इ	Strengthening (neuter gender)
ii	ई	Magnetic
u	उ	Energizing
uu	ऊ	Dislodging
r	ऋ	Upsetting and stunning
ly	ऌ	Arouses envy
e	ए	Controls and influences others
ai	ऐ	Controls the male element
o	ओ	Creates mass hypnosis
au	औ	Controls people in authority
a	अं	Controls the wild element
ah	अः	Fights death
ka	क	Poison at its acoustic root
kha	ख	Obstruction at its acoustic root
ga	ग	Ganesha at its acoustic root
gha	घ	Destruction at its acoustic root
ada	ङ	Demon at its acoustic root
ca	च	Moon at its acoustic root
cha	छ	Gain at its acoustic root

ja	ज	Brahma rakshas at its acoustic root
jha	झ	Fulfilment at its acoustic root
na	ञ	Mohan at its acoustic root
ta	ट	Remorse at its acoustic root
tha	ठ	Moon at its acoustic root
da	ढ	Garuda at its acoustic root
dha	ड	Kuber at its acoustic root
na	ण	Devil at its acoustic root
ta	त	Represents eight elements
		• guru Beej • shakti Beej
		• rama Beej • kam Beej
		• yog Beej • tejo Beej
		• shanti Beej • raksha Beej
tha	थ	Yama at its acoustic root
da	द	Durga at its acoustic root
dha	ध	Sun at its acoustic root
na	न	The rapeutic quality at its acoustic root
pa	प	Varuna at its acoustic root
pha	फ	Vishnu at its acoustic root
ba	ब	Brahma at its acoustic root
bha	भ	Kali at its acoustic root
ma	म	Fire at its acoustic root
ya	य	Air at its acoustic root
ra	र	Makes one indifferent or detached
la	ल	Indra at its acoustic root
va	व	Defeats death
sa	श	The goddess of wealth at its acoustic root
sa	ष	Sun at its acoustic root
sa	स	The goddess of learning at its acoustic root
ha	ह	Shiva at its acoustic root
ksa	क्ष	Bhairava at its acoustic root.

Shakti (power) This is the principle with whose help the Bija develops into a full fledged Mantra. The Nyasa of the Saktis is at the feet.

Kilaka It is said that Lord Shiva has nailed all the mantras.

(Nailing up) Hence there is a kilka for every mantra to denail the same. This is the vital link between, the Mantra and the devotee. Even if the devotee becomes inadvertent this nailing power kilaka holds the Mantra within the ambit of the aspirant and keeps the efficacy of the said Mantra well balanced. The Nyasa of a kilaka is all over the body.

Viniyoga (application) The devotee expressly states that he makes use of the particular Mantra in a particular rite. The texts on Tantra maintain that the knowledge of the Sage, meter etc. is a must for the efficacy of the Mantras as a mean to realise the intended benefit. The Mantra becomes weak if the devotee does not expressly state that he is making use of a particular Mantra in a particular rite.

Nyasa Through it Heart, Head, Tuft, Armour or the body as protected by armour, eyes, and the paint of the hand. These are the six limbs where the rite of Nyasa (ritualistic touch) is performed. The performance of these Nyasa helps in eradicating all hindrances and obstacles, thus, ensuring the achievement of the result. If out of ignorance or inadvertence the devotee does not perform Nyasa he is suet to be suffering by obstacles at every turn. In certain rites the Nyasa are only five. In that case "eyes" are omitted.

Samputa: - Samput are the specified words used in a mantra. These can be used in the beginning, middle or at the end of a mantra. The samput has a great value in mantras and be used carefully. It means covering up process in which repeating a mantra before and after a mantra. We use the *Mula* mantra to be covered by the *maya bija (Hrim / ह्रीं)* and repeated seven times before the prescribed mantra is taken up.

We will be providing the specific mantras for the specific use. Bija mantras too have been provided. The meanings of most common important words are provided below.

Hrim (**ह्रीं**) O, destroyer of time

Shrim (**श्रीं**) O, terific one.

Klim (**क्लीं**) Thou who are beneficeent, possessors of all the arts.

Aing (**ऐंग**) Thou are both form and formless.

Japa:- In this material world people at large are of destructive mind, selfish and do the acts through which they can gain, others may adopt it an misuse. If at the time of Japa someone is sitting by your side, then reicte the mantra in a *upansu* or *mansic* way. Japas are of following types.

Upansu Japa:- It is the method where japa is done very slowly so that nobody can hear it. Only lip movement should be there.

Mansic Japa:- The japa carried out only in the heart without any sound or lip movemnets.

Vachnik japa:- In this method one can recite the mantra in a low, medium or high tone of his/her sound.

One can recite "HIS NAME "OM" etc., in a Vachnik way but mantras are to be recited in this way only when one is alone at a secluded place.

It may be noted here that the yantras have been prepared as per directions prescribed in the tantras. Wherever it is not mentioned, the yantras be made on bhojpatra or copper plate with *asthgandh* as ink and stylus of pomegranate.

The preface may go long in describing the whole yantra procedure. It is advised to consult a practitioner before going for any ritual. We are confident that this occult science will be used by the practitioner, readers and by others methodically for good use.

We would again like to thank our readers for subscribing to our work and hope that this will go a long way in establishing a common man's faith in this field of yantra. We would look forward to your valuable suggestions, which we would certainly try to

incorporate in our forthcoming works.

Dr. M. H. K. Shastri

Janakpuri, New Delhi

Pt. Laxmi Kant Vashisth

190, Ambika Vihar

Paschim Vihar,

New Delhi-110087

Ph. (91) 011-25289814

09891621032

E-mail:laxmikant_vashisth@yahoo.co.in

Statutory warning: - A wrong and malicious practice of yantra may have devastating effects.

 # (For details please read our book "mantra shastra aur upiyog" published from Sagar Publications)

SHRI GANPATI YANTRAM

श्री गणपति यन्त्रम्

ॐ शरान्धनुः पाशसृणी स्वहस्तैर्दधानमारक्तसरोरुहस्थम् ।
विवस्त्रपात्न्यां सुरतप्रवृत्तमुच्छिष्टमम्बासुतमाश्रयेऽहम् ॥

❖

श्रीं गं सौमयाय गणपतये वर वरद सर्वजनं मे वशमानय स्वाहा ॥

SHRI DURGA BEESA YANTRAM

श्री दुर्गा बीसा यन्त्रम्

SHRI YANTRAM

श्री यन्त्रम्

बालार्कायुततेजसं त्रिनयनां रक्ताम्बरोल्लासिनीं
नानालंकृतिराजमानवपुषं बालोडुराट्शेखराम् ।
हस्तैरिक्षुधनुः सृणिं सुमशरं पाशं मुद्रां बिभ्रतीं
श्रीचक्रस्थितसुन्दरीं त्रिजगतामाधारभूतां स्मरेत् ॥

❖

ह्रीं ॐ नमः शिवाय ।
ॐ श्रीं ह्रीं श्रीं कमले कमलालये प्रसीद प्रसीद
श्रीं ह्रीं श्रीं महालक्ष्मयै: नमः ॥

SHRI MAHAMRITUNJAYEE YANTRAM

श्री महामृत्युंजय यन्त्रम्

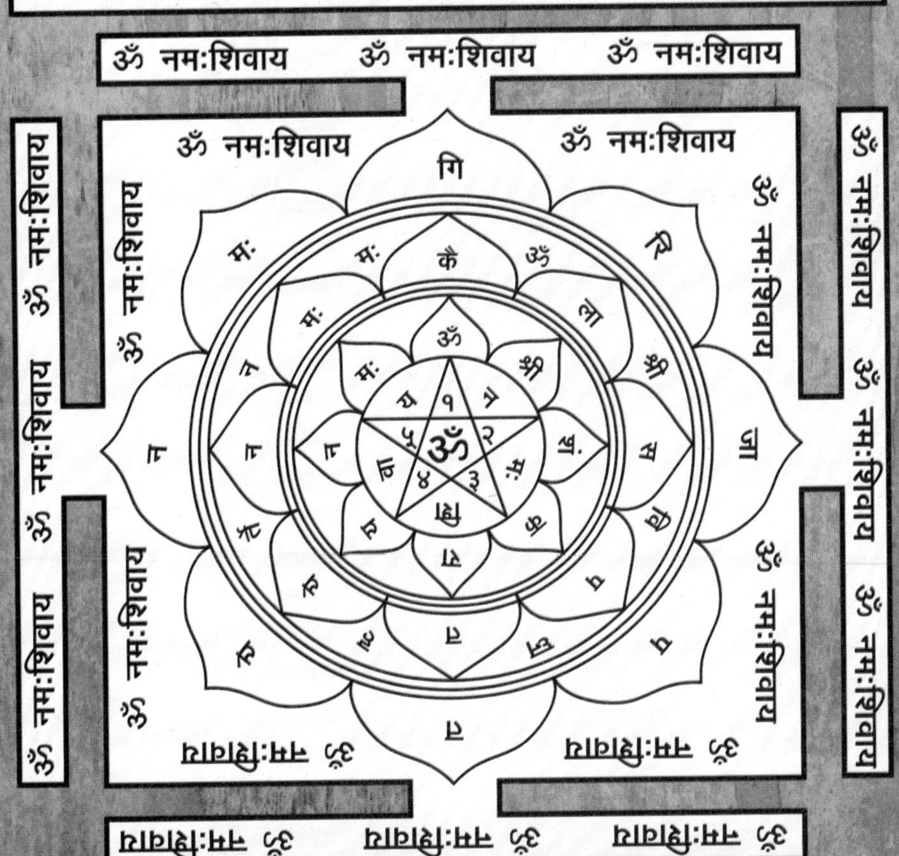

हस्ताम्भजेयुगस्थकुम्भयुगलादुद्धृत्य तोयं शिरः
सिञ्चन्तं करयोर्युगेन दधतं स्वांके सकुम्भौ करौ ।
अक्षस्रङ्मृगहस्तमम्बुजगतं मूर्धस्थचन्द्रस्रवत्पीयूषोन्नतनुं
भजे सगिरिजं मृत्युञ्जयं त्र्यम्बकम् ॥

❖

ॐ हौं जूं सः ॐ भूर्भुवः स्वः
ॐ त्र्यमबकं यजामहे सुगन्धिं पुष्टिवर्धनं
उर्वारुकमिव बन्धनान्मृत्योर्मुक्षीय माऽमृतात्
ॐ स्वः ॐ भुवः भूः ॐ सः जूं हौं ॐ

SHRI GAYATRI YANTRAM

श्री गायत्री यन्त्रम्

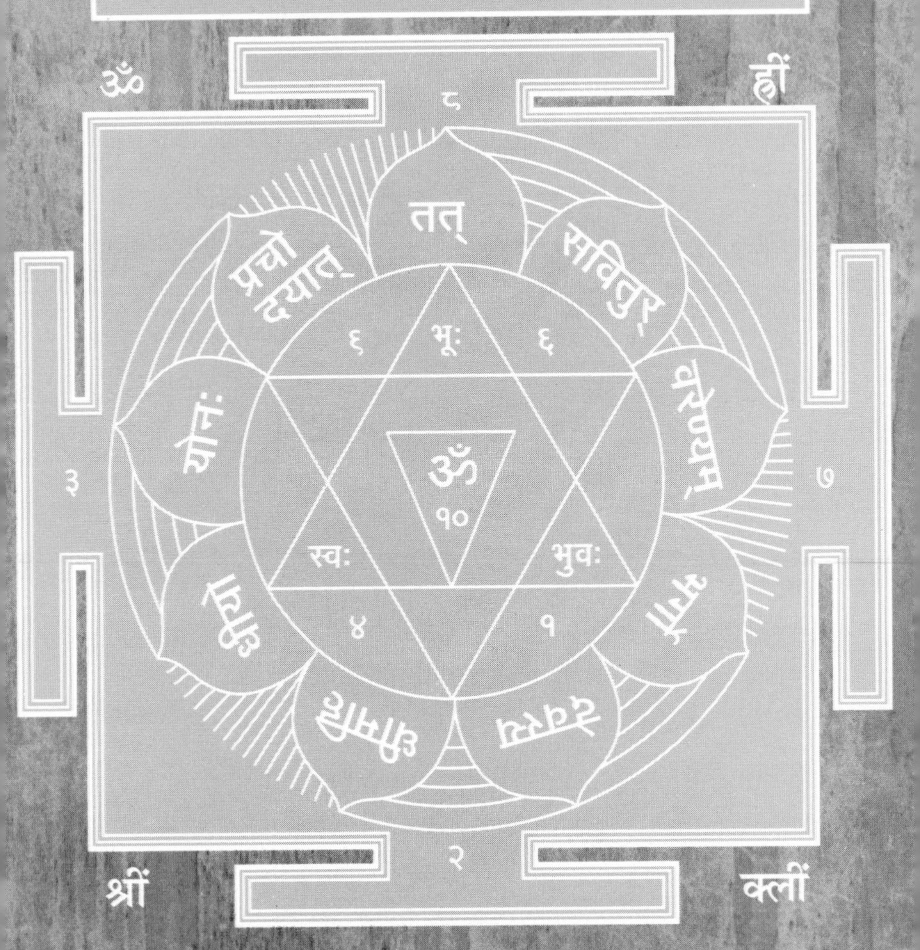

ॐ यद्देवैः सुरपूजितं परतरं सामर्थ्य तारात्मिकं
पुन्नागांबुजपुष्पनागवकुलौः केशैः शुकैरर्चितम् ।
नित्यं ध्यानसमस्तदीप्तिकरणं कालाग्निरुद्दीपनं
तत्संहारकरं नमामि सततं पातालसंस्थं मुखम् ॥

❖

ॐ भूभुर्वः स्वः तत्सवितुर्वरेण्यं भर्गो देवस्य धीमहि ।
धियो यो नः प्रचोदयात् ॥

SHRI DURGA SAPTSATI YANTRAM

श्री दुर्गा सप्तशती यन्त्रम्

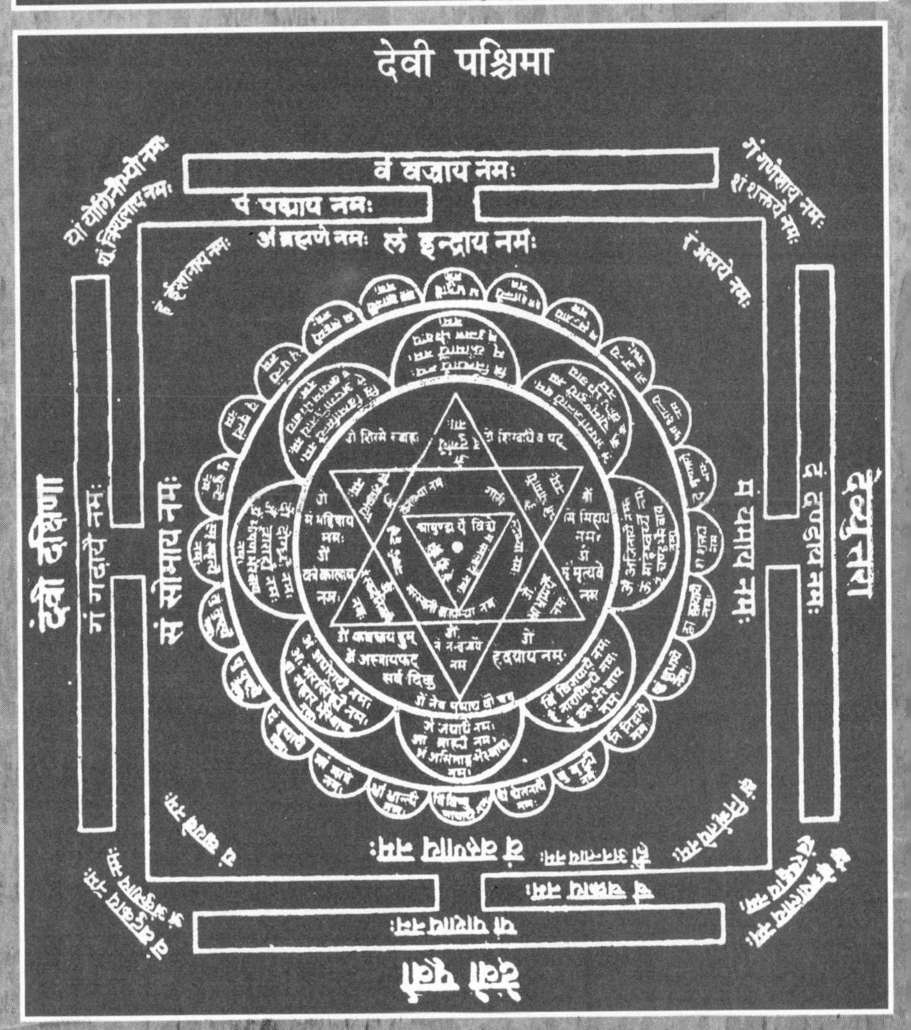

दुर्वानाम त्रिनयनां विलसत्किरीटां शङ्खाब्जखड्गशरखेटक शूलचापन् ।
सन्तर्जनीं च दधती महिषासनस्थां दुर्गा नवारकुलपीठगता भजेहम् ॥

SHRI SURYA YANTRAM

श्री सूर्य यन्त्रम्

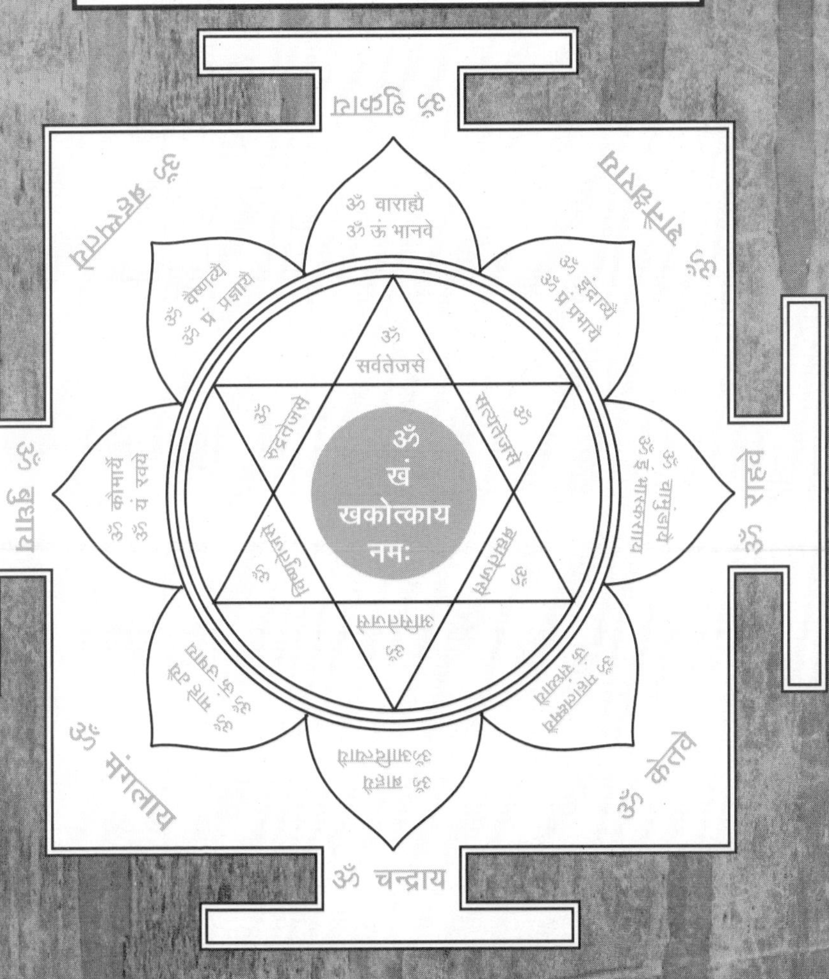

भास्वद्रत्नाढ्यमौलिः स्फुरदधररुचा रञ्जितश्चारुकेशो
भास्वान् यो दिव्यतेजाः करकमलयुतः स्वर्णवर्णः प्रभाभिः।
विश्वाकाशावकाशे ग्रहगणसहितो भाति यश्चोदयाद्रौ
सर्वानन्दप्रदाता हरिहरनमितः पातु मां विश्वचक्षुः ॥

ॐ ह्रीं घृणिनं सूर्य आदित्य श्रीं ॥

SHRI HANUMATPUJAN YANTRAM

श्री हनुमत्पूजन यन्त्रम्

बालार्कायुततेजसं त्रिभुवनप्रक्षोभकं सुन्दरं
सुग्रीवादिसमस्तवानरगणैः संसेव्यपादाम्बुजम् ।
नादेनैव समस्तराक्षसगणान्सन्त्रासयन्तं प्रभुं
श्रीमदामपादाम्बुजस्मृतिरतं ध्यायामि वातात्मजम् ।।

SHRI MAHALAKSHMI YANTRAM

श्री महालक्ष्मी यन्त्रम्

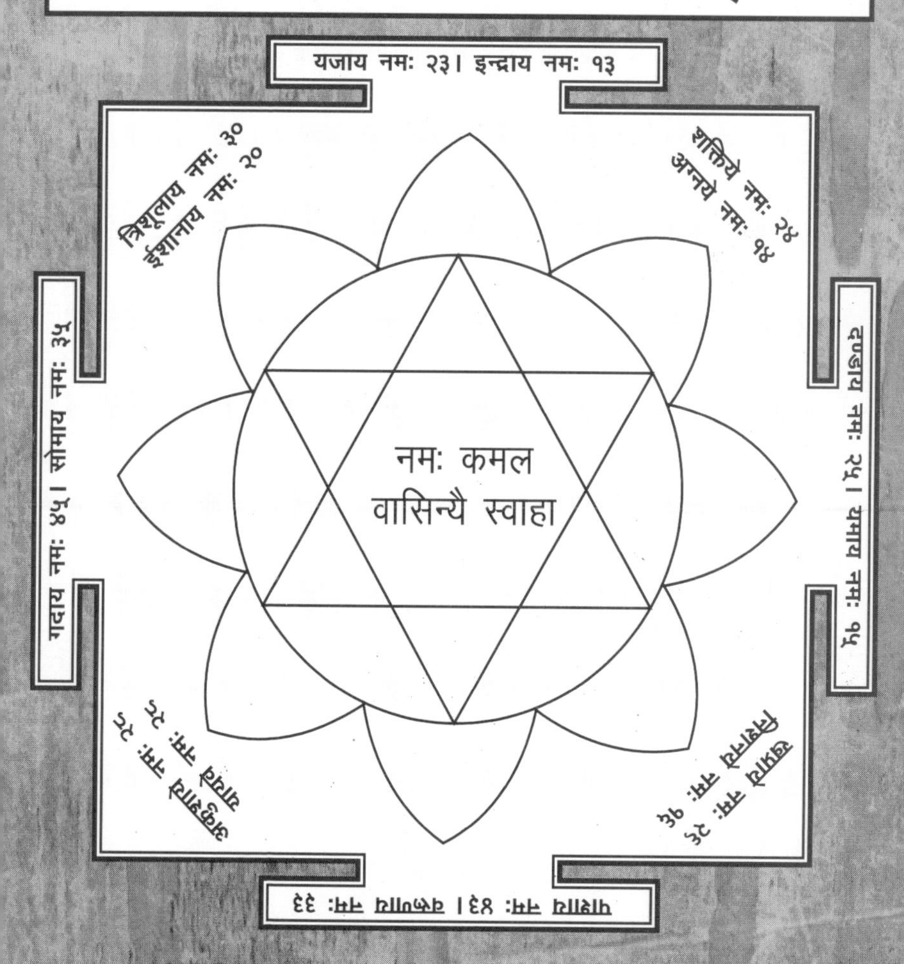

ॐ या सा पद्मासनस्था विपुल कटि तटी पद्मपत्रायताक्षी।
गंभीरावर्तनाभिः स्तनभर नमिता शुभ्रवस्त्रोत्तरीय ॥
या लक्ष्मीर्दिव्यरूपै मणिगण खचितै स्नापिता हेम कुम्भैः।
सा नित्यं पद्महल्ता मम वसतु ग्रहे सर्वमांगल्या युक्ता ॥

SHRI BAGLAMUKHI YANTRAM

श्री बगलामुखी यन्त्रम्

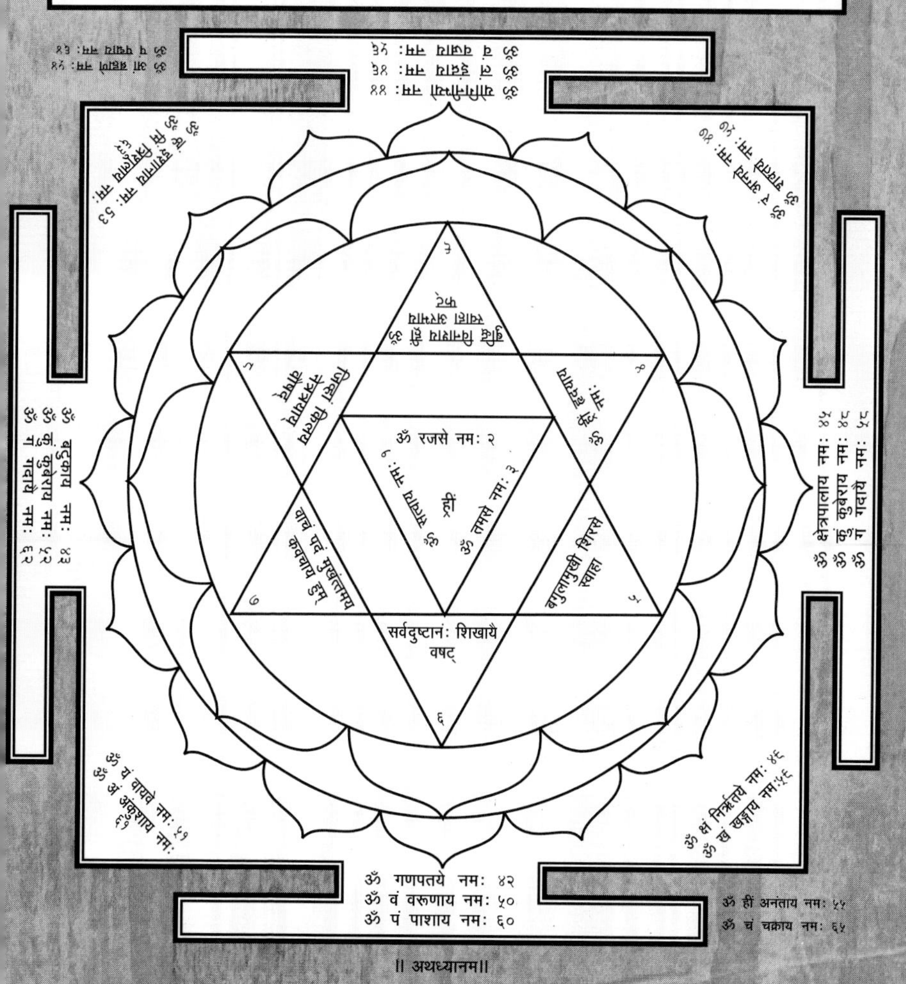

ॐ गणपतये नमः ४२
ॐ वं वरूणाय नमः ५०
ॐ पं पाशाय नमः ६०

ॐ ह्रीं अनंताय नमः ५५
ॐ चं चक्राय नमः ६५

॥ अथध्यानम॥

मध्येसुधाब्धि मणिमण्डपरत्ववेदीसिंहासनोपरिगतां परिपीतवर्णाम्।
पीताम्बराभरणमाल्यविभूषिताङ्गीं देवीं स्मरामि धृतमुद्गरवैरिजिह्वाम्॥

❖

ॐ ह्रीं बगलामुखि सर्वदुष्टानां वाचं मुखं पदं।
स्तंभय जिव्हां कीलय बुध्दिंविनाशाय ह्रीं ॐ स्वाहा॥

SHRI SARASWATI YANTRAM

श्री सरस्वती यन्त्रम्

ॐ तरुणशकलमिन्दोर्बिभ्रती शुभ्रकान्तिः
कुचभरनमिताङ्गी सन्निषण्णा सिताब्जे ।
निजकरकमलोद्यल्लेखनीपुस्तकश्रीः
सकलविभवसिध्यै पातु वाग्देवता ॥

❖

ॐ ह्रींश्रींऐं वाग्वादिनि भगवती अर्हन्मुखनिवासिनी
सरस्वति ममास्ये प्रकाशं कुरुकुरु स्वाहा ऐं नमः ॥

SHRI KUBER YANTRAM

श्री कुबेर यन्त्रम्

मनुजवाह्यविमानवरस्थितं गरूडरत्ननिभं निधिनायकम् ।
शिवसखं मुकुटादिविभूषितं वरगदे दधतं भज तुन्दिलम् ॥

❖

यक्षाय कुबेराय वैश्रवणाय धनधान्याधिपतये धनधान्यसमृद्धिं मे
देहि दापय स्वाहा ॥

SHRI VASTU YANTRAM

श्री वास्तु यन्त्रम्

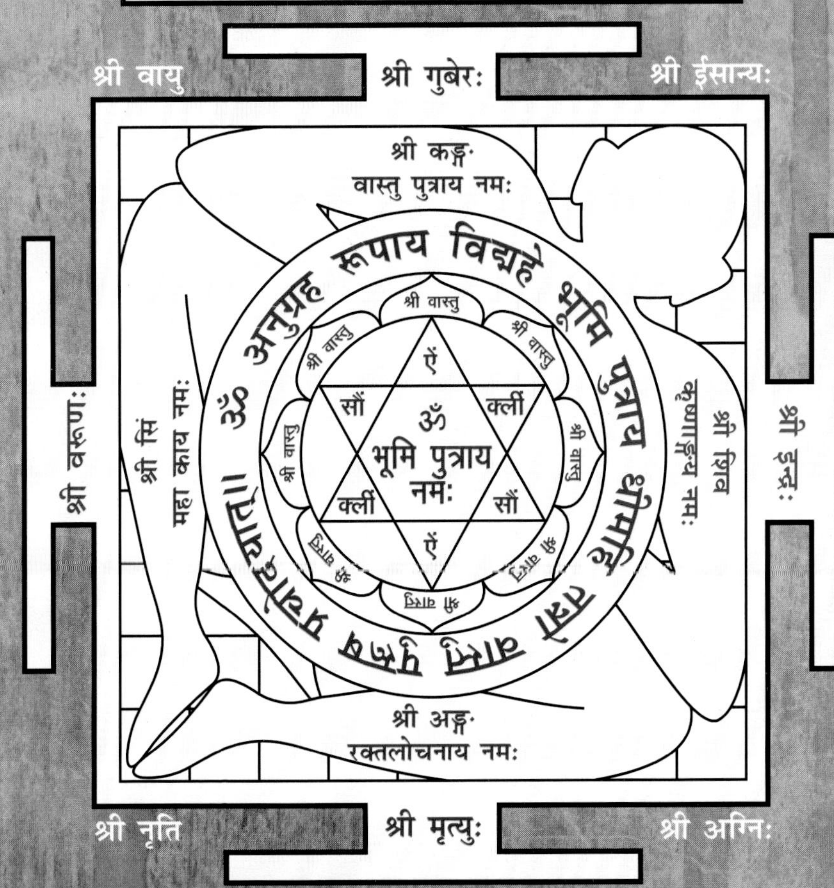

चतुर्भुजं महाकायं जटामण्डितमस्तकम् ।
त्रिलोचनं करालास्यं हारकुण्डलशेभितम् ॥
लम्बोदरं दीर्घकर्णं लोमशं पीतवाससम् ।
गदात्रिशूलपरशुखट्वाङ्गं दधतं करै ॥
असिचर्म्मधरैर्वीरैः कपिलास्यादिभिर्वृतम् ।
शत्रूणामन्तकं साक्षादुद्यदादित्यसन्निभम् ॥
ध्यायेद्देवं वास्तुपतिं कूर्म्मपद्मासनस्थितम् ॥

क्षां क्षीं क्षूं क्षैं क्षौं क्षः ।

SHRI DAKSHIN KALI YANTRAM

श्री दक्षिणकाली पूजन यन्त्रम्

ॐ सद्यश्छिन्नशिरः कृपाणमभयं हस्तैर्वरं बिभ्रतीं
घोरास्यां शिरसां स्रजा सुरुचिरामुन्मुक्तकेशावलिम् ।
सृक्कासृक्प्रवहां श्मशाननिलयां श्रुत्योः शवालंकृतिं
श्यामाङ्गीं कृतमेखलां शवकरैर्देवीं भजे कालिकाम् ॥

ॐ क्रीं क्रीं क्रीं हुं हुं ह्रीं ह्रीं दक्षिण
कालिके क्रीं क्रीं क्रीं हुं हुं ह्रीं ह्रीं स्वाहा ॥

SHRI NAVGRHA YANTRAM

श्री नवग्रह यन्त्रम्

६	१	८
७	५	३
२	९	४

Sun

७	२	९
८	६	४
३	१०	५

Moon

८	३	१०
९	७	५
४	११	६

Mars

९	४	११
१०	८	६
५	१२	७

Mercury

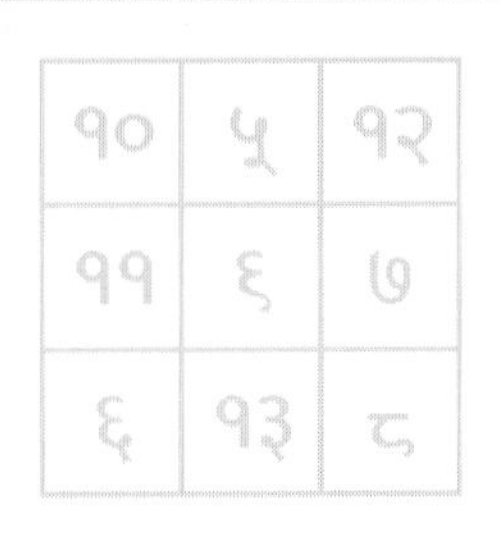

१०	५	१२
११	९	७
६	१३	८

Jupiter

११	६	१३
१२	१०	८
७	१४	९

Venus

१२	७	१४
१३	११	९
८	१५	१०

Saturn

१३	८	१५
१४	१२	१०
९	१६	११

Rahu

१४	९	१६
१५	१३	११
१०	१७	१२

Ketu

ॐ सूर्याय नमः। ॐ चंद्राय नमः। ॐ बुधाय नमः।
ॐ भौमाय नमः। ॐ बृहस्पतये नमः। ॐ शुक्राय नमः।
ॐ शनये नमः। ॐ राहुवे नमः। ॐ केतवे नमः। ॐ नवग्रहे नमः॥

KAALSARP YOGA YANTRAM

कालसर्प योग यन्त्रम्

नागपाश यन्त्रम्

ॐ नवकुलाय विद्महे विषदंताय धीमहि तन्नो सर्पः प्रचोदयात्॥

CHAPTER 1
INTRODUCTION

YANTRAS play significant role in the meditative practices as described in our classics. According to *Sanskrit* Dictionary *Vachaspatyam "Yantram"* is "an instrument" or an instrument for holding or restraining which may be used to denote a variety of linear diagrams. It is a geometric design acting as a highly efficient tool for contemplation, concentration and meditation. Yantras carry spiritual significance and point the user to higher levels of consciousness. Yantras often focus on a specific deity and so by tuning into the different Yantras one can interact with certain deities or creative force centres in the universe, our classics says.

Design of Yantras

Yantras may be of simple designs symbolising basic concepts such as cross, triangle, square, circle or lotus. They may be of more complex combinations of such elements in figures which represents abstract form, the particular creative forces in the cosmos, which are called divinities. These Yantras are closely related to the *mandals* used by persons following the *Vedic* religion in which geometric designs are supplemented by elaborate symbolic images of the deities by which their various forms and attributes indicate different aspects of the hidden order of reality. Yantras are used in the context of meditation and worship as visual-aids for concentration of mind leading to realisation of abstract principle which is the inner meaning of the visible representation. Yantras are usually designed so that the eye is carried into the centre, and very often they are symmetrical. They can be inscribed on paper, wood, metal, or earth, or they can be three-dimensional.

It is said that pious spirits (*Devas*) reside in Yantras and without performing *Pooja* of Yantra neither one can appease them nor attain desired results from Yantras

Effect of Yantras

Operation of Yantra is something called "shape energy" or "form energy". The idea is that every shape emits a very specific frequency and energy pattern. Certain 'powers' are ascribed to the various shapes. Some have 'evil' or negative energies and some have 'good' or positive energies, but in Yantras only the benefic and harmonious energies are used.

When one focuses on a Yantra, his mind is automatically tuned in by resonance into the specific form of energy of that Yantra. The process of intensification of vocal tones during articulation, as by the air cavities of the mouth and nasal passages is then maintained and amplified. The Yantra acts only as a "tune in" mechanism or a doorway. The subtle energy does not come from the Yantra itself, but from the system reflecting on a large scale or one of its component systems or parts.

Basically Yantras are secret keys for establishing resonance with the benefic energies of the macrocosm. Very often the Yantras can put us in contact with extremely elevated energies and entities, being of invaluable help on the spiritual path system reflecting on a large scale one of its component systems or parts

Types of Yantras

Bhu Prisht Yantra

Bhu in English is earth. Accordingly they are made from materials found within the earth, as the name implies. There are two subdivisions. The first is raised Yantras which include the *bija* mantras and *vern* mantras. The second is carved Yantra.

Meru Prastar Yantra

Meru in English is mountain. These Yantras are raised, like a mountain with a wide base, thinner especially the midriff of the human body and peaked top in the shape of a mountain.

Paatal Yantra

Paatal is inside the earth (nether world) in English. These Yantras are carved, in the shape of an inverted mountain, making it the opposite of the Meru Prisht Yantra.

Meru Prastar Yantra

These are of the "Meru" or mountain shape, but cut, rather than raised.

Ruram Prisht Yantra

Our classics classify these Yantras as forged one. They have tortoise shell like tops on a rectangular shaped base.

The above five types of Yantras are classified according to the different types of pooja (worship) conducted by the aspirants. Each has a separate and distinct purpose to gain a particular objective for the aspirant. Some Yantras are worshipped in temples, some are worshipped by individuals at home and some are worn on the body (usually of triangular or rectangular shape) either around the neck, the arm, or kept close to the body in another location.

Classification of Yantras

Sharir Yantras

Sharir means body in English language. There are six categories of these Yantras. According to yoga there are six *chakras* in our body which are know as *Muladhar chakra, Swadisthan chakra, Manipur chakra, Anahat chakra, Visudh chakra, Aggya ckakra.* Each of the "*Chakras*" has it own yantra through which *Kundalni* is awakened. Hence, they are worn on the body and each Yantra has its own mantra. By chanting these mantras one bestows various benefits to the aspirant.

Dhaaran Yantra

Dhaaran means wear in English language. These Yantras are also worn on the body and include particular rituals for producing the desired results.

Aasan Yantra

Aasan means seat in English language. These Yantras are positioned under the *aasana* (sitting place) during *pooja*. They are said to bear their fruit more quickly than other Yantras and therefore are generally placed under the foundations of homes and temples, sometimes even under the worshipped deity of the home or temple, to bring the favourable results in a fairly short span of time.

Mandla Yantra

Mandal is a group. These Yantras are created by nine people participating in the pooja. They arrange their sitting places in the form of the Yantra. One participant sits in the centre, another to the north, northeast, east, southeast, south, southwest, west and one to northwest. The aspirant in the centre position offers the pooja of the "*Ishat*" mantra (the mantra of the deity to be pleased) whereas the eight other members also chant individual specific mantras at the same time.

Pooja Yantra

Pooja is worship in English language. These Yantras are installed, either in temples or individuals' homes, while pooja is taking place. There are different Yantras to serve various desires. They may be for different religious deity worship, or for the different planets in our *Vedic* Astrological system. The worship and installation of these Yantras have five basic steps.

1. Before performance of the pooja, the Yantras are installed as icons, or worshipful deities. The Yantras are drawn numerically and while offering the pooja, the names of the respective "*devas*" (according to the numbers) are chanted throughout the mantras.
2. In the centre of the Yantra the name of the particular *deva* being worshipped is written, and then the pooja is performed.
3. Either the first word of the mantra, the bija mantra, or the full mantra is written while preparing the Yantra itself.
4. A carving, painting, or photograph of the *deva* and worshipful deity is attached to the Yantra before beginning the pooja.
5. Full-colour pictures of *deva* or worshipful deity are applied to the Yantra.

Chatar Yantra

Chatar means umbrella in English language or which is always on the top of the body. These Yantras are not placed upon the body, but kept in the pocket, or under a turban (or hat).

Darshan Yantra

Darshan is to view. These Yantras are generally found in temples. "Darshan" or view means to take advantage of association with a deity or other representative form of God, or His devotee. It is said that if an aspirant sees them during the morning hours, they will be benefic in awarding success. These are greatly "purified" Yantras and are installed in great historic temples such as the temple of "Lord *Jagannath*, *Balarama* and *Subhadra*" in *Shri Jagannath Puri* and *Shree Chakra* in *Shri Tirupati* temple, in Andhra Pradesh.

Composition of Yantras

It is best known that the *Vedas* described this Universe a composition of five elements which are known as Earth, Air, Fire, Water and Sky. In the Yantras where lines are used with the basic concept of *Bindu* or point, all these elements are used particularly earth, water and fire. The aspect of these figures is explained in the next chapter. The five elements which Yantras indicate for specific use are as follows:-

1. **Earth component :-** These Yantras are source of satisfaction and bestow contentment, comforts, an eager or strong desire to achieve something, and success. This component is stationed from the sole of the foot to the knee. It is diamond shaped in square form. The *Bija* mantra is *Lam* and colour is golden

2. **Water component :-** Such Yantras bless the native with respect, love, contentment, removes restlessness, smoothness, affection in life and wisdom. It is stationed from knee to navel. It is of white colour, *Bija* mantra

Vam and marked with two lotuses.

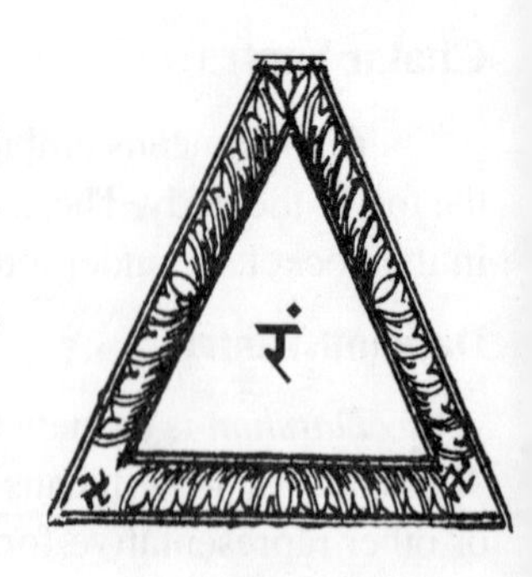

3. **Agni component :-** Yantras having this component are considered in gaining respect success, avert failures and troubles etc. The fire component is situated between navel and the heart. It is red in colour in the form of triangle with the *swastika.* The *Bija* mantra is *Ram.*

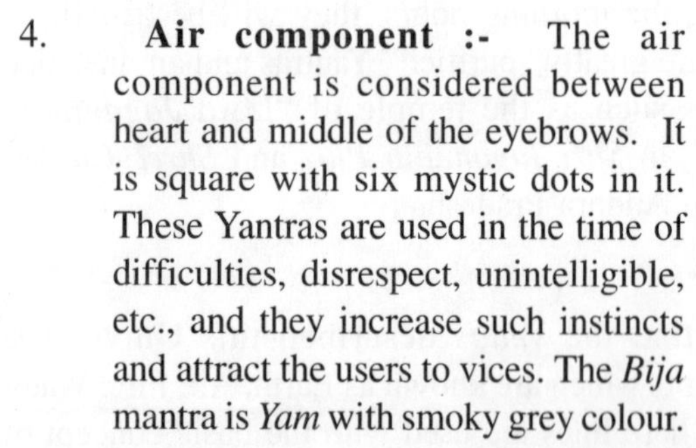

4. **Air component :-** The air component is considered between heart and middle of the eyebrows. It is square with six mystic dots in it. These Yantras are used in the time of difficulties, disrespect, unintelligible, etc., and they increase such instincts and attract the users to vices. The *Bija* mantra is *Yam* with smoky grey colour.

5. **Sky component :-** These Yantras are considered useful for creating affection, education, love for all, removing worries and success in efforts for spirituality in the state of being alone. It is between the middle of the eyebrows and aperture in the crown of the head. It's colour is crystal clear. It is circular in shape with *Ham* as its *Bija* Mantra.

It is noticed that some people place Yantras upside down, a monument of their ignorance. One cannot place a Yantra just any way he please. Anyone knows that when the cross (symbol of Christians) is held upside down, it is no longer a benefic symbol. A Yantra put upside down is no longer the same Yantra.

CHAPTER 2

ICONOGRAPHY IN YANTRAS

According to *Tantra* texts the practice of representing things by means of symbols or of attributing symbolic meanings or significance to objects, events, or relationship are the basic of yantras and these complex artistic forms and gestures are used as a kind of key to convey religious concepts. These visual, auditory, and kinetic representations of religious ideas and events have been utilised in old Hindu classics. The symbolic aspect of Yantra is considered by our saints as the main characteristic of religious expression. Our Saints have gathered and interpreted a great abundance of material on the symbolical aspects of Yantras and Mantras.

The importance of symbolical expression and of pictorial presentation of Yantras and Mantras has been confirmed, widened, and deepened both by the study of our old classics. Systems of symbols and pictures are constituted in a certain ordered and determined relationship to the form, content, and intention of presentation are believed to be among the most important means of knowing and expressing our old religious systems. Such systems also contribute to the maintenance and strengthening of the relationships between man and the sphere of the sacred or holy. The symbol is, in fact, the mediator, presence, and real (or intelligible) representation of the holy in certain conventional and standardised forms. According to *Tantra* texts, core of the Yantra is composed of one or several simple geometrical shapes shown as dots, lines, triangles, squares, circles and lotuses which represent different ways of energy which is considered so invisible to be detected or analysed.

The power of Yantras to induce or display a distinctive feature of vocal tones to an extreme degree during pronunciation, as by the air cavities of the mouth and nasal passages is based on the specific form of its appearance. Such a diagram can be composed from one or more geometrical shapes which combine into a precise model representing and transfiguring in essence, at the level of the physical universe, the subtle sphere of force corresponding to the invoked deity. It could be said that Yantras and Mantras are supplementary to each other. By amplification of vocal tones during articulation a certain energy from the practitioner's small representative system vibrates on the same wavelength which have analogies to a larger system in constitution with the corresponding infinite energy present in a small representative system which have analogies to a larger system in tandem is represented in the physical plane by the Yantra. The principle of resonance with any deity, cosmic power, aspect, phenomenon or energy owes its universal applicability to the perfect correspondence existing between the human being (seen as a true microcosm) and the creation as a whole universe.

Outline of Yantra (Bhupura)

Demarcation of Yantra from the exterior is done by a line or a group of lines which forms its perimeter. These marginal lines have the function to maintain, contain and prevent the loss of the magical forces represented by the core structure of the Yantra, usually the central dot. They also have the function to increase its magical and subtle force.

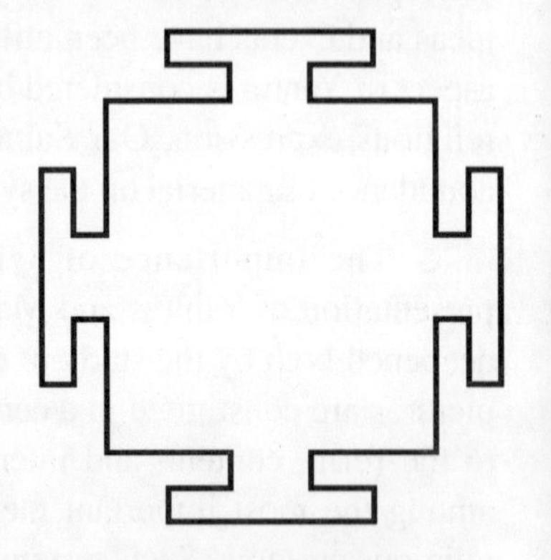

Dot (Bindu)

The dot (●) signifies the Lord *Shiva* or the concentrated energy and its intense concentration. It can be conceived as an image of kind of 'energy deposit' which can in turn radiate energy under other forms. The dot is usually surrounded by different surfaces, a triangle, a hexagon, a circle, etc. These forms depend on the characteristic of the deity or aspect represented by the Yantra.

Six Point Star (Sathkon)

A typical combination often found in the graphical structure of a Yantra is the superposition of two triangles, one pointing upwards and the other downwards, forming a star with six points. This form symbolically represents the union of *Purusha* {Human *(Shiva)*} and *Prakriti* {Nature *(Shakti)*}, or *Shiva-Shakti* (energy) without which there could be no creation.

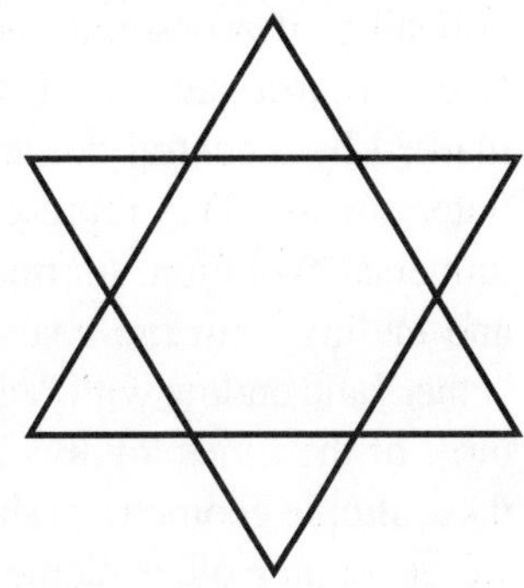

Triangle (Trikon)

The triangle is the symbol of Shakti. The triangle pointing down represents the *yoni*, (the feminine sexual organ and the) symbol of the supreme source of the Universe, and when the triangle is pointing upwards it signifies intense spiritual projection, modifies the natural expression (an instinctual impulse, especially a sexual one) in a socially acceptable manner of one's nature into the most subtle planes and the element of fire. The fire is always oriented upwards, thus the correlation with the upward triangle - Shiva Triangle. On the other hand, the downward pointing triangle signifies the element of water which always tends to be flown and occupies the lowest possible position. This triangle is known as Shakti *kona.*

Circle (Vrat)

Another simple geometrical shape often used in Yantras is circle, representing the rotation, a movement closely linked to the shape of spiral which is fundamental in the Macrocosmic evolution. At the same time, the circle represents perfection and the blissful creative void. In the series of the five fundamental elements it represents air element.

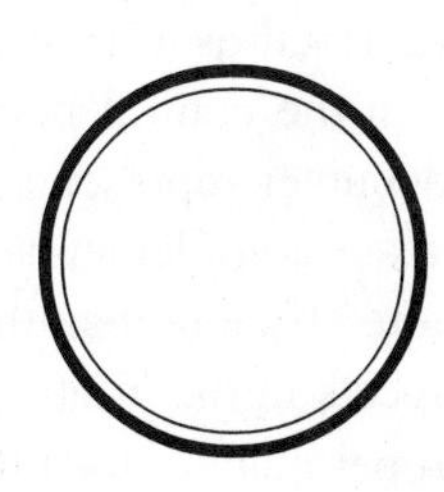

Square (Chaukor)

The square is usually the exterior limit of the Yantra and symbolically, it represents the element earth. Every Yantra starts from the center, often marked by a central dot and ends with the outer square. This represents the sense of universal evolution, starting from the subtle and ending with the coarse, starting from "ether" and ending with "earth". Even tough most of the times Yantras are composed of these simple geometrical shapes, sometimes we encounter other elements such as arrow points, tridents, swords, spikes included in the design of a Yantra with the purpose of representing vectors and directions of action for the *Yantric* energies.

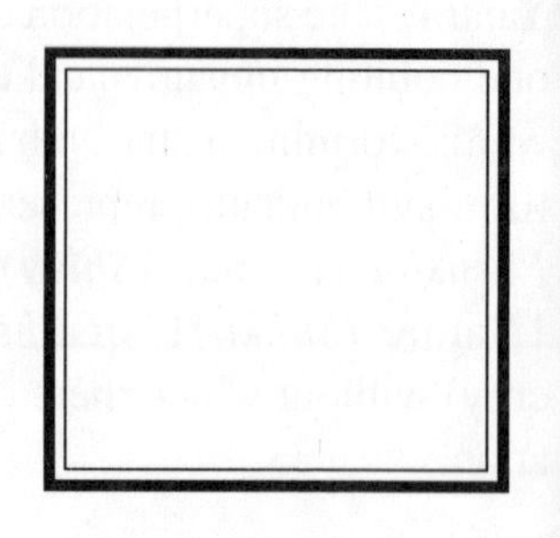

Lotus (Kamal)

The lotus symbol (or its petals) is a symbol of purity and variety, every lotus petal represents a distinct aspect. The inclusion of a lotus in a Yantra represents freedom from multiple interferences with the exterior (purity) and expresses the absolute force of the Supreme Self.

It may be worth to mention here that intersection of two geometric forms (lines, triangles, circles, etc.) represents forces that are even more intense than those generated by the simple forms. Such overlapping indicates a high level in the dynamic interaction of the correspondent energies. The empty spaces generated by such combinations are described as very efficient operational fields of the forces emanating from the central point of the Yantra. That is why we can very often encounter representations of *mantras* in such spaces. Yantra and mantra are complementary aspects of Shiva and their use together is much more efficient than the use of one alone. These signs represent different aspects in the Yantras. If these geometrical diagrams are sketched in a proper manner then the Yantras give their fruitful results.

CHAPTER 3

ASTROLOGY AND YANTRAS

Astrology is part of *Vedas*. Our saints while discovering different yantras also discovered their links with astrology. While writing the Yantras we have to follow the correct methods as told in our classics. The first thing which is to be taken into notice is correct *Hora* (*mahuarat*).

How Hora is used in writing the yantras?

Sl. No	Hora	Purpose of writing the yantra
1.	Jupiter	All yantras for good causes, love, affection, Cure for disease etc.
2.	Venus and Mercury	For object marked with magic signs and believed to confer on its bearer supernatural powers or protection, for opposite sex, conjuration, for bringing under control.
3.	Sun	For Love, affection, diseases, power, authority, favour from officers and Govt. servants. Meeting with ministers, officers etc.
4.	Saturn	Hatred, driven away, insult, death inflicting.
5.	Mars	Hatred, enmity, for enemies etc.
6.	Moon	Love affection for opposite sex etc.

According to above table, use of Hora of a planet is to be observed. For writing Yantra for good causes Hora of Jupiter is auspicious, this Hora is to be used for Yantras connected with love, affection , cure

HORA PERIODS

Hour	Duration	Sunday	Monday	Tuesday	Wednesday	Thursday	Friday	Saturday
1st	0 - 1	Sun	Moon	Mars	Mercury	Jupiter	Venus	Saturn
2nd	1 - 2	Venus	Saturn	Sun	Moon	Mars	Mercury	Jupiter
3rd	2 - 3	Mercury	Jupiter	Venus	Saturn	Sun	Moon	Mars
4th	3 - 4	Moon	Mars	Mercury	Jupiter	Venus	Saturn	Sun
5th	4 - 5	Saturn	Sun	Moon	Mars	Mercury	Jupiter	Venus
6th	5 - 6	Jupiter	Venus	Saturn	Sun	Moon	Mars	Mercury
7th	6 - 7	Mars	Mercury	Jupiter	Venus	Saturn	Sun	Moon
8th	7 - 8	Sun	Moon	Mars	Mercury	Jupiter	Venus	Saturn
9th	8 - 9	Venus	Saturn	Sun	Moon	Mars	Mercury	Jupiter
10th	9 - 10	Mercury	Jupiter	Venus	Saturn	Sun	Moon	Mars
11th	10 - 11	Moon	Mars	Mercury	Jupiter	Venus	Saturn	Sun
12th	11 - 12	Saturn	Sun	Moon	Mars	Mercury	Jupiter	Venus
13th	12 - 13	Jupiter	Venus	Saturn	Sun	Moon	Mars	Mercury
14th	13 - 14	Mars	Mercury	Jupiter	Venus	Saturn	Sun	Moon
15th	14 - 15	Sun	Moon	Mars	Mercury	Jupiter	Venus	Saturn
16th	15 - 16	Venus	Saturn	Sun	Moon	Mars	Mercury	Jupiter
17th	16 - 17	Mercury	Jupiter	Venus	Saturn	Sun	Moon	Mars
18th	17 - 18	Moon	Mars	Mercury	Jupiter	Venus	Saturn	Sun
19th	18 - 19	Saturn	Sun	Moon	Mars	Mercury	Jupiter	Venus
20th	19 - 20	Jupiter	Venus	Saturn	Sun	Moon	Mars	Mercury
21st	20 - 21	Mars	Mercury	Jupiter	Venus	Saturn	Sun	Moon
22nd	21 - 22	Sun	Moon	Mars	Mercury	Jupiter	Venus	Saturn
23rd	22 - 23	Venus	Saturn	Sun	Moon	Mars	Mercury	Jupiter
24th	23 - 24	Mercury	Jupiter	Venus	Saturn	Sun	Moon	Mars

of diseases etc. Venus Hora be used for talisman affairs, for opposite Sex, control of speech and dreams, *Mohan*, *Vashi Karan* etc. In Mercury Hora the items of Venus can also be written. Sun Hora is auspicious for love, affection, diseases, power, authority, favour from superiors and Govt., etc. In Saturn Hora Yantra for hatred enmity etc., are written and in Mars Hora Yantra for differences between friends, hatred, enmity etc., are written.

The table on page 12 has been prepared keeping in view durations in hours after local Sunrise time. Hora or each day starts with the lord of the day and other *horas* follow in an orderly manner such as Sun, Venus, Mercury, Moon and so on. The first Hora starts at the time of Sunrise. Necessary adjustments are required to be made for different places having different times of Sunrise.

Auspicious interval of time

Some particular period is assigned for writing the yantras. One should keep in mind these periods while writing the yantras.

Months :- The auspicious months for writing the yantras are *Sharavana*, *Bhadrapad*, *Aswin*, *Kartik*, *Margshir*, *Vaishak*, Pause, *Magha*, and *Phalgun*. These months are of Hindu *Vikram Samvat*. The yantras prepared during these months indicates successful results. They are beneficial for wealth, gold, gain, respect, comforts from children, promotion, success, education etc. The months of *Chaitra*, *Jyestha*, and *Asar* are middling for writing of yantras. Other months are not fit for writing of yantras.

For success in business, wealth, victory, fulfilment of desires etc., the yantras be written during first ten days of a month. For love, affection of opposite sex, etc., ten to twentieth days of month are auspicious. During last ten days of month, yantras for spiritual attainment, defeat of enemy, separation should be prepared.

Paksha :- Every month has two *pakhshas*. One is Shukla and the other is Krishna paksha. Bright half is known as Shukla Paksha and Dark half is known as Krishna Paksha. It starts after sunrise. *Shukla* Paksha is better than *Krishna* Paksha. The former is auspicious whereas latter is average. The yantras be prepared and written for vashi karan during

Shukal Paksha on seventh *tithi* morning. For success in business, the appropriate time is third or twelfth *tithis*. *Uchattan*, *Maran* etc., yantras are to be written during *Krishna Paksha* on second, sixth, seventh, or first, fourth, or fourteenth of *Shukal Paksha.* For Love affection etc., the best dates are eighth tithi in *Krishna Paksha* or fifth, tenth, eleventh, tithis in *Shukal Paksha.*

Nakshatra :- *Hast* and *Pushya Nakshatra* falling on Sunday are suitable for *Kashatriya*; *Rohini* and *Mrigasira* nakshatras falling on Monday are good for spiritual purposes; *Aswini* falling on Tuesday for jewellers; *Anuradha* on Wednesday for *Brahmins; Pushya* falling on Thursday for *Vaish*,; *Rewati* falling on Sunday is auspicious for persons in troubles, diseased and facing turmoil.

Day :- Monday morning is best for writing yantras for success in business *Vashi karan* and for recovery of diseases, the appropriate time is between morning and noon. Morning of Thursday and Friday is used for yantras relating to promotion, wealth etc. Saturday and Tuesday are termed appropriate days for *Maaran, Uchattan,* separation, enemy etc. Sunday and Wednesday are good days for controlling speech etc., and time is between noon and evening. The evening time is good for dream control etc.

There are some digits assigned to specific planets and deities. In case a particular deity is to be appeased, that particular digit is to be written first. This also applies to the directions.

Deity	**Direction**	**Digit**	**Planet**
Sun	East	1	Sun
Bhuvneshwari	North	2	Moon
Ganpati	North East	3	Jupiter
Hanumanji	North	4	Uranus (Negative Sun)
Vishnu	West	5	Mercury
Kartivirya	South west	6	Venus
Kali	South	7	Neptune
Bhairon	South West	8	Saturn
Bhairvi	West	9	Mars

At the time of writing Yantras, it should be borne in mind that one should himself be quite clean, wear clean clothes and place should also be purely clean. All material for writing the Yantra should be collected first to avoid any hindrance or break in the process of writing. Note the directions of writing yantra for each purpose along with Hora.

Purpose of yantra	Hora of planet	Direction	Articles
For love disease and Magic enchanting affection etc.	Moon	West	Mushak
Enmity, differences etc.	Saturn	East	Looban
Love, affection, patient and missing person	Jupiter	South	Camphor, Aud, Mushak and Barley
Love, controlling speech , sleep, dream and affection.	Venus	North	Amber, Sandal and Mushak
Love, controlling sleep, dream and affection.	Mercury	North	Camphor, Aud and Honey.
Cure from diseases, favour from superiors officers etc.	Sun	West	Looban, Camphor and Amber
Enmity, Vashikaran Enchanting.	Mars	East	Aud, Looban, and Sandal and Musk

Lagna for writing yantras

Tantras very much advise to perform the rites in right Hora. In the Rudrayamal Tantra it has been given in detail to perform pooja/sadhana of mantra/yantras in every lagan. There are twelve zodiac signs and every lagan (ascendant) has been assigned for different work.

1. **Aries (Mesha)** :- All yantras for wealth are written during this lagan.
2. **Taurus (Vrishbha)** :- If any devotee recite the mantras which are associated with their yantras during this lagan, for the purpose of Maaran, Vidveshan, it is good.
3. **Gemini (Mithun)** :- It destroys progeny.
4. **Cancer (Kark)** :- Auspicious for siddhi purposes.
5. **Leo (Simha)** :- It destroys the intelligence.
6. **Virgo (Kanya)** :- All mantras for *Lakshmi* (goddess wealth) etc. are to be recited.
7. **Libra (Tula)** :- Auspicious for all types of yantras.
8. **Scorpio (Varischak)** :- All yantras for gold gain etc. are to be recited as well as for victory over enemies.
9. **Sagittarius (Dhanu)** :- It indicates loss of respect etc.
10. **Capricorn (Makar)** :- It is an auspicious lagan for all works.
11. **Aquarius (Kumbh)** :- It is auspicious for yantras of wealth, religious type and *Siddhi* (power of mantras) etc.
12. **Pisces (Meena)** :- This lagan is termed as troublesome. So Taurus, Gemini, Leo, Sagittarius and Pisces lagans are to be avoided.

CHAPTER 4

YANTRA POOJA

As discussed in the previous chapter that there are different types of Yantras to please different deities for different works. For pleasing the deities we have to invite them, energise their idol or yantra and request for a favour or mercy from them. The *Shastras* says that the yantra without worship is just like a piece of article on which the yantra is drawn. Therefore our holy saints laid down some procedures to get the best through the Yantras. The process has different stages.

1. Purification of the aspirant
2. Selection of place
3. Drawing of yantra
4. Purification of yantra/mantra
5. Energising yantra
6. Worship of yantra

Get up early in the morning, one and a half hour before sun rise *(Brahm Mahurat)* and meditate upon your *Guru* (teacher of mantra *shastra*). Finish the daily essential routine work, change the clothes used during night. By reading the following verse sprinkle water on the body. By this act the *Mansik sanana* is done.

ॐ अपवित्रः पवित्रो वा सर्वावस्थां गतोऽपि वा।
यः स्मरेत् पुण्डरीकाक्षं स बाह्याभ्यन्तरः शुचिः॥

अतिनीलघनश्यामं नलिनायतलोचनम् ।
स्मरामि पुण्डरीकाक्षं तेन स्नातो भवाम्यहम् ॥

Om a'pavitra pavitro va sarvavastham gatoapi va ।
ya samret pundrikassam sa bhaya bhayantar suchi ॥
atinilghyanshyamam nalinayatlochnam ।
samrami pundikasham teen sanato bhavamayaham ॥

Now take bath in accordance with the directions as mentioned in our classics and mantra *Sanaana* thereafter. (There are seven types of bath which are named as *Mantra Sanaana, Bhaum Sanaana, Agni Sanaana, Vvayayva Sanaana, Divya Sanaana, Vaarun Sanaana, and Manasik Sanaana.*

Sanctification through the recitation of sacred verse आपो हि ष्ठा ***("Apo hi Vishthadi mantram)*** is called *Mantra Sanaana*, applying soil to the whole body is known as *Bhaum Sanaana*, applying ashes is known as *agni Sanaana*, applying the soil of the hoof of cow is *Vayavya Sanaana*, to take sun bath along with rain water is *divya Sanaana*, taking bath by taking a dip in the water is *varun Sanaana*, and performing self analysis is said to be the *manasik Sanaana*.

With the help of following first seven mantras sprinkle water on head. With the eighth mantra sprinkle water on the soil and again with the last one over the head. The mantra from yajurveda (11/50-52) for *mantra sanaana* is as follows:-

विनियोग : ॐ आपो हि ष्ठेत्यादित्र्यृचस्य सिन्धुद्वीप ऋषिर्गायत्री छन्दः आपो देवता मार्जने विनियोगः ।

१. ॐ आपो हि ष्ठा मयोभुवः । २. ॐ ता न ऊर्जे दधातन । ३. ॐ महे रणाय चक्षसे। ४. ॐ यो वः शिवतमो रसः ५. ॐ तस्य भाजयतेह नः । ६. ॐ उशतीरिव मातरः । ७. ॐ तस्मा अरं गमाम वः । ८. ॐ यस्य क्षयाय जिन्वथ । ९. ॐ आपो जनयथा च नः।

Viniyog :- Om Apoo hi shatetyaditrayarchasya sindhudweepe rishirgayatri chanda apoo devta marjane viniyoga.

1. Om Apoo hi shatha mayoobhuva । 2. Om ta na urje dadhatan।

3. Om mahe ranayee chakshee । 4.Om yoo va shivtamoo rase। 5. om tasye bhajye teh nah। 6. Om ushtiriv matra। 7. Om tasma aramgamam va । 8. Om yasya ksayaya jinvatha। 9. Om apoo janyatha cha nah।

At his place of worship the devotee shall perform the pooja at the door on all directions with the means of **अस्त्राय फट् (Astrya Phat)**. In the south direction **ॐ गं गणपतये नमः। ॐ दं दुर्गायै नमः। (Om gan ganpatye namah । Om dum durgayee namah।**), in the left side **ॐ वं वटुकाय नमः। ॐ क्षं क्षेत्रपालाय नमः। (Om vam vatukayee namah । Om ksam ksatrepalayee namah।**), on the door **ॐ सं सरस्वत्यै नमः। (Om sam Saraswatayee namah ।**), and on the door frame **ॐ अस्त्राय फट्। (Om Astraaye Phat)**. Now worship lord *Ganesha, Kurm, Anant, Vasudha, Ksaterpal*.

In the process of *Pranayama* inhale deeply repeating the *pranava (Om/ॐ)* Mantra thirty two times, retain the breath repeating the Mantra sixty-four times, and exhale repeating the Mantra sixteen times.

Thereafter perform *Bhuta Suddhi* (the purification of the five elements as physical constituents) in order to qualify for the worship of the deity. The mantra for *Bhuta Suddhi* is:-

ॐ सूर्यः सोमो यमः कालः सन्ध्या भूतानि पञ्च च ।
एते शुभाशुभस्येह कर्मणो मम साक्षिणः ॥१॥
भो देव प्राकृतं चितं पापा क्रान्तमभून्मम ।
तन्निस्सारय चित्तान्मे पापं तेस्तु नमोनमः ॥ २॥

Om Surya somo yama kala sandhya bhutani panch cha ।
Ete shubha subhshaye karmano mam sakshina ।। 1 ।।
Bho dev prakartam chitam papa krantmabhunmam ।
tannisasaraye chitaname papam testu namonamah ।। 2 ।।

After worshipping with these mantras say **ॐ गुरूभ्यो नमः। (Om Gurubhayoo namah।**), in the south and **ॐ गणेशाय नमः। (Om Ganeshaye namah ।**), in left side. After the performance of *Bhuta Suddhi* thus the devotee shall proceed to energise the yantra. The devotee should do the *Sadanga Nyaasa* (six limbed), *Nyaasa* (touching), enumerate the *pitha* *shaktis* and does resolution as under:-

देशकालौ संकीर्त्य ममामुकदेवतानूतनयन्त्रे मूर्तौ वा प्राणप्रतिष्ठां करिष्ये ॥

Deshkalo sankitarya mamamook devta nutan yantre murtau va pranparthistham karishasyee ॥

The Mantra for energising *(Pranparthistha)* is as follows:

विनियोगः अस्य श्रीप्राणप्रतिष्ठामन्त्रस्य ब्रह्माविष्णुमहेश्वरा ऋषयः। ऋग्यजुः सामानि छन्दांसि । क्रियामयवपुः प्राणाख्य देवता । आं बीजम् । ह्रीं शक्तिः । क्रां कीलकम् । अस्मिन्नूतनयन्त्रे मूर्तौ वा प्राणप्रतिष्ठापने विनियोगः।

Vinoyog :- Asya Shri Pranprathistha mantrasya brahma Vishunu Maheshwra Rishi, Ragyagu Samani Chandaasi, Kriyamayavapu, Pranakhaya Devta, Aam Bijam, Hrim Shakti, kram Kilkam, asminnutanyantre murtayee pranprathithapane viniyog.

If remembered (i.e. meditated upon) it bestows everything desired. After orating *viniyoga*, sprinkle water and recite the following mantra:-

ॐ आंह्रींक्रौंयंरंलंवंशंषंसंहंसः सोहं अस्याऽमुकदेवतासपरिवारयन्त्रस्य प्राणा इह प्राणाः । ॐ आंह्रींक्रौंयंरंलंवंशंषंसं हंसः सोहं अस्याऽमुकदेवतासपरिवारयन्त्रस्य जीव इह स्थितः । ॐ आंह्रींक्रौंयंरंलंवंशंषंसं हंसः सोहं अस्याऽमुकदेवतासपरिवारयन्त्रस्य सर्वेन्द्रियाणि इह स्थितानिः । ॐ आंह्रींक्रौंयंरंलंवंशंषंसं हंसः सोहं अस्याऽमुकदेवतासपरिवारयन्त्रस्य सर्वेन्द्रियाणि इह स्थितानिः । ॐ आंह्रींक्रौंयंरंलंवंशंषंसं हंसः सोहं अस्याऽमुकदेवतासपरिवारयन्त्रस्य वाङ्मनस्त्वक्चक्षुः श्रोत्रजिह्वा घ्राणपाणि पादपायुपस्थानि इहैवागत्य सुखं चिरं तिष्ठन्तु स्वाह ॥

Om am hrim krom yam ram lam vam sham sham sam hansa soham asya amuk devta saparivar yantrasaya prana iha prana । Om am hrim krom yam ram lam vam sham sham sam hansa soham asya amuk devta saparivar yantrasaya jeva iha sthithah । Om am hrim krom yam ram lam vam sham sham sam hansa soham asya amuk devta saparivar yantrasaya Sarve Indrayani ihahe sthithani । Om am hrim krom yam ram lam vam sham

sham sam hansa soham asya amuk devta saparivar yantrasaya vangmansatavkchakshu shotra jivha ghranpani pad payupasthani ihaevagtya sukham chiram tisthantu swah ॥

(In the above *shaloka* where *amuk* is written (underlined), replace it with the name of the deity of whom the yantra is concerned.)

Recite यः प्राणतोनिमिषतो महित्वे विधेम *(ya prantonimishto mahitve vidame)* three times and recite 108 times the yantra *gayatri* and do *dhyana* (mdeiate with concentration) of the concerned deity and invite him.

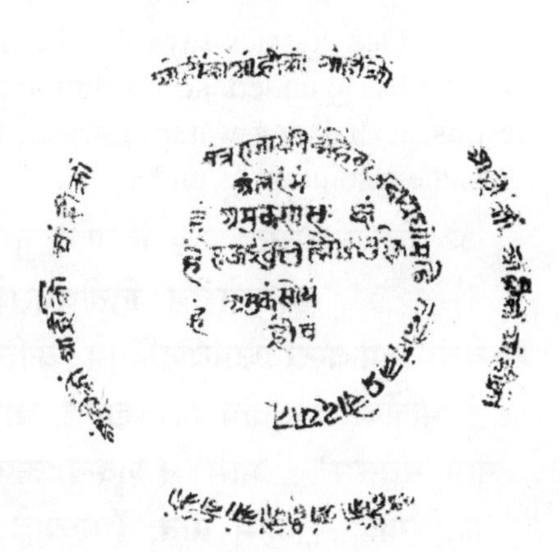

The Yantra Gayatri is:-

ॐ यन्त्रराजाय विद्महे महायन्त्राय धीमहि तन्नो यन्त्रः प्रचोदयात ॥

Om Yantra Rajaya Vidmahe Maha Yantrayee Dhimahe Tanno Yantra Pracodayat !!

After the performance of *Pranpratistha* (energising) the devotee shall perform *Matrika Nyaasa*. (The letters beginning with A (अ) and ending with *Ksa* (क्ष) are called *Matrikas*).

The sage of the Mantra for the performance of *Matrika Nyaasa* is *Prajapati*, the metre is *Gayatrii*, the deity is *Saraswati*. The *Viniyoga* (application) is the achievement of everything that one desires. All the consonants are the *Bijas* and the vowels *Shakti*. The *Nyaasa* should be done as told earlier.

Yantra pooja method

Before use and wear, pooja of every yantra is to be performed after energising for which there is a specific method. The method is provided here for the self use of devotee. The step wise method is to be adopted.

Since every yantra is associated to a particular *Deva* or *Devi*, so the devotee should first keep in mind, the particular Deity. *Dhyana* verse of each of the deities is given with every yantra. One should take flowers in the both hands; the flowers should be of *anjeel* and be offered to yantra reciting the *beej* mantra. This is worship of *Deva, ishat* or deity of the yantra.

Our classics says that before starting pooja of any deity the devotee has to undertake resolution other wise he did not get the desired results. By takaing water or water, flowers and some rice the devotee does the resolution as under:-

ॐ विष्णवे नमः, ॐ विष्णवे नमः, ॐ विष्णवे नमः । ॐ अद्य ब्रह्मणोऽह्नि द्वितीयपरार्धे श्रीश्वेतवाराहकल्पे वैवस्वतमन्वन्तरेऽष्टाविंशतितमे कलियुगे कलिप्रथमचरणे बौद्धावतारे भूर्लोके जम्बूद्वीपे भरतखण्डे भारतवर्षे.......क्षेत्रे[1] नगरे ग्रामे........ नाम-संवत्सरे[2]......मासे[3] (शुक्ल/कृष्ण) पक्षे......तिथौ[4] ...वासरे[5]......... गोत्र[6]......ऽहम् प्रातः (मध्याह्ने, सायं)[7] सर्वकर्मसु शुद्ध्यर्थं श्रुतिस्मृतिपुराणोक्तफलप्राप्त्यर्थं श्रीभगवत्प्रीत्यर्थं च अमुक कर्म करिष्ये ॥

Om Vishnave namah, Om Vishnave namah, Om Vishnave namah । Om Adh brahmanoahin dwitiyaeeprardhare shrishewat varahkalpe vavsavatmanvantreashtavinshtitme kaliyuge kaliprathamcharne bodhavataaree bhurlokee jambudweepe bharat khandee bharatvarshee.......ksashtree[1] nagree/ graame....name-samvantree [2]....... maase[3] (shukla/krishna) pakshee.........tihtoo [4]....vasaree[5]......gotree [6]......Sharma/verma/ guptoaham pratee (madhyaanee,saayeen) sarve karamsu suddharth shruti smrati puranookt phalpraptartham sshri bhagwatproitartham cha amuk karam karishashyee ॥

1. If one is doing pooja at some pilgrim centre then say the name of the place, if it is village or town say its name respectively.
2. The year of samvat is written on the panchang. Say the name of the year here. Always say the first name. For example 2005 A.D. is 2062 V.S.
3. Say the name of the Hindu calendar which is given in the glossary section. They are chaitra, Vaishakh etc.
4. Say the tithi such as pratipada, dwetya etc. as given in the glossary section as per panchang.

5. Say the name of the week ravi, som, bhom or mangal etc.
6. Say gotra as Vashisth, Gautam, Mudgil, etc.
7. Brahman should suffix Sharma; kshtrya should suffix Verma, and vashya gupt etc.

Poorva Pooja

1. Flowers be offered while speaking देवाय नमः आवाहमं सर्मपयामि ***Devaaye namah Aavahanam Samarpayam.***

2. Flowers are offered for *Assana* (seat) while reciting देवाय नमः आसनम सर्मपयामि ***Devaya namah Assanam Samarpayami.***

3. Water be offered to wash the feet of the Lord or deity while speaking देवाय नमः पाद्यं सर्मपयामि ***Devaye namah payadam samarpayame.***

4. Speaking देवाय अर्ध्य सर्मपयामि ***Devaye arghya samarpayame*** take three *achamans* and offer while reciting देवय आचमनीयं ***Devaye aachmaniyam.***

5. Bath be offered to Deva while reciting देवाय स्नानं सर्मपयामि ***Devaye sananam samarpayame.***

6. *Panch amrit* bath be offered with mantra देवाय पञ्चामृतस्नानं सर्मपयामि ***Devayave panchamrit sanaanam samarpayame.*** *Uddut sanan* be formed while reciting देवाय उदूतंन सर्मपयामि ***Devaye udutamn samarpayame.***

Uttar pooja

7. For *vastar* or clothes up *vastra* and *Yajya paveet*, recite the mantras.

- देवाय वस्त्रं सर्मपयामि ***Devaya Vastram samarpayame.***
- देवाय उपवस्त्रं सर्मपयामि ***Devaya upvastram samarpayame.***
- देवाय यज्ञोपवीतं सर्मपयामि ***Devaya Yajya paveet samarpayame.***

8. *Ghand* be applied while reciting देवाय गंधं सर्मपयामि ***Devaya Gandham samarpayame.***

9. Unbroken rice be offered while reciting देवाय अक्षतान् सर्मपयामि ***Devaya Akshtan samarpayame.***

10. For wealth this mantra be recited देवाय द्रव्यं सर्मपयामि ***Devaya Dravayam samarpayame.***

11. Flowers and garland be offered देवाय पुष्पाणि सर्मपयामि ***Devaya Pushpani samarpayame.***

12. *Dhoop* (incense stick) be lit and offered with mantra देवाय धूपं सर्मपयामि ***Devaya Dhupam samarpayame.***

13. Deep (lamp) be lit and offered with mantra देवाय दीपं सर्मपयामि ***Devaya Deepam samarpayame.***

14. Fruits etc., must be offered while reciting, देवाय नैवेद्यं फलं च सर्मपयामि ***Devaya Navaidyam phalm cha samarpayame.***

15. *Pan supari* be offered with mantra देवाय ताम्बुलं सर्मपयामि ***Devaya Tambulam samarpayame.***

16. For *arti* {fire flame offered in a clock wise direction (prayer)} recite the mantra देवाय प्रदक्षिणं सर्मपयामि ***Devaya Pardakshinam samarpayame.*** (*Pradakshina* means to walk around at the place be made thrice with following mantra.)

यानि कानि च पापानि जन्मान्तरकृतानि च ।
तानि सर्वाणि नश्यन्तु प्रदक्षिण पदे पदे ॥

Yani Kan cha papani janmantarkirtani cha ।
Tani Sarvani Nashyantu Pradakshin Pada Pade ॥

In the end offer flowers and *namaskar* with folded hands and prayer be performed with *beej* mantra with specific desires which be expressed. These sixteen steps are called *sodashupchar* pooja. If five steps are done they are called *panchupchar* pooja.

The above sixteen steps are for pooja of yantra. In case one can not do all for any reason, the devotee is advised to light *dhoop*, apply sandal red vermillion and scent while reciting *Beej* mantra after taking bath and wear new clothes. After the pooja the devotee is advised to read the following mantra for requesting pardon from the deity for any mistake done during the worship and requesting Him to bestow the desired fruits. Through this mantra the devotee is surrendring himself to the God. The mantra is as under:-

आवाहनं न जानामि न जानामि विसर्जनम् ।
पुजाभागं न जानामि त्वं गतिःपरमेश्वर ॥ १॥
मंत्रहीनं क्रियाहीनं भक्तिहीनं सुरेश्वर ।
यत्पूजितं मया देव परिपूर्ण तदस्तु मे ॥ २॥
यदक्षरपदभ्रष्टं मात्राहीनं च यद्भवेत् ।
तत्सर्वं क्षम्यतां देव प्रसीद परमेश्वर ॥ ३ ॥
कर्मणा मनसा वाचा त्वत्तो नान्या गतिर्मम ।
अन्तश्चरसि भूतानि इष्टस्त्वं परमेश्वर ॥ ४ ॥
अन्यथा शरणं नास्ति त्वमेव शरण मम ।
तस्मात्कारुण्यभावेन क्षमस्य परमेश्वर ॥ ५ ॥
मातृयोनिसहस्त्रेषु सहस्त्रेषु व्रजाम्यहम् ।
तेषु चेष्वचला भक्तिरच्युतेस्तु सदा त्वयि ॥ ६ ॥
गतं पापं गतं दुःखं गतं दारिद्र्यमेव च ।
आगता सुखसम्पत्तिः पुण्याच्च तव दर्शानात् ॥ ७ ॥
देवो दाता च भोक्ता च देवरूपमिदं जगत् ।
देवं जपति सर्वत्र यो देवः सोहमेव हि ॥ ८ ॥
क्षमस्व देव देवेश क्षम्यते भुवनेश्वर ।
तव पादाम्बुजे नित्यं निश्चला भक्तिरस्तु ॥ ९ ॥

Aavahanam na janami na janami visarjanam ।
poojabhagam na janami tavam gati parmeshwar ॥ 1 ॥
mantrahinam kriyahinam bhaktihinam sureshwar ।
yatpujitam maya dev paripurna tadastume ॥ 2 ॥
yadksarpadbrashtam matrahinam cha yadbhavet ।
tatsarv samayatam dev parseed parmeshwar ॥ 3 ॥
karmana mansa vacha tavto nanya gatirmam ।
Antascharsi bhutani iststavam parmeshwara ॥ 4 ॥
Anayatha sharnam naasti tamavev sharan mam ।
Tasmatkarunyabhaven shameshav parmeshvar ॥ 5 ॥
Matryoni sehasareyashu sehasareyashu varjayaham ।
Teshu cheshvachla bhaktijchayutestu sada tavayi ॥ 6 ॥

Gatam papam gatam dukham gatam daridrya mev cha ।
Aagta sukhsampti punyaccha tav darshnat ॥ 7॥
dedo data cha bhokta cha devrupmidam jagat ।
Devam japati sarvatra yo deva sohmev hi ॥ 8 ॥
Shameshva dev devesh shaymayate bhuvneshvar।
Tav paadambuje nityam nischla bhaktirastu me ॥ 9 ॥

Some instructions for the devotee while energising yantra and performing pooja.

1. Select a suitable place for the initiatory rites such as a Temple, holy centre, secluded spot etc. This is for the sake of getting the deity favourably disposed.

2 He shall cut the spot into nine straight line figures and write the seven sets of letters as well as La (ल) and (क) in the figures beginning with the eastern one with the Vowels in the centre.

3. Seat is to be in that direction for the performance of *Japa*, where the initial letter of the name of the place selected comes in the geometrical figures. It shall not be in any other spot that is likely to produce misery.

4. Japa in a low whispering voice or mentally. He shall take only *Havisya* (Rice mixed with ghee) at night and three baths every day. Oil bath is not allowed.

5. At the time of the Japa excitement, idleness, spitting, getting angry, stretching of legs, conversation with others and seeing unconcerned persons should be avoided.

6. Intimate talk with women and persons who do not have knowledge of *shastras*, censuring others, chewing betel leaves, sleeping during the daytime, acceptance of monetary gifts, dance, music and evasiveness of behaviour ought to be avoided.

7. Lying on the bare ground, celibacy (in strict sences includes no kissing or intimacy), worshipping of the deity thrice a day, special worship on stipulated occasions, singing of the hymns of the deity and faith should strictly be adhered to.

8. Everyday he shall repeat the names (Japa) for the same number

of times, neither less nor more. After concluding the Japa *Homa* should be performed for one tenth of the number of *Japas*.

9. The articles to be used for Homa are those mentioned in the respective ritualistic and ceremonial codes.

10. By means of the *Mula mantra* the devotee shall perform *Pranayama* and *sadanga Nyaasa*.

11. The sacrificial pit be made holy or the selected spot by the Mula mantra etc. for performing the four rites namely *Iksana* (seeing) *Proksana* (sprinkling), *Tadana* (beating) and *Secana* (scattering in continuous drops). The Iksana rite is by means of the Mula mantra. The *Prokshna* rite is by means of the Mantra *Astriiya Phat*. The Tadana rite is gentle beating with the *Kusa* grass. The pouring rite of secana is by means of the closed fist uttering the Mantra Hum (हुं).

12. Now *Vahni* yantra is drawn. This Yantra consists of triangle, hexagon, circle, eight petal figure and square. In the centre write ॐ ह्रीं ॐ (**Om Hrim Om**) and worship the base. Now begin the pooja of the deities of Pitha beginning with *Manduka* and ending with *Paratattva* and also the *Pithasaktis*, beginning with *Jaya*. By means of this mantra the seat shall be offered to both of them.

Method of drawing Yantra

The *tantras* have directed the devotee to begin the special worship of the deity of his own choice on an auspicious day (Refer the chapter astrology and yantras for details). By keeping full control over his characteristic of the body organs the devotee shall lie down on the uncovered ground. Havisya would remain his food and he should always be engaged in the reverberation of mantras.

Before start of his everyday worship he should ask, "How shall this yantra written by me be?" Then the deity should be worshipped. The devotee would witness the required dream on the night of the third day as to whether it is *Siddha*, *Saadhya*, *Susiddha* or *Satrubhuuta*. He shall never endeavour to write *Satrubhuta* (that is enimical). He can never write any of the others. In case no dream is forthcoming, the devotee shall never write the unfavourable one but only the others.

General procedure regarding all the Yantras

1. The Yantras must be written with the specific materials in the places mentioned in a scheduled spot. The writing materials used for writing the Yantras are :-

   Agar, tagar, gorochan, jatamansi, safeed chandan, lal chandan,Kessar. All these items are grounded well to form *Ashat Gandh* powder. It is mixed with water of Ganges (or of any sacred river) to form ink. For making ashat Drava (eight liquids) Ikshu, sattu, banana, chiuda, sesame seeds, modak, coconut and lava of rice is used.

2. The word intended victim ending in the genitive case should be written on the middle *Bija*. The Saadhya (person or activity) in the Accusative shall be written beneath it. The word *Kuru* is written twice in the sides.

3. The Bija {(*Hsauh*) it is considered soul of the Yantra} is to be written beneath the middle portion. Then *Hamsah* Soham (the vital airs) be written in the corners e.g., north east etc.

4. On either side *Netra* (I and I) and *Srotra* (U and O) are to be written and the Bijas of the guardians of the quarters. [Lam (लं) Ram (रं), Mam (मं), Kam (कं), Yam (यं), Yam (यं), Sam (सं), Ham (हं), Am (अं) and Hrim (ह्रीं)] should be written in the quarters. The Yantra Gayatri should be written all rounds at the rate of three

syllables per quarters. Externally the *Pranapratistha* Mantra is to be written encircling everything.

5. If the object on which Yantra is to be written is not mentioned, then it shall be written on *Bhojpatra*, silk cloth or palm leaf, folded up and tied up with a thread.

6. The deity is to be worshipped with the central *Bija* of the deity or the initial letter of the name of the deity, the concerned Mantra should be repeated, the requisite number of *Homas* should be performed the Yantra should be soaked in, the *Sampata* (residue ghee) and put into an amulet made of gold, silver or copper sealed well with lac. Thereafter it can be put into regular use by wearing it on the head, arms or neck for the purpose of realizing the desired benefit.

7. The *Bhutalipi* (script of the spirit consists of 42 letters) should be worship (repeated in japa) by one who is assured of making use of the Yantra. By means of this *Upasti* the devotee will be capable of perfecting the mastery of all *Siddhis*.

ॐ अं आं इं ईं उं ऊं ऋं ॠं लं लॄं एं ऐं ओं औं अं अः कं
खं गं घं डं चं छं जं ञं टं ठं डं ढं णं तं थं दं धं नं पं फं बं भं मं
यं रं लं वं शं षं सं हं लं क्षं ॥

Om, am, aam, im, iim, um, uum, rrm, rrrm, lam, larm, Em, Aim, Om, Aum, Am, Am, kam, kham, gam, gham, dam, cham, cham, jam, anam, tam, tham, dham, ddham, anam, Tam, Tham, Dham, Dam, Mam, Pam, Pham, Bam, Bham, Mam Yam, ram, Lam Vam, Sham, Sam, Sm, ham, lam, Ksam ॥

(Bhutalipi : The five short vowels, A, E, Ai, O and Au; the five groups of consonants; the semivowels, aspirate and the sibilants).

Yantras should always be used on the level. If drawn on paper the colours preferable are red, orange, yellow or a combination of these. A Yantra without bija mantras is dead. They can be drawn to whatever size is required. In worship they should be placed level on a pedestal or pitha.

CHAPTER 5

GANESH YANTRA

In Hindu mythology Shri Ganesha is revered as the son of the *Shiva and Parvati,* and is always honoured first in most worship services and rituals. Ganesha is also known as *Ganapati, Vigneswara* (one who destroys hurdels), *Vinayaka, Gajamukha and Ainkaran.* He is worshipped for *siddhi*, success in undertakings, and *buddhi*, intelligence. His worship is considered auspicious before any venture is started, may it business, the building of a house or the writing of a book or even undertaking a journey. He is also the God of education, knowledge wisdom, literature, fine arts, the design God of wisdom who removes all obstacles.

Benefit from Ganesha worship

The one who worships Ganesha is blessed with success in his work, business, undertaking and desires. Ganesha pooja can be performed through idol or through Ganesha yantra. Ganapati or Ganesha, the Lord of *Ganas*, the elephant headed God, represents the power of the Supreme being that removes obstacles and ensures success in human endeavours.

Ganesh yantra

Ganesha pooja can be performed through idol, photo or through Yantra. *Swastika* is the sign of Lord Ganesha. In case one can not have yantra, pooja of *swastika* is also auspicious and mantras be recited. The yantra is carved on gold or silver plate. Ganesha yantra is written in accordance to canons in auspicious *hora* and *mahurta* and *mantra* should be recited and yantra is purified. It could also be drawn on any metal with red vermillion or asthgandh.

Ucchist Mahaganpati yantra

This yantra is of Maha Ganapati. This yantra bestows sons wealth, comforts, grand sons and all cherished dreams. From *Ashtmi* of bright half till *chaturdashi* if some one does eighty five hundred *japas* and 1/10 of japas as homa, his all wishes are fulfilled. If this yantra is being used in attraction purpose of higher Govt. officials or minister then take four thousand flowers of *Dhatura* and offer them to lord Ganesha while reciting the mantra as given below. Ucchatan is done with one thousand offering with the twigs of *neem*. While worshipping Shri Chakra (Shri Yantra) this yantra is also worshipped. The mantra for recital is :-

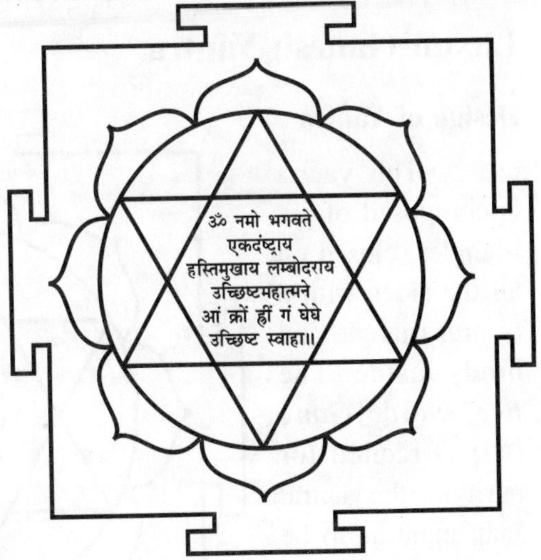

ॐ नमो भगवते एकदंष्ट्राय हस्तिमुखाय लम्बोदराय उच्छिष्टमहात्मने
आं क्रों ह्रीं गं घेघे उच्छिष्ट स्वाहा॥

Om namo bhagwate ekdanstraya hastimukhaya lammodraya uchchistmahatmane aam krom hrim gan ghege ucchist swah ॥

The sage of the mantra is *Matang bhagwan rishi*, metre *gayatri, ucchist mahaganpati devta, gam bijam, swah shakti, hrim kilkam,* application of the mantra is for all cherished dreams. The mantra is to be recited for one hundred thousand times. The yantra is carved on copper, gold, silver or *bhojpatra* with *asthgandh* with the stylus of pomegranate.

Dhyana verse

ॐ शरान्धनुः पाशसृणी स्वहस्तैर्दधानमारक्तसरोरुहस्थम् ।
विवस्त्रपात्न्यां सुरतप्रवृत्तमुच्छिष्टमम्बासुतमाश्रयेऽहम् ॥

Om shrandhanu pashsarni savhasteerddhanmarktsaroruhstham।
Vivsatrpatnyam suratparvartmuchistmmbasutmasharayaham ॥

Laxmi Ganesh Yantra

Design of Yantra

This yantra is composed of six triangles, closed on all the sides with a central triangle and binds inside. The *Beej* word {*Gang (गं)*} is recited for purifying the yantra. Jaap mantras to be recited for purifying the Laxmi Vinayak Yantra.

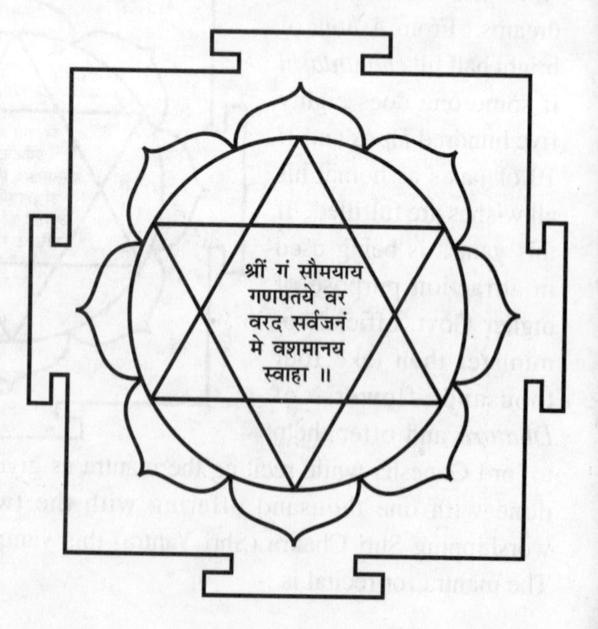
श्रीं गं सौमयाय
गणपतये वर
वरद सर्वजनं
मे वशमानय
स्वाहा ॥

Mantra for recital is:-

श्रीं गं सौमयाय गणपतये वर वरद सर्वजनं मे वशमानय स्वाहा ॥

Om gang somvaye Ganpatiye var vard Sawjanam me Vashmanaye Savaha ॥

The sage of the Mantra is Antaryami (The imminent Soul).The metre is Gayatri. The deity of the' Mantra is Lakshmi Vinayaka. The Bija is Srim and the Shakti is Swaha. the mantra has to be repeated for four hundred thousand times. The food for offerings are honey, milk, and coconut.

Dhyana Verse

दन्ताभ्ये चक्रवरौ दधानं कराग्रगं स्वर्णघट त्रिनेत्रम् ।
धृताब्जयालिङ्गितमब्धिपुत्र्या लक्ष्मीगणेशं कनकाभमीडे ॥

Dantebhaye chakrevaao dadhaanam karagargam swaran ghat trinetram ।
Grithabajyalingitambaniputrya laxmiganesham kankabhmide ॥

With the twigs of the Bilva tree homa is performed. At the outset he performs the *Aanga pooja* (ancillary worship) and then worship the eight Shaktis *Balaka*, *Virnala*, Kamala, *Vanamaliki*, *Vibhiika*, *Malika*, *Sailkari* and *Vasubaliki*.The devotee sits at the root of the Bilva tree and repeats the mantra three hundred thousand times. He reaps the same benefit as told in the beginning. By performing Homa with rice grains smeared with ghee in the fire kindled with *Ashoka* twigs, the devotee can bring the entire universe under his control. During the summer *Arka* twigs can be used. If the Homa is performed with milk pudding in the fire kindled with *Khadira* twigs the devotee brings the govt. officials or ministers under his control. He obtains glory and fortune also.

Haridra ganpati yantra (for marriage and son)

One who worships haridra ganpati all his cherished desires are fulfilled. On the Chaturdashi of the bright half, the devotee should smear his body with turmeric, powdered by a maiden and take bath in holy water before worshipping lord Ganesha. A barren lady is blessed with a son if she worships hardira Ganesha. On can conquer water, fire, thieves, lions, and weapons by with standing then he can even stun the speech of enemies. The mantra for recital is:-

ॐ हुंगंग्लौं हरिद्रागणपतये वर वरद सर्वजनहृदयं स्तम्भय स्तम्भय स्वाहा ॥

Om Hum gam glaum Hariddraganpati vara varda sarvajanahridayam stambhaya stambhaya swaha ॥

The sage of the mantra is *Madana*, the meter is *anustup* the deity is *haridragananayaka.* The mantra is to be recited for four hundred thousand times and after that perform forty thousand homa with rice grains mixed with powdered turmeric. Then feed *Brahmins*. After tarpan he shall repeat the mantra thousand and eight times. If the homa is done with sweet pies prepared in ghee a hundred times and feed them to religious student and propitiate virgins. Through this all desired would be fulfilled. If the Homa is performed with fried grain the devotee gets a bride and the bride would get a bride groom.

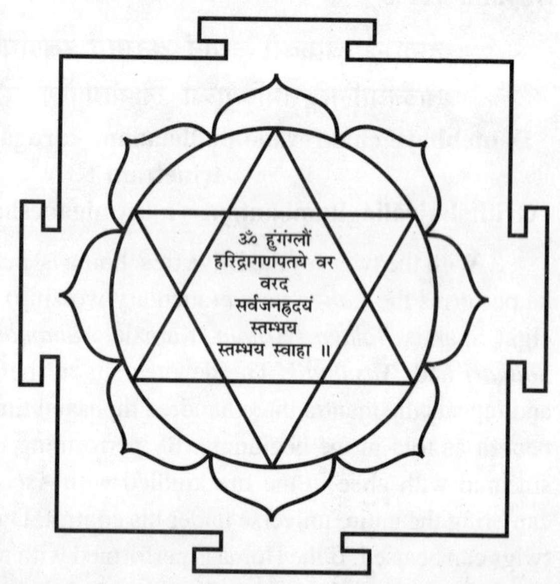

Adhochist ganpati nivaran yantra

For worshipping this yantra first of all the devotee should make an idol of Lord Ganesha either of red sandal wood or white arka tree and that has to be the size of the thumb of the devotee. After energizing, the idol should be bathed in the honey. Person who worships this yantra gets all benefits from the govt., and enemies never destroy him. The mantra for recital is:-

हस्तिपिशाचिलिखेस्वाहा ॥

Hasti Pisaci likhe swaha ॥

The sage of this mantra is *kamkola*, the meter is virat and the deity is ucchistaganpati. The mantra is to be recited for one hundred thousand times and the homa with gingelly seeds is performed for ten thousand times.

Dhyana verse

चतुर्भुजं रक्ततनुं त्रिनेत्रं पाशांकुशौ मोदकपात्रदंतौ ।
करैर्दधानं सरसीरुहरथमुन्मत्तमुच्छिष्टगणेशमीडे ॥

Chaturbhujam rakttanum trinetram pashamkushoo midakpatram danto ।
kreerdhadhanam sarsiruharthmumtuchisthganeshmidey॥

The devotee should wear red cloth, or apply red unguents. He shall chew betel in the night and while chewing it repeat the mantra. He shall offer fruits along with betel leaves. The devotee can repeat the mantra while eating sweet meat offered during the prayers as *naveidya* to the lord. After realization the yantra do the rites for achievement of desired objectives.

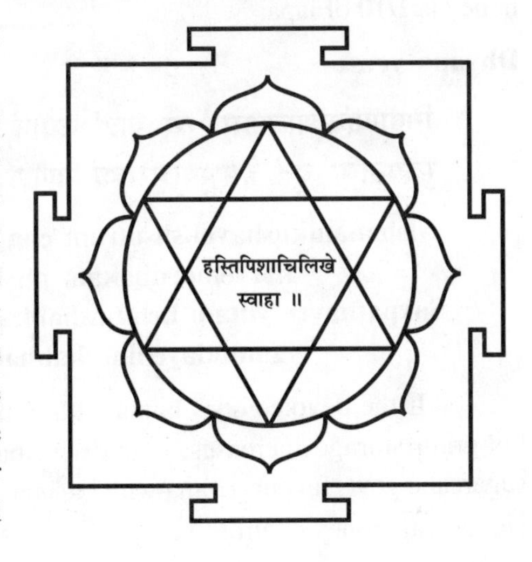

Shakti Vinayak Yantra

By worshipping this yantra a person would never die due to starvation. Storage of food is always full at his home. It also gives *siddhi* to the devotee and through regular worship of this yantra a person gets all what he desires. The mantra for recital is:

ॐ ह्रीं ग्रीं ह्रीं ॥

Om Hrim grim hrim ॥

The sage of this mantra is Bhargva, the meter is *virat*, and the deity is *Shakti Vinayaka, gram bija, hrim shakti,* application of this mantra is for fulfilling of all cherished desires. The mantra is to be recited for four hundred thousand times and homa with honey is 1/10 of japa.

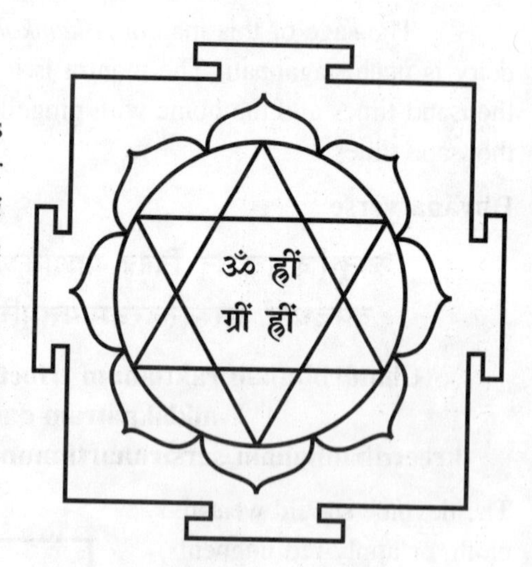

Dhyana verse

निषाणांकुशावक्षसूत्रं च पाशं दधानं करैर्मोदकं पुष्करेण ।
स्वपत्नया युतं हेमभूषाभराढ्यं गणेशं समुद्यद्दिनेशाभमीडे ॥

Nishanamkushavakshsutram cha pasham dadhanam kareemordhakam pushkraen ।
Savpatnayee yutam hembushabharadayam ganesham samudayedineshabhameda ॥

If the devotee does homa with grains smeared with pure ghee his grain storage increases, homa with palas increases wealth, with sugarcane govt. favour. Homa with banana and coconut attracts people, Homa with honey controls a lady.

CHAPTER 6

GAYATRI YANTRA

Gayatri Devi is Maha Devi and deity of Shri Gayatri yantra. Reference of Gayatri Mantra comes in *Shukla Yajurveda* (36: 3) and the mantra is considered most auspicious in the *Vedic* chronology.

Gayatri Yantra is bestowal of knowledge of *Vedas*, religion, business and salvation. This yantra is kept in house or business place. By the sincere use of this yantra, one cannot be affected by souls, spirits and is blessed with health, wealth and happiness. In case, a house or man is afflicted by souls and spirits, the yantra after pooja be dipped in water, and water is sprinkled in house for a week, all spirits etc., will vanish. This yantra washes away all sins of the devotee if he worships the yantra in letter and spirit.

Gayatri worship

The Gayatri worship is done on the top of the mountain, bank of a river, temple, under the shade of *peepal* tree etc. When the Moon is in auspicious hora, Gayatri worship is considered best for the devotee. For Gayatri yantra *sadhana* one has to be complete vegetarian. Take only

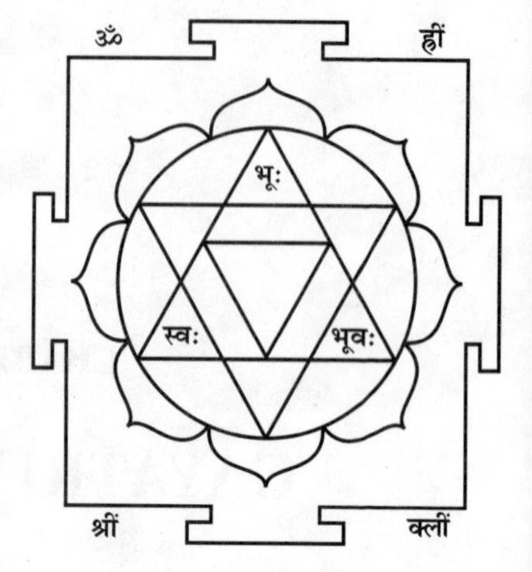

rice and milk once during a day during the pooja period of the yantra as food. The bed used during the Gayatri sadhna should be of durva grass and the devotee has to remain isolated for forty days.

During Gayatri yantra *sadhna jyestha*, *asadh*, *badhrapad*, *pusha* and *malmasa*; Tuesday, Saturday; *Vayatipat*, and *vaidarti yoga; ashtami, navmi, chartuthi, trodashi, chaturdashi*, *Amavasya*, *pardosh*, night, *yam, agni, Rudra*, *sarp*, *inder*, *vasu*, *shravan*, and birth constellation , Aries, Cancer, Taurus, Aquarius, and Capricorn all are prohibited. The Gayatri worship should be started during *poornima* in the *Hora* of Moon.

Design of the Yantra

The Yantra contains eight petal lotus, one triangle, a hexagon and one beautiful *bhupura*. The Gayatri Devi is seated on a Lotus. This yantra is carved on gold, silver or copper plate.

Gayatri mantra has twenty four sages, and metre and deities are in the same corresponding numbers. The mantra is to be recited for thirty two hundred thousand times. Some texts are of the view that the mantra should be recited as per the number of alphabets in the mantra in the multiples of hundred thousand times. The devotee should divide the *japas* equally and the number should not change. The Gayatri mantra is cursed by our sages (Brahma, Vashisth and Vishvamitra) hence, the devotees are advised to first do the *Shapvimochan* (An appeal or prayer for good fortune) of the mantra before recital, to reap the desired fruits.

Brahama shapvimochan

ॐ अस्य श्रीब्रह्मशापविमोचनमन्त्रस्य ब्रह्मा ऋषिर्भुक्तिप्रदा ब्रह्म शापविमोचनी गायत्री शक्तिर्देवता । गायत्री छन्दः । ब्रह्मशापविमोचने विनियोगः ॥

Om Asya Shri Brahm shapvimochanmantrasaya brahma rishi. bhukti brada brahmshapvimochni, gayatri shaktirdevta। Gayatri chanda। Brahma shapvimochni viniyog।

The sage of the Brahma shapvimochan mantra is Brahma, deity is salvation giving devi gayatri, metre is gayatri, and application of the mantra is Brahma shapvimochan. Through the following mantra one has to do *shapvimochan* of gayatri mantra and recite the same for three days.

ॐ गायत्रीब्रह्मेत्युपासीत यद्रूपं ब्रह्मविदो विदुः ।
तां पश्यन्ति धीराः सुमनसा वाचामग्रतः ॥

ॐ वेदान्तनाथाय विद्महे हिरण्यगर्भाय धीमहि। तन्नो ब्रह्म प्रचोदयात्
। ॐ देवी ! गायत्री त्वं ब्रह्मशापाद्विमुक्ता भव ।

Om gayatri brahmotyupasit yadrpam brahmvido vidu। tam pasayanti dhira sumansa vachaamgrata। Om vedantnathaya vidhmahe hirangrabhaye dhimahi। tanno braham parchodayat। Om devi ! Gayatri tavam brahamshapadivimukta bhav।

Vashisth shapvimochan

ॐ अस्य श्रीवसिष्ठशापविमोचनमन्त्रस्य निग्रहानुग्रहकर्ता वसिष्ठ ऋषिर्वसिष्ठानुग्रहीता गायत्री शक्तिर्देवता । विश्वोद्भवा गायत्री छन्दः । वसिष्ठशापविमोचनार्थं जपे विनियोगः ॥

Om Asya Shri Vashisth shapvimochanmantrasaya nigrah anugrah karta Vashisth rishi. Vashisth anugrahhita gayatri shaktirdevta. vishvodbhava Gayatri chanda. Vashisth shapvimocharth jape viniyog.

The sage of the Vashisth shapavimochan mantra is *Brahma*, deity is salvation giving devi gayatri, metre is gayatri, and application of the mantra is vashisth *sapvimochan*. Through the following mantra one has to do *shapvimochan* of the gayatri mantra and recite the following mantra for three days.

ॐ सोऽहमर्कमयं ज्योरात्मज्योतिरहं शिवः।
आत्मज्योतिरहं शुक्रः सर्वज्योतिरसोऽस्म्यहम् ॥

ॐ देवी ! गायत्री त्वं वसिष्ठशापाद्विमुक्ता भव ।

Om sohamkarmayam jyoratamjyotirham shiva । Aatamjyotirham shukra sarvjyotirsosamayaham । Om Devi Gayatri tavam Vashisth shapadivimukta bhav।

Vishvamitra shapvimochan

ॐ अस्य श्रीविश्वामित्रशापविमोचनमन्त्रस्य नूतनसृष्टिकर्ता विश्वामित्र ऋषिः। विश्वामित्रानुग्रहीता गायत्री शक्तिर्देवता। वाग्देहा गायत्री छन्दः । विश्वामित्रशापविमोचनार्थं जपे विनियोगः ॥

Om Asya Shri Vishvamitra shapvimochanmantrasaya nigrah anugrah karta Vishvamitra rishi. Vishvamitra anugrahhita gayatri shaktirdevta. vagdeha Gayatri chanda. Vishvamitra shapvimochnarthe jape viniyog.

The sage of the Vishvamitra shapvimochan mantra is Brahma, deity is salvation giving devi gayatri, metre is gayatri, and application of the mantra is Vishvamitra sapvimochan. Through the following mantra one has to do *shapvimochan* of the gayatri mantra and recite the following mantra for three days.

ॐ गायत्री भजाम्यग्निमुखीं विश्वगर्भां यदुद्भवाः ।
देवाश्चक्रिरे विश्वसृष्टिं तां कल्याणीमिष्टकरीं प्रपद्ये ॥
यन्मुखान्निःसृतोऽखिलवेदगर्भः । ॐ गायत्री त्वं विश्वामित्रशापाद्विमुक्ता भव ।

Om sohamkarmayam jyoratamjyotirham shiva । Aatamjyotirham hukra sarvjyotirsosamayaham । Om Devi Gayatri tavam Vashisth shapvimukta bhav।

Before mantra recital perform sadanga nayasa.

Dhyana verse

ॐ यद्देवैः सुरपूजितं परतरं सामर्थ्य तारात्मिकं
पुन्नागांबुजपुष्पनागवकुलौः केशैः शुकैरर्चितम् ।
नित्यं ध्यानसमस्तदीप्तिकरणं कालाग्निरुद्दीपनं तत्संहारकरं नमामि सततं पातालसंस्थं मुखम् ॥

Om yaddavee surpujitam partaram samarthaya taramitkam punnagabujpushpnagvakulau keshee rachirtam । Nityam dhyan samastdipti karnam kalaginiruddipanam tatsanharkaram namami satam patalsanstham mukham ॥

Now do prayer with folded hands as given below:

ॐ अहो देवि महादेवि संध्ये विद्ये सरस्वति ।
अजरे अमरे चैव ब्रह्मयोनिर्नमोऽस्तु ते ॥

ॐ देवि गायत्रि त्वं ब्रह्मशापाद्विमुक्ता भव, वसिष्ठशापाद्विमुक्ता भव, विश्वामित्रशापाद्विमुक्ता भव ।

Om Aho devi mahadevi sandhye vidye saraswati Ajre amre chaiv brahamyonirnamoastu te ॥

Om Devi gayatri tavam brahmashapadivimukta bhav, vashisthadi shapa divimukta bhav, Vishvamitrashavpaidimukta bhav ॥

Now do the viniyoga (application) of gayatri mantra:

Viniyoga

ॐकारस्य ब्रह्मा ऋषिर्गायत्री छन्दः परमात्मा देवता, ॐ भूर्भुवः स्वरिति महाव्याहृतीनां परमेष्ठी प्रजापतिर्ऋषिर्गायत्र्युष्णिगनुष्टुभश्छन्दांसि अग्निवायुसूर्या देवताः ॐ तत्सवितुरित्यस्य विश्वामित्रऋषिर्गायत्री छन्दः सविता देवता जपे विनियोगः ॥

Om karasya brahma rishirgayatri chanda parmatma devata, om Bhurbhuva svariti mahavyahritinam parmesthi prajapatir rishir gayatriushninustubhschandashi agni vayusurya devta Om tatsavituritasya vishvamitra rishir gayatri chanda savita devta jape viniyoga । ।

Mantra for recital

ॐ भूर्भुवः स्वः तत्सवितुर्वरेण्यं भर्गो देवस्य धीमहि । धियो यो नः प्रचोदयात् ॥

Om Bhoorbhuvah Swah Tatsyavitur Vareniyam, Bhargo Devasya Dhi Mahi Dhiya Yona Prachodyat ।।

Some usages of Gayatri yantra after realisation

1. After realization of the yantra in case of disease, recite the mantra for ten times and exorcism the patient, who will be cured.
2. As and when one has to do any job, recite the mantra and every thing would be in order. When a house is affected by souls etc., recite the mantra for four days and sprinkle the water in the house, all evils will go.
3. In case of *siddhi* of any Yantra, recite the mantra and draw a line and sit inside the line and perform *japa* of yantra. Siddhi of yantra will be attained. Many other uses can be made of Gayatri Yantra.
4. Before pooja of any yantra worship Gayatri yantra with the mantra. It helps in attaining success.
5. If a man dies with unnatural death, japa of this mantra leads him to salvation.
6. A native afflicted with souls, can be treated successfully. Give a smoke of gugal, dhoop and white mustard to native and recite ten times the mantra, purify the water, sprinkle the water and water be taken by the native. All effects will go.
7. For gain of wealth use fresh flower of Juhi or Red Lotus. Also can use *samidhas* (portion of wood use in Homa for agni) of Bilva tree, its leaves, flowers fruit or its root with pure ghee in Homa.
8. *Samidhas* of Shami, Bilva or Visheshar Aak or their flowers with ghee be used in Homa for aacqusition of Gold wealth etc.
9. Dip the leaves of bilva in ghee and use in Homa. This makes the devotee wealthy.
10. Round balls of Gugal be used in Homa with Ghee to be a fortunate.
11. One is blessed with wealth and prosperity when *til* and barley are used with ghee in Homa.
12. Following samput are used in Gayatri Mantra for reaping more benefit from it. After the word ॐ भूभुर्वः स्वः (**Om Bhoorbhuvah Swah**) use the following words as samput for the specific purposes indicated below and then the mantra be recited.

⇒ ॐ ऐं क्लीं सौं (**Om aeeng kaleeng soo**) This Samput is used for proficiency in words.

⇒ ॐ श्रीं ह्रीं श्रीं (**Om Shareeng hareeng shareeng**) This samput is used for wealth and comforts.

⇒ ॐ ऐं ह्रीं क्लीं (**Om Aeeng hareeng kaleeng**) Enemies are destroyed, troubles and worries vanish and native is blessed with joy and happiness through the use of this samput.

⇒ ॐ श्रीं ह्रीं क्लीं (**Om Shareeng hareeng kaleeng**) Through the use of this samput, one is blessed with progeny and one enjoys sexual bliss.

⇒ ॐ ह्रीं (**Om hareeng**) By candid use of this samput, one recovers from diseases.

⇒ ॐ आँ ह्रीं क्लीं (**Om aeeing hareeng kaleeng**) This samput when used blesses the devotee with protection from all evil forces. His hopes and wishes are realised.

Brahma gayatri yantra

This yantra fulfils all desires of the devotee. Students get good education and can have good memory power, it bestows wealth, all comforts in life, long life, and is also used in six rites. Persons who regularly worships the Brahma Gayatri yantra remains healthy and the goddess bestows long life to him.

The mantra for recital is:-

ॐ भू ॐ भुवः ॐ स्वः ॐ महः ॐ जनः ॐ तप ॐ सत्यं ॐ तत्सवितुर्वरेण्यं भर्गो देवस्य धीमहि। धियो यो नः प्रचोदयात् । ॐ आपोज्योतीरसोमृतं ब्रह्मभूर्भूवः स्वरोम् ॥

Om Bhu Om bhuva Om shuva Om Maha Om Jana Om Tapa Om Satyam Tatsyavitur Vareniyam, Bhargo Devasya Dhimahi । Dhiyo Yona Prachodyat । Om Aapojyotirsomartam Brahambhurbhuvasuvha savrom ॥

Dhyana verse

ॐ मुक्तविद्रुमहेमनीलधवलच्छायैर्मुखैस्त्री
क्षणैर्युक्तामिन्दुनिबद्धरत्नमुकुटां तत्त्वात्मवर्णात्मकाम् ।
गायत्रीं वरदाभयांकुशकशापाशां कपालं गुणं शंखं
चक्रमथारविन्दुयुगलं हस्तैर्वहन्तीं भजे ॥१॥
कुमारीमृग्वेदयुतां ब्रह्मरूपां विचिन्तयेत् ।
हंसस्थितांकुशकरां सूर्यमण्डलसंस्थिताम् ॥२॥
मध्याह्ने विष्णुरूपाञ्च तार्क्ष्यस्थां पीतवासिनीम् ।
युवतीं सयजुर्वेदां सूर्यमंडलसंस्थिताम् ॥३॥
सायाह्ने शिवरूपाञ्च वृद्धां वृषभवाहिनीम् ।
सूर्यमंडलमध्यस्थां सामवेद समायुताम् ॥४॥

**Om muktvidrumahemanildhawalchchayairmukhai stari shaniyr yukta mindu nibadh ratan mukutaam tatvatmavarnatmakam ।
Gayatrim vardyabhayam kushkashapasham kapalam gunam shankham
Chakramatharvinduyuglam hasteevarhantee bhajee ।। 1 ।।
Kumari margvedyutam brahamrupam vichintayate ।
Hanssiththam kushkaram surya mandal sansthitham ।। 2 ।।
madhyane vishnu rupanch taksharya satham pitvasnim ।
yuvtim sayajurvedam suryamandal sansthitham ।। 3 ।।
sayahane shivrupanch vradhaam vrashbhavahinim।
surya mandalmadhyastham samved samayutam ।। 4।।**

The devotee should start the Gayatri worship at some temple during some auspicious *Hora* of Moon. He should wear white cloths during the Gayatri worship and use the white articles. The yantra is drawn with the ink of *Asthgandh* on *Bhojpatra* or silver plate. The yantra consists of a triangle then a circle with eight petals and a beautiful *bhupura*. The devotee should write following mantra in the triangle:-

ॐ ब्रह्माविज़्णुरुद्रबिमबात्मकीय सौराययोगपीठीय नमः ॥

He should observe celibacy during the Gayatri *sadhna*. The mantra is to be recited for twenty four thousand times. The daily counting of the mantra should remain same during the whole exercise. If the devotee keeps fast for three continuous nights does homa with pure ghee and twigs of *Khair* he will get one thousand benefits. If the devotee does homa during solar eclipse with pure ghee and twigs of *plash*, he will be benefited in his cherished desires. After realisation of the yantra if the devotee recites the mantra after having bath in sacred water his all curses will be washed away. If one recites the mantra after having milk during the recital period he will get salvation. If the devotee, while facing Sun, stands in the sacred water at the level of navel does homa with sacred ash then there would not be any fear of abortion. Even barren lady would be blessed with progeny and all sorts of gynaecology problems would be solved through this yantra.

CHAPTER 7

DEVI YANTRAS

In this chapter we would discuss various *yantras* of *Shakti*, the supreme power. According to *Brathopnioshad* it is said that only *Devi* exists before the creation of the Universe who is also known as *Kamkala*. She gave birth to *Vishnu*, *Rudra*, and *Brahma*. All the gods, demons, *gandharvas*, *kinnars* (musicians) were born. Hence, the formation of universe came into existence.

Shakti which is also known as *Durga, Parvati, Mahalaxmi, Mahasasraswati, Mahakali* etc. is known through different names. The reincarnation of Shakti as *Dus Mahavidyas* is also discussed in this chapter. First of all we will discuss Durga yantras.

Durga

Durga Saptsati Yantra (Satchandi Use)

Durga which is considered the goddess of power has reference in *Devi Rahasay* in which Devi Herself said that when she will kill a demon named *Durg*, She would be called *Durga*. *Durga* in Sanskrit: means the Inaccessible, in Hindu mythology, one of the many forms of Shakti (the goddess), and the wife of *Shiva.* Her

best-known feat was the slaying of the buffalo-demon *Mahisasura*. According to legend she was created for this purpose out of flames that issued from the mouths of Brahma, Vishnu, Shiva, and the lesser gods. She was born fully grown and beautiful; nevertheless, she presents a fierce menacing form to her enemies. She is usually depicted in painting and sculpture riding a lion (sometimes shown as a tiger), with 8 or 10 arms, each holding the special weapon of one or another of the gods, who gave them to her for her battle against the buffalo-demon. The Durga-*pooja*, held annually in September-October, is one of the greatest festivals of northern and eastern India. A special image of the goddess is made that is worshipped for nine days, then immersed in water, all accomplished with large processions and much public and private festivity. In *Markandaya purana* there are 700 *sholakas* for worshipping Goddess. It is said that without *Durgasaptsati* yantra the worship is half and the devotee did not get the full fruits of his worship. First of all we will give the *Durgasapsati* Yantra which is used during worship of devi during *navratras*. This yantra is carved on copper plate or on *Bhojpatra*. After energizing the yantra the devotee should recite the *Durgasapsati* during as per details:

Chapter 1	(*Madhu kaitabha samhaara*) is to be read for 1st day,
Chapter 2 to 4	(*Mahishhasura* samhaara) to be read on 2nd day,
Chapter 5 and 6	(*Dhuumralochana vadha*) on the 3rd day,
Chapter 7	(*Chanda Munda* vadha) on 4th day,
Chapter 8	(*Rakta biija* samhaara) on 5th day,
Chapter 9 and 10	(*Shumbha Nishumbha* vadha) on 6th day,
Chapter 11	(Praise of *Narayani*) on 7th day,
Chapter 12	(*Phalasruti*) on 8th day,
Chapter 13	(Blessings to *Suratha* and the Merchant) on 9th day
Chapter 14	(*aparaadha shamaapana*) on 10th day

The reading of Durga *saptasati* is to be done during Navratri. Navratri is celebrated four times a year. They are *Ashada* Navratri, the *Sharada* Navratri, the *Maha* Navratri and the *Vasantha* Navratri. *NAVARATRA* ("nine nights"), in Hinduism, a festival of nine days occurring during the month of *Asin*, or *Ashvina* (September-October). It usually ends with the *Dussehra*, or celebration on the 10th day. Among followers of the goddess , who are particularly predominant in Bengal and Assam, the *Durgạ-pooja* ("Rite of Durga") is celebrated during this period. Special images of Durga celebrating her victory over the buffalo-headed demon Mahisasura are worshipped daily, and, on the 10th day (Dussehra), they are taken in jubilant processions to rivers or reservoirs for immersion in water. In addition to family feasting and visiting, the pooja, or ritual, days are also celebrated with public concerts, recitations, plays, and fairs. Of these, the Sharada Navratri of the month of *Puratashi* and the Vasantha Navratri of the Vasantha kala are very important. If you refer to the *Agni* Purana, then it is said that the Puratashi and *Panguni* (in *Tamil* months) i.e. *Asvin* and *Chaitra* are like the two jaws of Lord *Yama*. If one wants to escape the mouth of Yama, then one should celebrate Navratri on these two occasions. A similar analogy is presented in the *Devi bhagavatam*. *Devi bhagavatam* also talks in detail on how one should observe fasts, and how one should meditate/work on these days.

Durgasapsati or the glory of the goddess is a final expression of God's will and purpose for man. It has a unique position in Hindu devotional literature. Though it appears as an insertion in virtually all editions of the *Markandaya Purana* it is also circulated as an independent text. Metaphysically the goddess represents *Shakti*, the guided power, the transcendental source and support of all creatures and of entire creation. The Rig-*Veda* (10/125) calls the great goddess as *vak* the universal power.

The goddess is the ultimate reality knowledge of whom liberates from the cycle of birth and death, yet she is also the in snaring veil of the great illusion, *Mahamaya* binding all being. As the power which enslaves and liberates, She is Shakti, the energy or power of Shiva.

The mantra, the significant formula which for the uninitiated may be an incomprehensible sequence of syllables or a sentence of no obvious relevance we find the highest, spiritual attribute-laden energy.

Goddess Durga is worshipped under different names in the different parts of the country. A common term for the goddess is simply mother.

Throughout South Asia the goddess is referred as mother or *Maa* in the *Hindi* speaking north, *Ammaa* in the Southern Indian languages. *Navratri*, Durga pooja, and *Mahanavmi* are the important festivals associated with the Goddess.

In other parts of India, the 10th day, Dusehra, is associated with the victory of the god over the demon-king *Ravana*. Many other, lesser observances are associated with the festival of navaratra in varying ways across the country. On the first day of Navratri, a rite is celebrated in honour of the goddess of learning, in which she is worshipped together with the sacred books of the house; this is a favourite observance among the *Bengali* population of India. In parts of Maharashtra, the fifth day is given to the worship of the goddess *Lalita* and is known as Lalita-*pañcami* ("Lalita's Fifth Day").

According to legend, Durga sat on the tip of a needle for nine days, doing a severe penance to destroy the evil demon *Mahisha*. On the first three days, she meditated as Herself, the next three days as *Mahalakshmi* and the last three days as *Sarasvati*. This signifies progression from *tamsik*, to *rajasik* to *satvik* and eventually obtaining salvation. The tenth day during Sharada Navratri is called *vijaya dashami* to signify the victory on the day of dashami.

It is, however, a long tradition that one reads the *Durga saptasati,* (700 verses on Durga) during this period. Devi bhagavaṭam notes that *Rama* meditated and fasted for nine days after *Sita* was kidnapped by Ravana. There are numerous such incidents on how people's wishes were granted.

As per the chapter 12 of *Durga saptasati,* Devi herself tells the merits of reading Durga Saptasati. She said that whoever with a concentrated mind shall pray to her constantly with these hymns, she shall without doubt put down every trouble of his. 'And those who shall laud (the story of) the destruction of Madhu and Kaitabha, the slaughter *Nisumbha* likewise. Those also who shall listen with devotion to this sublime poem on her greatness on the eighth, the fourteenth and on the ninth days of the fortnight with concentrated mind, to them nothing wrong shall happen, nor calamities that arise from wrong doings nor poverty and never separation from beloved ones. The person shall not experience fear from enemies, or from robbers and kings, or from weapon, fire and flood. Hence this poem of her greatness must be chanted by men of concentrated minds and listened to always with devotion; for it is the supreme course of well-being. May this poem of her glories desimate all epidemic calamities, as also the threefold natural calamity? 'The place of her sanctuary where this poem so duly chanted everyday, She will never forsake and there her presence is certain. 'When sacrifice is offered, during worship, in the fire-ceremony, and at a great festival, this entire poem on her acts must be chanted and heard. She would accept with love the sacrifice and worship that are made and the fire-offering that is offered likewise, whether they are done with due knowledge (of sacrifice) or not.

During autumn season, when the great annual worship is performed, the man hearing this glorification of her with devotion shall certainly through her grace, be delivered without doubt from all troubles and be blessed with riches, grains and children. Hearing this glorification and auspicious appearances of mine, and her feats of prowess in battles, a man becomes fearless. Enemies perish, welfare accrues and the family rejoices for those who listen to this glorification of mine. Let one listen to this glorification of mine everywhere, at a propitiatory ceremony, on seeing a bad dream, and when there is the great evil influence of planets. (By that means) evil portents subside, as also the unfavourable influence of planets, and the bad dream seen by men turns into a good dream. It creates peacefulness in children and it is the best promoter of friendship among men when split occurs in their union. It diminishes most effectively the power of all men of evil ways. Verily demons, goblins, and ogres are destroyed by its mere chanting. 'This entire glorification of her draws (a devotee) very near to her. And by means of finest cattle, flowers, *arghya* and incenses, and by perfumes and lamps, by feeding *Brahmanas*, by oblations, by sprinkling (consecrated) water, and by various other offerings and gifts (if one worships) day and night in a year-the gratification, which is done to her, is attained by listening but once to this holy story of mine. The chanting and hearing of the story of her manifestations remove sins, and grant perfect health and protect one from evil spirits; and when her martial exploit in the form of the slaughter of the wicked *daityas* is listened to, men will have no fear from enemies.

Durga Saptsati Yantra (Satchandi use)

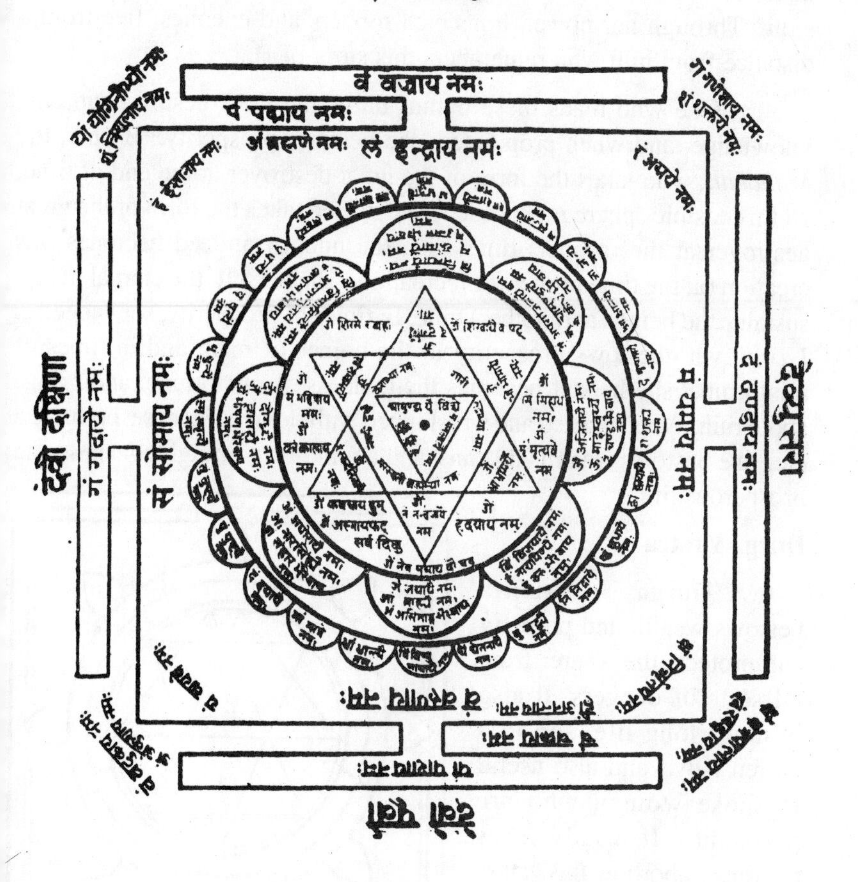

The hymns of Devi bestow a pious mind. He who is (lost) on a lonesome spot in a forest, or is surrounded by forest fire, or who is surrounded by robbers in a desolate spot, or who is captured by enemies, or who is pursued by a lion, or tiger, or by wild elephants in a forest, or who, under the orders of a wrathful king, is sentenced to death, or has been imprisoned, or who is tossed about in his boat by a tempest in the vast sea, or who is in the most terrible battle under shower of weapons, or who is amidst all kinds of dreadful troubles, or who is afflicted with pain - such a man on remembering this story of mine is saved from his strait. Through her power, lions etc., robbers and enemies, flee from a distance from him who remembers this story of Her.

One who reads these hymns daily, the Devi bestows supreme knowledge, and when propitiated, she bestows prosperity. By her, the *Mahakali*, who takes the form of the great destroyer at the end of time, all this cosmic sphere is pervaded. She indeed takes the form of the great destroyer at the (proper) time. She, the unborn, indeed becomes this creation (at the time proper for recreation), she herself, the eternal being, sustains the beings at (another) time. In times of prosperity, she indeed is *Laxmi*, who bestows prosperity in the homes of men; and in times of misfortune, she herself becomes the goddess of misfortune, and brings about ruin. When praised and worshipped with flowers, incense, perfumes, etc., she bestows wealth and sons, and a mind bent on righteousness and prosperous life.

Durga Yantra

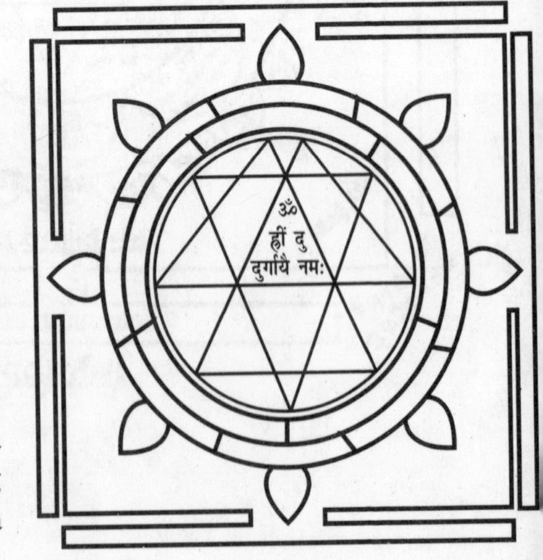

Durga Yantra bestows wealth and property and protects the wearer from all sorts of dangers. It also bestows long life, son to a barren lady. and also useful to those women who are pregnant. If a lady faces continues abortion, this yantra is very useful in checking such incidents. If the yantra is realised, the devotee can use it for six rites also (for six rites please refer chapter on six rites). The mantra for recital is:-

ॐ ह्रीं दुं दुर्गायै नमः ॥

Om Hrim Dum Durgayee namah ॥

The sage of this Mantra is *Maheshwar*, deity is *Durgaastaaksharitmika, Dum Bija, hrim sakhti,* Om *Kilkam.*

Dhyana Verse

दुर्वानाम त्रिनयनां विलसत्किरीटां शङ्खाब्जखड्गशरखेटक शूलचापन् ।
सन्तर्जनीं च दधती महिषासनस्थां दुर्गा नवारकुलपीठगता भजेहम् ॥

Durvanam trinayanaam vilsastkiriitam
sankhabajkharagsharkhetek shulchapan ।
Santargani ca dadhti Mahisasanstham
Durga Navarkulpithgatha Bhajeham ॥

The mantra is to be recited for one hundred thousand times. Devotee who is desirous of Durga Siddhi can recite the mantra for eight hundred thousand times. Durga yantra is written on *Bhojpatra* or carved or embossed on Gold or silver plate and be worn.

Durga Navaran mantra yantra

This yantra is of *Trirupa Maha Shakti* i.e., *Mahakali, Maha Saraswati, Mahalakshmi.* This yantra is good for attraction. Only by realisation of the yantra women, king, Govt. officials could be attracted by the devotee. He will not be sacred of devils, demons, animals and thieves. Devi *Chandika* bestows all power in him and he will never face any sort of disease in his life. If this yantra is worshipped in letter and sprit then Mahalakshmi bestows all comforts in life. He is blessed with son, and grandsons. Maha Saraswati blesses the devotee with education, good memory and voice. The mantra for recital is:-

ॐ ऐं ह्रीं क्लीं चामुण्डायै विच्चे ॥

Om Aan Hrim Klim Chamundaayee Vichche ॥

The sage of this Mantra is *Brahma, Vishnu , Maheshwar*, Gayatri vishnu anustup metre, deity is *Mahakali, Mahasaraswati,*

Mahalakshmi, worship of *Agnivayusurya Raktdantika durga bramaryao Bija, Nand jash akmbhri bhima sakhti, Hrim Kilkam.*

The devotee has to perform extensive nayaas of *rishi, Matrika, Sarswati, matrika angnayas, Nandjadinayas, Brahamakhyannayas, mahalakshm*i Nayaas, Mantravarna nayaas, *Sadaang* nayaas before dhyana.

The mantra is recited for one hundred thousand times for one month. Foods for offering are pure ghee, honey and *belive* leaves. If lotus petals mixed with milk are used in *homa* it bestows prosperity. The best period for realisation of yantra is *panchmi tithi* of *Shukla paksha* in the month of *Ashwin*. This process should continue till *asthmi*. If the devotee recites the mantra along with *Durga saptasati* the Devi fulfils all desires.

Dhyana Verse

खड्ग चक्रगदेषुचापपरिधाञ्शूलं भुशुण्डीं शिरः
शंङ्खसन्धतीं करैस्त्रिनयनां सर्वाङभूषावृत्ताम् ।
यांमस्तौत्स्वपिते हरौ कमलजो हन्तुं मधुं कैटभं
नीलाश्मद्युतिमास्यपाददशकां सेवे महाकालिकाम् ॥१॥
अक्षस्त्रक्परशु गदेषुकुलिशं पद्मं धनुष्कुण्डिकां
दण्डं शक्तिमसिं च चर्मजलजं घण्टां सुराभाजनम् ।

शूलं पाशसुदर्शने च दधतीं हस्तैः प्रवालप्रभां
सेवे सैरिभमर्दिनीमिह महालक्ष्मीं सरोजस्थिताम् ॥२॥
घण्टाशूलहलानि शंङ्खमुसले चक्रं धनुः सायकं
हस्ताब्जैर्दधतीं धनान्तविलसच्छीतांशुतुल्यप्रभाम् ।
गौरीदेहसमुद्भवां त्रिजगतामाधारभूतां महापुर्वामत्र
सरस्वतीः मनु भजे शुम्भादिदैत्यार्द्दिनीम् ॥३॥

Kharak Chakra gadeshu chap paridhashulanam bhushandi shira
Sankhsandhtim karayestrinayanam sarvang bhushavartpam ।
Yamastootasavpate haroo kamaljoo hantum madhum kaitbham
Nilasmadhutimasyapaddashkam seve Mahakalikam । । 1 । ।
Aksaraskaparshu gadeshu kulisham padam Dhanushkundikam
Dandam shaktimasim cha charamjalajam ghantam surabhajnam।
Shulam pashsudershne cha dhatim hastee parvalprabham
Seve seirabhMardinimih Mahalakshmi Sarojsthithim । । 2 । ।
Ghantashulhalani shankh musele Chakram dhanu sayakam
Hastabajerdhadhtim dhantvilaschitamshutulyaparbham ।
Gauri Deh Samudhbhavam Trijata madharbhutam maha purva matr
Saraswati manu bhaje shuadidetya mardnim । । 3 । ।

This yantra is drawn on bhojpatra with the ink of *Asthgandha.* Devotee can also carve the yantra on gold plate. The yantra has triangle, sixteen, eight, twenty four and lastly sixty four petal lotus. The yantra is covered with a beautiful *bhupur.*

Shulini Durga Yantra

This yantra fulfils all desires of the devotee. This yantra is also good for decreasing the malefic effect of the planets in the native's natal chart. If somebody is poisoned by snake, rat or any poisons insect or reptile this yantra can show its effect. The mantra for recital is:-

ॐ ज्वलज्वलशूलिनिदुष्टग्रहान् हुं फट् स्वाहा ॥
Om jawal jawal shulini dustgrahan hum phat swaha ॥

The sage of this Mantra is *Dirgtam*, deity is *Shulini Durga* and *Kukup* metre.

Dhyan Verse

अद्ययारूढां मृगेन्द्रं सजलजलधरश्यामलां पद्महस्तैः
शूलं बाणं कृपाण मरिजलजगदाचापपाशांवहंतीम् ।
चन्द्रोत्तंसां त्रिनेत्रां चतसृभिरिसिमत्खेटकं बिभ्रतीभिः
कन्याभिः सेव्यमानां प्रतिभटभयदां शूलिनीं भावयामि ॥

Adyarudam Mrgendram sajal jaldharshymalam padamhaste
Shulam banam karpan marijaljagdachappashamvanhitim ।
Chandrotnsam trinetram chatsarbhirisietkhetkam bhibrthibhi
kanyabhi sevyamanam partibhatbhaydam shulini bhavyami ॥

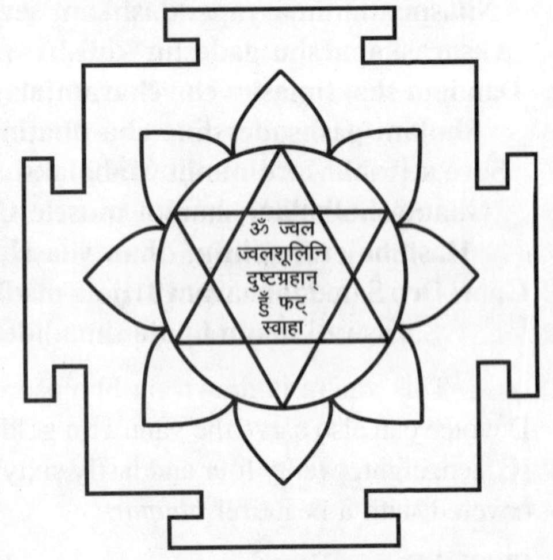

This mantra is recited for fifteen hundred thousand times. If the devotee offers daily homa with ghee and food articles to Devi for hundred and eight times, his desires are full filled and devi bestows wealth and comfort on him.If homa is done with honey, sugar, *til* smeared in ghee for hundred and eight times he will get *Devi Siddhi.* If the devotee wants to create rift between two know persons then make hundred and eight balls of cow dung and do homa for a week.

Mahasaraswati

Goddess Saraswati the consort of Lord Brahma is considered the bestowal of intellect, music, education and intelligence. Knowledge is power. Everybody needs to enhance his knowledge through various ways like academic pursuits, private study of religious/ spiritual treatises etc. From Vedic times, Goddess Saraswati is regarded as the giver of wisdom. She is also referred as *Vak* Devi (goddess of speech) and *Sakala kaladhishtatr.* One can gain all these things including fame by offering worship to the Goddess.

Saraswati yantra be made on copper plate and worship is offered with white cloths, white lotus flowers and white coloured eatables are used as offerings. By constant worship of Devi Saraswati one becomes learned, famous and is praised by all. By worshipping Saraswati Yantra students will perform well in the examinations. Concentration and memory power will increase. Only good thoughts will spring up form their minds. For acquiring spiritual wisdom, the grace of Goddess Saraswati is very essential.

Neeltara saraswati yantra

This yantra is considered *Mahavidya.* If it is properly served it bestows enjoyment and salvation. If the devotee worships the yantra he can be a genuine scholar. The mantra for recital is:-

ऐं ह्रीं श्रीं क्लीं सौं क्लीं ह्रीं ऐं ब्लूं स्त्रीं निलात्रे सरस्वति द्रां द्रीं क्लीं ब्लूं सः ऐं ह्रीं श्रीं क्लीं सौः सौः ह्रीं स्वाहा ॥

Aim Hrim Srim Klim Saum Klim Hrim Aim Blum Strim Nilatare Saraswati Dram Drim Klim Blum Sah Aim Hrim Srim Klim Sauh Sauh Hrim Svaha ॥

The sage of the mantra is *brahma*, metre is *anustup,* deity is *saraswati.*

This mantra is to be recited for four

hundred thousand times and shall perform 1/10 part of mantra recited as homa with sweetened *Kimsuka* flowers with great faith and free from lethargy. The yantra consists of hexagon so as to make six cornered figure. Then eight, sixteen, thirty-two and sixty four petals lotus are drawn on outside the other. The *bhupura* is drawn with three lines all round.

Dhyana Verse

शवासनां सर्वविभूषणाढयां कर्त्री कपालं चषकं त्रिशमलम् ।
करैर्दधाना नरमुण्डमालां त्र्यक्षां भजे नीलसरस्वतीं ताम् ॥

Shavasanam sarvavibhusanadhayam kartari kapalam chaskam trishalam ।

Kareerdhadhana narmundmalam trayaksam bhaje neelsaraswati tam ॥

After realising the yantra if one writes the mantra on the tongue of a child soon after the umbilical cord has been cut with a stylus made of *durva* grass dipped in *Gorochana* pigment the child would become a great scholar at the age of eight.

Saraswati yantra for education

On Deepawali night, the devotee after taking bath wears white clothes and face towards north direction. Place the yantra on pedestal covered by rice. Worship the yantra with *panchopchar* with the following mantra using rosary of crystal *(safatik)* for twelve thousand times. Through this mantra the Devi bestows power for better understanding, intellect and good memory.

The mantra for recital is:-

ॐ ह्रींश्रींऐं वाग्वादिनि भगवती अर्हन्मुखनिवासिनी सरस्वति ममास्ये प्रकाशं कुरुकुरु स्वाहा ऐं नमः ॥

Om Hrimshrimaim vagvadani bhagwati arhanmukhniwasani

Saraswati mamasaya parkasham kuru kuru swah aim namah ॥

Dhyana Verse

ॐ तरुणशकलमिन्दोर्बिभ्रती शुभ्रकान्तिः
कुचभरनमिताङ्गी सन्निषण्णा सिताब्जे ।
निजकरकमलोद्यल्लेखनीपुस्तकश्रीः
सकलविभवसिध्यै पातु वाग्देवता ॥

Om Tarun shakalminda birbhriti shubrakanti
Kuckbharni mitangi sannisnnaa sitabaje ।
Nij kar kamlodhl lakhni pustak shri
Sakal Vibhav siddhayee patu vag devta ॥

Mahalakshmi

Mahalakshmi the goddess of wealth and prosperity is worshipped on deepawali. She is worshipped with Mahalakshmi Yantra which is auspicious yantra for wealth and comforts in life. Devi Mahalakshmi is depicted as seated on blossomed lotus. Mahalakshmi Yantra is placed in cash box, almirah, purse or in temple of house after worship. The pooja of the yantra is performed with flowers, saffron, sandal etc.

Mahalakshmi Yantra is embossed on copper plate, *bhojpatra* or on gold plate. Mahalakshmi Yantra must be offered pooja with cleanliness and full confidence and faith. Mahalakshmi Yantra brings success and wealth through regular pooja and mantra chanting. It is believed that mere sight of this unique Mahalakshmi Yantra in the morning blesses the person with Wealth. The mantra for recital is:-

ऐं ह्रीं श्रीं क्लीं सौं जगत्प्रसूत्यै नमः ॥

Aem hrim shrim klim som gajatparsutaye namah ॥

The sage of this Mantra is *Brahma*, deity is *Mahalakshmi* and

Gayatri metre. *Shrim Beej*.

The mantra is to be recited for twelve hundred thousand times.

Dhyana Verse

ॐ या सा पद्मासनस्था विपुल कटि तटी पद्मपत्रायताक्षी।
गंभीरावर्तनाभिः स्तनभर नमिता शुभ्रवस्त्रोत्तरीय ॥
या लक्ष्मीर्दिव्यरूपै मणिगण खचितै स्नापिता हेम कुम्भैः।
सा नित्यं पद्महल्ता मम वसतु ग्रहे सर्वमांगल्या युक्ता ॥

Om yah sa padmmasanasatha vipul kati tati padampatrayatakshi ।
Gambhiraavarnabhi satanbhar namita subhrvastrotariya ॥
ya lakshmirdivyarupyi manigan khataiya sanapita hem kumbhai।
sa nityam padamhalta mam vastu grahe sarve manglaya yukta॥

For long life the devotee should do homa for hundred and eight times for continues ten nights with durva grass dipped in pure ghee. The devotee who at the time of Sun rise does homa while standing in the water upto neck recovers from all sorts of diseases and all his desires are full filled. Daily homa with rice gets the blessings of goddess Lakshmi. Homa with yellow mustard gives fame to the devotee.

Jyestha Lakshmi

Jyestha Lakshmi is worshipped for all dimensional desires. The mantra for recital of Jyestha Lakshmi is:-

ऐं ह्रीं श्रीं ज्येष्ठालक्ष्मि स्वयंभुवे ह्रीं ज्येष्ठै नमः ॥

Aim Hrim Srim Adyalakshmi Svayambhuve Hrim Jyesthayai Namah ॥

The sage of this Mantra is Brahma; the metre is *Asti* and the deity is Jyestha Lakshmi, the Bija is Hrim and the Shakti is *Srim*. Hands are to be washed and wiped off repeating the *Mula* mantra and *anga* nayaas is performed.

ऐं ह्रीं
श्रीं ज्येष्ठा
लक्ष्मिस्वयंभुव
ह्रीं ज्येष्ठै
नमः

Dhyana Verse

ॐ उद्यद्भास्करसन्निभा स्मितमुखी रक्ताम्बरालेपना सत्कुम्भं धनभजनं सृणिमथो पाशं करैर्बिभ्रती पद्मस्था कमलेक्षणा दृढकुचा सौंदर्यवारान्नि- धिर्ध्यातव्या सकलभिलाषफलदा श्री ज्येष्ठालक्ष्मीरियम् ॥

Om udyabhadisjarsannibha samitmukhi raktambralepna satkumbham dhanbhajnam sarnimatho pasham kareebirbhati padmasatha kamlekshna dradcucha saundryavaraanni dhidharyatavya sakalbhilashphaldha shri Jyesthalaxmiriyam ॥

The devotee shall repeat the Mantra a hundred thousand times and perform ten thousand Homa with milk pudding smeared with ghee. This yantra is conducive to the increase of wealth.

Lakshmi Yantra

This yantra is composed of three words which are inscribed in the yantra. The mantra reads as:

ॐ ऐं क्लीं सौः॥

Om Aeem Kleem Soham ॥

Dhyana of this mantra as given above.

Recite the above mantra over yantra which is written on *Bhojpatra* with *ashatgand* or carved on gold or silver plate for one thousand and eight times for twenty one days. The pooja of the yantra is performed with flowers, saffron, sandal etc. especially on deepawali day. The yantra is kept on person or in a cash book for getting blessing from Devi Lakshmi.

Dusmahavidya Yantras

Dusmahavidyas which are considered to be reincarnation of goddess Shakti are taken in very high esteem in the world of tantra. These are considered the ten Cosmic Powers in the universe. The Universe has a pyramidal vibratory structure. Different worlds are placed on different levels. Each stratum has a definite rate of vibration and expresses a definite level of consciousness. At the top of this gigantic pyramidal structure there are certain Cardinal Energies (*Vidya*-s) called "Cosmic Powers" or "Goddesses", which have a paramount role in creating, maintaining and reabsorbing the Cosmos. The disciplines that lead to the inner communion with these Cosmic Powers are known as Mahavidya Yoga or Shri Vidya Yoga. These are the supreme fundamental paths of profound knowledge and wisdom. The Supreme Goddess, the Mother of the Universe, the essential femaleness is a dynamic Power which complements the stillness of Consciousness. Each female is a Shakti. She embodies and manifests the secret fundamental subtle forces which animate and control the Cosmos.

According to a legend these *mahadvidya* were born from the Shakti when she did not get an invitation from her father *Daksh* and was bent upon to attend the *yagna*. On her stubborn attitude Lord Shiva tried to check her from going there and the Devi formed her ten clones which were protector of ten directions. Besides this there are other legends about birth of *Dusmahavidyas*. ***(For details please read our book Dusmahavidyas.)***

Kali Yantra

In the mahavidyas first is *Mahakali* the black complexioned goddess which kills the enemy. Kali accord the supernatural powers of speech immediately. If Kali is worshipped, a person can obtain all the desired things in this world. Devi Kali bestows on the devotee fulfilment of all his desires, wealth, and comforts of life and is used for Mohan or Vashi karan purposes. Kali Yantra is considered auspicious for protection from black magic, Saturn and evil influences.

According to *Swangam Tantra*, *Kali Tantra* and *Bhairo Tantra* this Yantra is known as swanam yantra, kali yantra, Mahakali yantra or Bhadra Kali Yantra. Goddess Kali in a fierce pose is deity of this yantra. Special *pooja* of this yantra is performed on Eighth day of *Chaitra*, *Asar*, *Sharavan* and *Magh* Months of *Vikrami* year. The worship of this yantra is performed in a specialised way.

Kalika pujan Yantra

To draw a Kali pujan yantra first of all a hexagon is drawn, then three triangles the eight-petal lotus, finally the *Bhupura*. The devotee shall worship the goddess therein.

The Mantra for recital is:-

ॐ क्रीं क्रीं क्रीं हुं हुं ह्रीं ह्रीं
दक्षिण कालिके क्रीं क्रीं क्रीं हुं हुं
ह्रीं ह्रीं स्वाहा ॥

Om Krim Krim Krim Hum Hum Hrim Hrim Dakshine Kalika Krim Krim Krim Hum Hum Hrim Hrim Svaha. ॥

The sage of this Mantra is *Bhairava,* the metre is *Usnik,* the deity is *Kali,* the Bija is *Maya* (i.e. Hrim) and the Shakti is *Dirgha Varma (i.e. Hum).*

Dhyan verse

ॐ सद्यश्छिन्नशिरः कृपाणमभयं हस्तैर्वरं बिभ्रतीं घोरास्यां शिरसां स्रजा सुरुचिरामुन्मुक्तकेशावलिम् ।
सृक्कासृक्प्रवहां श्मशाननिलयां श्रुत्योः शवालंकृतिं शयामाङ्गी कृतमेखलां शवकरैर्देवीं भजे कालिकाम् ॥

Om sadyashichannshira kripanambhayam hastiverram bibrithim ghorashyam shirsam sraja suruchi ramunmuktkeshavalim ।
Sarakkasarakparvaham shamshannilayam shurtyo shavalamkritim shayamangi kritmekhlam shavkarairdevim bhaje kalikam ॥

After meditating thus the devotee repeats the Mantra a hundred thousand times and performs ten thousand Homas with *Kanner* flowers for realisation of yantra.

Tara yantra

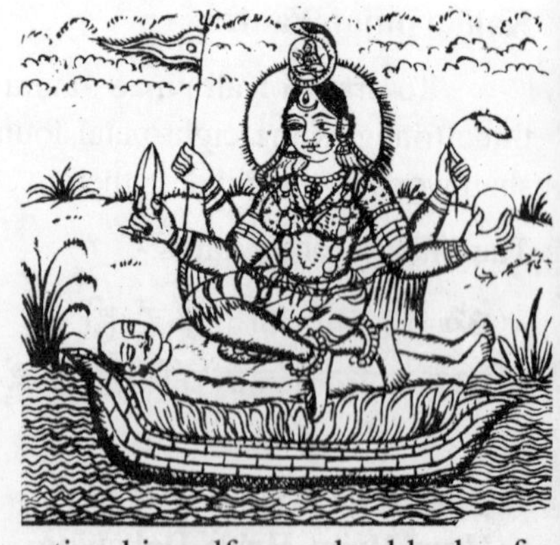

Tara, the second in Dusmahavidyas should be worshipped through some learned preceptor. She is bestowal of supernatural powers and men on the earth can have fulfiled them. The Tara yantra consists of a circle, eight petals, triangles and a bhupura. There is no restriction as to the time and position at the time of the mantra. The devotee can practise and assimilate this mantra seating himself on a dead body of a solider killed in a battle or a six months old child in the cremation ground, in a deserted house , in a temple or in secluded spot on the mountain or the middle of the forest. The mantra for recital is:-

ॐ त्रीं ह्रीं हुं त्रीं हुं फट् ॥

Om Trim Hrim Hum Trim Hum Phat ॥

Dhyana verse

ॐ विश्वव्यापकवारिमध्यविलसच्छ्वेताम्बुजन्मस्थितां कर्त्रीं
खड्गकपालनीलनलिनैराजत्करां नीलभाम् ।
काञ्ची कुण्डल हार कङ्कणल सत्केयूरमञ्जीर
तामाप्तैर्नागवरैर्विभूषिततनूमारक्तनेत्रत्रयाम् ॥१॥
पिङ्गोग्रैकजटां लसत्सुरसनां दंष्ट्राकरालाननां हस्तैश्चापि
वरं कटौ विदधतीं श्वेतास्थिपट्टालिकाम् ।
अक्षोभ्येणविराजमानशिरसं स्मेराननांभोरुहां तारां शावहृदासनां
दृढकुचसमंबां त्रिलोक्या स्मरेत् ॥२॥

Om vishva vayapak varimadhya vilsachchuvetambujnamsithtam
katri khakragpalnilnalineirajtkaramnilbham
Kanchi kundalhar kangal lastquerea njirtamiptayeer
nagvareevirbhusit hnumartnetratam !!
Pingogreckjatam lastsursanam danstrakaralannam hastischapi
varam katoo viddhati shewtasthithpattalikam
akshobhyanvirajmanshjirsham samrennimbhoruham taram
shavhrdsanamdaddkuchsambha trilokya samret.

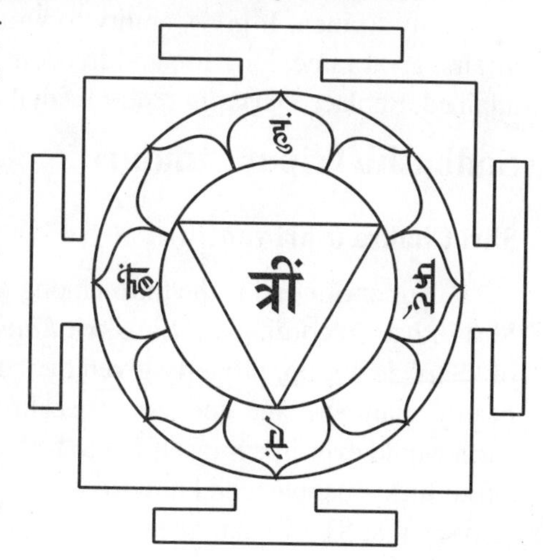

After realisation of the yantra the devotee can use the yantra for some purposes.

Within three days from the date of birth the devotee shall write the Tara mantra on the tongue of the new born child with a golden stylus or wild *durva* grass smeared with honey and ghee, the son would be like a prince at the age of eight. He cannot be conquered by others. The devotee who puts yellow pigments inspired hundred times by the mantra shall become favourite of goddess of speech and fortune. He will be capable of pleasing common people. If he sees anyone that man will instantly become his slave.

Tara Dharan Yantra

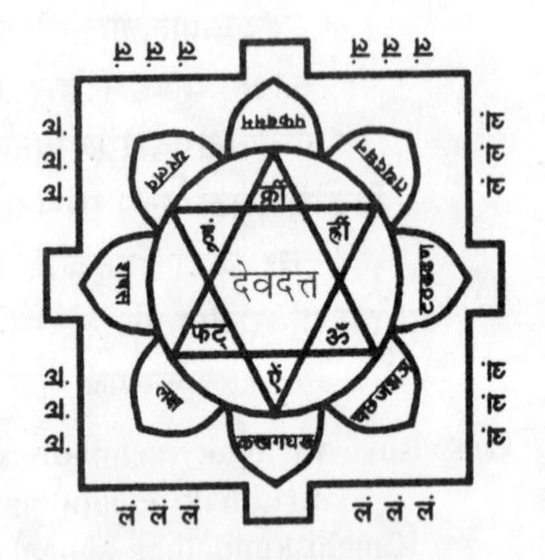

The Yantra consisting of hexagon, eight petals, and *bhupura* should be written on the *bhojpatra* with *kusum* juice. In the middle of the hexagon the *Mula* Mantra should be written along with the name of the beneficiary. In the filaments all the sixteen vowels are to be written. In the eight petals the letters of the eight classes are written. The entire yantra is enclosed in a *Bhupura* which is wrapped in a yellow cloth and tied with yellow threads. If this amulet is tied to the neck of children it becomes a protection from the terror of evil spirits to women, when tied on left arm it ensures birth of sons and conjugal bliss. On the right arm of men it ensures wealth to the poor, knowledge to those who yearn for it and victory to the kings. It accords all desired prosperity to men. It gives ability to write poems, honour in the Govt. affairs, great fame, long life and freedom from sickness all these can be attained. Replace *Devdatta* (**देवदत्त**)with the name of the intended person.

Sodhashi/Tripur sundari

Shri Chakra (Shri yantra)

Tripur Sundari is the third among Mahavidyas. She is also called Shri Vidya. According to " **Sanskrit *Kaustub* Dictionary** " the meaning of "Shri" is wealth, property given by the Govt., fame, higher position, beauty, glamour, and goddess of wealth "***LAKSHMI***" etc. Nobody on earth would ever like himself not to be blessed by goddess and it is only a few lucky people who know to invoke the goddess blessings. We can also say that Shri Chakra means the 'Wheel of the Mother Goddess' but actually, it represents the symbolic energy form of the Goddess.

From time immemorial, our holy saints have done a lot of research work on it and found ways and means to welcome *Shri* to the homes of her disciples. The sages transferred this art to their disciples which was stored in our old classics in the form of Yantra, Tantra, and Mantra.

God created so many system of principles and methods which are employed in the performance of a set of activities in the universe through our saints which are considered of immense help. According to a legend, ईशानः सर्वविधानाम् *(Ishana sarvidyanama)* means God created all schools of knowledge. Besides creating these faculties , he blessed some people with the knowledge of implementing this knowledge for the benefit of humanity. In the process of this spiritual knowledge, Shri *Vidya*, Shri Mantra, Shri Chakra (**also known as Shri Yantra**) were a discovery of our holy saints, which were used for solving the problems of mankind.

What is Shri Chakra ?

The famous Sanskrit dictionary *"vachaspatyam"* while referring to *Yantra Lok* gave the meaning of Shri Chakra as " Shri Chakra, the Yantra of *Tripur Sundari* is a symbol of the entire cosmos that serves to remind the practitioner of the non-difference between subject and object." In addition, it is also a symbol of body or the nine substances in it which are known as skin (*trak*), blood (*asrk*), flesh (*mamsa*), fat (*medher*) and bone (*asthi*) which are given by Shakti; and the other four are from Shiva being semen (*sukla*), marrow (*majja*), vital breath (*prana*) and the individual soul (*jivatman*). This is also consider as *"Yantra raj"*. Shri Chakra is said to be of the greatest use and has prime importance. It is reputed to give fulfilment of ambitions for power, financial gains and influence.

Design of Shri Chakra

If we properly watch the Shri Chakra we will find that this diagram consists of nine interwoven triangles having two sides, four pointing upwards, representing Shakti, the original female essence of dynamic energy, and five pointing downwards, representing Shiva, the actual male essence of fixed wisdom. The triangles are managed in such a way that they produce forty three subsidiary triangles, at the centre of the smallest of which there is a big dot (known as the *bindu*). These smaller triangles are supposed to form the abodes of different gods, whose names are sometimes entered in their respective places. In common, with many depictions of the Shri Chakra, it has outer rings consisting of an eight-petal lotus, enclosed by a sixteen petal lotus, griddled in turn by three circles, all enclosed in a square with four doors, one on each side. The square represents the boundaries within which the deities reside, protected from the chaos and disorder of the outside world. Tantric tradition suggests that there are two ways of using the Shri Chakra for meditation. In the 'outward approach', one begins by contemplating the bindu and proceeds outwards by stages to take in the smallest triangle in which it is enclosed, then the next two triangles. The three *bindus* which joins triangle are know as:-

(1) Wish power
(2) Action power
(3) Knowledge Power.

These three powers regulate the whole universe. Where these three bindus join is known as *Devnagar* and the corresponding script is known as *Devnagri* script.

For getting different type of advantages, Shri Chakra could be drawn on different metals.

Advantage of Shri Chakra

According to *Rudrayamal* Shri Chakra could be inscribed on Gold Silver or Coral by red vermillion as per the instructions told in our classics Shri Chakra drawn on Gems blesses with wealth; on gold, it blesses with beauty, smartness; on silver, it blesses with fame; on copper blesses with son, wealth, and health. For getting these benefits one should follow the instructions carefully as told in the book.

It may be worth to mention here that the Yantras reached us through Shakti who got it from Shiva for the benefit of mankind. As it was said in *Yamal* :-

आगतं शिववक्त्रेभ्यो गतं च गिरिजामुखे। मतं श्रीवासुदेवस्य तस्मादागमुच्यतें॥

Aagatam Shivvaktrobhya matam cha girigamukhe !
Matam Shri Vasudevasya tasmadagammamuchte !!

In this process, Devi Shakti described the Shri Chakra. It could be drawn on Rock, *Shaligram, Gandaki* river stone and benefit could be drawn accordingly. Shri Chakra drawn on earth with red vermillion blesses with all comforts. Shri Chakra on Crystal *(Safteek)* blessed with all desires; on Ruby blesses *Rajyoga*; Shri Chakra on Emerald destroys the enemy. Shri Chakra on *Lohatray* (iron mixed with three metals) blesses all type of *siddhi*

In her conversation with Shiva, Devi Shakti asked Him about *lohatray.* She said that this is not a common metal therefore the common man should know about it. She asked that how this metal is created and how it works ? Shiva replied that by mixing ten parts of Gold, with 16 parts of silver and 12 parts of copper a *Manohar pitihika* is drawn. Shri Chakra drawn on this *pitihika,* blesses peace of mind, long life, health, wealth and all comforts to the person.

Extension of Shri Chakra

Extension of Shri Chakra is described in following manner :-

1. On the land by extending it upto the desired area.
2. On big rocks and half part of the mountain

In his conversation with Shakti, Shiv said that low lines drawn on the surface are meant for the people of *Paatal* (residents of nether world), the raised lines are meant for the people of *Mrityulok* (earth) and the lines drawn on the half part of the mountain are meant for the people of *swarg* (Heaven). Therefore, Shri Chakra could be made of Meru size, or of *prastar* size or on any metal as told.

Prohibited metals

Following metals are prohibited in making Shri Chakra:-

1. Glass and bell metal *(kansa)* are prohibited for Shri Chakra
2. No metals other than told be used for making Shri Chakra .

Length of worship

According to *Rattansagar* Shri Chakra on Gold should be worshipped for whole life; on silver it should be worshipped for 22 years; on copper it should be for 12 years; and on *Bhojpatra* the Chakra should be worshipped for 6 years. According to *Lakshyasagar and Tantralok* the Crystal *(Safteek)* Yantras should be worshipped for whole life which bless with all comforts.

Precautions while drawing Shri Chakra

The Lines in the Shri Chakra should be straight According to *"Sautramani Tantra"*, the straight line bestows wealth and curved, angular or diluted, lines brings poverty. If the Chakra is carved on gold person can sit facing any direction. When the purpose of Shri Chakra is for universal order *(Shrishti karma)* or for Status Quo *(Sthiti Karma)*, then the person should sit in a temple or at some auspicious place. When the Chakra is meant for destroying the enemies, *(Sanhar karma)* then the articles should be synonym to that act. It is well known that God has three qualities.

1. Creation
2. Bringing up
3. Destroyer

In the same manner the Shri Chakra is drawn for three purposes. Creation means solving the problems, maintaining status quo and destroying the factors responsible for the problems.

Importance of lines in Shri Chakra

There are nine triangles in Shri Chakra, out of these five are facing upwards and four are facing downwards. After joining these triangles some lines are automatically formed in the Shri Chakra which are described as rhythmical. The downwards lines destroys the problems faced by the person, checks the mishappenings etc., hence they are called rhythmical. The upwards facing lines are meant for inculcating new ideas, reviving the capabilities of a person and forcing the hidden spiritual powers to come out for checking the any misshappenings. It also works as a source of energy for the person also.

Shri Chakra on ground

As told earlier Shri Chakra could be drawn on ground but before erecting the diagram there are some precautions to be observed.

1. The ground should be clean, protected and in an isolated place.
2. The surface of the ground should be levelled (if not, get it done before drawing the Shri Chakra) plaster it with cow dung.
3. Throw red solid mixed with vermillion and red antimony over it.
4. Fill coloured rice in the triangles and other formations.

After drawing the Yantra energize the Yantra as told in the book and perform pooja accordingly. As a result it will become effective in few days and start giving its result.

Auspicious time for drawing Shri Chakra

The auspicious time for writing the Yantra is Deepawali or *Sharad Navratra*. If the Chakra is drawn in *Chaitra Navratri* then the night of *panchmi*, *Saptami* and *Ashtami* are considered auspicious. Besides this, the Chakra could be drawn on some auspicious day after consulting the *panchang*. If someone have some apprehension about it then it is advised to consult some known person for drawing and energising it. Then only one can start performing pooja of the Chakra. The Chakra could be placed in pooja rooms, office, business establishments or meditation place. It is worth mentioning here that there is no need to perform the entire practice daily. The person by offering red, yellow flower and other pooja material along with a lamp of *ghee* (clarified butter) should recite the following mantra. One should always keep in mind the image of Tripur Sundri while worshipping the Shri Chakra.

After performing pooja it would be much better if the devotee is in possession of lotus stem rosary if not, then, take rosary of *Rudraksha* or coral and complete eleven rounds of the rosary while reciting the mantra. The mantra for recitial is:

श्रीं ह्रीं क्लीं ऐं सौः ॐ ह्रीं श्रीं कएइलह्रीं हसकहलह्रीं सकलह्रीं सौः ऐं क्लीं ह्रीं श्रीं ॥

Shrim Hrim klim aim som om hrim shrim keiilhrim haskahlhrim sakalhrim som aim klim hrim shrim ॥

The sage of the mantra is *Dakshinamurti,* metre *pankti*, deity is *shri tripur sundri, aim bij, som shakti, klim kilkam.* The mantra is recited for one hundred thousand times. Homa is to be performed with *kaneer* flowers mixed with three sweets. Another mantra for this yantra is which is commonly used is:

ह्रीं ॐ नमः शिवाय ।

ॐ श्रीं ह्रीं श्रीं कमले कमलालये प्रसीद प्रसीद श्रीं ह्रीं श्रीं महालक्ष्मयैः नमः ॥

Hrim om namah Shivaya ।

Om shareeng hareeng Shareeng kamla kamlalye Prasiid Prasiid Shareeng Hareeng Shareeng Mahalakshmaye Namah ॥

Dhyan Verse

बालार्कायुततेजसं त्रिनयनां रक्ताम्बरोल्लासिनीं नानालंकृतिराजमानवपुषं बालोडुराट्शेखराम् ।

हस्तैरिक्षुधनुः सृणिं सुमशरं पाशं मुद्रां बिभ्रतीं श्रीचक्रस्थितसुन्दरीं त्रिजगतामाधारभूतां स्मरेत् ॥

Balakaryuttejsam trinenyam raktambrollasnim nanalankartirajmanavpusham baloduratsekhram ।

Hastairiksudhanusarnim sumsaram pasham mudram bibrahtim shrichakra stith sundrim trijagtamadharbhutam samret ॥

It is the claim of our saints and scholars that if the Chakra is worshipped in the above manner then the person, establishment would not face any poverty and goddess *Lakshmi* would permanently stay in that house (procedure of the mantra is already discussed in our earlier chapters).

Wearing Shri Chakra and its benefit

Shri Chakra is not only drawn on ground, rock, mountain, or worship place but as per some of the texts it could also be worn in any finger as directed or in the neck. Before wearing the Chakra following method be followed for proper use.

Before wearing it should be purified with Ganges water. After that put a *tilak* of red Vermillion and put in the smoke of incense while sitting in a comfortable *Aasana*. At last the yantra be dipped in scent or sprinkle scent over it.

Recite the following mantras according to the part where it was directed to use :-

1. For Thumb: **ह्रीं श्रीं अं अंगुष्ठाभ्यां नमः ।** ***Hareeng Shareeng Aeeing Angushtabhyam Namah*** **।**
2. For First finger: **ह्रीं श्रीं अं तर्जनीभ्यां नमः ।** ***Hareeng Shareeng Aeeing Tirjaniabhyam Namah*** **।**
3. For Second finger **ह्रीं श्रीं सौः मध्यमाभ्यां नमः ।** ***Hareeng Shareeng Soing Madhyam Namah*** **।**
4. For Third finger **ह्रीं श्रीं अं अनामिकाभ्यां नमः ।** ***Hareeng Shareeng Aeeing Anamikabhyam Namah*** **।**
5. For Fourth finger **ह्रीं श्रीं अं कनिष्ठिकाभ्यां नमः ।** ***Hareeng Shareeng Aeeing Kanishthabhyam Namah*** **।**
6. For neck, arm or any other body part: **ह्रीं श्रीं सौः करतलकरपृष्ठाभ्यां नमः ।** ***Hareeng Shareeng soing Kartalkarparishthabhyam Namah*** **।**

Some more Shri Chakras

According to *Rudrayamal* Lord Shiva disclosed to Devi Shakti that *Sumeru*, *Kailash*, and *Bhumi* (Ground/Earth) are other three forms of Shri Chakra. These *Chakras* were formed after levelling the surface of *Sumeru*, *Kailash* and *Bhumi*.

These Shri Chakras were worshipped by the Gods and their mothers who were attendants of Lord Shiva. These were some mystical things which were disclosed by Lord Shiva to Devi Shakti which were later discovered by our saints and sages. These are the same Yantras which are described as rare.

Shri Chakra of *Sumeru* (mountain type), if drawn, on some gem then it is thousand times beneficial than other Yantras. The gems

recommended in our classics are emerald and ruby. This type of yantra could be used by any person, especially who undertakes mental work. This yantra is also useful in mental agony, distress, tiredness, impatientness etc. This Shri Chakra could be installed in office, business establishment, vehicle, home, etc. This is also useful in maintaining full spirituality and checks any type of mishappening. It gives a boost to disgruntle and disgusted people and make them happy, provide peace of mind, maintains health. If this type of yantra is worshipped religiously daily with Lakshmi *Stuti*, *kanak ghas*, Shri *Sukt* or *Mahaguari path*, we assure you that no sign of poverty would be there and health and wealth would be restored in the family for ever.

In *Shrividyaarnav* while referring to Shiv-Shakti dialogue it was said:

श्री चक्रमपि देवेशि मेरूरूपं न शंसयः ॥

Shri Chakramapi Devashi Merurupam na sanshya ॥

No doubt devi Shri Chakra is also of *Sumeru* Type.

Precaution for Shri Chakra

If Shri Chakra is defaced, broken, not being worshipped properly, stolen or lost, comes under the foot of some undesirable animals or birds, placed on the back of such animals, dropped at some inauspicious place, or worshipped with some wrong mantras or touched by some disgraced person then the yantra should be removed from the installed place. The person is advised to keep fast for a day honestly, recite the Shri *Vidya Sukta* for one hundred thousand times, perform homa for one tenth part of the mantra, offer food to *Brahmins, Gurus,* or persons enjoying equal status, persons having knowledge in the field of Yantras and mantras.

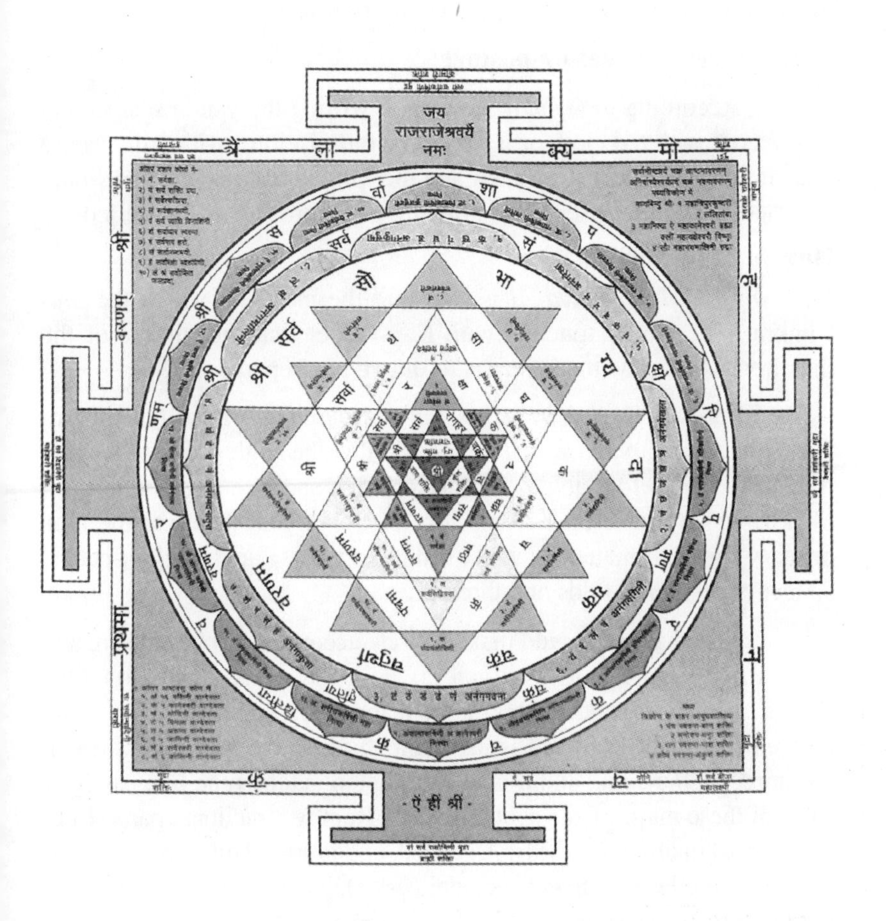
जय
राजराजेश्वर्यै
नमः
- ऐं ह्रीं श्रीं -

If the lines of Shri Chakra have become dim in course of times or some inauspicious things have fallen over it then it would certainly give its malefic effect. If a insane person wilfully defaces it then he/she have to face dire consequences. In this case the person is advised to throw it in the river at any pilgrim centre or sea.

Arrangement of seat or posture

According to *Gyanarnava* while writing the yantra seat should be covered with red cloth or it should be red. Before writing the yantra one should remember the Shakti and the first word to be written would be (शान्ति) ***Shanti.*** Afterwards drawing of yantra should be started.

How to draw Shri Chakra

In the *Malaarnava* it is said that the metal on which the Shri Chakra is drawn be touched with fire. After that the surface of the metal on which side the yantra is to drawn be prepared.

In *Saundriya lahari's* first Part '*Aanand lahri* written by Adi Guru Shankracharya in which it was said that the angles of your feet are transformed into four angles related to Shiva and five angles related to Shakti, which are distinct from those of Shiva, and thus into the nine primary forms of matter, as well as into forty-three angles, eight-petals, sixteen-sides, three-folds and three-lines.

It said that one should make a circle according to one's desire and draw a line from east to west and divide it into forty-eight parts. One should make nine marks on this diagram and on the sixth, on the sixth and on the fifth, on the third and again on the third, on the fourth and then on the third, on the sixth, and on the sixth again extend nine lines on both sides of these marks, from south to north. Remove fractional parts (from these lines) in order. On the first, second, and fourth, then on the fifth and sixth, and on the eighth and last agni (three), bana (five), kala (sixteen), purana (eighteen), sixteen, veda (four), and agni (three). One who have profound knowledge should join these lines. Hence a Shri Chakra is formed with nine mandals , with a centre having trembling fire with eight, twelve and fourteen lights. Apart from the Chakra there are eight *vasus* lotus petals and sixteen leaves. The group of three circles enhanced the distinction of the Chakra and has an earthly house distinguished by three lines. The dwelling consists of a threefold road and is beautifully adorned with four fold doors. This way the Chakra is beautifully adorned with fourfold doors is divine, completely splendorous, consisting of the nature of Moon, Sun and fire.

The nine mandals of Shri Chakra

According to *Subaghide* there are nine mandalas in Shri Chakra which are geometric abstract symbolising the cosmos of the body of Devi Shakti. The goddess is supposed to reside in her physical, visible form in the dot at the centre of the Chakra while simultaneously flowing through out the entire universe. This 'double presence' concept is vital in grasping the Shri Chakra. Her seat has four 'pillars': *Brahma* - the creator, in the Northeast, *Vishnu* - the preserver, in the Southeast; Mahesh - the destroyer, in the Southwest; and *Sadasiva* in northwest. The dot is the core of the Chakra and represents the principles or activities known as the *Pancha Kriya* known as, Emanation of the cosmos from its primal source; Projection of creation into the primal void; Preservation of the created universe; Withdrawal of the creative and preservative energies in cosmic dissolution; and lastly, retention of the withdrawn energy of the universe for the next cycle of recreation.

Three Chakras constitute the square, the sixteen petal lotus and eight-petalled lotus on the periphery form the centre of a gradual flow, the fourteen cornered figure and the two ten angled figures in the middle, form the centre for preservation, the eight-angled figure, the primary central triangle and the central point or *bindu* make the centre of reabsorption and retention.

The first Mandal

This mandala represents the enclosing walls or fence of a small zone of a practitioner which is named as *Bhupur* and is called *Trailokya Mohana* Chakra. On the outer line are the eight *Lokapalas* (Inder-East, *Vahani*-Agni, Yam-*Pitrapati*, *Varun*-Water, *Naqarat*-Shakti, *Marut*-Air, *Kuber*-Money, Ish-The best ruler) which are guardian spirits of the all directions. The Eastern gate is the way of the mantras. The Southern gate is the way of devotion or *bhakti*. The Western gate is for the performance of rites and rituals, or karma-*kanda*. The Northern gate is the way of wisdom, or *Jnana*. The gate 'below' is the 'path of words' whereas the gate 'above' is the way or 'road of liberation'. These are located at the Southern and Northern gate, respectively, i.e. 'above' is north, 'below' is south. Each of these gates also stands for one of the six primary *Chakras* in the body. 'Below' is the root or *Muladhara* Chakra; the Eastern gate to the sacral or *Svadhishthana* Chakra; the Southern to the navel or *Manipura* Chakra; the Western corresponds to heart or *Anahata* Chakra; the Northern to the throat or *Visuddha* Chakra, and the 'above' to the brow or *Ajna* Chakra.

The three lines of the earth square of Shri Chakra each has a set of subsidiary aspects of the goddess. On the middle line are eight *Siddhi* Shaktis identified with the senses which are known as . On the inner line are eight Shaktis ruling *Adana*, *Garima*, Mahima, *Laghima*, *Ishtiv*, *Vashitiv*, *Prapti*, *Prakrya*. They are the eight *matrikas* or little mothers. These Shaktis are collectively known as the *Prakata Yoginis*.

The second mandal

This is technically named *Shodashal* (16 petals) and is called the 'Fulfiller of all Hopes' or *Sarva Ashapurak* Chakra. The Shaktis in this circle are known as the Hidden Ones. Since frustrated desire is the strongest obstacle to spiritual progress, the next stage is wisely concerned with satisfying them. Only he who has experienced can renounce. The values of virtue, wealth and

pleasure are granted at this stage.

The petals are representations of 16 sacred vowels, each one starting from the east in an anticlockwise direction. Each of the 16 vowels corresponds to the Shakti. The 16 *yoginis* in this mandal are associated with the attainment of desires by the cultivation or strengthening of power, over mind, ego, sound, touch, sight, taste, smell, intellect, steadiness, memory, name, growth, etheric body, revivification, and physical body. The Shaktis manifest their powers in the Five Elements, the 10 senses of perception or *Indriyas* (being further divided into five organs of action and five sense organs) and the Mind. This stage, too, corresponds to the Muladhara Chakra and is the second part of Emanation.

The third mandal

The third mandal is known as *Ashtadal* and considered as Agitator of All or Sarva *Sankshobhan* Chakra. The Shaktis in this mandala are called the Very Secret *Yoginis*. The eight large petals of this mandal represent a state of relationships between physical stimuli and sensory response in dynamic equilibrium.

Each petal of the mandal has a consonant inscribed within it that begins with '*Ka*' - the name of the Unknown God. In the East, the petal stands for speech and expression; in the South, apprehension and reception; in the West, locomotion; in the North, bodily urges ; in the Southeast, pleasure; in the Southwest, rejections and reactions; in the Northwest, conscious attention; and in the Northeast, detachment and dispassion.

The eight Shaktis in each of the eight petals of the mandala are described as Shaktis of speech, holding, walking, excreting, pleasure, abandoning, concentration and detachment. They are described as sapphire blue, holding noose, goad, dispelling fear, and holding blue lotus.

Their names (*Ananga Madana* etc.) all convey terms of loving sexuality. The third Mandal corresponds to the Manipura Chakra and is a transition stage between emanation-preservation symbolically representing both of them. This stage sees the aspirant succeed even further towards reaching the ultimate goal.

The fourth Mandal

The fourth mandala is called *Chaturdashar*. The Yoginis are called 'Concealed by Tradition'. It is called the 'Provider of Prosperity' or Sarva *Saubhagya Dayak* Chakra. It is a *14-cornered* figure. It represents the first 14 letters of the Sanskrit alphabet, regarded as a sacred revelation of words of power which are known as 14 Shaktis of the triangles and associated with the chief *nadis* or currents of bio energy known as the mind (*Manas*), the intellect (*Buddhi*), being (*Chitta*), the conscious ego (*Ahamkara*) and the 10 indriyas.

The chakra associated with it is the *Anahata* and it is the first stage of Preservation-Emanation. Hope of spiritual success is firmly established at this stage in the aspirant. Here we move from the petals of the flower into the 43 triangles of Shri Chakra, formed from the four fires and the five Shaktis.

The fifth mandal

This mandala is called Sarva *Artha Sadhak* Chakra 'The *Cakra* Bestowing All Objects to the *Sadhaka*'. The Shaktis are called the *Kula Kaulas. It* is also called *Bahiradashar* 'Achiever of all Objects'. It is a ten cornered figure. It corresponds to the Visuddha chakra and is the stage called preservation-a strong Vishnu energy.

The Ten cornered figure represents the 10 types of Vital Breaths (*Prana* or *Ki*). This is inevitable as Vishnu. These 10 Shaktis in the

triangles are described as having thrilled faces, holding noose and goad and adorned with various crystal and heavenly gems. These are the Yoginis of the 10 vital breaths. The possibility, not the actual experience, of inner spiritual realization is firmly established here.

The sixth mandal

According to *Yoni Tantra* this mandala is called Sarva *Rakshakar* Chakra. The Chakra protecting all. It is also a Ten cornered figure. They are the Shaktis of the 10 Vital fires. The gem is emerald. The *ore* is Marrow. The time is Lunar Fortnight. The *Mudra* is the Great Goad. The nature is moon of sun. Here Tripur is garlanded in her red flowers, also equated with the blood of menstruation.

There is some ambivalence about it as it corresponds to the Manipura Chakra, but is apparently experienced by mystics who have internalised the Sri Chakra as being between the eyebrows, which is where one would expect the Ajna Chakra to be. Its nature is that of fire (Agni), the 10 specific 'fires within the body' being the fire of purgation (*Rechak*), digestion (*Pachak*), absorption (*Shoshak*), burning (*Dahak*), the secretion of enzymes (*Plavak*), acidification (*Ksharak*), to take out or excrete (*Uddharak*), the fires of pessimism and frustration (*Kshobhak*), the fire of assimilation (*Jrambhak*) and creating lustre (*Mohak*). This enclosure symbolizes the third stage of Preservation called Preservation-Absorption.

The Seventh Enclosure

This Mandal is known as Sarva *Roga Hara* Chakra, the Chakra destroying all disease. The yoginis are known as the Secret or *Rahasya* yoginis. It is also known as *Ashtar* an eight-cornered figure and is considered as remover of all diseases. It is represented by five letters of the '*pa*' group as also the letters 'sa', '*sha*' and 'sa' again. These are the yoginis of Tripur *siddha* which are the colour of pomegranate flowers, wearing red clothes, smeared with red scent, each carrying five arrows and a bow.

These Shaktis are the rulers of cold, heat, happiness, sorrow, desire, and the three *gunas sattvas*, rajas, *tamas*. They are also called the eight *Vasinis*. The gem is diamond (*Vajra*). The time is month. The Mudra is *Khecari* Mudra. The nature is fire of moon. The eight letters are also supposed to represent the eight weapons held by the *Kameshwara* - *Kameshwari* (Shiva-Durga) which destroy disease. Shiva as Mahesh was specifically a healer, thus this mandal merely adds the Shakti's healing energy to the mix. A statement contrary to received opinion corresponds to two Chakras of the human body, both the forehead Ajna as well as the *Svadhisthana* Chakras. It may have something to do with the sort of energy required to bring about healing. Energy workers are aware that it sometimes begins to flow from the womb or genitals, where the Svadhisthana is located. This *Mandla* symbolizes the first stage of absorption, namely absorption-emanation. At this level the aspirant is free of all earthly bondage and is, literally, on the threshold of the inner circle of realization.

The Eighth Enclosure

This is the Primary Triangle technically named the Kama-kala and known as Sarva *Siddhiprada* Chakra 'The bestower of all Attainments'.

The Kama-kala is the first outcome or effect of the central dot's energy outflow. Since it is an inverted triangle, it is also described as 'the wandering between horns', the two lines meeting at a point below being the horns.

The three lines of the triangle are also held to represent the three qualities or Gunas: Purity and Calm (*Sattva*), Activity (Rajas), and Inertia (Tamas). Alternatively, the three lines are held to symbolize three goddesses - Kameshwari, *Brijeshwari* and *Agamalini*. They also represent the three stages of consciousness: Conscious Awareness (*Jagriti*), Dreaming (*Swapna*), and Deep Slumber (*Sushupti*). The fourth stage of Consciousness is literally *Turiya* - the Fourth! This is a transcendent state found only in the ultimate realization of the final enclosure. The Kama-kala represents the head (and womb!) of the Mother and symbolizes also the three fundamental tendencies of existence - desire, knowledge, activity - which also have to be transcended for the final liberation. This is the penultimate stage before complete realization of the Self. The primary triangle represents the second stage of absorption, namely absorption-preservation, and it is white in colour denoting purity or sattva.

The ninth Mandala

This is the central point and is aptly called Sarva *Anandamayai Chakrn* 'Filled with all Bliss'. Since it is too minute to be clearly seen, the Primary Triangle exists as a manifestation of this bindu. This point is the actual spot where the Mother resides though, to make matters interesting, this point is supposed to pervade all creation too.

This, in a temple, would be the sanctum sanatorium, with all the other circles or enclosures representing various parts of the temple as you move inwards. Every classic temple has this nine-enclosure design to enable the mind to be successively purified and focused, by the time it gets the actual vision of the deity. By this point, the seeker should be in mystical union with the God-field. The point is also called the 'Field of Deliberation', the spot wherein takes place the indissoluble union of the individual soul with the divine.

Benefits of worshipping the Shri Chakra

In the worship of Shri Chakra, one proceeds from the outer square to the innermost bindu. This process almost invariably involves the awakening of the *Kundalini* power within. However, the Shri Chakra need not be used that way. It can be simply worshipped and allowed to radiate its energy outwards to create prosperity and harmony for the worshipper. The immense complexity of the Shri Chakra makes it a veritable unified pantheon of the Gods. Worshipping the Shri Chakra ensures worshipping of all forms of divinity. It is an immense intellectual discipline, as well as a towering achievement of Indian spiritual thought. By repeating the Mantra nine hundred thousand times the man will have the same form as Mahesh. By performing Homas with the flowers of *Mallikii* and *Malati* he shall be the lord of speeches. By performing Homa with *Kaneer* flowers he can enchant and fascinate the entire universe. By performing the *Homa* with camphor, saffron and musk the devotee shall excel the lord of Love. . The *Homa* with the flowers of *Campaka* and *Patala* shall make the universe come under his control soon. The *homa* with fried grain bestows kingdom that with honey brings about the annihilation of harassments. The *homa* at night with the flesh of goat brings about the destruction of the armies of the enemy. If *Homa* is performed with curd, ghee, milk and honey one shall obtain respectively health, richness, village and wealth; through sugar obtains happiness, through lotus flowers wealth and fortune and through pomegranate the favour of the king. Attainment of money and grain through milk puddings; all living beings brought under control through *Bandhuka* flowers; if

Homa are performed with ripe mango fruits a hundred thousand times the entire earth comes under control. By performing *Homa* with salt together with mustard evil persons can be destroyed; by performing *Homa* with camphor a man erelong attains mastery of speech. Through the *Homa* with *Karaiija* fruit evil spirits, ghosts etc., come under control; through *Bilva* fruits one attains enormous wealth and attainment of happiness through sugarcane stems. Through the *Homa* with ghee one attains the desired object; peace can be achieved through gingelly seeds and rice grain. Everything desired is achieved by men through the goddess of the Devas.

Energising *(pranapratishta)* the Shri Chakra

It is necessary to energize the Shri Chakra without which it is futile to worship it. This process, in fact, holds true for initiation of a candidate into Shri Vidya. This process installs the 35 elements into the yantra. It also gives the yantra the full set of senses and the *Antahkarana*, or subtle body. The process also inspires the yantra with the Matrika, the letters of the Sanskrit alphabet which are the goddess as sound.

Balatripur Yantra

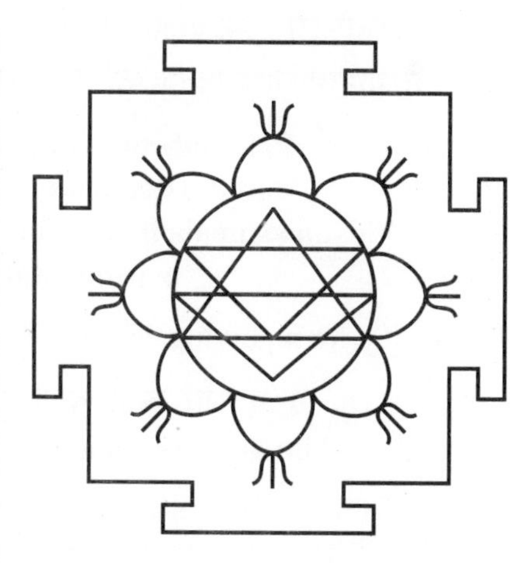

One who worships this yantra becomes possessor of wealth and learning. If *homa* with red lotus flowers are done women become favourites, if with mustard kings can be brought under control. The devotee can conquer premature death by performing *Homa* with *Guduchi* flowers together with milk. By performing *Homa* with the *Durva* grass soaked in milk one attains longevity with freedom from ailments. The devotee after attaining siddhi of this yantra becomes *Brihaspati* (scholar) and *kubera* (wealthy with all comforts). The mantra for recital is:-

ऐं क्लीं सौः ॥

Aim klim Sauh ॥

The sage of this mantra is *Dakshinamurti,* metre is *pankti,* and the deity is *Tripur Bala.*

The mantra is to repeat for three hundred thousand times and perform *Homa* thirty thousand times with the flowers of *palas lata* or *plash* socked in honey. The yantra for the purpose of adoration consists of nine cornered figure with triangles with eight petal lotus enveloping it and the whole figure is surrounded by a *bhupura*. At the tips of the petals, tridents are to be written and lotus be surrounded by the letters of the alphabets.

The devotee should note here that the mantra is cursed by the Devi; hence, it does not bestow the desired results. There the devotee shall does redemption from curse and *utkilana* rites then only begin the japa. The devotee shall wear white garments, apply white sandal and bedeck himself in pearl ornaments.

Dhyana Verse

रक्ताम्बरां चन्द्रकलावतन्सां समुद्यदादित्यनिभां त्रिनेत्राम् ।
विद्याक्षमालाभयदानहस्तां ध्यायामि बालामरुणाम्बुजस्थाम् ॥

Raktambram chanderkala vatansam
samudh daditaya nibham trinetram ।
Vidyaa kshmala bhaya dan hastam dhayayami bala
marunambujsatham॥

The mantra for nullifying the curse is:-

ऐं ऐं सौः क्लीं क्लीं ऐं सौः सौः क्लीं ॥

Aim aim sau klim klim aim sau sau klim ॥

This mantra is recited for hundred times and, hence, the curse is abolished. The mantra for denailing is:-

ॐ क्लीं नमः ॥

Om klim namah ॥

This mantra is recited for hundred times, hence, the mantra is denailed.

Tripurbala dhaaran Yantra

Now we will discuss the tripurbala dharan yantra. This yantra bestows son, fame, wealth and all worldly comforts in life. The mantra for recital is:

क्लीं क्लीं क्लीं श्रीं श्रीं श्रीं ह्रीं ह्रीं ह्रीं त्रिपुरसुन्दरी सर्व जगत् मम वश कुरु कुरु मह्यं बलं देहि स्वाहा ॥

Klim Klim Klim Shrim Shrim Shrim Hrim Hrim Hrim Tripursundari sarv jagat mam vash kuru kuru maham balam dehi swaha ॥

The sage of the mantra is *Dakshinamurti,* metre *gaytri,* deity is *tripurbala.* This mantra is to be recited for one hundred thousand times. *Homa* be done with the flowers of *kaner.*

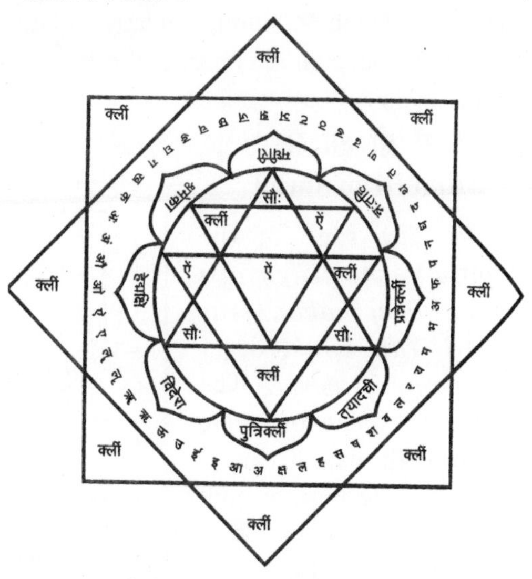

Dhayana Verse:-

पाशांकुशौ पुस्तकमक्षसूत्रु करैर्दधाना सकलामराच्र्या ।
रक्तात्रिनेत्रा शशिशेखरेयं ध्येयाऽखिलद्धयैं त्रिपुरात्र बाला ॥

Pasham kushoo pustakmakshsutru karedhadhana saklamaracharya ।
Raktatrinetra sahsishetrayam dheyayaakhildhadye tripurt bala ॥

Bhuvneshwari Yantra

Goddess Bhuvneshwari is fourth among dus mahavidyas. By worshipping her one can attract the whole world. She is also known as *Rajrajeshwari*. She is *sidhdatri* and *sidh vidya* and also known as the goddess of eternal world. By worshipping goddess Bhuvneshwari one can attract the world, the Govt. servant. One can become poet by worshipping the goddess and get intelligent daughter. A pregnant lady will not have labour problems if she goes to the hospital after seeing the Bhuvneshwari yantra. The mantra for recital is:-

ऐं ह्रीं श्रीं ॥

Aim Hrim Shrim

The sage of the mantra is *shakti, gayatri* metre, *beej hakar, ikar shakti, raif kilak*, deity *Bhuvneshwari devta*. The mantra is to recite for twelve hundred thousand times. Food for offering are pure ghee, honey, sugar mixed rice boiled in milk.

Dhyana Verse

सिंदुरारुणविग्रहां त्रिनयनां माणिक्य मौलिस्फुरत्तारानायकशेखरां
स्मितमुखीमापीन वक्षोरुहाम् ।
पाणिभ्यां मणिपुर्णरत्नचषकं रक्तोत्पलं बिभ्रतीं सौम्यां
रत्नघटस्थसव्यचरणां ध्यायेत्परामम्बिकाम् ॥

Sindurarunvigraham trinayam manikya

maulisafoortaranayakshekram samitmukhimapin vakshoruham Panibhyam manipuranratanchaskam raktotpalam bibrahtim saumayam ratanghatsathsavyacharanaam Dhayatparambikam

After realising the yantra if the devotee does the *homa* with good gragrance and flowers of *plash* he becomes a good singer. If *homa* with salt, yellow mustard is done then he can attract men and women. If the devotee does the *homa* with honey, pure ghee, sugar, red flowers, then he would certainly get benefits from govt.

Chinnamasta Yantra

Goddess Chinnamasta is fifth among Dus mahavidyas. She is also know as *Parchand-chand chandika.* It is said that Lord *Parshuram* and Guru *Gorakhnath* of *Nath* sect were devotee of this vidya. One can yield benefits quickly by worshipping her. If the devotee worships her the Devi bestows all desires immediately. Devi bestows eloquence of speech; he can captivate all people and practise all six rites. Goddess bestows enjoyment of worldly pleasures and salvation to the devotee. By means of correct comprehension of this Vidya the devotee shall attain the knowledge of all scriptures and lures, destruction of all sins and all types of happiness.

The mantra for recital is:-

ॐ श्रीं ह्रीं ह्रीं क्लीं ऐं वज्रवैरोचनीये ह्रीं ह्रीं फट् स्वाहा ॥

Om Srim Hrim Hrim Klim Aim Vajravairocaniye Hrim Hrim Phat Svaha ॥

The sage of the mantra is *Bhairva;* metre is *samrat,* deity is *Chinnamasta devta, hinkardevyam* Beej, *swah* Shakti. The mantra is to be recited for four hundred thousand times. Articles for offerings during homa are fruits and flowers of *palasa* or *biliva.* The yantra for worship consists of two triangles, a circle then an eight petal lotus and a *bhupur* surrounds everything.

Dhyana verse

भास्वन्मण्डलमध्यगां निजशिरश्छिन्नं विकीर्णालकं स्फारास्यं प्रपिबद्गलात्स्वरुधिरं वामे करे बिभ्रतीम् ।
याभासक्तरतिस्मरोपरिगतां सख्यौ डाकिनीवर्णिन्यौ परिदृश्य मोदकलितां श्रीछिन्नमस्तां भजे ॥

Bhasavmandalmadhyagam nijshirshichannam vikirnklkam safarasayam parpibadhgalatsavrudhiram vame kare bibarthim।
Yabhasakt ratisamroparigatam sakhyo dakini varninayoo paridarshaya modaklitam shri chinnmastam bhajee ॥

Tirpurbharvi Yantra

Devi Tripur bhairvi is sixth among Dus mahavidyas. She full fills all the desires of the devotee. One who worships Devi he never falls ill and all type of diseases do not affect the devotee. If some one worships this yantra with *gorocharan*, saffron or red sandal and offer white flowers on Tuesday, Saturday and Sunday the Devi fulfils all desires. If the yantra is worshipped in cremation ground or temple it gives more effect. The mantra for recital is:-

हसैं हसकरीं हसैं ॥

Hasee hanskari hasee ॥

This Mantra is to be recited for twenty four hundred thousand times. The sage of the mantra is *Dakshinemurte*, pankti metre, *tripurbharvi* deity, *aim* beej, *hrim* Shakti, *klim* kilak.

Dhyana verse

उद्यद्भानुसहस्त्रकान्तिमरुणक्षौमां शिरोमालिकां
रक्तालिप्तपयोधरां जप परीं विद्यामभीतिं वरम् ।
हस्ताब्जैद्दधतीं त्रिनेत्रविलसद्वक्त्रारविन्दश्रियं
देवीं बद्धहिमंशुरत्नमुकुटां वन्देऽरविन्दस्थिताम् ॥

Udyadbhanusahasr kantimarunkshomam shiromalikam
raktaliptpayodharam jap parim vidyambhitim varam ।
Hastabjaidaddhtim trinetravilasdvaktrirvindshriyam
devi badhhimshuratan mukutam vande arvindstithtam ।।

Dhumavati Yantra

Devi Dhumavati is seventh among Dus mahavidyas. Yantra of Dhumavati is used to check the nefarious activities of the enemy. The yantra is used for six rites and through different ways the yantra could be used after realisation. Worship of this yantra is also useful when someone is facing sentence and chances of being put behind the

bars due to some unknown reason, then this yantra is very useful. The devotee could also reap fruits like son, wealth and other problems related to six rites. The mantra for recital is:-

धूं धूं धूमावती स्वाहा ॥

Dhum Dhum Dhumavati Swaah

The sage of this mantra is *pippalad*, metre is *nivarch*, *jyestha* devta, dhum *bija* swah Shakti, dhumavati kilak. The mantra is to be recited for one hundred thousand times. Pure ghee and sesame seed to be used for offerings.

Dhyana verse

अत्युच्चा मलिनाम्बराखिलजनोद्वेगावहा दुर्मना
रूक्षाक्षित्रितया विशालदशना सूर्योदरी चञ्चला ।
प्रस्वेदाम्बुचिता क्षुधाकुलतनुः कृष्णातिरूक्षाप्रभा
ध्येया मुक्तकचा सदाप्रियकलिर्धूमावती मन्त्रिणा ॥

Attyucha malinambrakhiljanodvegavaha durmana
Rukshashitritya vishaldasha suryodari chanchala ।
Parasvedambuchita akshudha kultanu krishna tirukshaprabha
dhayeya muktchhha sadapriya kalirdhumavati mantrina ॥

During fourteen days of dark half of the lunar month the devotee should observe fast. He should be naked with the hairs united and dishevelled and he should keep the mantra reciting at a desolated house, cremation ground, forest or a mountain. Food should be taken in night time. After completing a hundred thousand times the devotee can destroy his enemy. More benefit could be attained by performing *homa* with *rai* mixed with salt at night.

Baglamukhi Yantra

Devi Baglamukhi is eighth among Dus Mahavidyas. Baglamukhi yantra is very powerful. It bestows victory over enemies, law suits, success in quarrels and competitions. This yantra also offers protection for cuts, scars, operations and accidents. The presiding deity goddess Baglamukhi is the controller of this powerful Yantra which recharges Yantra with occult forces.

Baglamukhi pujan Yantra

The Yantra is to be drawn with sandal powder, *Agar*, camphor etc. It consists of Triangle, hexagon, eight petal lotus, sixteen petal lotus and *Bhupura*. The devotee shall worship the goddess in the middle. The mantra is recited for one hundred thousand times. The mantra for recital is :-

ॐ ह्लीं बगलामुखि सर्वदुष्टानां वाचं मुखं पदं स्तम्भय जिह्वां कीलय
बुद्धिं विनाशय ह्लीं ॐ स्वाहा ॥

Om Hlim Bagalamukhi Sarvadustanam Vacam Mukham padam Stambhaya Jihviimkilaya Buddhim Vinasaya Hlim Om Svaha ॥

The sage of the Mantra is Narada the metre is *Bharti*; the deity of the Mantra is *baglamukhi*. The *Bija* is *hrim* and the *Shakti* is *Svaha*.

Dhyana Verse

ॐ सौवर्णासनसंस्थितां त्रिनयनं पीतांशुकोल्लासिनीं
हेमाभाङ्गरुचिं शशाङ्कमुकुटां सच्चम्पकस्रग्युताम् ।
हस्तैर्मुद्गरपाशवज्ररशनाः संविभ्रतीं भूषणैर्व्याप्ताङ्गी
बगलामुखीं त्रिजगतां संस्तम्भिनीं चिन्तयेत् ॥

Om Sauvarna sanestithtam trinayanam pitanshu kaulasani hemabhangruchim sashankmuktanam sachhmpaksargyutam

hasteermudgarpashvajrarsashansanvebrathi
bhushanevyarpatangi
baglamukhitrijagatam sansthbhini chintyat

The devotee should wear yellow clothes with yellow garland. While performing *japa* he shall always be seated. *Homa* is done with the flowers of *champa* which stunns the Devi. Repeat the Mantra ten thousand times with turmeric rosary. The goddess is to be conceived yellow in complexion while meditating. The *Homas* with gingelly seeds smeared with three sweets. (i.e., Sugar honey and ghee) is considered alluring human beings. Certainly the *Homa* with salt smeared with the three sweets is also captivating. The *Homa* with *neem's* leaves smeared with oil causes hatred. The *Homa* with *Haritila*, salt and turmeric brings about the amazement of enemies. At night the devotee performs *Homa* in the funeral pyre at the cremation ground with charcoal, smoke, mustard, buffalo milk and goggle and thereby he ere long destroy his enemies. By performing *homa* in the funeral pyre with the feathers of vultures and crows, bitter oil, *Baheda* and domestic smoke the devotee extirpates enemies. The devotee who performs *homa* with *dorva*, *guduci*, and *laja* together with the three sweets can cure all ailments by merely looking at the patient.

For the sake of achieving all types of supernatural powers the devotee shall maintain celibacy and repeat the Mantra a hundred thousand times on the top of a mountain, in a great forest, at the confluence of two rivers or in a Shiva temple. The devotee shall inspire three hundred times with the Mantra the milk of a cow having only one colour and drink it with sugar and honey. He can get rid of the ill effect of person. The devotee shall inspire a hundred thousand times with the Mantra two wooden sandals made out of white *Palasa* timber and paint them with *alta*. The man who wears those sandals can go 1200 km. in a trice.

Baglamukhi satmbhan yantra

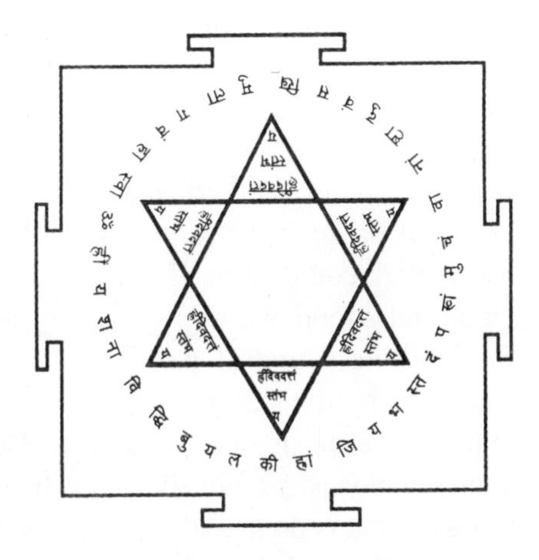

In the entire six small triangle formed by two vertically intersecting triangles the devotee shall write the name of the intended person ह्लीं अमुकं स्तम्भय ***(Hlim amukam stambhaya)*** with the *Mula* Mantras by means of *haritala* and powdered turmeric together with *dhattura* juice. Ritualistically inspire it with vital airs after writing all remaining syllables all round the hexagonal figure but within the *Bhupura*. Then tie it with a yellow string. .Take some clay from the spinning potter's wheel and make a beautiful image of a bull. The Yantra must be placed in it. This clay bull must be muddy with *Haritila* every day and worshipped. This shall bring about the retardation of the speech movement and all activities of the enemies. Then fetch a skull from the cremation ground lifting it with his left hand with the charcoal from the funeral pyre.

Now draw the Yantra in it. It shall be inspired with the Mantra and buried in the enemy's ground. It shall retard their movement. The devotee writes the Yantra with charcoal on the cover of a dead body. Then he shall put it in the mouth of a frog and tie it with a cloth. The frog is then worshipped with Yellow flowers. This will bring about the retardation of the speech of the enemies.

The Yantra is to be written on the ground where the *Divya* (spiritual incidents) is held. It shall then be stroked with the leaves of *Adusa*. It shall then retard the *Divya* process. The devotee takes the root of *Indervaruni* and inspires it seven times with the Mantra. Now throw it into the water where the *Divya* ordeal is to take place. It shall retard the process in the water of the *Divya* organizers.

Matangi Yantra

Devi Matangi is ninth among mahavidyas. She is also known as daughter of Sage *Matang*. She is considered the goddess of *Vani* (voice) and luxuries. She is also known as *chandali* or *ucchist chandali*. She is dark complexioned like cloud and is fond of listening to the chirping sound of parrot. The Devi bestows all enjoyment in life. If there is any problem in the married life of anyone, worship of Devi is considered the best. This yantra is mostly used in six rites. The mantra is recited for ten thousand times. Homa is done with the flowers of *Mahua* smeared in honey. The mantra for recital is:-

ॐ ह्रीं ऐं श्रीं नमो भगवति उच्छिष्टचाण्डालि श्रीमातङ्गेश्वरि सर्वजनवशंकरि स्वाहा ॥

Om Hrim Aim Srim Namo Bhagwati Ucchistacandali Sri Matangesvari Sarvajanavasamkari Svaha॥

The sage of the mantra is *Matanga*, the metre is *anustup* and deity is *Matangi*. The yantra consists of triangle in the middle, two lotuses of eight petals one circling the other, then sixteen petal one surrounding it and a *bhupura*.

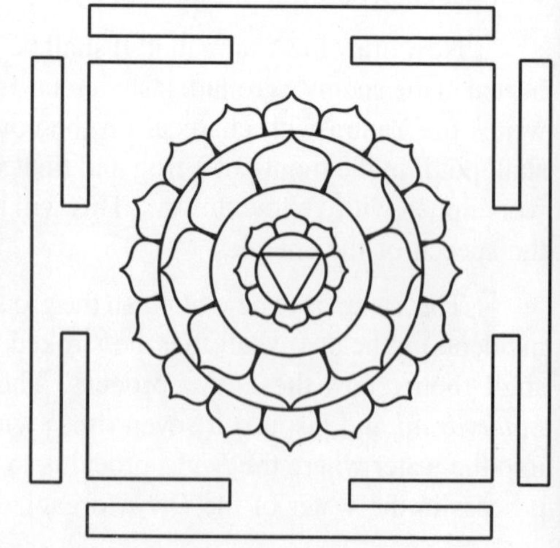

Dhyana verse

ॐ घनश्यामलाङ्गीं स्थितां रत्नपीठे शुकस्योदितं शृण्वतीं रक्त वस्त्राम् ।
सुरापानमत्तां सरोजस्थितां श्रीं भजे वल्लकीं वादयन्तीं मतङ्गींम् ॥

Om Ghanshyamalangi stitham ratanpithe shukshyoditam shranvatim rakta vastratam ॥
Surapanmatam sarojsthithtam shrim bhaje vallikim vadyanti maatangi ॥

If the devotee perform *homa* with *malika* flowers the devotee will have all enjoyment and if the fruits and leaves of *palasa* tree are used people will be under control; with banana fruits the devotee attains all desires. Homa with the twigs of *giloy* one always remain fit. Homa with the twigs of neem and pieces of rice one gets blessings of goddess lakshmi.

Kamalatmika Yantra

Devi *Kamalitmika* is tenth among the Dus mahavidyas. She is also known as *Trilokya Mata* (mother of the three worlds). She is also said Lakshmi Rupa. She is maha ratri vidya. She is Vashnvi Shakti. She is also known as companion of MahaVishnu. Dev, demons and human beings all worship her and sought her blessings. She is worshipped in *Aagam* and *Nigam* equally. She bestows all comforts, luxuries in life.

The mantra for recital is:-

ॐ नमः कमलवासिन्यै स्वाहा ॥

Om Namah Kamalvasaniye Swaha ॥

The sage of the mantra is *Daksh,* metre is *virat,* and deity is *Lakshmi.* The mantra is to be recited for ten hundred thousand times.

Dhyana Verse

ॐ आसीना सरसीरुहे स्मितमुखी हस्ताम्बुजैर्बिभ्रती
दानं पद्मयुगाभये च वपुषा सौदामिनिसन्निभा ।
मुक्ताहारविराजमानपृथुलोत्तुङ्गस्तनोद्भासिनी पायाद्वः कमला
कटाक्षविभवैरानन्दयन्ती हरिम् ॥

**Om Aassina sarsiruhe smitmukhi Hastambujai virbrihti danam padamyugabhaye cha vapusha saudamini sannibha ।
mukta har virajman prathulotung satnodbhasini payadva kamla kataksh vibhavaranandyanti harim ॥**

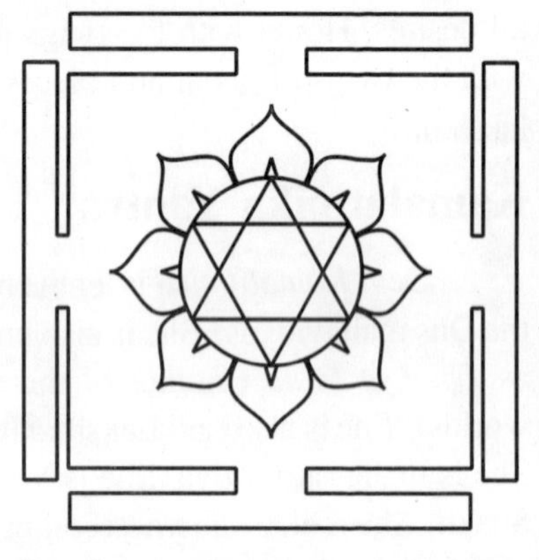

The *homa* be performed with honey, pure ghee, and sugar mixed with red flowers. Devotee, who performs worship with three hundred thousand mantras at a place where river falls in the sea, Devi bestows all luxuries in life. If the worship is performed during *uttarshada*, *uttra bhadrapada* and *uttra phaguni nakshatras* with rosary and sandal the devotee gets all spiritual powers. On full Moon day the devotee perform japa and *homa* with honey, pure ghee, and sugar and *belive* fruit his purpose is fulfilled. On fifth and Friday the worship is performed with lotus and other flowers.

CHAPTER 8

SHIV YANTRA

Shiva who is also known as *Panchmukh*, *Mahamritunjaye*, and *Rudra* is worshipped for different purposes. It is said that he is fulfiller of all desires. Hence, he is also known as *Bholanath*. He is a *Vedic* deity and our saints worshipped him for getting different fruits from him. The demons got all wishes fulfilled through him. He is said to be the orator of *Agam sahastras* which are found in dialogue form between *Parvarti* and Shiva. In this chapter we would discuss various types of *Yantras* of lord Shiva.

Shiva worship and astrology

In *Brahat Parashar Hora Shastra* forty types of *Dashas* are discussed but only *Vimshotri*, *Asthothri* and *yogini* are in actual use. However, only vimshotri *Dasha* is mostly used by the astrologers. In these Dasha systems *Antardahsa*, *partayantr* dasha, *sukshma*, and *pran dahsas* are discussed. In these *dashas* the book referred to the Shiva's worship for removing malefic effect of the planets. Here we would discuss some of the salient points for the use of our readers.

1. During the *mahadasha* of Sun, if Sun is giving malefic effect in its Antardahsa then to check this effect Mahamritunjaye yantra/ mantra to be used. This checks all evil effects of the Sun and the Sun god bestows wishes on him. In the same manner during the *mahadasha* of Saturn and *Ketu*, worship of Mahamritunjaye is recommended.
2. If the native is having the mahadasha of Moon and Antardahsa of Jupiter and the yoga is not good, then the native will have premature death. Then the native is recommended to worship lord Shiva with his *sahasrnam* (thousand names) and Shiva Yantras. During the Saturn Antardahsa the native is likely to fell ill. Mahamritunjaye yantra is recommended as a remedy for it. During the Moon dasha and Venus or Sun *Antardasha* Rudra worship or Shiva worship is recommended.
3. Mahamritunjaye yantra is useful when Saturn, Mars is enjoined, in opposition or in aspect to each other in a birth chart or in transit to avoid any accident or accidental death.

Mahamritunjaye Yantra

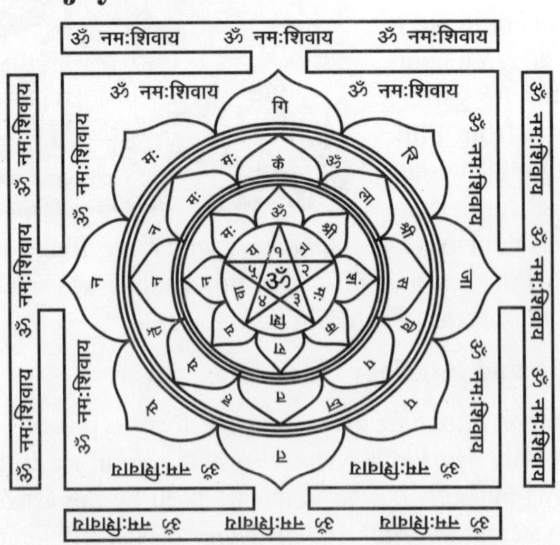

Lord Mahamritunjaye *Shankar* is the winner of death. On *worshiping* Mahamritunjaye Shankar one can escape from miseries and troubles of this materialistic world as well as the problems related to inner soul. He checks our troubles, tensions, stress as well as our ego. Lord Mahamritunjaye is the doctor of soul and sentiments. This Yantra is used to free the fear of death, grave dangers, and fatal diseases and makes one courageous and healthy. It bestows the person with wealth, health and happiness, good fortune and fame. Mahamritunjaye yantra dispels all sort of fears, influence of evil planets, fear of ghosts, accidental death and disease etc. It particularly relieves one from all dreadful diseases. It is carved on copper plate or gold plate or it can also be written on *Bhojpatra* and energised with mantras. The person who perform *pooja* of Mahamritunjaye yantra, remains in good health and free from all ailments.

After pooja, the yantra if dipped in water and the water is taken as *"Charnamrit"* (sacred water), it controls and cures diseases. If the water is sprinkled in the house, it creates amity and comfort in home. The pooja of Mahamritunjaye yantra is like that of *Kali* or *Durga* yantra. To avoid effects of souls and other calamities, Mahamritunjaye yantra, after pooja and energising, is fixed on the outer Gate of the house.

Mahamritunjaye mantra, which is remover of all sins and calamities, was obtained by *Maharishi Bhargava (Sukra)* from Shiva and thereby he could gave breathe a new life into the demons.

This Mantra for recital is:

ॐ हौं ॐ जूँ सः भूर्भुवः स्वः त्र्यम्बकं यजामहे सुगन्धिं पुष्टिवर्धनम् । उर्वारुकमिव बन्धनान् मृत्योर्मुक्षीय मामृतात् । भूर्भुवः स्वः जूँ सः हौं ॐ ॥

Om Haum Om Jum Sah Bhurbhuvah Svah Tryambakam Yajamahe Sugandhim Pustivardhanam Urvarukamiva Bandhanan Mrtyormuksiya Mamrtat Bhurbhuvah Svah Jum Sah Haum Om ॥

The sages of this Mantra are Vamadeva, *Kahola* and *Vashisth*. The metres of this mantra are *Panikti*, *Gayatri* and *Anustup*. The deities are *Sadasiva*, Mahamritunjaye and Rudra. *Hrim* is the *Shakti* and *Srim* is *Bija*. The application of this Mantra is for the realization of desired objects.

The Vedic Mantra within this Mantra under reference should be split at syllables 3, 4, 8, 9, 5 and 3. The nine initial syllables of the present Mantra are to be added before the specified sections of the Vedic Mantra for the purpose of *nayasa* along with certain other phrases as well. The mantra is to recited for one hundred thousand times. The *tarpan* is to be done with milk mixed with water. The *homa* is to be done with ten articles which are as under:-

1. Belive fruit
2. Til
3. *Khir* (Rice cooked with milk and sugar)
4. Pure ghee
5. Milk
6. Curd
7. Durva grass
8. Bar twigs }
9. Plash twigs }
10. Khair twigs }

These articles are used after smearing in Ghee, Honey and sweets

Design of the Yantra

The Pooja Yantra of Lord Mahamritunjaye is eight petal lotus in the inner most area, then sixteen petals one, then twenty four petal one, then thirty two petal one-and then forty petal lotus.

Dhyana Verse

हस्ताम्भजेयुगस्थकुम्भयुगलादुद्धृत्य तोयं शिरः सिञ्चन्तंः करयोर्युगेन
दधतं स्वांके सकुम्भौ करौ ।
अक्षस्रङ्मृगहस्तमम्बुजगतं मूर्धस्थचन्द्रस्रवत्पीयूषोन्नतनुं भजे सगिरिजं
मृत्युञ्जयं त्र्यम्बकम् ॥

Hastambhej yugasth kumbhyuguladudgrathya toye shiree sinchantam karyoryugan dadhtam swanke sakumbho karoo।
Akshsardmrighastmmbuj jagtam mugrhasth chander sarvatpi yushtontanu bhajee sagirijam mritunjayeem triyambkam ॥

Thus after realising the yantra following desires could be full filled:-

To wipe off all his ailments and enemies, rejoicing with prosperity, sons and grandsons and long life, the devotee shall perform *Homa* on the day of the birth star, or on its tenth day or nineteenth day with four inch long twigs of *Sudhavalli.* For achievement of wealth, *homa* with the twigs of *Bilva* fruit is conducive and with Bar twigs for the acquisition of wealth and with *Khair* twigs for brilliance, with gingely seeds for destructive of impiety, *sarsoon* causes destruction of enemies; with ilk pudding bestows splendour, glory and renown; curds removes the sins incited by others and premature death as well as bestows victory in arguments. In all these cases the number of *homa* is fixed at ten thousand.

By performing *Homa* with groups of three of *durva* grass blades for hundred and eight times one can achieve the removal of all ailments. *Homa* performed on the birthdays with milk puddings and sweets wealth, health and renown increase: with the twigs of *guduci* or *mollsiri* on the birth star, its tenth star or nineteenth star wards off primitive death and ailments. For preventing the possibility of unnatural death the devotee shall perform *homa* with *durva* grass blades everyday. For eradicating fevers the *homa* is to be performed with the twigs of *latjira* as well as ready-cooked food. For the purpose of getting everything the *homa* recommended is that of *giloy* twigs soaked in milk. The *homa* should be continued for a month.

Mritunjaya Dharan Yantra

If one desires to protect oneself from a wrong person/ govt. official bent on murder one has to make use of *Mritunjaye* Yantra. The devotee shall draw twelve-petal lotus. In the pericarp in a square the name (of the intended victim by replacing *devdatta*) along with the activity undertaken (Death etc.) is to, be written. That excelient square shall have seven parallel lines on all sides. In the petals beginning with the northeast one the letters La with all the vowels except (Ai, Au) should be written (La, Lu, Li, Li etc.). Thereafter the lotus shall be surrounded with another square-tridents should be drawn in the four corners of the outer square. This Yantra should be written separately on the *Bhojpatra*. The two Yantras are placed face to face. Facing the north the devotee places the pair of Yantras under the ground. A rock is placed over it. The devotee sits there and repeats the *Matrkias* (letters). If this rite is performed, the aspirant can become free from fear of even the *yama*, as well as from all types of ailments.

Rudra pujan yantra

This yantra is a supplementary of Rudra *Japa*. The devotee who worships Lord Rudra together with the five bodily *Nyasa* and is eagerly engross in the repetition of the Mantra will never find any difficulty in achieving what is desired. His house will be fine; he will have beautiful women and money for the fulfilment of all his desires. The mantra for recital is as follows:

ॐ नमो भगवते रुद्राय ॥

Om Namo Bhagavate Rudraya ॥

The sage of this Mantra is *Bodhayana*; the metre is *Pankti* and the deity is Rudra. In order to attain the state of being Rudra the devotee here shall perform five different types of Nyasa. The devotee shall repeat the Mantra one hundred thousand times and perform ten thousand *Homa* with milk pudding and ghee in the sacred fire and perform tile adoration rite in the pedestal.

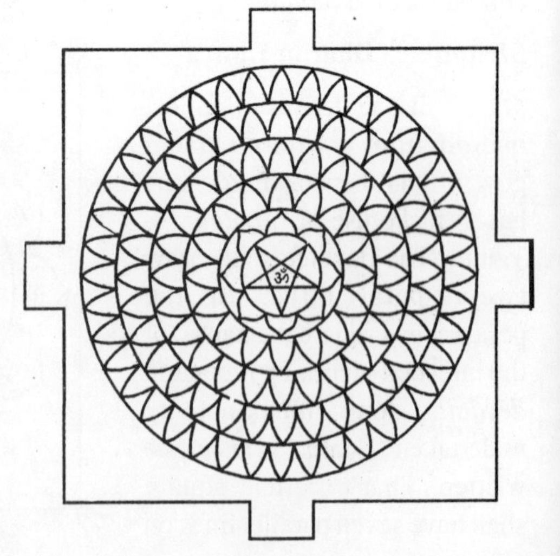

Dhyana Verse

**कैलासचलसन्निभं त्रिनयनं पञ्चास्यमम्बायुतं नीलग्रीवमहीशभूषणधरं व्याघ्रत्वचा प्रावृतम् ।
अक्षस्रग्वरकुण्डिकाभयकरं चान्द्रीं कलां बिभ्रतं गङ्गाम्भोविलसज्जटं दशभुजं वन्दे महेशं परम् ॥**

**Kailash chalsannibham trinayam panchaasyamambayatum nilgriv mahishbhushan dharm vyagrtvacha pravartam ।
akshar gavarkundikabhyakaram chandrim kalam bhibartam gangambhovilsajjatam dasbhujam vande mahesham param ॥**

The Pooja Yantra consists of Eight petal lotus in the inner most area, then sixteen petal one, then twenty four petal one, then thirty two petal one-and then forty petal lotus.

Dakshina Murti Poojan Yantra

The devotee who worships this yantra becomes scholar and Lord Dakshina Murti bestows healthy and prosperous life to him. The mantra for recital is:-

ॐ नमो भगवते दक्षिणामूर्तये मह्यं मेधां प्रयच्छ स्वाहा ॥

Om Namo Bhagwate Dakshinemurte mahayam megham paryach swaha ॥

The sage of the mantra is *Chaturmukh*, metre Gayatri, deity is *vedvyakhantatpar dakshinamurti devta*. The mantra is to be recited for one hundred thousand times.

Dhyana Verse

**स्फटिकरजतवर्णं मौक्तिकीमक्षमाला ममृतकलशविद्याज्ञानमुद्राः कराग्रैः।
दधतमुरगकक्षं चन्द्रचूडं त्रिनेत्रं विधृतविविधभूषं दक्षिणामूर्तिमीडे ॥**

**Safteekrajatvaran mautikkimakshmala
mamrakkalashvidyasagyan mudra karaggree ।
dathatmurgkaksham chandrchudam trinetram vidhtarth
vividthbhasham dakshinmurtimuidhe ॥**

The devotee has to observe celibacy during this period. The *homa* is to be performed with lotus. After realisation the devotee who worships this yantra before sun rise becomes scholar. If a person who is in need of wealth does dhyana of Lord *Shiva* along with his consort and does ten thousand japa of the said mantra is blessed by *Devi* Lakshmi with wealth and prosperity. If the water sanitised with this mantra is rubbed on the body, the devotee will get wealth and all luxuries in life.

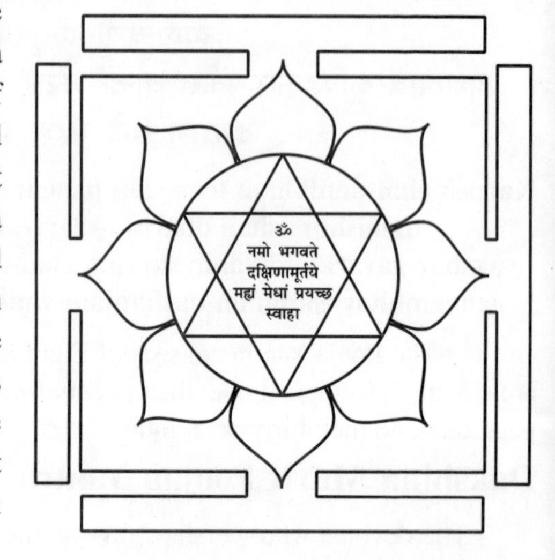

CHAPTER 9

VISHNU YANTRA

Lord Vishnu who is one of the *tridevs* is worshipped for different purposes. He is known as the saviour of the world. In Shri *Madbhagwat* there is a reference of twenty four reincarnation of Lord. In this chapter we will discuss the main reincarnation of the Lord Vishnu. He is known as *Narshiman, Varahi, Ram, Krishna* etc.

Narayan Yantra

Narayan Yantra can enable us to achieve all objects of desires. *Brahma* and others made use of it for worship and created different kinds of people. It is the wish yielding *Kalpa* tree for men. The mantra for recital is:-

ॐ नमो नारायणाय ॥

Om namo Narayanaya ॥

The sage for this mantra is *Sadhyanarayan* and the metre is *Gayatri*. The deity is *Vishnu devta*. The mantra is to be repeated for sixteen hundred thousand times and perform one hundred and six thousand *homa* with ghee and milk pudding.

Dhyana Verse

**उद्यत्कोटिदिवाकराभमनिशं शङ्ख गदां पङ्कजं चक्रं
विभ्रतमिन्दिरावसुमतीसंशोभिपार्श्वद्वयम् ।
कोटिराङ्गदहारकुण्डलधरं पीताम्बरं कौस्तुभोद्दीप्तं विश्वधरं स्ववक्षसि
लसच्छ्रीवत्सचिह्नं भजे ॥**

**Udyatkotidivakarabmanisham shank gada pankajam chakram
vibrahtmindiravsumatisanshobhipashvaradayam ।
Kotirangdaharkundaldharam pitambaram kaustubhoddiptam
vishwdharam lasajcharivatschinam bhaje ॥**

After realisation of yantra if the devotee performs one thousand and eight *homa* in water with three tight *durva* grass all his calamities perish. This *homa* is destructive of great calamities and it bestows all desired objects to men. For the purpose of removing the grief caused by poisons, the devotee shall duly place a water pot and repeat the mantra a thousand and eight times. Then he shall pour the water over the victim of poison. If man has to pass through a forest infested by thieves, tigers and serpents one shall continue to repeat mantra.

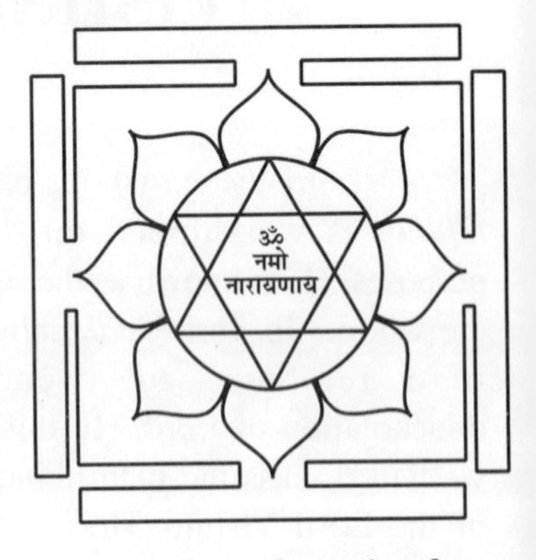

Narshima yantra

This yantra of *Narashima* removes all fears and accomplishes everything. The *Narasimha* Yantra offers an exceedingly effective protection yantra for *vastu Dosha* which not only be applied to the south, but also to other directions where special protection is desired, such as the entrance or the sleeping

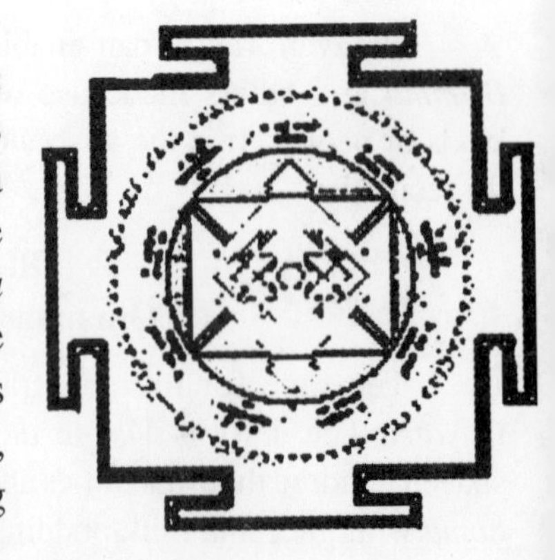

area. The mantra for recital is:-

जय जय श्री नृसिम्हः ॥

Jaya Jaya Sri Nrsimha॥

Dhayan verse as told earlier.

The sage of this *mantra* is Brahma and the metre is Gayatri. The deity is *Nrkesari. Im* is the *Sakti* and Ham is the *Bijam*. The mantra is to be repeated for eight hundred thousand times and perform eight thousand *homa* in the fire with milk pudding.

Sudershan Mahachakra Yantra

This yantra is of *Narsinghdev* which fulfils all desires. It is the door of salvation. The devotee who worships this yantra daily is like a pious man and gets blessings of *tridevas* i.e., Brahma, Vishnu and *Mahesh*. This yantra also dispels the evil effect of malefic planets in the natal chart of the native and increases the effect of benefic planets. The mantra for recital is:-

ॐ उग्रवीरं महाविष्णुं ज्वलन्तं सर्वतोमुखम् ।
नृसिंहं भीषणं भद्रं मृत्युमृत्युं नमाम्यहम् ॥

Om Ugarvir MahaVishum jawalantam Sarvatomukham ।
Narshimam Bhishanam bhadram martyu Martyu Namamyham ॥

The sage of the mantra is *Prajapati*, metre is *anustup*. The mantra is recited for thirty two hundred thousand times. *Homa* is done with the *kheer* mixed with pure ghee. *Homa* with belive leaves will bless the devotee with wealth and all luxries in the life.

Narsingh Dharna yantra

This yantra destroys enemies, eradicates prison and brings good fortune to the wearer. *Beeja* and *Sadhyam* etc., are written inside a lotus and the mantra as given above in the eight petals. These petals are to be surrounded by rectangle with the mantra shim (क्ष्रीं)put in each corner. The petals are also encircled by alphabets etc. The yantra is to be worshipped with the mantra as detailed above after performing the usual ritual. Thirty two hundred thousand japas are required to be performed for purascharan of this mantra. After the pooja thirty two thousand *homa* are necessary.

Lakshmi Narayan yantra

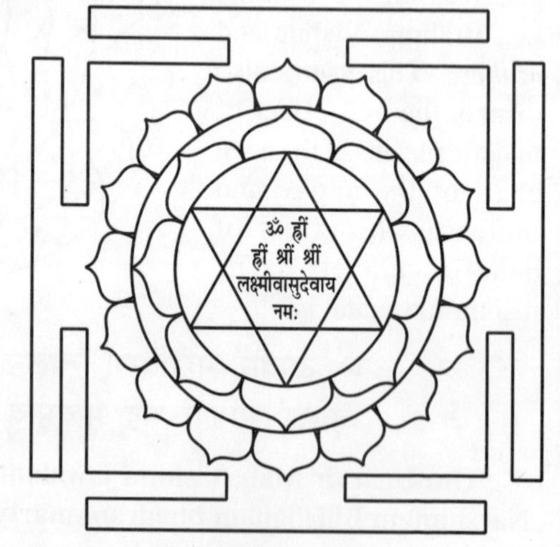

This yantra is bestowal of all luxuries in life. Devotee of this yantra leads a healthy and wealthy life. It fulfils all desires of the devotee. The mantra for recital is:-

ॐ ह्रीं ह्रीं श्रीं श्रीं
लक्ष्मीवासुदेवाय नमः ॥
Om hrim Hrim Shrim Shrim Lakshmi Vasudevaya namah ॥

Dhyan Verse

ॐ विद्युच्चन्द्रनिभं वपुः कमलजा वैकुण्ठयोरेकतां प्राप्तं
स्नेहवशेन रत्नविलासद्भूषाभरालंकृतम् ।
विद्यापङ्कजदर्पणान्मणिमयं कुम्भं सरोजं गदां शङ्खं चक्रममूति

बिभ्रदमितां दिश्याच्छ्रियं वः सदा ॥

Om Vidacchandernibham vapu kamalja vaikunthyorekatam praptam snehvashem ratanvilasdbhubharalankrtam ।
Vidyapankajdarpananmanimayam kumbham sarojam gadam sankh chakrammuti vibhardamitam dischyachchariyajm va sada ॥

The mantra is to be repeated for fourteen hundred thousand times. The *homa* is to be done with lotus, honey, pure ghee, and sweets. *Homa* with rice boiled in milk and sugar will attract Devi Lakshmi, *homa* with sesame will attract all.

Ram Pujan yantra

Lord *Rama*, the hero of *Ramayana* and principal deity of *Hanumanji* is worshipped for different purposes. The mantra for recital is:-

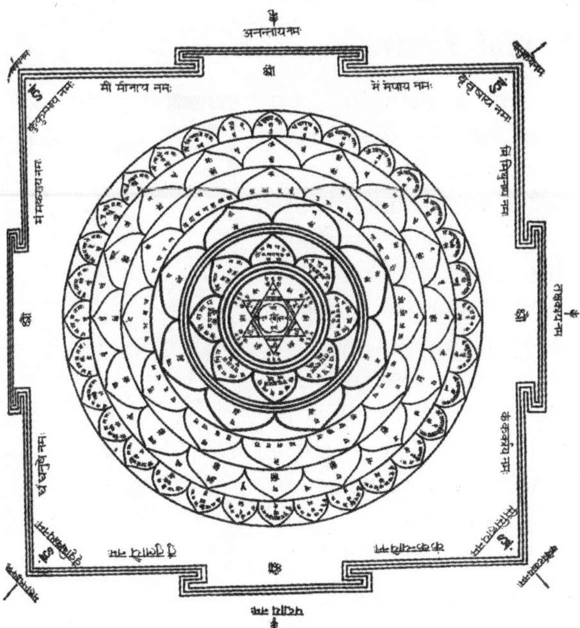

रां रामाय नमः ॥

Ram Ramaya Namah ॥

The sage of the mantra is Brahma, metre is Gayatri, and deity is Shri Ram; *Ram* bijam, namah Shakti. The mantra is to be recited for six lakh times.

Dhyana verse

कालाम्भोधरकान्तिकान्तमनिशं वीरासनाध्यासिनं मुद्रां ज्ञानमयीं दधानमपरं हस्ताम्बुजं जानुनि ।

सीतां पार्श्वगतां सरोरुहकरांविद्युन्निभां राघवं पश्यन्तीं
मुकुटाङ्गदादिविविधाकल्पोज्वलाङ्गं भजे ॥

kalambhodhar kanti kant manisham virasanadhyasinam
mudram gyanmayi dadhanmapram Hastambujam januani ।
Sitam pasvargatam saroruhkaramvidhiynnibham raghvam
pashyanti mukutangdadivividhakalpohjawalang bhaje ॥

After realisation of yantra if the devotee does *homa* with the jasmine flowers smeared in sandal water he can attract the ministers/ Govt. officers. For getting wealth he should perform *homa* with lotus. *homa* with blue flowers he can attract any one. *homa* with durva grass can lead the devotee a healthy life. *Homa* with red lotus, the devotee can has desired wish fulfilled.

Gopal Yantra

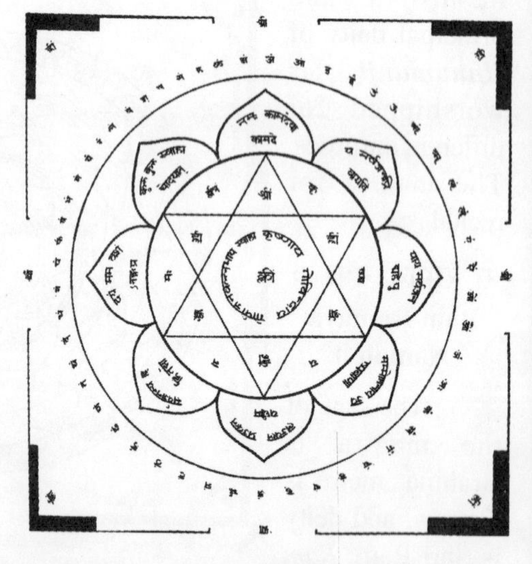

This yantra of Lord Krishna bestows the desired benefits. If there is any hurdle in the marriage and the devotee if worships this yantra he will get married, one can attract a girl, good for those who are in love with some one and are facing difficulties in marriage. The yantra consists of one hexagon, eight petal lotus enveloped by one circle and *bhupura*. The yantra may be carved on copper, silver or *bhojpatra* by the stylus of pomegranate with the ink of *asthgandh*. The mantra for recital is:-

गोपीजनवल्लभाय स्वाहा ॥

Gopijana Vallabhaya Svaha ॥

The sage of this mantra is *Narada*. The metre is *Virat* and Lord

Krishna in the deity, *Klim* is the *Bija* and *Svaha* is the *Shakti*. The mantra is to be repeated for a hundred thousand times and ten thousand *homa* are performed with lotuses

Dhyana Verse

स्मरेद्वृक्षवने रम्ये मोहयन्तमनारतम् ।
गोविन्दं पुण्डरीकाक्षं गोपकन्याःसहस्त्रशः ॥ १ ॥
आत्मनो वदनाम्भोजप्रेषिताक्षिमधुव्रताः पीडिताः
कामबाणेन विरमाश्लेषणोत्सुकाः ॥ २ ॥
मुक्ताहारलसत्पीनतुङ्गस्तनभरानताः ।
स्त्रस्तधम्मिल्लवसना मदस्खलितभाषणाः ॥ ३ ॥
दन्तपंक्तिप्रभोद्भासिस्पन्दमानाधराश्चिताः ।
विलोभयन्तीर्विविधैर्विभ्रमैर्भावगर्भितैः ॥ ४ ॥
फुल्लेन्दीवरकान्तमिन्दुवदनं बर्हावतसं प्रियं
श्रीवत्साङ्कमुदारकौस्तुभधरं पीताम्बरं सुन्दरम् ।
गोपीनां नयनोत्पलार्चिततनुं गोगोपसङ्घावृतं गोविन्दं
कलवेणुवादनपरं दिव्याङ्गभूषं भजे ॥ ५ ॥

Samredvrakshvane ramye mohyantamnartam ।
Govindam pundrikasham gopkanya sahasram ॥ १॥
Atmano vadnambhojpreshetakshimadhuvrate piditha ।
kambanen virmashleshnotsuka ॥ २ ॥
Muktaharlastapintungstanbharanata ।
sarsatdhammillvasana madsakhlitbhasana ॥ ३ ॥
dantpangti prabodhbhasanisapandmanadharaanchita ।
vilobhayantivirvidhayeevirbharmairbhavgarbhaitee ॥ ४ ॥
phullendivarkantmiduvadnam bheravatsam priyam
shrivatsangmudarkaustubdharam pitambaram sundaram ।
Gopinam nayanotpalachirttanum gogopasnghavartam govindam
kalvenuvadnparam divyangbhusam bhajee ॥ ५ ॥

To crush fevers perform *homa* with the pieces of *Giloy* in the fire; to do separation between, two friends, meditate on Lord Krishna as being angry with *Balabhadra* and *Rukmini* held in playing the game of dice and perform the *homa* with balls of dried cow dung. For quelling of enemies perform ten thousand *homa* with the twigs of *Aksa* trees smeared with *neem* oil in night. Repeat the mantra ten thousand times meditating on *Hari*, identifying himself with the lord, the enemy with *Kansa* (his maternal uncle) who was dragged by the lord and who slipped down from his conch with vital airs extinct. Now perform ten thousand *homa* at night with the twigs from the tree corresponding to the star of the enemy. If this is done in letter and spirit even the fierce enemy shall die. For achieving learning the man shall perform a hundred thousand *homa* with the *Palasa* flowers. For attraction the devotee shall perform *homa* regularly with rice grains mixed with mustard and white flowers etc. At the end of seven days apply the ashes there or on forehead and head. This enables the devotee to exercise a fascinating control over groups of young women straight away, young women doing like this shall control men. If flowers, garments collyrium, betel leaf, sandal paste etc. inspired thousand times with this mantra is given to anyone he shall erelong come under the influence of the devotee along with his sons, kinsmen and cattle-wealth. He who meditates on Hari stationed in *Vrndavana* and engaged in singing along with the cowherd lasses and performs *homa* with the twigs of *latgira* shall fascinate the entire universe. If the devote meditates on Lord Krishna engaged in Love making and repeat the mantra ten thousand times then one can marry the girl of his choice within six months. The girl who meditates on Hari seated on the *Kadamba* tree and repeats the mantra thousand times (everyday) shall obtain the desired husband within 49 days. By performing *homa* with the leaves, fruits or twigs of the *Bilva* tree mixed with honey or with lotuses mixed with sugar the devotee shall be the lord of wealth.

Santana Gopala yantra

Legend says that one who worships Shri *Mahavishnu*, the supreme protector will be free from all sorrows. When he is propitiated in the form of Lord Krishna, He is all the more ready to bestow gifts to the devotees. Surrender to Lord Krishna, especially when one is yearning for progeny. Contemplate on the form of *Nanda Gopal* (little Krishna) to get the gift of progeny.

When *putrakaraka* Jupiter and the 5th house are not well disposed

in a natal chart, blessing of offspring is delayed or even denied sometimes. To overcome this affliction, worship of Santana Gopala Yantra is recommended.

The yantra can be made on Gold or drawn on butter which is favourite offering of Lord Nanda Gopala (lord Krishna). When butter is used draw the yantra on the fresh butter and the butter is to be consumed daily by the couple after the *pooja*. Strict vegetarian food is advocated for the couple during the days of worship. The following mantra is to be chanted for one hundred thousand times for fourty eight days. The worship is done with lotus, *tulsi* leaves, rose, jasmine and food for offering are butter, honey, mixture of cooked rice, sugar and cow's milk.

The mantra for recital is:-

देवकीसुत गोविन्द वासुदेव जगत्पते।
देहि मे तनयं कृष्णत्वामहं शरणं गतः ॥

Devaki Sutha Govinda Vasudeva jagatpathe
Dehi me tanayam Krishna twamaham sharanam gathah ॥

During the mensuration the lady have to take a break as she is not clean. Now the husband should continue with it.

Dhyana Verse

ध्यायामि बालकं कृष्णं मात्रके स्तन्यपायिनम् ।
श्रीवत्सवक्षसं कान्तं नीलोत्पलदलच्छविम् ॥

Dhyayami balakam Krishnam Matrake Sthanyapayiam
Srivastavakshsam Kantham Neelothpala dala chavim ॥

Seed mantra for the worship is:-

ॐ श्रीं ह्रीं क्लीं ग्लौं ॥

Om Shreem Hreem kleem Gloum ॥

The other method of this mantra is, on *dashmi tithi* of *shukal paksh* perform pooja of Lord Krishna, Shiva or your deity. For pooja draw or procure *swastika* yantra (page 31) and pour over it a lamp full of ghee and light the lamp with cotton wick. Make a eight petal lotus and put idol of Lord Krishna etc., inside it and perform pooja. Fill two bowls or jug with water and install them. Perform their pooja these are called kalash.

After that invocate Lord Krishna in those kalashes and perform pooja. Recite one hundred eight times above mantra. On *dwadshi tithi* perform pooja of deity. Prepare *khir* of *Anghai* rice in cow milk and jaggery and offer to deity as *Bhog* or diet. Along with fruits, pulse sweetened and tasteful diet, curd of milk of *kapila* cow is also to be included. Put them in Golden plates (or as you can afford) and offer to your deity. The clear water mixed with rose water is offered along with diet.

After that, according to the financial position invite Brahmins for lunch. Perform *homa* with above *khir* by putting hundred and eight offerings or twenty eight times while reciting the mantra. The balance *khir* be preserved. Put eight hundred offerings of ghee in sacred fire of *homa*. The balance ghee should be put in both kalashes containing water. The water should be sprinkled over husband and wife. The devotee should recite hundred and eight times the mantra and balance *khir* kept be given in the hands of couple, couple should sit on a comfortable seat.

During the worship keep the idol in their thoughts and eyes and keep the desire for birth of a child and pay homage to Brahmins, who bless the couple for the birth of a child. The couple should take lunch. In this way the child born will be quite lucky. In case, any body can not spend as above they should recite the above mantra and perform *tarpan.* He too will be blessed with a child. The devotee is advised to read *santan gopal stotra* along with the mantra.

CHAPTER 10

SURYA YANTRA

Lord Sun is among *panch deva*. He is soul of all living beings. He is at par to *Narayan* hence is also called *Surya* Narayan. He is *vedic devata* and has reference in *Regveda* (1/115/1). He is lord of the eight planets Our saints were of the opinion that the devotee who recites *Surya Gayatri* regularly will not face any problems through out his life. Sun god dispels ailments, poverty, eye related problems and increases fame etc. The mantra of Sun for recital is:

ॐ ह्रीं घृणिनं सूर्य आदित्य श्रीं ॥

Om Hrim Ghrnih Surya Adityah Srim ॥

The sage of this mantra is *Devabhaga*; the metre is Gayatri and the deity is Sun-god, the lord of the day. Hrim is the *Bija* and Srim is *Sakti*. The application is for realisation of cherished desires.

Dhyana verse

भास्वद्रत्नाढ्यमौलिः स्फुरदधररुचा रञ्जितश्चारुकेशो
भास्वान् यो दिव्यतेजाः करकमलयुतः स्वर्णवर्णः प्रभाभिः।
विश्वाकाशावकाशे ग्रहगणसहितो भाति यश्चोदयाद्रौ
सर्वानन्दप्रदाता हरिहरनमितः पातु मां विश्वचक्षुः ॥

Bhasavdarratnadayamoli safoorddharrucha rangitscharukeshoo
Bhaswan yo divsteja karakmalyuta sawaranvarna parbhabhi ।
vishwakashavakashe grahgansahitoo bhati yaschodayadroo
sarvaanandpardata hariharnamita patu ma vishwachakshu ॥

The mantra is repeated for one hundred thousand times and *Homa* is performed for one hundred thousand times with lotus and *gingelly* seeds and libations are offered. If the yantra is worshipped through *aditya Hridyam* Sun God bestows all his blessings on the devotee. Thereafter feed Brahmins. One should offer *Argha* to Sun after the yantra has been perfectly realised. After the regular performance of *Pranayama*, *Qanga Nyasa* and other Nyasa as well Lord Sun is to be adored mentally with the requisite ancillary items in his own yantra consisting of dot, hexagon, two circles, eight petal lotuse enveloped by one *bhupura*, drawn on copper, gold or *bhojpatra*.

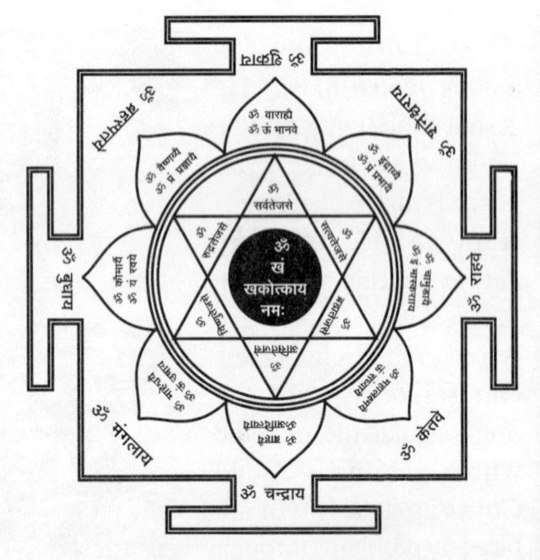

Offering arghya to Sun God

Place a beautiful copper vessel in the *mandala* smeared with red sandal paste and utter the letters of the alphabet, the *mula mantra* in the reverse order. Fill it with water mentally conceiving it to be the nectar coming out of the solar disc and utter the *mula mantra.* Put the following articles into the pot viz. *keesar, gorochan, rai, lal chandan, banslochan, kaneer* flower, flower of *adool, shali, kusha* tips, and rice of *sawa.*

Now invoke Sun god from the external solar disc into the water and worship the pedestal with all the ancillary items of worship the devotee adores the deity, all the subsidiary, and deities of the *Avarana*. Thereafter perform *Pranayama* three times and *sadangaa Nyasa,* the *Nyasa* of *Sudhabija* (*Vam*) on the right hand with sandal paste. The right hand is placed on the left and the vessel of *Arghya* is covered. Inspire the water hundred and eight times with the *mula mantra* and worship with all the five ancillary items of reverence uttering *mula mantra.* Hold the vessel with both the hands and kneels down. The vessel is raised up to the head. The devotee then gazes at the solar disc and mentally worships the Sun god there along with his retinue. Now meditate on Sun, offer *arghya* on the *mandala* of *lal chandan* paste and floral offerings are made to Sun seated on the mandala. Seated on mat or plank the devotee repeats the *mula mantra* hundred and eight times. The devotee who offers *arghya* to the Sun god every day in the morning thus shall attain prosperity, fame, sons, learning and glory. The devotee who regularly meditates with *gayatri mantra* and performs *sandhya vandana* and repeats mantra shall never become miserable.

Surya Chakshushi yantra

The main source of light for the world is Sun and due to this light our eyes get light to see further in this beautiful world. Light and sight are very synonymous to each other. In olden days our saints and *ayurved acharyas* did extensive research in the field of eyes and found that besides medical attention if the person also worships Lord Sun, then he could get more benefits from it. In the *krishana yajurvedaya* it is said that whoever worship Lord Sun through *Chaksushi Vidya* will never have eye related problems throughout his life.

Procedure of Chakshusi Vidya

On any Sunday (if *Ravi Pushya* yoga or *Hasta Nakshatra* is there, then it is best) take seat while facing east direction and mediate on Sun God through the following mantra and think that all eye related problems should not come to me. This *sadhana* should continue for twelve weeks. The devotee should take water in a copper pot and mix red *kaneer* flowers with red sandal and offer *arghaya* while reciting following mantra:-

ॐ एहि सूर्यो सहस्त्रांशोः तेजोराशि जगत्पते ।
अनुकम्पय माँ भक्तया गृहाणामर्घ्यं दिवाकरः ॥

Om aehi suryo sahasransho tejorashi jagatpatye ।
anukampaya maa bhagtaya grahanamarghaya divakara ॥

After offering arghya the devotee should do dhyana and application of the mantra as under. The sage of the mantra is *bhargava*, *nana* metre, *chakshumati* deity, and application of the mantra is to get rid of eye related problems.

Dhyana Verse

चक्षुस्तेजोमयं पुष्पं कन्दुकं विभ्रतीं करैः।
रौप्यसिंहासनारूढां दैवीं चाक्षुष्मतीं भजे ॥

Chakshusatejomayam pushpam kandukam vibrahtim kareee ।
Ropyesinghasanaarudam devim chakshumatim bhajee ॥

Chakshushi vidya stuti

विनियोगः - ॐ अस्याश्चाक्षुषी विद्याया अहिर्बुध्न्य ऋषिर्गायत्री छन्दः सूर्यो देवता चक्षूरोगनिवृत्तये विनियोगः ॥

ॐ चक्षुः चक्षुः चक्षुः तेजः स्थिरो भव । मां पाहि पाहि। त्वरितं चक्षुरोगान् शमय शमय ॥ मम जातरूपं तेजो दर्शय दर्शय । यथाहम् अन्धो न स्यां तथा कल्पय कल्पय। कल्याणं कुरु कुरु ॥ यानि मम पूर्वजन्मोपार्जितानि चक्षुः प्रतिरोधकदुष्कृतानि सर्वाणि निर्मूलय निर्मलय॥ ॐ नमः चक्षुस्तेजोदात्रे दिव्याय भास्कराय ॥ ॐ नमः करुणाकरायामृताय । ॐ नमः सूर्याय । ॐ नमो भगवते सूर्यायक्षितेजसे नमः । खेचराय नमः। महते नमः । रजसे नमः । तमसे नमः । असतो मा सद्गमय । तमसो मा ज्योतिर्गमय । मृत्योर्माअमृतं गमय। उष्णो भगवान् शुचिरूपः । हंसो भगवान् शुचिरप्रतिरूपः ॥

य इमां चाक्षुष्मती विद्यां ब्राह्मणो नित्यमधीते न तस्याक्षिरोगो भवति। न तस्य कुले अन्धो भवति। अष्टौ ब्राह्मणान् सम्यग् ग्राहयित्वा विद्यासिद्धिर्भवति। ॐ नमो भगवते आदित्याय अहोवाहिनी अहोवाहिनी स्वाहा ॥

Om chakshu chakshu chakshu teja sthiroo bhav। Ma pahi pahi । Tavritam chakshu rogan shamay shamay । Mam jatrupam tejo darshay darshay । Yatha ham andho na shayam tatha kalpay kalpay । kalyanam kuru kuru । yani mam purvajanmoparjitani chakshu partirodhak dushkritani sarvani nirmulaya nirmulaya। Om namo chakshutejodate divya bhaskaraya। Om namah Arunnkariyamritaya। Om namah suryaya। Om Namo Bhagwate Suryanyakshitejase namah। Khechraya namah। Mahete namah rajse namah। Tamse namah। Asto ma sad gamayee। Tamso maa jyotirgamaye। Mrityomam amritam gamayee। Ushnoo bhagwan shuchi rupee। Hanso bhagwan suchirpratirupa। Ya imamchakshusmati vidyam brahmno nityamdhitee na tasyashirogo bhavti। na tasya kule andho bhavti । ashtoo bhrahmanam samyag grahitva vidya siddhirbhavti । om namo bhagvate aditaya ahovahini ahovahini swaha ॥

The sage of the mantra is *Ahirbudhnaya, metre* is *gayatri,* deity is Sun God and the application of the mantra is to get rid of all type of eye related problems. This *japa* is to be performed daily and after completion of the japa the devotee has to recite the following mantra and perform homa ten times with the ghee of cow. If the ghee is not available then he should offer mental offerings. The devotee has to offer

८	१५	२	७
६	३	१२	११
१४	९	८	१
४	५	१०	१३

arghaya to Sun god after the process daily.

Chakshushi Bej mantra

ॐ ह्रीं हंसः ॥

Om Hrim Hansa ।

Design of yantra

The chakshushi yantra is a digital yantra as explained in Chakshushi *Upanishad.* On an auspicious Sunday the devotee should write this yantra facing east direction . Before writing the yantra the devotee should do dhyana of Sun God and make ink of turmeric powder. He should write the yantra on bell metal with the stylus of pomegranate. After worshipping the yantra recite the *Chakshushi mantra* and do twelve *japas* with the rosary of turmeric having hundred and eight pieces. The *chakshushi stuti* is to be recited for twelve times.

Surya Namaskar

Though this book purely deals with yantra, however, for getting complete benefit from Sun yantra is would be worth to mention the mantras used in Surya namaskar. To ward off the malefic effects of Sun, Surya Namaskar in 12 poses should be performed atlest 5 times daily. While performing this yogic exercixe, the relevant mantras should be uttered for each posture as mentioned below. After *Surya namaskar, shavaasan* should be performed for about five minutes. The twelve mantras are as under:

1. **ॐ मित्राय नमः ॥ (Om Mitraya Namah)**
2. **ॐ रवये नमः ॥ (Om Ravaye Namah)**
3. **ॐ सूर्याय नमः ॥ (Om Suryaya Namah)**
4. **ॐ भानवे नमः ॥ (Om Bhanawe Namah)**
5. **ॐ खगाय नमः ॥ (Om Khagayaya Namah)**
6. **ॐ पूष्णे नमः ॥ (Om Pushane Namah)**
7. **ॐ हिरण्यगर्भाय नमः ॥ (Om Hirnayagarbhayaya Namah)**
8. **ॐ मरीचये नमः ॥ (Om Mreechaye Namah)**
9. **ॐ आदित्याय नमः ॥ (Om Aaditya Namah)**
10. **ॐ सवित्रे नमः ॥ (Om Saveetrye Namah)**
11. **ॐ अर्काय नमः ॥ (Om Arkaya Namah)**
12. **ॐ भास्कराय नमः ॥ (Om Bhaskaraya Namah)**

CHAPTER 11

HANUMAN YANTRA

Hanumanji who is esteemed disciple of Lord *Rama* is very much worshipped for realisation of all cherished desires. He is also know as *Bajrang Bali* and *Mahavir*. People also call him *pawan sut Hanuman* i.e. son of *Vayu*. He is considered the lord of wars and political stability. He is known as commander in-chief. Lord hanumanji is bachelor and all evil spirits fear from him and where hanumanji is worshipped all such spirits remain away. A house which is devoid of children is blessed with children where hanumanji is worshipped daily. He bestows good health, beauty and vigour. Hanumanji is also called *putradatta*. He is also worshipped to propitiate planet Mars and Saturn in astrology.

Points to remember during Hanuman Sadhana

1 One should be of good character. Do not talk ill of any body. Keep your mind calm and clear. Avoid vices.

2. *Sadhaka* should be vegetarian and be fasting on Tuesday.

Hanuman Yantra

This yantra is good for checking the harassments due to great evil spirits, poison and thieves. If the planets are showing their adverse results then this yantra gives its full result. If fever is caused by black magic or evil spirits the devotee shall angrily strike the patient with water and hold ashes inspired with the mantra, the patient gets relief. The yantra is to be drawn on *bhojpatra* with *Asthgandh* or carved on copper plate. The mantra for recital is:-

हौं हस्फ्रें ख्फ्रें हसौं हस्खफ्रें हसौं हनुमते नमः ॥

Haum Hsphrem khphrem Hsraum Hskhphrem Hsaum Hanumate Namah ॥

The sage of this Mantra is *Ramachandra*, the metre is *jagati* and the deity is Hanuman. The *Hsaum* is the *Bija* of the whole Mantra and *hsphrem Bija* is *Shakti*.

Dhyana Verse

बालार्कायुततेजसं त्रिभुवनप्रक्षोभकं सुन्दरं
सुग्रीवादिसमस्तवानरगणैः संसेव्यपादाम्बुजम् ।
नादेनैव समस्तराक्षसगणान्सन्त्रासयन्तं प्रभुं
श्रीमदामपादाम्बुजस्मृतिरतं ध्यायामि वातात्मजम् ॥

Balakarayuttejsam tribhuwanparshobhkam sundram
Sugrivadisamastvanarganee sansevaypadambujam ।
nadeneev samast rakshakganansantrasanayatam prabhu
Shrimadampadambujsamartiratam dhayami vatatmjam ।।

Having perfectly realised the yantra, the devotee can accomplish the realisation of his own as well as others' desires. He shall perform a thousand homa banana, pomegranate and mango. Then he shall feed twenty two *brahmin* religious students leading celibate life. If this is done all cherished desires are fulfilled.

Hanumad dharan yantra

This Yantra is unsympathetic to fever, plague, deadly diseases and black magic. It quells all types of harassments. If it is worn by children and women it delights them effectively.

An eight petal lotus shall be described all round and (हुं) Hum should be written in all the petals. The circle should be described outside and the square outside that. At the points of the sides of the square the devotee writes trident figures. In the eight inner cardinal edges of the square he shall write the Bija "*hsaum*". In' the outer corners *Ankusa* (*Krom*) is written. The whole thing is then enveloped by the "*Malamantra*" This Yantra can be written on a cloth, rock slab, wooden plank, copper plate, *Bhojpatra*, palm leaf or on the wall with *Gorochana* orpiment, *musk* and *keesar*.

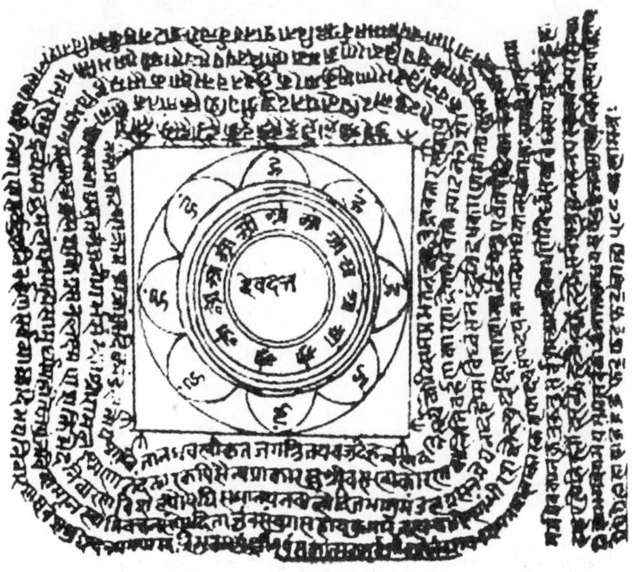

After writing the yantra observe the vow of celibacy, fasting and should not entertain any special craving. In this manner he shall energise it and duly worship it. For the purpose of eradicating all miseries the devotee shall wear that Yantra as an amulet.

Hanuman yantra for defeating enemies

This yantra is a remedy for the ailment of swelling of the bad temper and defeating the enemies. The mantra for recital is:-

ॐ यो यो हनुमनतः फलफलिताः धगा धगिता आयुर्सपरूधा ॥

Om Yo Yo Hanumanta Phalaphalita Dhaga Dhagita Ayurasaparudaha ॥

The sage and the metre of the mantra is as above. The devotee should place an auspicious betel leaf on the belly with enlarged spleen and cover it with a cloth folded eight times. Now mediate on Lord Hanumanji by placing a piece of bamboo. Fire is to be kindled by rubbing two pieces of rock from the forest. A stick of *Badari* branch shall be warmed seven times over that fire. Repeating the mantra given above hit the bamboo piece with this *Badari* stick seven times. The ailment of enlarged spleen shall get healed instantaneously. Take an excellent cloth cut in the form of a tail. The feather of the cuckoo is used as stylus and the beautiful picture of lord hanumanji is drawn with the eight fragrant substances as material for writing. In the middle the devotee shall write the eighteen syllable Mantra along with the name of the enemy. The cloth shall be inspired with the Mantra. The person shall wear that cloth as a turban. Certainly at the very sight of that person the enemies shall be defeated.

Hanumad Yantra

This Yantra of Hanuman brings about safety. By wearing the yantra the devotee shall become victorious in battle, win in law suits and gaming table; he is never suffered by adverse planets, obstacles, poisons substances, weapons or thieves. He shall get rid of all ailments and be fortunate. He shall live a long life. The mantra for recital is:-

ॐ ह्रां ह्रीं ह्रुं ह्रैं ह्रौं ह्र ॐ ॥

Om Hram Hrim Hrum Hraim Hraum Hrah Om ॥

The devotee shall make an eight petal lotus with the pericarp containing the name of the intended, victim.

The should be written in the petals and enveloped with the Mala Mantra. This shall then be covered externally by Hrim (written many times). Then the rite of energising shall be performed. With a gold stylus the yantra is to be written on the auspicious *bhojpatra* using *Gorochana* and *keesar* as materials for writing. It shall then be sanctified by the residue of Homa ghee. Then the entire piece shall be enclosed in an amulet of gold or other metals. This amulet is to be worn on the head or on the arm.

Hanuman yantra for all purposes

This yantra is good for relief from all minor ailments, destruction of evil spirits, ghosts, genii etc., bringing together two mutually opposing parties and making life more enjoyable. For worshipper of this yantra prosperity will increase and calamities become extinct. The yantra is carved either on copper, silver or gold or on bhojpatra. The mantra for recital is:-

ॐ नमो भगवते आञ्जनेयाय महाबलाय स्वाहा ॥

Namo Bhagavate Anjaneyaya Mahabalaya Svaha

The sage of this Mantra is *Ishvara*. The metre is *Anustup*. The deity is Hanuman. *Hum* is the *Bija* and *Svaha* is *Shakti*. The mantra is to be repeated for ten thousand times and perform thousand *Homa* with gingelly seeds. After realising the yantra the devotee can do the following usages.

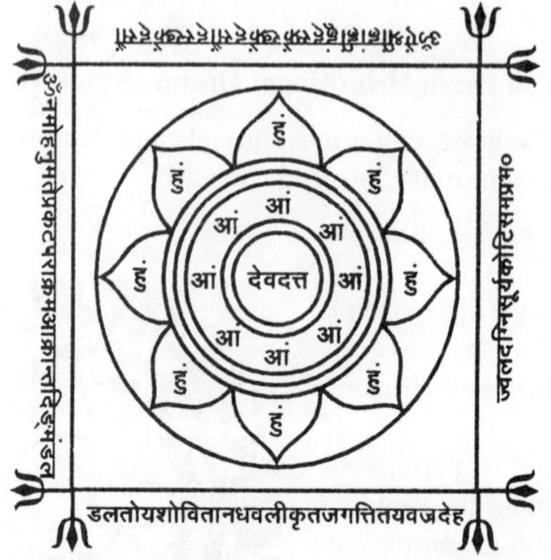

If the mantra is repeated for hundred and eight times while abstaining from sensual pleasures and having food only at night every day, he gets relief from all minor ailments in three days. For destruction of evil spirits, ghosts, genii etc. the same rite has to be performed. For relief from major ailments repeat the Mantra thousand times every day. Restriction in diet should be observed and repeat the Mantra ten thousand times every day meditating on Hanumanji killing the hosts of demons. He shall defeat his enemy. To bring together two mutually opposing parties the devotee shall meditate on Hanumanji effecting the alliance between Rama and *Sugriva* and repeat the Mantra ten thousand times. When starting on a journey the devotee shall meditate on Hanuman and repeat the Mantra to accomplish his desired objective and return home. If a devotee is devoutly engaged in repeating the Mantra and worships Hanumanji always in his house his life and prosperity increase and calamities become extinct.

Hanumat kalp yantra

The worshipper of this yantra gets all blessings from Lord Hanumanji and the lord comes to him. The devotee of this yantra should take pledge that he has to meet the Lord. He should do worship on the bank of the river or in a *Vishnu* temple or on an isolated place or a forest or any place where he did not get disturb. He should use the seat of grass while practising this yantra. The yantra is drawn on copper plate with the stylus of red sandal and ink of saffron and red sandal. The yantra consists of eight petal lotus and *mula* mantra is written in between the lotus. The names *Sugriv*, *Laksahman*, *Angadh*, *Nal*, *Neel Jamwant*, *Kumud* and *Kesari* should be written in the each of the petals. The mantra is to be recited for one hundred thousand times. When the recital of one hundred thousand is completed the devotee has to perform *pooja* at large scale. The mantra for recital is :

ॐ हनुमते रुद्रात्मकाय हुं फट् ॥

Om Hanumate Rudraatmakay hum Phat ॥

Dhyana Verse

ॐ महाशैलं समुत्पाटय धावन्तं रावणं प्रति ।
तिष्ठतिष्ठ रणे दुष्ट घोररावं समुच्चरन् ॥ १ ॥
लाक्षारसारुणं गात्रं कालान्तकयमोपमम् ।
ज्वलदग्निलसन्नेत्रं सूर्यकोटिसमप्रभम् ॥ २ ॥
अङ्गदाद्यैर्महावीरै वेष्टितं रुद्ररूपिणम् ।

Om Mahashelam samutpataye dhavantam ravanam priti tisth
tisth rane dust ghorravam samuchcharan ॥ 1 ॥
laksharasaarunam gaatram kalantkaymopnam
jawaldaganilsannetram suryakotisamprabhem ॥ 2 ॥
Angadidhairmahavireevaishtitam rudrrupinam ॥

Vishwalochan charkaraj Hanuman yantra

In *Agastaya sanhita* this yantra has reference during *Suthin* and sage *Agastaya* dialogue. It says that if some one wants his desires fulfilled and wants to know the result of his worship this yantra is used for the same. The yantra consists of one triangle, eight petal lotus covered with sixteen petal, all enveloped with two circles covered by a beautiful *bhupura*. The circles would have alphabets written between the two circles. The mantra for recital is:

ॐ नमो भगवते रुद्रावताराय महाबलाय आंजनेयाय वायुपुत्राय कौशलेन्द्रानुचराय साम्प्रतं स्वात्मानं दर्शय दर्शय सत्यं वद वद स्वाहा हां हां ॐ ॥

Om namo bhagwate rudraavtarayee mahabalaya Anjanayee vayuputrayaee Kaushalendraanucharaya sampratam swatmanam darshya darshaya satyam vad vad swaha ham ham Om ॥

The sage of the mantra is Agastaya, metre is *atijagti*, and deity is *kaushalendra maheshwra Hanuman*, *ham bija swah Shakti*, *Namah kilak*. The mantra is recited for one hundred thousand times. The *homa* is done with *ber*, and pure ghee. After homa do *tarpan* with pure ghee, honey and sugar.

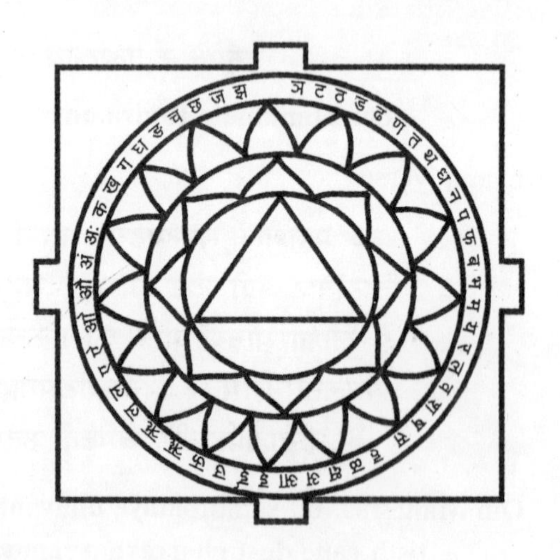

Dhyana verse

ॐ मनोजीवं मारुततुल्यवेगं यतेन्द्रियं बुद्धिमतां वरिष्ठम् ।
वातात्मजं वानरयूथमुख्यं श्रीरामदूतं शिरसा नमामि ॥

Om Manojvam marutitulyavegam yatendriyam budhimatam varistham ।
Vatatmajam vanaryudhmukhyam Shri Ram dutam sirsa namami ॥

On Friday, Saturday and Tuesday lit a lamp in a metal. The metal is preferably gold. Write the mula mantra on *bhojpatra* and wrap agar-tagar, red vermillion camphor by mixing them in shape of powder in the bhojpatra. Worship this with the *mula mantra* by offering *sodashupchar* (sixteen rituals) worship. After that whisper this mantra in the ears of a boy preferably *Brahmin* and ask him to dream. If he sees lord hanuman or any of the characters of *Ramayana* (from the army of Lord *Rama*) or any thing considered auspicious then his desires are fulfilled. The question is to be asked at the night time. The devotee is advised not to ask any thing which is not under the preview of law and if he asks such questions then he has to recite the mula mantra for one hundred thousand times more. For *Shanti* rites the devotee has to wear white clothes, and recite the mantra with white rosary. Other persons who are sitting with the devotee should wear red clothes.

Hanuman yantra

This yantra is written on paper or *bhojpatra* for 1.25 hundred thousand times. This yantra pleases Hanumanji and he bestows all wishes on the devotee.

नंo	छंo	जंo	चंo
दंo	दंo	चंo	चंo
जंo	छंo	जंo	वंo
छंo	नंo	जंo	हंo

CHAPTER 12

ASTROLOGICAL YANTRAS

In *Nirayana system*, all the planets have their astrological characteristics. They are not just solid matter, but have a different kind of vibrations, which influence life, on this planet. They are friendly (*mitra*) or enemy (*shatru)* depending upon their *mooltrikona rashis* (signs) falling in certain houses of the horoscope i.e. if the *mooltrikona rashi* of a planet falls in any of the 6th, 8th or 12th houses of a chart, all such planets become *shatru grahas* and will confer malefic results. *Mooltrikona rashis* falling in any of the remaining nine *rashis* (signs) make lords of all such houses, the friendly ones and will confer benefic results, during their periods, depending of course, upon their strength in the natal as well as transit charts. Our *shastras* have prescribed *upayas* (remedial measures) for strengthening of our weak friendly planets as well as for propitiation of the malefic ones by performing problem/situation specific *kriyamaan karmas* so as to derive most optimal results, during their life.

Sun Yantra

Of all the planets, the Sun's position in Indian astrology is supreme. The Sun is the king of our solar system. It does not tolerate negligence. The Sun is the Lord of Leo. This is the fifth in serial order, in the zodiac and signifies habits and temper of a lion. According to Astrology, the Sun is debilitated when posited in Libra and therefore most compassionate and soothing for the native. In debilitation if the sun is otherwise benific it will not deliver the disired results. Should it be

malefic it will be highly damaging for the native. Such people see many ups and down during their lifetime. The Sun posited in the sixth, eighth and twelfth houses make it the worse. In a horoscope, the afflicted Sun can give many diseases. The Sun stands for power and authority. When one is deprived of happiness through termination of service, suspension or through opponents or diseases etc., worship of the Sun through *Surya Namashkar* etc., is always advised (for surya namaskar please refer Surya yantra page 122). Such difficulties are overcome and cure from diseases is achieved. Of course, good health is also achieved through *pooja* of the Sun *yantra*. The Sun *Yantra* enhances peace of mind, gets favour from superiors, officers and the Govt. The Sun *yantra* is carved on gold, silver or copper plate and after *pooja* it is worn in the neck, kept on the body or is worshipped in the temple of the house. By the use of the Sun *Yantra*, the enemies are suppressed and it eliminates the malefic effects of the Sun. When the Sun is malefic in the birth chart of a native or according to the transit or Moon sign indicates malefic effects, the Sun *Yantra* is very effective & useful.

On *Ravi-pushya yoga,* start writing the *yantra* with the stylus of pomegranate with *asthgandha* or *lal chandan.* This *yantra* is either carved on bronze or gold plate. After drawing the *yantra* install it on a pedestal made of wood and recite the following mantra:

Surya Gayatri Mantra:

ॐ आदित्य विद्महे दिवाकराय धीमहि तन्नो सूर्यः प्रचोदयात्॥

Om Aditya Vidmahe Divakraya Dhimahi tanno Surya Parchodayat ll

The Sun mantra for recital :-

ॐ ह्रीं घृणि सूर्य आदित्य श्री ॥

Om Hrim Ghrani Surya Aditya Shri ll

The sage of the Mantra is *Brighu.* The metre is *Gayatrii.* The deity of the Mantra is Sun God. The *Bija* is *Hrim* and the *Shakti* is *Shrim.* The above mantra is to be recited ten hundred thousand times. The other Surya mantra is:-

ॐ ह्रां ह्रीं सः सूर्याय नमः ॥

Om Hram Hrim Sa Suryaye namah ll

This mantra is to be recited seven thousand times, starting from Sunday. 1/10 of the mantra to be done as *tarpan* and 1/10 of that it should be *marzan.* After that the devotee should donate articles of the Sun. The yantra is worshipped with *Surya stotra.*

Jupiter Yantra

When Jupiter is malefic, use of Jupiter yantra is very benefic and favourable. If Jupiter is occupying the sign Capricorn or is in the 6th, 8th or 12th house or in conjunction with Rahu/Ketu (the head/tail of the dragon), it is considered weak for the individual. Jupiter yantra is to be kept on rising moon Thursday, in pooja place. Jupiter *Yantra* negates the malefic effects of planet Jupiter and bestows power, rank and authority. Jupiter Yantra is best for profession and business.

The Yantra is either drawn on *bhojpatra* or on a piece of silver with *astgandha* or *kessar* mixed with red vermillion or white *chandan* with the stylus of pomegranate or *chandan*. After drawing the *yantra* is placed on a yellow cloth on a bronze pedestal. The seat to be used in worshipping the *yantra* is *kusa asana* (seat made of grass). And the devotee has to recite the following mantra.

ॐ बृं बृहस्पतये नमः॥

Om Brahm Brashpatye Namah ॥

The above mantra is to be recited for eighty thousand times. The sage of the Mantra is *Brahma*. The metre is *Anustup*. The deity of the Mantra is *Sukracharya*. The *Bija* is *brahma* and the *Shakti* is *namah*.

The other mantras for Jupiter are:

Jupiter Gayatri Mantra:

ॐ अंगिरोजाताया विद्महे वाचस्पति धीमहि तन्नो गुरू प्रचोदयात्॥

Om Angirozaataaya vidyamahe vachaspati dhimahi tanno guru parchodayat ॥

The Jupiter mantra for recital :-

ॐ ह्रां ह्रीं ह्रौं सः बृहस्पतये नमः ॥

Om hram hrim hrom sah Braspataye namah ॥

ॐ ग्रां ग्रीं ग्रौं सः नमः॥

Om gram grim grom sah namah ॥

This mantra should be chanted nineteen thousand times. During worship, it should be chanted at six in the morning everyday. The one tenth of the mantra should be done *homa*, and one tenth *of homa be tarpan* and *marzan*. The flowers to be offered for Jupiter are yellow, fruits and other offerings should also be yellow. If the devotee wears yellow clothes, it would give better results. The yantra is to be worshipped daily to ward off evil effects and increase the benefic effects of Jupiter, in the horoscope.

Mars yantra

The worship of Mars Yantra should be done during *Siddha* Yoga, on any Tuesday. If Mars is posited in the ascendant, fourth, seventh, or eighth or the twelfth house, it is bad for the maritial happiness. In such a situation, the immediate remedy is propitiation of Mars with its yantra and mantra. All those who are deprived off marriage even upto 30 to 40 years due to certain obstacles or married life is full of miseries or difficulties, threatened separation or divorce, should worship Mars Yantra to ward off these evils. Also Mars *Yantra* works remarkably in case of repeated abortions, denial of children, for someone in debt and not able to repay in spite of honest intentions rather debt increases making life hell. All these difficulties can be overcome by the worship of Mars Yantra. Mars Yantra helps the devotee to overcome the above difficulties and one succeeds in all his efforts to achieve happiness and lead a comfortable life. When one is of rash temperament, Mars yantra is very useful. With this, one overcomes his enemies, gets protection from effects of poisonous articles. The yantra also removes the evil effects of Mars like injury, accident etc. Those who are suffering from high blood pressure should keep the Mars yantra in their house and worship it daily.

The yantra is carved on copper or written on *bhojpatra* with the stylus of pomegranate and ink of red *sandal*. After drawing the *yantra*, the devotee should do *dasopchar* pooja. It may be noted here that the *yantra sadhana* should end on Tuesday.

Mangal Gayatri Mantra:

ॐ क्षितिपुत्राय विद्महे लोहितांगाय धीमहि तन्नो भौमः प्रचोदयात्॥

Om Shitiputraya vidyamahe lohitangaya dhimahi tannoo Bhowmaa Parchodayat ॥

Worshipping the yantra with the following mantra bestows sons and wealth. This mantra also bestows desired objects and eliminates debts. The Mantra is as follows:

ॐ हां हंसः खं खः ॥

Om Ham Hamsah Kham Khah ॥

The sage of this Mantra is *Virupa*, the metre is *Gayatri* and the deity is *mangal*. The aspirant devotee shall perform *sadanga Nyasa* with the six syllables of the Mantra.

The devotee shall repeat the mantra six hundred thousand times. The requisite number of Homas with the twigs of *Khadira* shall be performed. Mars should be worshipped in *Saiva Pitha*. When the mantra is perfectly realized, he should perform repeat rites for realization of specific desires.

A woman who desires to beget a son shall observe the requisite vow on Tuesday. The beginning of this vow in the month of *Mrigasira* (Nov.-Dec.) or *Vaisakha* (April-May) is held to be praiseworthy.

The mantra for recital :

ॐ क्रां क्रीं क्रौं सः भौमाय नमः ॥

Om kara kri kro sah bhomaya namah ॥

ॐ अं अंगारकाय नमः॥

Om an angarkaya namah ॥

The mantra is to be recited ten thousand times. If the mantra is recited at two in the afternoon, it is more benefic. The worship should be done with red flowers, red sandal, and fruit of red colour. After *japa*, the *homa* should be done with the rice boiled in milk, sesame, barley, rice, pure ghee, crushed sugar and *panchmewa*. 1/10 of homa be done as *tarpan* and 1/10 of that it should be *marzan*. After that the devotee should donate the articles of mars.

Mercury Yantra

When Mercury is malefic, use of Mercury yantra is very benefic and favourable. If Mercury is occupying the 6th, 8th or 12th house in anybody's horoscope, or is in conjuction with a melific planet, it needs help through the Mercury Yantra. This Yantra protects from fire and electric shock etc. It is especially favourable for a pregnant woman against abortion and for safe delivery of a child. Those having problems of stammering and speech should perform daily pooja of Mercury yantra.

The Mercury Yantra *Sadhana* should be started on *sarwarthsiddhi* yoga day falling on Wednesday. The devotee should wear clothes of green yellowish colour (colour of banana's new leaf) of cotton or silk. The devotee should carve Mercury's yantra on *bhojpatra*, bronze plate or on copper plate. The yantra on *bhojpatra* is drawn with *astgandha,* white sandal or juice of *Tulsi* with the stylus of pomegranate.

Mercury Gayatri Mantra:

ॐ चंद्रपुत्राय विद्महे रोणीप्रियाय धीमहि तन्नो बुधः प्रचोदयात्॥

Om Chanderputraya vidyamahe Rohinipriyaya dhimahi tannoo Budha Parchodayat ॥

The Mercury mantra for recital :-

ॐ ब्रां ब्रीं ब्रौं सः सौम्याय नमः ॥

Om bra bri bro sa somyaya namah ॥

ॐ बुं बुधाय नमः॥

Om bum budhaya namah ॥

The mantra is to be recited nineteen thousand times. The time to recite the mantra is five in the evening. Sugar balls are offered to the yantra deity as offerings. The *sadhna* should end on Wednesday. On the last day, articles of mercury are donated to Brahmins, within the first four hours of sunrise.

Moon Yantra

When Moon is malefic, the Moon *Yantra* is kept in the house or pocket to negate the malefic effects of the planet. If the Moon is posited in the sign of Scorpio, is in the 6th, 8th or 12th house or is with Rahu or Ketu, it needs to be strengthened, otherwise the person will either be killed due to the bad influence of the planet, or the person's wife/husband will die. The Moon *Yantra* blesses the native with respect, friendship and creates contacts with opposite sex in harmoniums way. The Moon *Yantra* shall be installed on any rising Moon Monday and shall be kept with Lord *Shiva's* photograph or image.

Monday is considered best for worshipping the Moon. Some scholars are of the opinion that the sadhana could be performed during *Guru-pushya* or *Ravi-pushya yoga*. The *sadhna* should start from a Monday falling during *shukla paksha*. The devotee should wear white clothes, have a white seat and food for offering should also be white. This *yantra* is always carved on silver being an article of the Moon but persons who can not afford a silver *yantra*, may use a bhojpatra. The *yantra* be written with the stylus of pomegranate or *Tulsi* with the ink made of white *sandal* mixed with camphor.

The mantra for recital is:

सौं सोमाय नमः॥

Som somay namah ॥

The sage of the Mantra is Brighu. The metre is *pangti*. The deity of the Mantra is the Moon god. The Bija is Som and the Shakti is namah.

The above mantra is to be recited six hundred thousand times. The other mantras for Moon are:

Chander Gayatri Mantra:

ॐ अत्रि पुत्राय विद्महे सागरोद्भवाय धीमहि तन्नो चन्द्रः प्रचोदयात्॥

Om Atriputraya vidyamahe Sagrobhadvaya dhimahi tannoo Chandra Parchodayat ॥

The Moon mantra for recital :-

ॐ श्रां श्रीं श्रौं सः सोमाय नमः ॥

Om shram shrim shrom sah somaya namah ॥

ॐ स्वाँ सोमाय नमः॥

Om swa somaya namah ॥

These mantras are to be recited eleven thousand times. 1/10 of this figure be done as *tarpan* and 1/10 of that should be *marzan*. After that the devotee should donate articles of Moon.

Saturn Yantra

Saturday is considered best for worshipping Saturn. If *Pushya Nakshatra* is also on Saturday then it is the best day to worship the *yantra. The yantra* is used to propitiate an afflicted Saturn and achieve *Rajayoga* through complete blessings of Saturn. When Saturn is malefic in a horoscope, in transit or causes the 7½ years cycle, use of Saturn *yantra* is very beneficial. In whatever house Saturn is posited, it makes it stronger whereas Jupiter destroys the house in which it is posited. But whatever house Jupiter aspects or overlooks, it makes it stronger whereas Saturn destroys the house it aspects. This is the rule mentioned in *Bhrigu Samihta*. Apart from this, if Saturn is in the house of Sun that is in Aries or one house before or after the Moon, it is bad. And as for any other planet, it is also bad if posited in the sixth, eighth and twelfth houses. So in the case of Saturn's malefic position, this *yantra* is used. Saturn *Yantra* is useful, when one feels depressed. It indicates success in worldly affairs, success in business and the man touches dizzy heights.

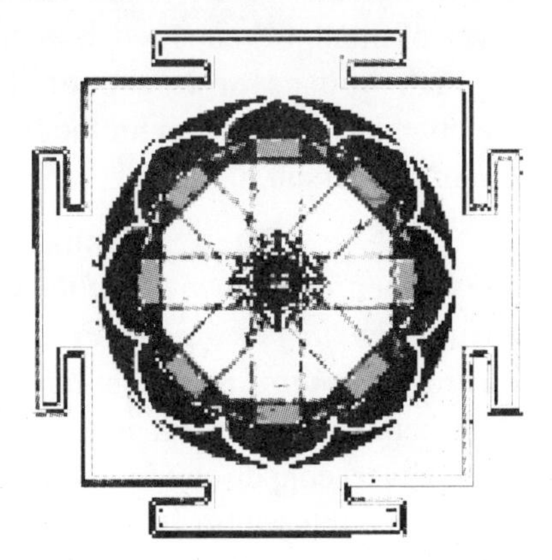

On a Saturday, on which *sarwarth siddhi yoga* is there and Moon is favourable to the devotee, worship of saturn yantra is to be started. The *yantra* is drawn either on zinc or iron plate, blue paper or bhojpatra with black ink. The rules for observance of the mantra are same as told earlier.

Shani Gayatri Mantra:

ॐ कृष्णांगाय विद्महे रविपुत्राय धीमहि तन्नो सौरिः प्रचोदयात्॥

Om Krishnaangay vidyamahe Raviputraya dhimahi tannoo Sooria Parchodayat ॥

The Saturn mantra for recital :-

ॐ खां खीं खौं सः शनैश्चराय नमः ॥

Om kha khi kho sah snacharaya namah ॥

ॐ शं शनिश्चराय नमः ॥

Om sham shanicharaya namah ॥

The above mantra is to be recited twenty three thousand times. 1/10 of homa be done as *tarpan* and 1/10 of that should be done as *marzan*. After that the devotee should donate the articles of Saturn.

Venus Yantra

When Venus is malefic, the use of Venus *yantra* is very benefic and favourable. Venus Yantra bestows respect, love of opposite sex and peace of mind. If Venus is debilitated in Virgo, or is posited in the 6th, 8th or 12th houses or is aspected by malefic planets, it is bad for the sexual life of the person.

The Venus is worshipped on *sarwarth siddhi* yoga during *shukla paksha* on Friday. If *Pushya Nakshatra* is on that day, it is even better. The *yantra* is drawn on gold, silver, copper or *bhojpatra.* On *bhojpatra*, the yantra is written with *asthgandha, yakshkardam*, or pure sandal juices used as ink with the stylus of pomegranate. After drawing the *yantra,* it is installed on a pedestal made of wood with white cloth as a cover on it. The rosary of *safatik* (crystal), or pearl is used. Some scholars advise use of *rudraksha*

or *tulsi mala* for *japa* of the mantra. The mantra for recital is:-

ॐ वस्त्रं मे देहि शुक्राय स्वाहा ॥

Om Vastram me dehe shukraya swah ॥

The sage of the Mantra is *Brahma*. The metre is *Virat*. The deity is *Shukra*. The *Bija* is *Om* and the *Shakti* is *Swah*.

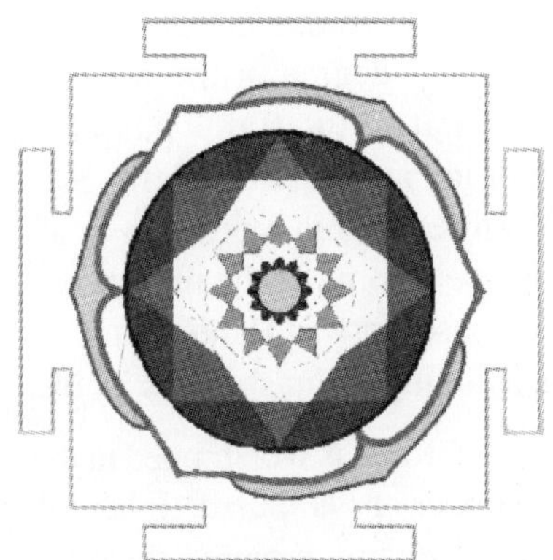

This mantra is to be chanted ten thousand times. For better results, the devotee is advised to do homas with scented white flowers for twenty one Fridays.

Shukra Gayatri Mantra:

ॐ भृगुवंशताजाय विद्महे
स्वेतवाहनाय धीमहि तन्नो कवि प्रचोदयात्॥

Om Bharguvanshtajaya vidyamahe Shevatvahanaya dhimahi tanna Kavi Parchodayat ॥

The Venus *mantra* for recital :

ॐ द्रां द्रीं द्रौं सः भृगवे नमः ॥

Om dra dri droo sah bhraguve Namah ॥

ॐ शुं शुक्राय नमः॥

Om Shum shukraaya Namah ॥

The above mantra is to be recited sixteen thousand times. 1/10 of *homa* be done as *tarpan* and 1/10 of that should be *marzan*. After that the devotee should donate articles of Venus.

Rahu (Dragon's head) Yantra

Rahu as well as Ketu are universally malefic planets. They adversely affect all those planets they are conjoined with or are aspecting closely i.e. within 5 degrees of the ascending degree or the house they are posited in. Rahu has similar qualities as that of malefic Saturn. When Rahu is in a position to affect adversely some of the planets and/or the houses, use of Rahu yantra is very benefic and favourable. However, unafflicting Rahu showers its blessings to the house it occupies.

Rahu is worshipped in the night on Saturday. The yantra is carved on copper or *bhojpatra.* It is written with black ink as in case of Saturn. Rahu *sadhana* is more effective & beneficial if performed on *Sarvarth siddhi yoga* falling on Saturday. After drawing the yantra, it is installed on a pedestal made of wood covered with black cloth. The worship is done with the articles of Rahu with the lamp of mustard oil. After sadhana, articles of Rahu like Hassonite, lead, blue cloth etc., should be donated. Feeding an elephant is also considered beneficial for propitiation of Rahu.

Rahu Gayatri Mantra:

ॐ नीलवर्णाय विद्महे सैहिकेयाय धीमहि तन्नो राहु प्रचोदयात्॥

Om Nilvarnaye vidyamahe sehikeyay dhimahi tannoo Rahu Parchodayat ll

TheRahu mantra for recital :-

ॐ भ्रां भ्रीं भ्रौं सः राहवे नमः ॥

Om bram brim broom sah rahuve namah ॥

ॐ रां राहवे नमः॥

Om Ram Rahuve namah ॥

The above mantra is to be recited eighteen thousand times. 1/10 of *homa* be done as *tarpan* and 1/10 of tarpan be done as *marzan*. After that the devotee should donate articles of Rahu.

Ketu (Dragon's tail) *Yantra*

As stated above, like Rahu, Ketu is also a universally malefic planet provided it is not aspecting any of the planets or houses, closely i.e. within five degrees. When Ketu is malefic, use of Ketu *yantra* is very benefic and favourable. In someone's chart, if Ketu is in the eighth house with the Moon, it is said that the person must attempt suicide at least once in life time. As in the case of Rahu, unafflicting Ketu also showers its blessings to the house it occupies.

Ketu is worshipped in the night on Saturday. The yantra is carved on copper or *bhojpatra*. It is written with black ink as in the case of Saturn. After drawing the yantra, it is installed on a pedestal made of wood covered with black cloth.

Ketu Gayatri Mantra:

ॐ अत्रवाय विद्महे कपोतवाहनाय धीमहि तन्नो केतु प्रचोदयात्॥

Om Atrvayee vidyamahe Kapotvaahanhaye dhimahi tannoo Ketu Parchodayat ॥

The Ketu mantra for recital :

ॐ प्रां प्रीं प्रौं सः केतवे नमः ॥

Om pram prim proom sah ketuve namah ॥

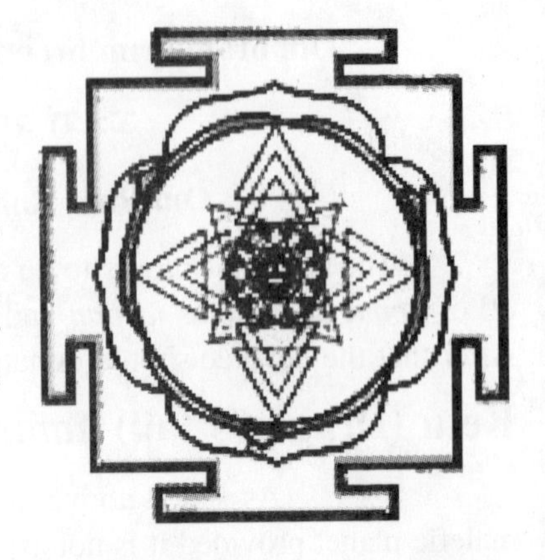

ॐ कें केतवे नमः॥

Om kam ketuve namah ॥

The above mantra is to be recited seventeen thousand times. 1/10 of *homa* be done as *tarpan* and 1/10 of that should be *marzan*. After that the devotee should donate the articles of Ketu.

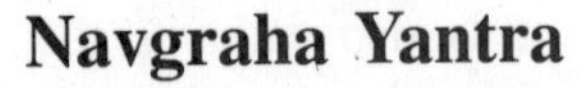

Navgraha Yantra

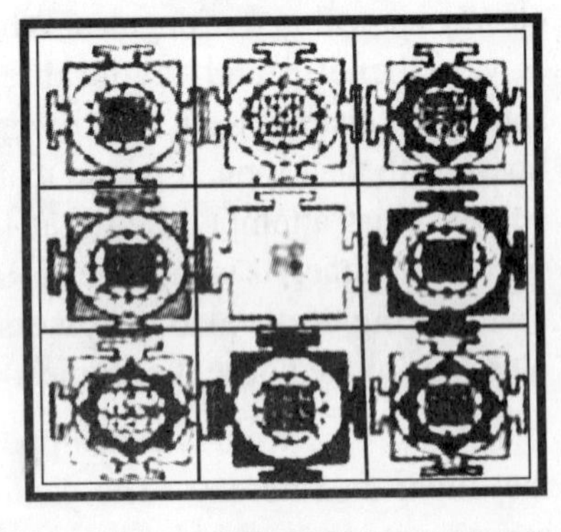

Navgraha *Yantra* is a combined *Yantra* for all the nine planets and is divided into nine squares, each one with a talisman representing one planet. This is an extremely useful & beneficial *Yantra*, since it's worship, on the one hand, strengthens benefic planets and increases their positive influences and on the other, propitiates malefic planets which not only reduces their malefic affects but also start blessing with their benefic affects, instead. Navgrah Yantra is recommended for all, particularly those whose benefic planets (*mitra grahas*) are weak and therefore unable to deliver. The malefic planets in their case are quite potent to do maximum damage. Navgraha Yantra should be worshipped life-long to ensure that one always gets optimum benefits from all the planets.

This yantra is inscribed on gold plate and worn in the neck. Fruits, honey and spiced rice of various kinds be offered during pooja. The yantra be purified with navgraha mantra for thousand times daily for forty five days. The mantra for recital is:-

ॐ सूर्याय नमः। ॐ चंद्राय नमः। ॐ बुधाय नमः। ॐ भौमाय नमः।
ॐ बृहस्पतये नमः। ॐ शुक्राय नमः। ॐ शनये नमः। ॐ राहुवे नमः।
ॐ केतवे नमः। ॐ नवग्रहे नमः॥

Om Suryaye namah। Chanderaae namah। Budhaye namah। Bhomaae namah । Brahaspatiaae namah । Shukeraae namah । sanieaae namah । rahuaae namah। ketuaae namah । navgrarahaae namah ॥

Navgrah Shanti Mantra

ब्रह्मा मुरारी त्रिपुरांतकारी भानु शशि भुमिसुतो बुधश्च।
गुरूश्च शुक्रो शनि राहु केतवे सर्वेंग्रहा शान्तिकरा भवन्तु ॥

Brahma Murari Tripurantkari bhanu shashi bhumisuto budascha।
Guruscha shukro shani rahu ketva sarvegraha santkara bhavantu॥

Kaalsarp yoga shanti yantra

In Hindu Astrology *yogas* play an important role and enjoy a very prominent position. Kaalsarp yoga is regarded as one of the dreaded evil yogas having significance in Mundane Astrology. Hindu ancient astrological literature is more or less silent about it. None of the astrological classics have any reference of *Kaal sarpa Yoga.* Even the learned commentators did not make any detailed scrutiny as to the effects of this yoga in natal astrology. Lately some of the scholars have come forward to evolve a pattern for assessing the evil effects of Rahu-Ketu positioned diagonally. This yoga is not fairly common but can be traced in the horoscopes of both great and small.

What is Kaalsarp yoga?

In *Karmic* Astrology, it has been found that Rahu is *kala* or earth-life while Ketu is the *Sarpa* or Serpent. In Indian Astrology too Ketu is also considered as serpent. Rahu is afraid of Ketu. The symbol of serpents is basic in Indian Occult Literature. On the basis of this symbolism, the importance of *Kaalsarp Yoga* in Hindu Astrology could be understood.

Astrologically it becomes an indication of great importance attached to Kaalsarp yoga, as this yoga has the reference to encirclement of all the planets by these two nodes (Rahu and Ketu) i.e., when all the planets are hemmed between Rahu and Ketu i.e., the moon's north node and the moon's south node *Kaalsarp Yoga* is formed. Complete Kaalsarp yoga is formed only when half of the chart is unoccupied by planets. Even if one planet is outside the Rahu-Ketu axis there is no Kaalsarp Yoga. (Before you do any remedies for the Kaalsarp Yoga make sure that all planets are between Rahu and Ketu.) Even if there is one planet outside the Rahu-Ketu axis, the Kaalsarp Yoga does not exist. When we talk of *Kaalsarp yoga* the reader is advised not to confuse this with *Naga Dosha* or *Karaka Dosha.*

Problems with Kaalsarp yoga

The Kaalsarp yoga, leads sometime to unbearable strains and tensions, delaying success or making success look insignificant in relation to efforts made to achieve it. This yoga is also found to be associated with frustrations and losses although efforts are made in pursuit of food. This yoga perhaps selects the pure and simple, honest and truthful and loyal and hard-working souls as its victims. Such individuals suffer indignities of outrageous fortune despite their purest ray quality and character.

Types of Kaalsarp Yoga

→ **Anant Kaalsarp Yoga :-** When Rahu is in the 1st House and Ketu in the 7th house and the rest of the planets are left to this axis is the Anant Kaalsarp Yoga or *Vipareeta* Kaalsarp Yoga (opposite Kaalsarp yoga). Though this yoga has the power to give windfall gains to the native, it is bad for marital life. Generally natives with this yoga get married late in life.

→ **Kulik Kaalsarp Yoga :-** When Rahu occupies the 2nd house and Ketu the 8th house Kulik Kaalsarp Yoga arises. This combination is bad for health. The probability of losses and accidents is high with natives of this combination. It is bad for financial prosperity too. The native is worried on account of an insecure financial standing.

→ **Vasuki Kaalsarp Yoga :-** When Rahu occupies the 3rd house and Ketu the 9th house and the rest of the planets are located to the left of the Rahu Ketu axis this yoga is born. The native is burdened with problems relating to job and business

→ **Shankpal Kaalsarp Yoga :-** When Rahu occupies the 4th house and Ketu the 10th this yoga is formed. The native gets trouble relating to work sphere and has to go through stress and anxiety. Sometimes the native has an illegitimate child or can be an illegitimate child. However this yoga also has the power of conferring high political success and windfall gains.

→ **Padam Kaalsarp Yoga :-**When Rahu occupies the 5th house and Ketu the 11th house this Yoga is formed. The native is worried on account of children. There is difficulty in getting a progeny. If the moon is also afflicted then there is the possibility of being troubled by spirits. In this case if a native falls ill the recovery time is slow. There are also chances of being let down by friends in this case.

→ **Mahapadam Kaalsarp Yoga :-**This yoga is formed when Rahu is in the 6th house and Ketu is in the 12th house. The native has many enemies and has problems on account of diseases. However if this yoga acts beneficially it has the power to confer power and political success.

→ **Takshak Kaalsarp Yoga :-**When Rahu is in the 7th house and Ketu in the 1st house this yoga is formed. The native has got speculative tendencies and can lose wealth by way of wine, women and gambling. There is marital discord in the life of the native.

→ **Karkotak Kaalsarp Yoga :-**When Rahu occupies the 8th house and Ketu the 2nd house this yoga is formed. The native is short tempered and has many enemies. Such a native has friendship with the anti social elements. The native does not get paternal wealth.

→ **Shankachood Kaalsarp Yoga :-**When Rahu occupies the 9th house and Ketu is in the 3rd house this yoga operates. Natives who have this yoga in the chart have many ups and down in life. They have a habit of speaking lies. They are also short tempered.

→ **Ghatak Kaalsarp Yoga :-**This yoga arises when Rahu is in 10th house and Ketu in the 4th house. Litigation problems are common is this case. The person is likely to be punished by law or by the Government. However if this yoga operates in a beneficial manner then it has the power to confer the highest form of political power, special in Virgo and Leo ascendant.

→ **Vishdhar Kaalsarp Yoga :-**When Rahu occupies the 11th house and Ketu the 5th house the yoga which arises is the Vishdhar Kaalsarp Yoga. The native travels frequently and is never fixed at on place. Problems also arise from children. However these natives get some peace in the latter half of their life.

→ **Sheshnag Kaalsarp Yoga :-**When Rahu occupies the 12th house and Ketu the 6th house the native has problems relating to litigation. There may be enemies and health problems.

Here we would like to say that like so many other subjects in Astrology, even this subject is not free from controversies. Different scholars have given different versions as to the formation of this Kaalsarp yoga. While considering the *Kaalsarp yoga,* according to us, following things may be kept in the mind.

- The planets should be hemmed in between Rahu and Ketu and not in between Ketu and Rahu.
- From the ascendant, Rahu must be in the first six houses and Ketu in the remaining houses.
- Kaalsarp yoga is saved, if at least one planet is outside the Rahu/ Ketu axis.
- There is no Kaalsarp yoga if there is any planet with Rahu or Ketu though it may be between Rahu and Ketu axis. For example, if Rahu is 15° Libra and Moon is 28° Sagittarius and Saturn is 11° Sagittarius, there is no yoga present.

Remedy

There are lot of remedies for Kaalsarp yoga but this book deals only with yantra we would deal only with the yantra part. After energising the yantra the devotee should start his pooja on *panchmi tithi* (fifth day of any *paksh* of Hindu calendar) or *Amaavasaya* or Saturday. The most auspicious day considered for Kaalsarp yantra pooja is panchmi of *shukla paksha* in *sharavan* month. The Mantra for recital is *Mahamritunjaya* (please refer Shiva yantra) for hundred and twenty five thousand times and after that the *nav nag pooja* is done. The yantra which is also know as *nagpash* yantra is worshipped for *kaalsarp dosha* daily.

KAALSARPYOG (NAAG PAASH) YANTRA

Nag Gayatri mantra

ॐ नवकुलाय विद्महे विषदंताय धीमहि तन्नो सर्पः प्रचोदयात्॥

Om navkullaya vidhmahe Vishdantaaye dhimahee tanno sarpa parchodayat ॥

Manglik Yantra

What is Mars *Dosha*?

Mars/Manglik/Kuja/Bhom/Angaraka Dosha is formed when it is posited in any of the 1st, 4th, 7th, 8th, or 12th houses, of the chart. The first house is for self, 4th for marital happiness and peace of mind, 7th house for the partner in life, 8th house, the most malefic house is the 2nd from 7th and is also known as *Mangalya Bhav* and 12th for the pleasures of bed. So, all these houses are connected with the marital happiness and harmony. To this, we also add the second house, as it represents family. Married life without progeny will often become a nightmare. But Mars in these houses will have an adverse affect only if it is malefic planet for the native.

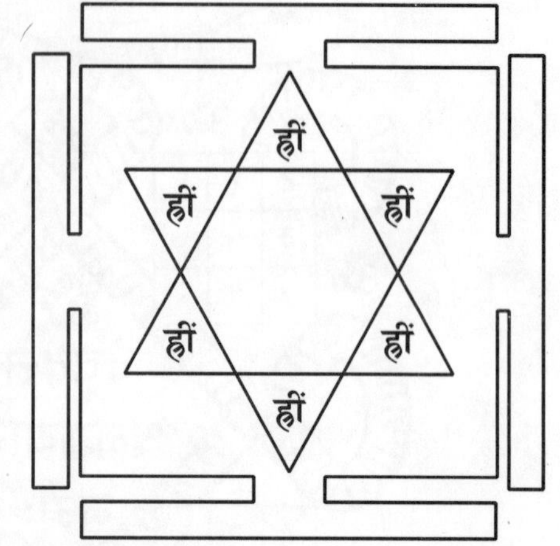

Remedy for the Mangal Dosha

*Mangal Gau*ri Yantra is the only remedy for *Manglik Dosha*. If the native is facing problems such as late marriage, then the native is advised to do the *Mangal Gauri Anusthan*.

Mangal Gauri Mantra:-

ॐ ह्रीं मंगलेगौरी विवाहबाधां नाशाय स्वाहा ॥

Om hrim Manglegauri Vivahbaadhaam naashaaya swah ॥

The above mantra is to be recited for a minimum of sixty four thousand to a maximum of hundred twenty five thousand times. The sage of the Mantra is *Aja*. The metre is *Gayatri*. The deity of the Mantra is *Manglagauri*. The *Bija* is *Hrim* and the Shakti is *Swah*. The yantra is to be installed on a pedestal covered with yellow cloth. The yantra is worshipped with *panchopchara* which includes the articles like vermillion, rice, flowers, *dhoop*, pure *ghee* and deep (earthen lamp). Articles of Mars to be donated after the *anusthan*.

Mangal Trikon Yantra

Now we will discuss *Mangal trikon* yantra**.** This yantra is good in preventing accidents, blesses with son, frees the devotee from debts, cures blood pressure and rash temper. It hastens the marriage of ladies. It also offers protection from enemies, cuts, wounds, operation and enables the devotee to recover speedily from above causes.

When Mars is afflicted one suffers. Since Mars is significator of husband in female chart (not Jupiter) and when found afflicted, the marriage of a girl is delayed, this yantra is being used successfully.

This yantra is in shape of a triangle and is embossed or engraved on copper plate. It is composed of twenty one sub-triangles, enclosed in a big circle. In each triangle different names of the lord Mars are inscribed.

After installing the yantra in pooja place in the house the yantra is worshipped with red flowers and sweets made from jaggery or rice are offered. The mantra for recital is:-

ॐ हों हँ सः खं खः ॥

Om Hom han sa kham kha ॥

The sage of the mantra is *virupaksh*, metre is gayatri, deity is mars and application of the mantra is for propitiating the planet mars. The mantra should be recited for six hundred thousand times. In case of severe diseases, the yantra be worshipped daily starting from tuesday with following mantras.

ॐ क्रां क्रीं क्रौं सः भौमाय नमः ॥

Om karang kareeng karoong sah bhoomaye namah ॥

ॐ क्रां क्रीं क्रौं सः भौमाय नमः क्रौं क्रीं क्रां ॥

Om karang kareeng karoong sah bhoomaye namah karoong kareeng karang ॥

Some usages of *mangal rikon* yantra

- Mars is significator of husband in the case of ladies. When position of Mars in birth chart is weak, afflicted or posited in 6th, 8th, or 12th houses, the lady's marriage is invariably delayed. In such cases yantra is prepared with *pooja* and then girl should start performing *pooja* of the yantra from Tuesday for forty one days, except day of periods, and then on every subsequent tuesday, then a suitable match is found within a short span of time.
- In cases where lady's maritial life becomes strained, leading to divorce or separation between the couple, *pooja* of this yantra by lady has shown remarkable results in patching up relations between the couple.
- In case where man or woman is of harsh tamper then, by wearing

this yantra, troubles arising from such person's behaviour are controlled after *pooja.*

- When a man is lacking in courage and boldness or is shy and unable in expressing himself, very good results have been seen by performing the *pooja* of this yantra and keeping it on person's body.

It may be noted here that person who is wearing this yantra on his or her body or performing its pooja should avoid fish, meat, etc., and sexual act or contacts with opposite sex on tuesday. Keep a fast on this day in order to get rapid results.

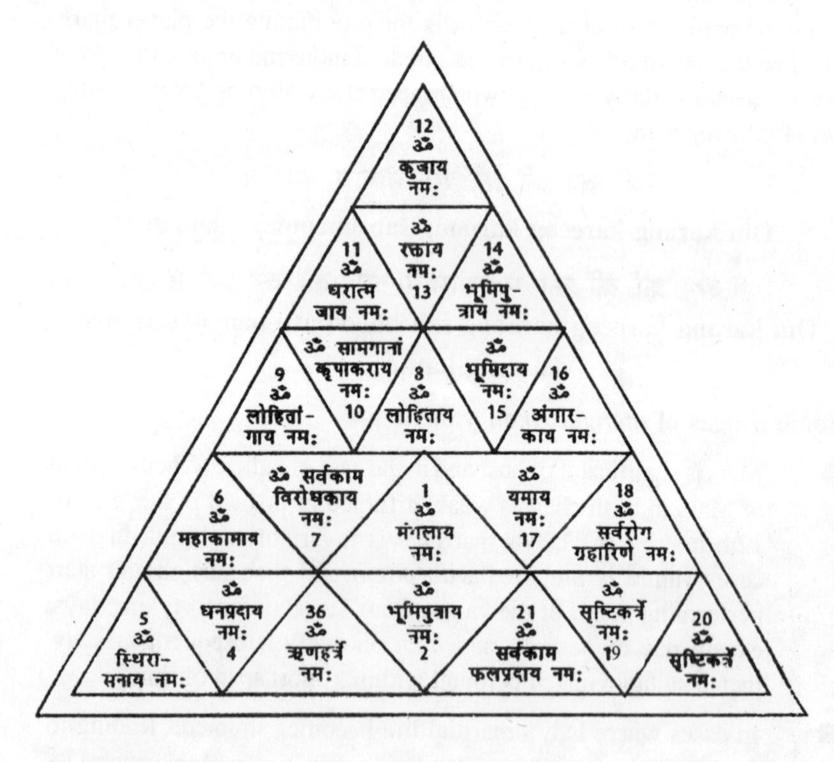

CHAPTER 13

NUMERICAL YANTRAS

Numerical Yantras are designed with the help of numericals. These digits carry some significant values. These Yantras are *Beesal Vishank* Yantra (Sum total twenty), *Pandhriya* Yantra (Sum total fifteen), *Bhatreeya* Yantra (sum total seventy two) etc.

While writing the digits, starting from the smallest digits to highest, this is called *Aroh Karam* except where specific directions are indicated keeping in view the specific purpose. The digits are assigned to specific planets and *Devas*. In case a particular *Deva* or deity is to appease that particular digit is written first. This also applies to the directions. *Sadhaka* should refer and memorise the following table.

Digits of yantra	Results of Yantra
15	For comforts and various uses.
16	Saves from theft etc.
20	When kept with Sadhaka, it removes all types of fears and bestows all comforts
28	For cure of diseases and removes fear of *Shakni*
30	For removal of fear from Shakni
32	To be used at the time of Child birth and bestows all comforts.
34	This should be written when *Dev yagya* is being performed. It removes all fears. If written on the

	entrance of a house it protects the house from dangers and influence of evil souls. It is used for *Serv Siddhi*.
36	Useful for speculation purpose and children are cured.
40	For headache. Also useful for respect and victory over enemies.
56	Useful for *Mohenen* and *Vashikaran* purposes.
62	It is beneficial for the pregnancy for the ladies who does not conceive.
64	Removes all sorts of fears and of souls etc.
70	One's rank is elevated.
72	Removes the fear of souls. One wins in quarrels, war etc., and helps in pregnancy.
85	Bestows all comforts and removes all worries etc.
87	Cures all diseases.
120	This is every important yantra. It bestows wealth and comforts.
152	If the face is washed after dipping and washing yantra in water, one is respected. The relations between brother, sister becomes cordial.
170	It is used for intelligensia.
172	It is useful for gain or birth of Son. Removes fear also.
200	This is written and pasted outside shop to increase the business.
300	Increases good relations between opposite sex. The broken relations are tied up again.
400	Removes all homely fears. If used, buried or thrown in the field, increases the quantity and quality of crops.
500	The use of this yantra is beneficial for pregnancy of a women. Men can also use for good luck.
600	Beneficial for comforts and wealth.
700	Victory over law suits, quarrels and enemies etc.
900	Removes all fears.
1000	Fear vanishes, one is never defeated. Gains through Govt.
1100	If one is troubled through souls, by wearing this yantra fear is removed.

1200	The prisoner is released early from jail.
5000	Respect power and authority from Govt. all worries etc. are removed.
10000	The accused is acquitted by court of law and good for *Sarv* Siddhi.

Beesa/Vishank Yantra

Vishank which is commonly known as *Beesa* means a Yantra having sum total of twenty from all sides. This Yantra bestows all type of leisure in the life. According to *Vishwalok Tantra*, this Yantra is also used in six rites. Through this Yantra one can get all his desires full filled. A barren woman can have babies, one can have sons, job, and kings can get their lost kingdoms. Not only the devotee is blessed with all luxuries, but also the malefic effects of the planets do not disturb him. He can enjoy the blessings of the eight *siddhis*. While practising this Yantra there is no need for *Dhyana*, *nyaas*, *homas*, *pooja*, *stotra path* etc. During the use of this Yantra only mantra *Jap* can yield the desired results.

Design of the Yantra

This Yantra is drawn by drawing four lines from east to west and north to south. These lines form nine squares. These squares are filled with following digits.

Sl. No.	Digit of yantra	Its significance
1.	8	*Vasu*
2.	9	Nand
3.	3	*Hutashan*
4.	2	Eyes
5.	7	Saints
6.	11	*Parmath*
7.	10	*Adhip*
8.	4	*Vedas*
9.	6	*Ras*

Through these figures the Beesa Yantra is drawn. This Yantra, drawn in nine squares bestows all powers of earth and nether world. The sum total of these nine digits is 60, every angle counts 20 but from one angle the total comes to 21.

८	१	३
२	७	११
१०	४	६

Characteristic feature

It may be worth to mention here that while drawing this yantra the devotee might face many hurdles such as ghosts in the dreams, songs of *gandharwas,* dance by the royal dancers of the heaven and all other things which may not be dear to the person who is practising the yantra. Here it is advised that the devotee should not get frightened from all these things and should continue with his work. The devotee is advised not to fear from these things as these things are created by the Almighty God to test the skills of the devotee. During the *purascharan* period, the devotee should continue with his work. On the completion day, the deity of the Yantra Lord *Janardhan* would bless the devotee with all desires.

Writing of the Beesa yantra

On an auspicious day, at auspicious place or on a mountain or near the bank of a river or any other lonely place which is considered auspicious for this rite, the devotee, after completion of his daily routine should sit on a seat made of Durva grass facing east or north direction and recite the following:

ॐ गुरवे नमः ॥ ॐ गणपतये नमः ॥

Om Guruve namah ॥ Om ganapatye Namah ॥

In this manner the devotee should start writing the yantra and pray to Lord *Shiv* as follows:-

ॐ प्रजानाथ नमस्तेस्तु प्रजापालनतत्पर ।
प्रसन्नो भव मे देव यन्त्रसिद्धिं प्रयच्छ मे ॥ १ ॥
ये केचित्प्रेतकूष्माण्डा भैरवा भूतनायकाः ।
ते सर्वे विलयं यान्तु प्रजानाथ नमोऽस्तु ते ॥ २ ॥
प्रयच्छ सिद्धिमतुलां यन्त्रराजात्सुदुर्लभाम् ।
त्वत्प्रसादादहं नाथ कृतकृत्यो व्रजे परम् ॥ ३ ॥

Om prajanath namasteastu prajapalantatpar ।
Prassano bhav me dev yantrasiddhan prayachme ॥ 1 ॥
Ye kechitpretkushmanda bharva bhutnayaka ।
Te sarve vilyam yantu prajanath namoastu te ॥ 2 ॥
Paryach siddhimtulam yantrarajasudurlbham ।
Tavtprasadaham nath kritkrityo vajre param ॥ 3 ॥

After worshipping the Ganesh, worship lord *Shiva* and write the yantra with the stylus of *jaati* and *chandan*, *agar*, *kasturi*, red *chandan*, *kapur*, red vermillion, *devdaroo, kusth,* and *asthgandh*. The yantra is written on *Bhojpatra* and while orating ***Om Hrim Om*** (ॐ ह्रीं ॐ) the nine squares be filled with numericals. In the first three lines 8, 9, 3 in the second line 2, 7, 11, and in the third line 10, 4, and 6. In this manner, hundred and eight Yantras be drawn and different type of flowers are offered along with essence of black *agar* and lamp of oil be lit. In this manner, worship the yantra. Again, facing west direction lit the lamp and worship lord *Varuna*. After worshipping Lord *Varuna,* worship the yantra with its *mula* mantra. The mantra for worshipping beesa yantra is as follows:-

ॐ ह्रीं श्रीं क्लीं मम सर्ववांछितं देहिदेहि स्वाहा ॥

Om Hrim shrim klim mam sarvavarchitam Dehidehi swaha ॥

The *rishi* of the mantra is *brahma, Anustup* metre, *Vishanka Bhawani Devata*, *Om* is *bija, hrim shakti, shrim kilkam.*

After doing *viniyas* recite the mantra for one thousand times for eighty eight days. Homas be done of 1/10 of *japas* and 1/10 of japas as *tarpan* and 1/10 of tarpan as *marjan* respectively. On last day, all the

Yantras be rapped in the pills of wheat flour in the shape of a ball and be flown in water. The fish will eat the pills and by doing so, Lord *Varuna* blesses the devotee with wishes and hence, the yantra is energised.

Procedure for realising the yantra

The devotee should go to any reputed place of pilgrim and on a plain ground with total concentration focus his attention on Guru and *Ganesha*. Using a stylus made out of jasmine wood draw the yantra with *Asthgandh* on white *Bhojpatra*. Starting with oration of ***Om*** (ॐ) ***(Pranav)*** write *Maya beeja* and put the digit in the prescribed boxes of the Yantra. By facing west, incense the yantra with black agar. The yantra be worshipped with different types of flowers for hundred and eight times and the mantra is recited for one thousand times. The food items for offering are pure ghee, honey, cheese, and rice boiled in milk. The devotee has to write the yantra until the figure lasts. On the eighty-eighth day after worshipping the *Devi*, it is flown in the water. The yantra needs to be wrapped in the ball of the flour and flown in the water. When the fish eats it, the yantra is realised and the devotee is blessed. During this period the devotee has to abstain from sensual pleasure and should take food made of flour of wheat and oil. Pure ghee is prohibited during this practise.

Some usages of Beesa yantra

1. Six Rites

First, we should start with six rites through these yantras. These rites are explained in the six rites chapter. For undertaking six rites through these yantras, one should note that during *Ucchatan* rites, the devotee should face towards north direction, during *Vidveshan*, it should be southwest, and in all other rites, he should face towards northeast direction.

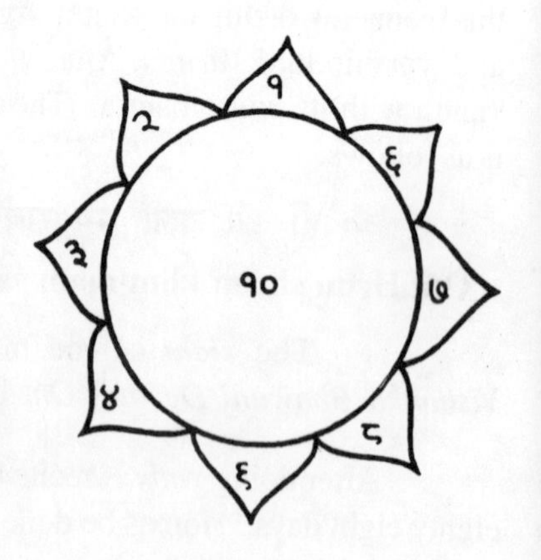

♦**For Attraction:** -Take an earthen pot and write the yantra on it. Kick the pot and again put it in inverted position. Then recite the following mantra hundred and eight times. Replace *amuk* with the name of the intended person.

१
४ ७ ६
३
८ १० २
५

ॐ ह्रीं श्रीं क्लीं अमुकमाकर्षय स्वाहा ॥

Om Hrim shrim klim
amukmakarshaye swaha ॥

♦**For Maaran: -** After writing the yantra write the name of the enemy. Energise it through mantra and orate the name of the enemy. If the yantra is put in fire the intended person would suffer from illness, and other diseases. Moreover, if the yantra becomes red hot the enemy may die.

४	२	८	६
६	८	२	४
२	४	६	८
८	६	४	२

♦**For Ucchatan: -** The devotee should write the yantra in an angry mood with the juice of *Dhatura* mixed with *massi.* The devotee should throw the yantra in a cremation ground or a dense forest. This act would cause Ucchatan.

♦**For Stambhan:** - The yantra is written with the turmeric powder mixed with salt on Bhojpatra and bury it in a pit. Now recite the mantra along with the names of the intended persons. All the persons named during oration of mantra would get Stambhan.

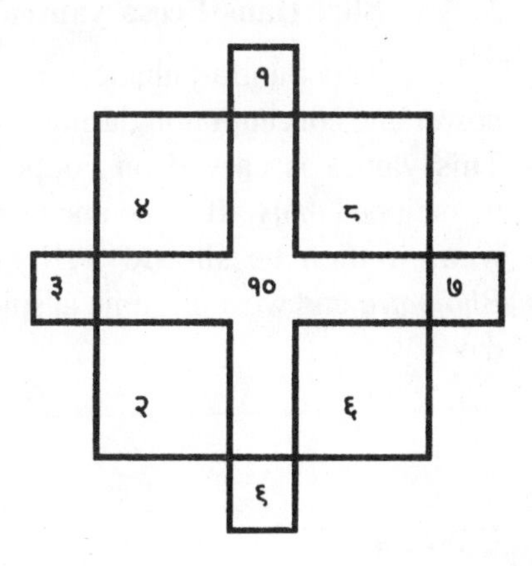

♦**For Vidveshan:** - The devotee should write the yantra with the feather of owl as stylus on the cloth of cremation ground or shroud. By reciting the mantra, he should crush the yantra with left leg. The Vidveshan is complete.

♦**For Shanti:** - The devotee

interested in shanti rites should recite the mantra for three thousand times while writing the yantra. This rite would help in getting rid from diseases, anger, attraction, propitation of evil planets in the natal chart and all other such ill habits that are not welcomed by the society.

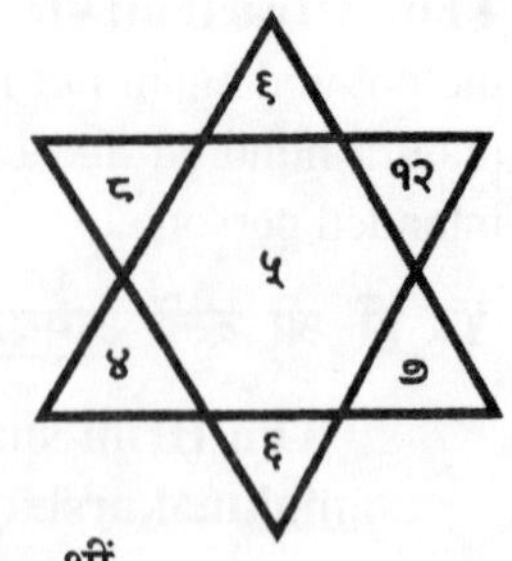

2. Shree Beesa yantra

This yantra is used for pleasing goddess Laxmi. The goddess bestows all luxuries, wealth and comforts in life. It is carved on copper plate. In the morning, at the time of sunrise, the devotee should worship it with saffron mixed with sandal powder with mantra:-

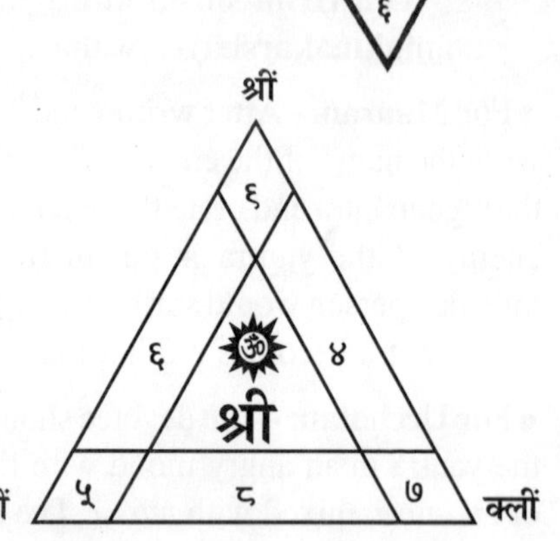

ॐ ह्रीं क्लीं लक्ष्मी देव्यै: नम: ॥

Om Hrim klim lakshmi Devia namah ॥

The mantra be recited for two thousand times daily along with *Shri sukta.*

3. Shri Hans Beesa yantra

This yantra enhances memory power and concentration during studies. This yantra is carved on copper and worshipped daily. If some one wants to wear it then he should write it on *Bhojpatra* and wear on some auspicious day

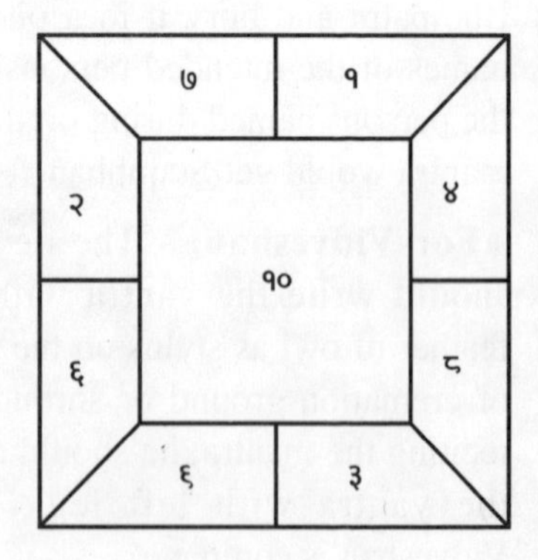

4. Singh (Lion) Beesa yantra

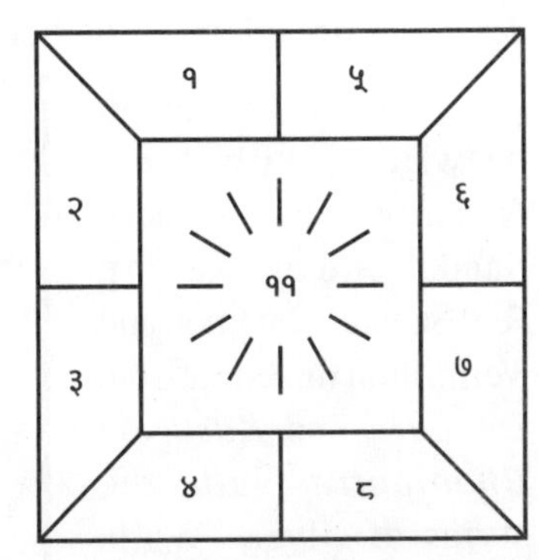

This Beesa yantra enables a person to win over his enemies, get rid of fears developed in the mind of a person due to some unseen problems. This Yantra is drawn on *bhojpatra* and tied on the right arm to increase self confidence.

5. Shri Kuber Beesa yantra

The yantra is drawn on the wall of the business establishment, office with ghee and red vermillion or on bhojpatra with asthgand and saffron mixed ink. If the yantra is tied on the right arm, it increases age.

१	८	३	८
७	४	५	४
७	२	१	२
५	६	३	६

6. Shri Saubhagya (Good luck) Beesa yantra

Those persons who did not get dues out of their labour in the field of business, job or education this yantra is good for them. The yantra is drawn with pure ghee and red vermillion or on bhojpatra. If the yantra is tied on the right arm, it increases good luck.

८	१	३
२	७	११
१०	४	६

6. Shree Amogh Beesa yantra

This yantra is tied as an amulet in the neck of a child and write the yantra on bhojpatra to save from ill sight or diseases.

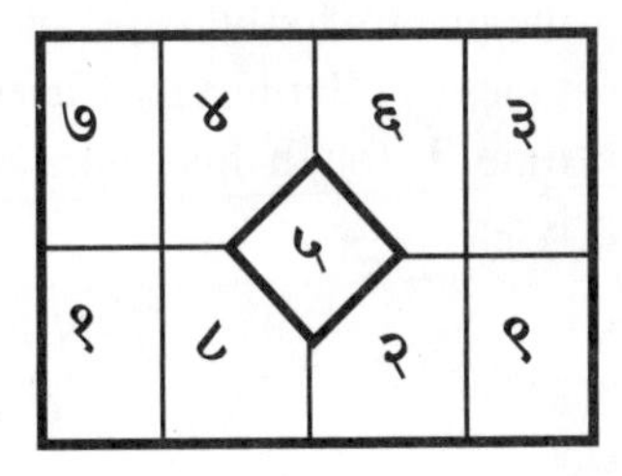

7. Kalyankari Sidh Beesa Yantra

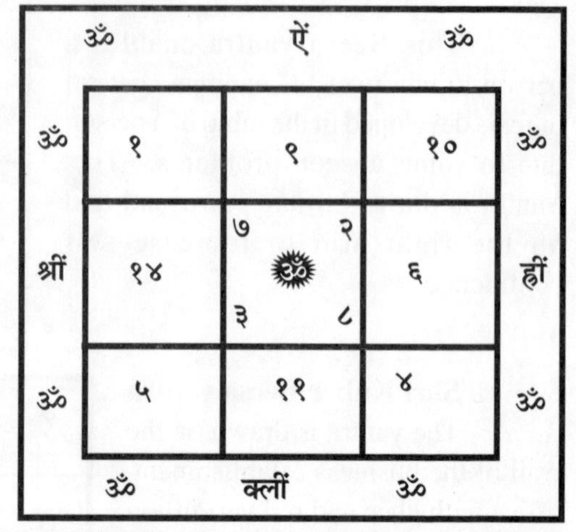

This yantra is to be written with *Ashat Gandh* which consists of Sandal, *Aagar*, Kasturi, Red Sandal, Camphor, and Vermillion mixed saffron. Dev*daru* and *Kusth* on *Bhoojpatra* with the stylus of silver. While writing the yantra the devotee should recite the mantra. This yantra be written for hundred and eight times, and *pooja* is performed with various kind of flowers and put in the smoke of lamp lighted with black agar and flowers. It bestows all round success. The mantra be recited for 27 days. Sadhaka's all desired are fulfilled. The mantra is as follows:-

ॐ ऐं ह्रीं श्रीं क्लीं नमः ॥

Om Aeeng Hareen Shareeng Kleeng Namah ॥

8. Shri Vishnu Beesa Yantra

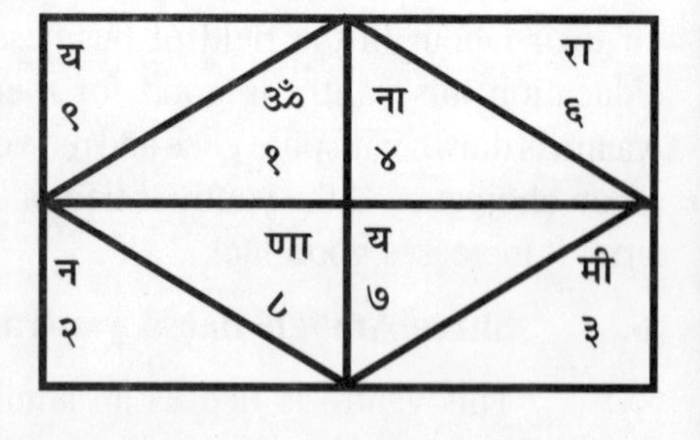

This yantra as shown be written with white sandal and stylus of Tulsi (basil) sitting on the seat made of sandal or mango wood or it be engrossed on copper plate be put to daily pooja by offering tulsi leaves and recite the mantra for hundred and eight times by offering tulsi leaves each time. Through this yantra all desires are fulfilled. The mantra for worship is :-

ॐ नमो नारायणय ॥

Om Namo Narayana ॥

9. Shri Krishan Beesa Yantra

This yantra is also written as Vishnu yantra is written. Besides bestowing a son, it also gives power to win over the enemies.

श ९			र ६
	१ श्री	४ शं	
	२ कृ	३ ष्णः	
म ८			णं ७

श्री कृष्ण शरणं माम् ॥

Shri Krishna Sharnam Maam ॥

10. Shri Durga Navaran Beesa yantra

Shri Durga Beesa yantra is drawn as of Vishnu beesa Yantra. The yantra is worshipped through the following mantra.

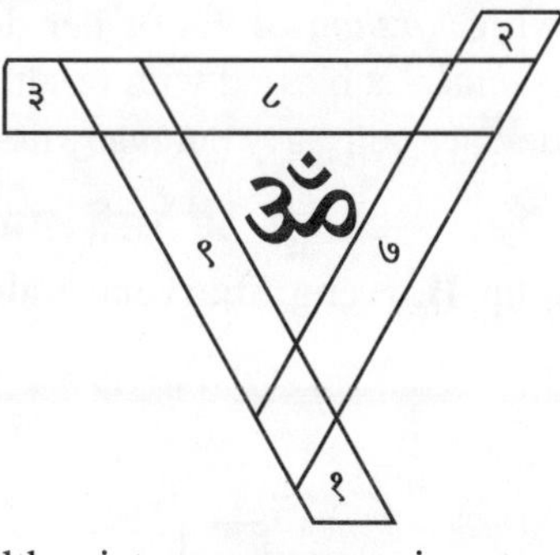

ऐं ह्रीं क्लीं चामुण्डायै विच्चे ॥

Aaeng kareeng kaleeng Chamundaye Vichche ॥

The mantra is recited for hundred and eight times daily. This yantra can be worn by writing on *Bhojpatra*. It bestows wealth, good health, victory over enemies etc.

11. Navaran Beesa yantra

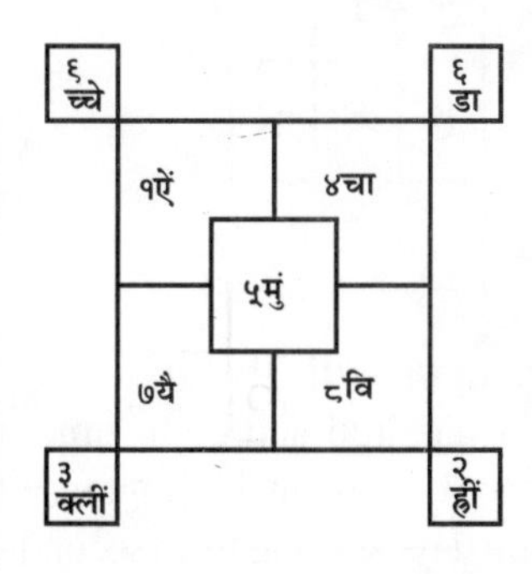

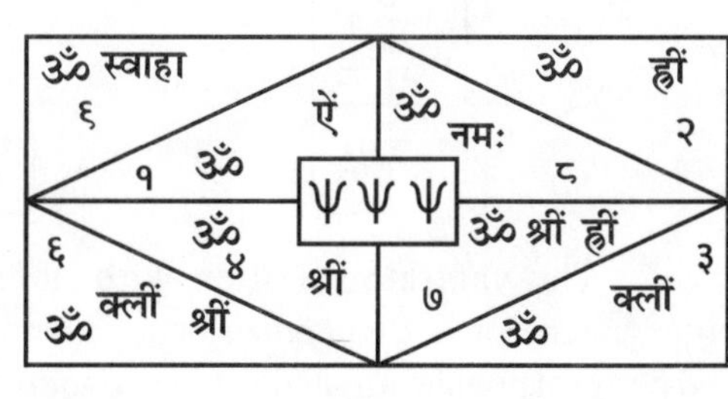

This yantra can be prepared as per instructions above. The yantra of Devi full fills all desires of sadhaka. Another form of Navaran *Beesa* yantra is as follows. In this yantra three tridents are shown which shows the presence of *Mahakali*, *Mahalakshmi* and *Mahasaraswati* which are three parts of Shakti. The material used in writing the yantra is same. The yantra pooja is done with following mantra by reciting it for twelve thousand times to be completed in twelve or nine days.

ॐ ह्रीं श्रीं क्लीं नमः ॐ क्लीं श्रीं ह्रीं नमः मम मनोवाञ्छितं फल देहि स्वाहा ॥

Om hareeng shareeng keleeng namaha om kaleeng shareeng hareeng namah, mam manovanchhatam phal dehi svaha ॥

12. Navkoshtak Beesa yantra

On the completion of rituals of pooja of this yantra one is blessed with *darshan* of his or her deity who appears in the dream and the *sadhaka* is blessed with wealth and happiness. Through this yantra, the devotee can carry out many usages. The mantra for recital is as follows:-

ॐ ह्रीं श्रीं क्लीं मम सर्ववांछितं देहि देहि स्वाहा ॥

Om Hareeng Shareeng kaleeng mam sarvanechtam Dahe Dahe Savaha ॥

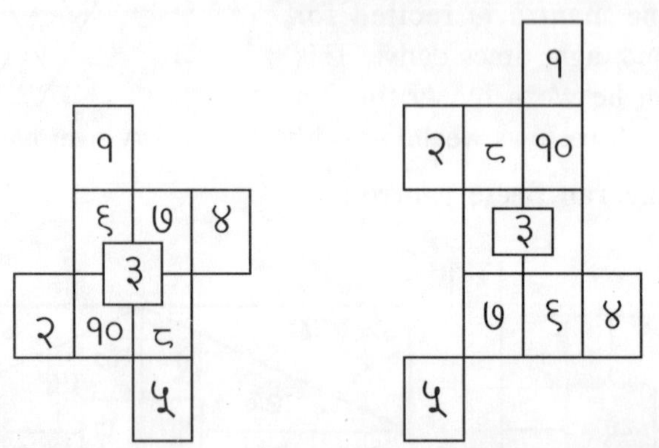

The yantra be written with *Ashtgandh* with the stylus of pomegranate on a *Bhojhpatra* or a paper for hundred and eight times and perform pooja with sandal, lamp, *dhoop* and flowers having fragrance etc. The process should continue for eighty eight days starting from second *tithi* in *Shukla paksh* and *japa* of above mantra be performed for one thousand times daily and if possible, perform *Homa* while reciting the mantra for hundred and eight times. Use *kheer*, sugar, ghee, honey, and *bilva* leaves in Homa. After homa 1/10 of japa should be *marjan* and *tarpan* respectively

To get better results the devotee is advised to make a yantra on gold plate and over the plate place hundred and eight yantras already written on *Bhoojpatra* or paper and offer pooja. Homa be then performed with these hundred and eight yantras and other material to be used during Homa.

13. Lakshmi Data Beesa yantra:- Spread *Gulal* on the plank of the Mango wood and write yantra with the stylus of *chameli* wood for hundred and eight times. Perform *pooja* for the realising of the yantra. The mantra for recital during the pooja is:-

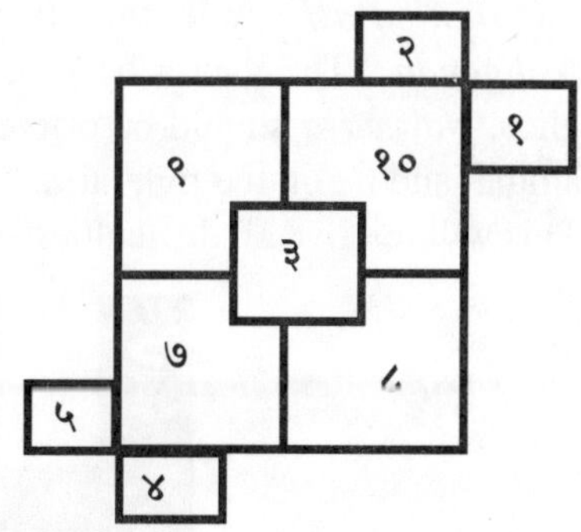

श्रीं श्रीं ह्रीं श्रीं कमले कमलालये
प्रसीद प्रसीद श्रीं ह्रीं श्रीं महालक्ष्मयै
नमः ॥

Shrim Shrim Hrim Shrim Kamle kamlalye Parsid Parsid Shrim Hrim Shrim Mahalakshmaye namah ॥

After realising, the yantra could be worn on the body as an amulet when written on *bhojpatra* with *asthgandh.*

14. Lakshmi Siddh Beesa yantra: - The Devotee should start this practise on Thursday during the hora of *Pushya Nakshtra* is there.He should wear yellow clothes and sit on yellow seat and use yellow coloured rosary for mantra recital given below.

<table>
<tr><td>महालक्ष्मयै</td><td colspan="2">५</td><td>नमः</td></tr>
<tr><td>९</td><td colspan="2">श्रीं</td><td>६</td></tr>
<tr><td rowspan="2">ॐ</td><td>१</td><td>४</td><td rowspan="2">ह्रीं</td></tr>
<tr><td>७</td><td>८</td></tr>
<tr><td>३</td><td colspan="2">क्लीं</td><td>२</td></tr>
</table>

ॐ श्रीं ह्रीं क्लीं महालक्ष्मयै नमः ॥

Om Sreem Hareeng Kaleeng mahalakshmaye namah ॥

This mantra is recited for hundred and eight times daily for 62 days and it is written in fixed numbers. On 63rd day engross the yantra on a silver plate and put already written yantras on it and perform *pooja*. One yantra out of them be put in the neck in a silver talisman. Yantra made on silver plate be kept in the cash box. Other yantras be thrown in the river in the pills of wheat flour.

15. Beesa yantra for removal of difficulties

On *Deepwali* or *Holi* festivals the devotee should write the yantra on *Bhooj Patra* with the stylus of pomegranate with the ink of *Asthgandh.* The yantra be worshipped with *dhoop* and lamp of pure ghee. *Naveedya* should be offered to the yantra. Use the yantra as an amulet and tie on the right arm. It should be covered in silver covering. This will remove all difficulties and favourable results will be shown.

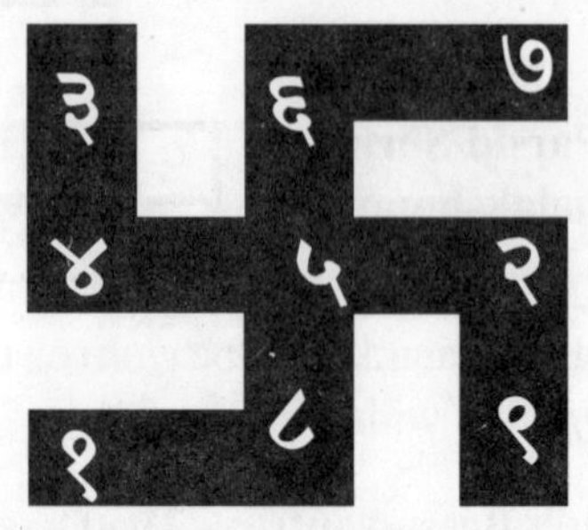

16. Shree Mahalakshmi Beesa yantra

During some auspicious period the devotee should draw this yantra with the stylus of pomegranate and ink of *Asthgandh.* This yantra is to be inscribed on bhojpatra. If bhojpatra is not available then the devotee should use the copper plate and apply *Asthgandh* over it. The yantra is to be placed on a pedestal covered with red cloth. The devotee should recite the following mantra for 21 days for one hundred thousand times. During worship the devotee should lit the pure ghee lamp and

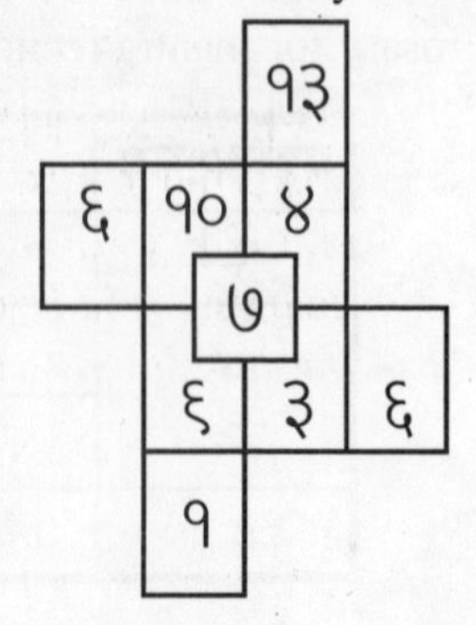

offer sweets, honey *bel* leaves etc. This yantra is as good as the idol of goddess Lakshmi. The mantra for recital is:-

ॐ श्रीं ह्रीं क्लीं ह्रीं श्रीं महालक्ष्मयै नमः ॥

Om Shrim Hrim Klim Hrim Shrim Mahalakshmaye namah ॥

17. Bala Tripur Beesa Yantra

The yantras given below are of *Bala Tripur Sundari.* During some auspicious *lagna* these yantras are inscribed on a silver plate. The pooja is performed with the following mantra for hundred and eight. This yantra bestows wealth and all luxuries. The mantra is as given under Sl.No. 16.

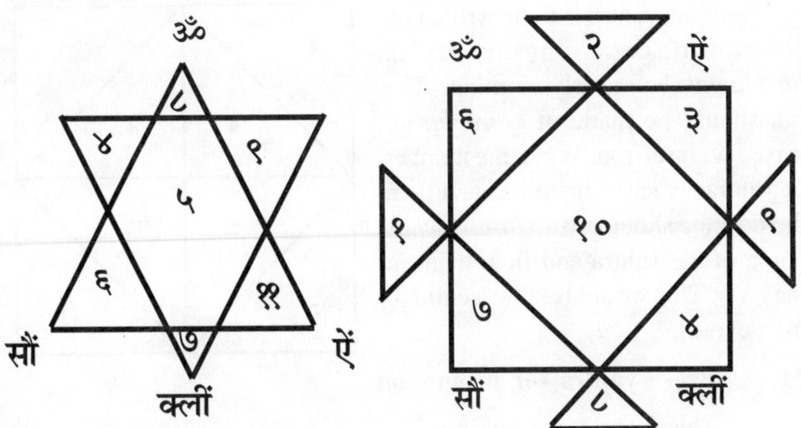

18. Shree Laxmi Beesa yantra

While worshipping this yantra the devotee should use saffron colour. All the articles should be of saffron colour. The yantra realises after one hundred thousand mantra. It bestows all comforts in life. The mantra for recital is:-

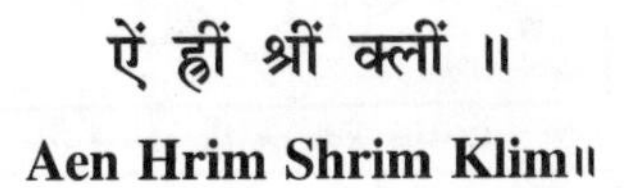

ऐं ह्रीं श्रीं क्लीं ॥

Aen Hrim Shrim Klim॥

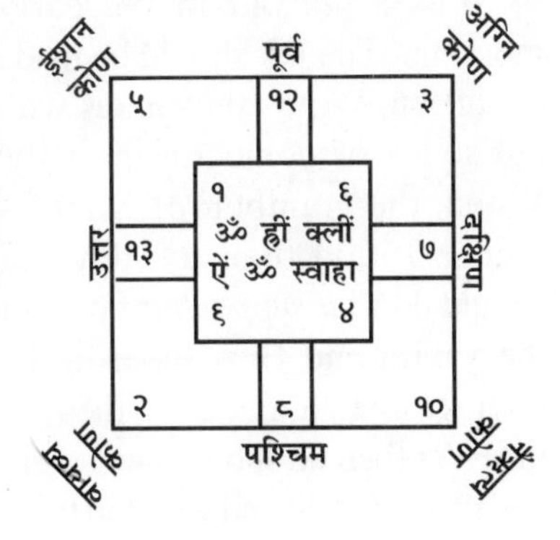

19. Beesa yantra for comfortable life

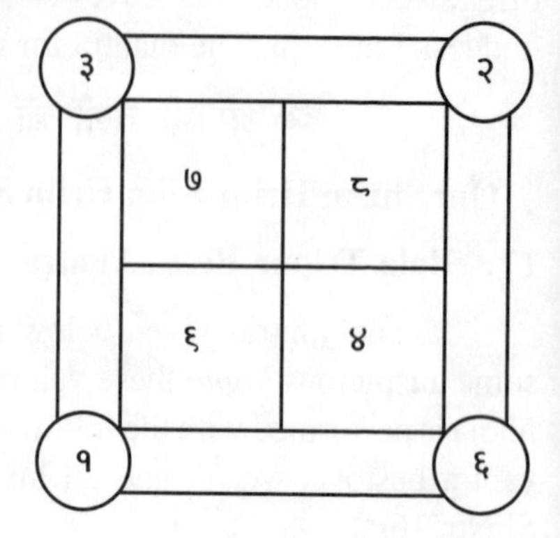

This yantra is to be written for 101 times daily with the stylus of pomegrenate on the *bhojpatra*. The devotee should do the *shodasuppchar* pooja. After the ceremony the devotee should flow the yantra in water. Comforts returns to the home and all pending work start taking its shape.

20. Beesa yantra for children

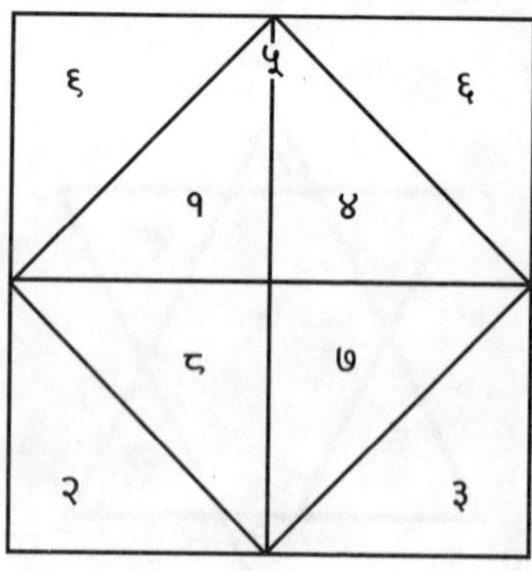

This yantra is to be written on *Deepawali*, or on any Sunday in *Shukla paksha* in early morning. The ink should be made of *Gorocharan* mixed with saffron. When the number of yantras reaches five thousand then the devotee should do *sodasuppachar* pooja of the yantra and flow them in the river. This would bestow a child to the devotee.

21. Beesa yantra for promotion

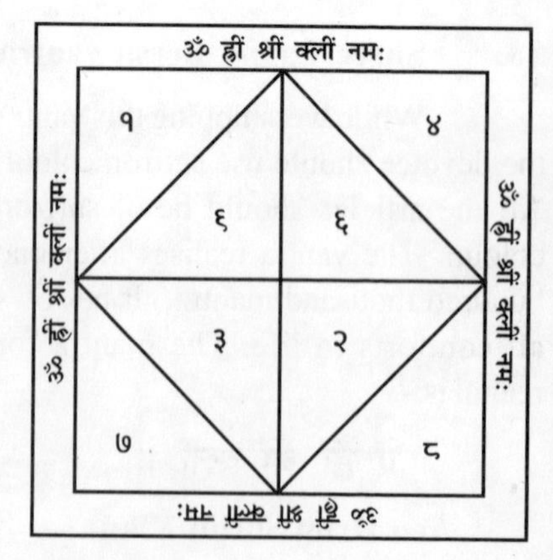

This yantra is to be written on Deepawali, or on any Tuesday in *Shukla paksha* in the early morning. The ink should be made of saffron. Write 100 yantras with the stylus of pomegranate daily. When the number of yantras reaches 5000 then the devotee should do *sodasuppachar* pooja of the yantra and flow them in the river. If one cannot flow them in the river then he should keep them tied in a red cloth and worship them with the following mantra:-

ॐ नमो भगवती त्रिलोचनं त्रिपुरां देवी अंजलीम् मे कल्याणं कुरू कुरू स्वाहा ॥

Om Namo Bhagwati Trilochanam Tripuram Devi Anjalim me kalyanam Kuru kuru Swah ॥

22. Beesa for transfer

This yantra is to be written on Deepawali, or on any Tuesday in *Shukla paksha* in the early morning. The ink should be made of saffron or red in colour. Write 100 yantras on bhojpatra or on white paper with the stylus of pomegranate daily. When the number of yantras reaches 2100 then the devotee should do *sodasuppachar* pooja of the yantra and flow them in the river.

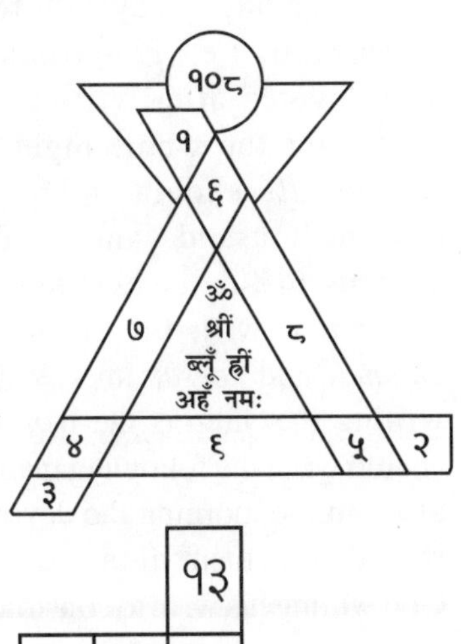

23. Beesa for getting a job

This yantra is to be written on Deepawali, or on any Tuesday or Thursday. The ink should be made of saffron. Write hundred and one yantras with the stylus of pomegranate daily. When the number of yantras reaches five thousand then the devotee should do *panchoppachar pooja* of the yantra and flow them in the river. This would lead to getting some job or means of earning.

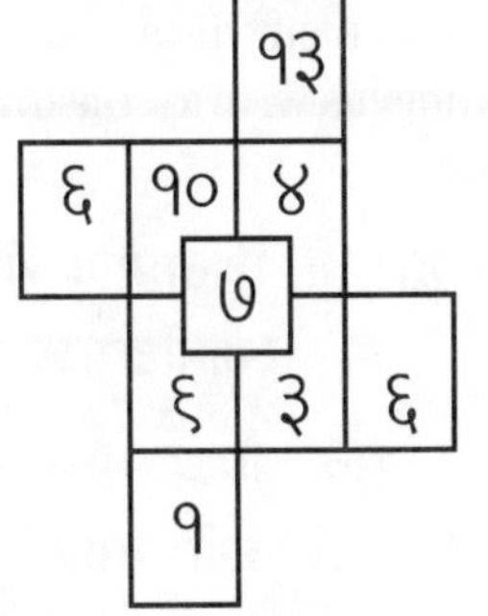

24. Beesa for getting a vehicle

This yantra is to be written on *Deepawali,* or on any Tuesday. The yantra is to be drawn on *bhojpatra* with the ink made of saffron. Writer 101

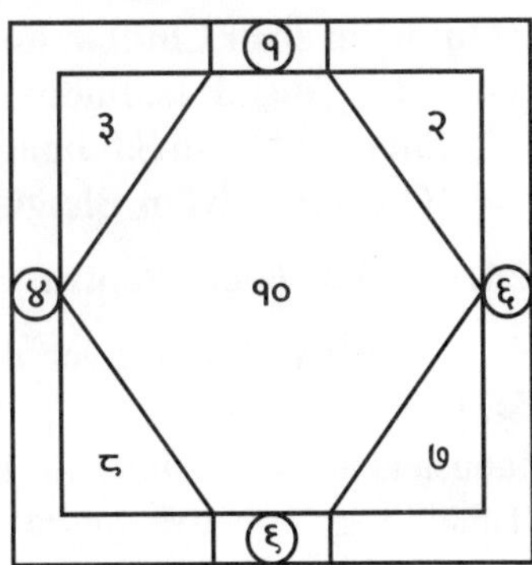

yantras daily for 39 days and keep them at the pooja place in the house. On 39th day flow them in the flowing water.

25. Beesa for construction of house

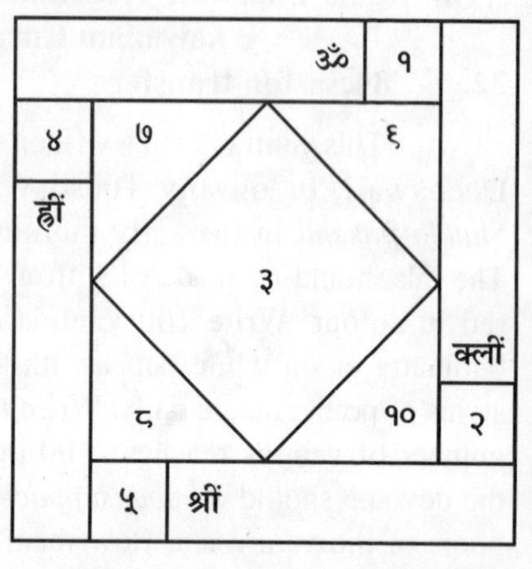

This yantra is to be written one day before Deepawali, i.e., *chaturdashi*. The devotee after writing the yantra for the whole night on *Deepawali* should complete eleven thousand yantra. The yantras are to be written on *bhojpatra* with the stylus of *chameli* and *keesar* ink. While writing the yantras the devotee should write the following mantra also. In the morning the devotee should flow them in the river after *sodashupchar pooja* of the yantra. God willing his wish to construct the house would be fulfilled. The mantra is as under:-

ॐ ह्रीं श्री चिंतामणि गणपतये वांछितार्थ पुष्य लक्ष्मी दायक
लक्ष्मीदायक ऋद्धि वृद्धि कुरु कुरु ।
सर्व सौख्य सौभाग्यं कुरु कुरु श्री ह्रीं स्वाहा ॥
ॐ ह्रीं क्लीं भगवती मम वांछित देही देही स्वाहा ॥

Om hrim srim Chintamani Ganpatape Vanchitarth pusya laxmi dayak laxmidayak Riddhi vridhi kuru kuru।
Sarv saukhaya Saubhagyam Kuru Kuru Shri Hrim Swah॥
Om Hrim Klim Bhagwati mam vanchit dehi dehi swah ।

26. Sun Beesa Yantra

Sun is the life giver of the Universe. So for attaining good health Surya yantra is used after performing pooja. The mantra is recited for thousand and eight times for twenty one days as provided in the yantra. This is very effective yantra. By the personification of Sun Lord, one will maintain good health. The yantra be written on *Bhojpatra* with Asthgandh or carved on a copper or silver plate and be worn in neck. This can be carved on a similar metal ring and be worn in Sun finger of right hand. The mantra for recital is;

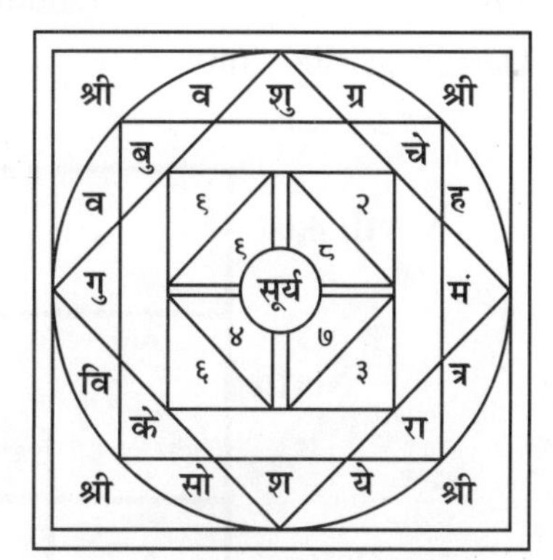

ॐ वासुग्र चंहा मंत्र रायं शासो केवि गुवबु ॥

Om vasugra choha mantra rayam shasho kavee goovabo ॥

27. Navgrah Beesa Yantra

This Yantra is of nine planets and wards off all difficulties and bestows good luck on the user. This yantra is worshipped with navgraha stotra.

Panchdashi Yantra (Sum fifteen/Pandhriya yantra)

The second and most important in the digital yantras is *Panchdashi* or *Pandhriya* yantra. The sum total of this yantra from all angles comes to fifteen. Like the Beesa yantra this yantra does not require pooja mantra. Mere collection of the yantra blessed the devotee with all worldly comforts. The devotee should be pious while writing the yantra.

According to *Shiv Rahasaya Tantra* this yantra is a nine squares yantra and the devotee should know the digits through which the boxes are to be filled and the significance of the numbers. According to the tantras, all the yantras and mantras have been nailed by lord Shiva so that no one can misuse them but this yantra was spared from being nailed for the welfare of the masses.

Design of the yantra

	East		
North east	८	१	६ South east
North	३	५	२ South
North west	४	९	७ South west
	West		

This Yantra is drawn by drawing four lines from east to west and north to south. These lines form nine squares. These squares are filled with digits one by one. One should also know the rules about these numbers. It is said that the figures from 1-6 are filled in the yantra and afterwards the remaining figures but in some of the tantras it is written that first 1-5 and 9 are written, afterwards 8-3-4, and lastly 2-7-6. Hence, the yantra is formed as shown above.

Realising the yantra

For realising of the yantra the devotee should do the *purascharan* of the yantra. When *Hasta, Pushya, Mula* or *Sharavan nakshatra* is falling on Sunday the devotee on an isolated place should sit on a seat made of grass facing east or north direction. The seat should be covered with red cover; red rosary for mantra *japa* and start *pranayam* after resolution *(Sankalp).* He should do japa of *Bhut lipi* for hundred and eight times. (The *Bhutlipi* is given on page no. 29 of Chapter 4).

After the japa of *bhutlipi* the devotee should take the leaf of *gular*, stylus of *gyanvraksh*, *jasbandh*, or *plash* which should be of the size of eight fist of the devotee. The ink should be made of *kessar*. After forming the nine boxes the devotee should start filling the numbers. 2 in south west, 3 in north, 5 in northwest, 6 in south east, 7 in south, 8 in northeast, and 9 in West. In this manner the devotee should complete the yantra by filling the figures in the boxes as told above. Now the devotee should do the hundred and eight japa of *Bhadreshavra* mantra with the following mantra:-

ॐ भद्रेश्वर भद्रं पूरय पूरय स्वाहा ॥

Om Bhadreshavra Bhadram puray puray swah ॥

The *rishi* of the mantra is *Swaran Aakarshan bhairav, Virat* metre, *Bhadshevra Devata*, *Hrim* is *bija*, *Bhadram shakti Puryate kilkam*.

With the above mantra the devotee should do the *pooja* of Lord *Bhadreshavra.* The devotee should also worship *navdurga*, all the nine planets, lord *Indra* and his weapon *vajra.* This yantra is realised after five thousand *japs* of this mantra. *Dhoop* of black agar with scented oil or ghee with food articles is offered to Lord *Bhadreshavra*. After that the yantra is realised and used as an amulet to be worn in neck or tied on arm. The cover of the amulet should have three metals.

Some more uses of this yantra

1. Ground *hartal* and *mansal* and mix juice of *belive* leaf. Sit on an auspicious and lonely place and write the yantra on the ground with the stylus of Bel for two thousand times. All the desires of the devotee are full filled.
2. With saffron the yantra be written for thousand times on the leaves of *shatavar* tree. The devotee is blessed with progeny
3. Write the yantra for thousand times on the leaves of *bar* tree. By this the devotee is blessed with wealth and all comforts of life and good luck.
4. Wealth is obtained if one writes thousand times this yantra on Lotus leaves
5. Write the yantra on copper plate for thousand times. One's virility and sexual power is increased.
6. Poverty is removed if this yantra is written with the stylus of *peepal* wood for thousand times.
7. Write this yantra for thousand times with the ink made of cow urine, *mansal*, *tagar*, *kapur* and *gorochan* on *Bhooj patra* with

the stylus made of root of *peepal* tree etc. The desire of the devotee is fulfilled.

8. Write this yantra for hundred and eight times with the turmeric powder mixed in water on a stone. The stone is buried under the entrance of enemy's house. There will be quarrels between enemy and his father, brothers, children wife and relations etc.

9. Write this yantra on pieces of *Bhoojpatra* for hundred and twenty five thousand times. It may be noted here that when the yantra is written for fulfilment of all desires the stylus of *chameli* plant is used, for the purpose of attraction the stylus should be of *dhatura*, for *Stambhan* the stylus should be of *bar* tree, for *Vashikaran* it should be of *kush* plant and for *Shantikaran* the stylus should be of gold or silver. The ink should be made of *chandan*, *agar*, *kapur*, *kasturi* and saffron mixed with auspicious water (Ganges water is considered most auspicious in tantra. The reader is advised to take water of some sacred river of his/her area which would also serve the same purpose). Each yantra is put in a ball of flour. The balls are thrown to fish while reciting the following mantra.

४	९	२
३	५	७
८	१	६

ॐ ह्रीं क्लीं पारस्वपक्षया नवनागकुल सेवनाय स्वाहा ॥

Om Hareeng kaleeng parsvapakoshaya navanagakul sewnaya Svaha ॥

10. If the devotee fills the yantra with one digit it is certain that Lord *Hanumanji* (the Lord of the yantra) comes to him; with two digit the king comes under the control of the devotee; three digit gives benefit in the trade; with four digit the house of the enemy is shifted; with five digit Ucchatan could be done; for *maran* 8-

9-6-1-2-4-3-5-7 are used; for Vashikaran 2-3-4-5-6-7-8-9-1 are used; if the yantra is written with figures 3-2-8-5-4-9-1-6-7 and the same is tied in a piece of cloth around the neck the lady is blessed with a son.

२	९	४
७	५	३
६	१	८

Yantra for different purposes

1. For Maaran:- On Sunday *Aakh* milk and ash of cremation ground be mixed together and with the stylus of *kekar* or of iron write any yantra of 15 digits on *aakh* leave starting with the digits from 9 to 1 at evening time and write the name of intended person on it. Recite the mantra for thousand and eight times and put in the funeral pyre. By doing so boils will appear on the body of the person who will not survive. The second use of this yantra for Maaran purpose is, make ink from coal of cremation ground on Saturday and with the stylus of wood of funeral pyre write the yantra on a paper. Write the name of enemy on the yantra and bury in the cremation ground, the enemy will die.

४	३	८
९	५	१
२	७	६

८	३	४
१	५	९
६	७	२

2. Vashikaran: - On Monday mix white *Dhoob* grass white *Dhamchi* and milk of *Kapila* cow and the ink thus is made. Write on *Bhoojpatra* and wear in neck. Ministers and other govt. servants and others will favour.

3. Ucchatan: - On Tuesday with blood of crow using wing of crow as stylus write the yantra on paper. Write the name of the enemy on it. Keep silent at the time of writing yantra. Bury this yantra on the entrance of enemy. It will create *uchattan* in his family.

4. Mohanan: - Mix *Nagkesar* and *gorochan* on Wednesday. With stylus of pomegranate write the yantra on a paper. Make a wick of yantra and in the lamp of mustard oil burn it at noon or in the evening. Write the name of the intended person who will be infatuated.

5. Aakarshan: - During the night of Thursday, make ink of *Gorochan, tagor* and *Ghat*. Write on *Bhooj patra* with ink and stylus of pomegranate. Write the name of the person on the yantra. Bury it at place where you sit. This will cause aakarshan (attraction).

6. For wealth: - On Friday make ink mixed with *Kapur*, *bichh*, *kuth* and honey. Write the yantra on *Bhoojpatra* with stylus of pomegranate or jasmine and wear it in the neck. One is blessed with wealth.

The yantras shown above are some of the examples of *pandhriya* yantra. They may be of other types also.

Gauri Shankar Yantra

This is most powerful yantra for success in all desires, comforts and worldly object. The yantra be written on *Bhojpatra* with Red Sandal and be used in neck or on person, and be written on Monday or Thursday. It can also be engraved on copper or stainless plates.

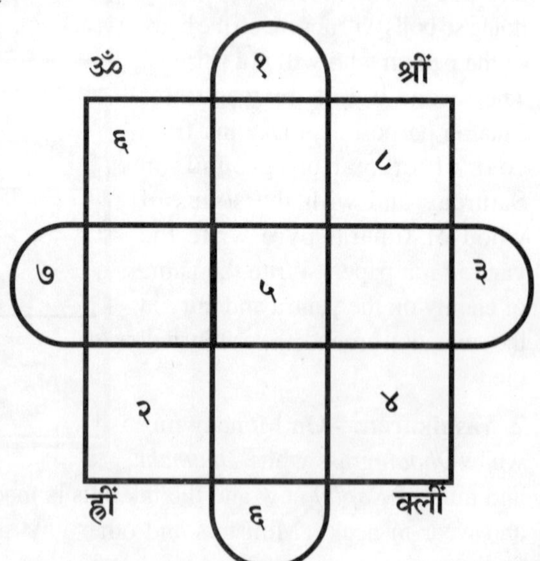

Pandrah Shakti Yantra

The use and method of this yantra is same as above for Gauri Shankar yantra. This is known as Shakti yantra of panchdashi. In addition to the above it bestows victory over enemies.

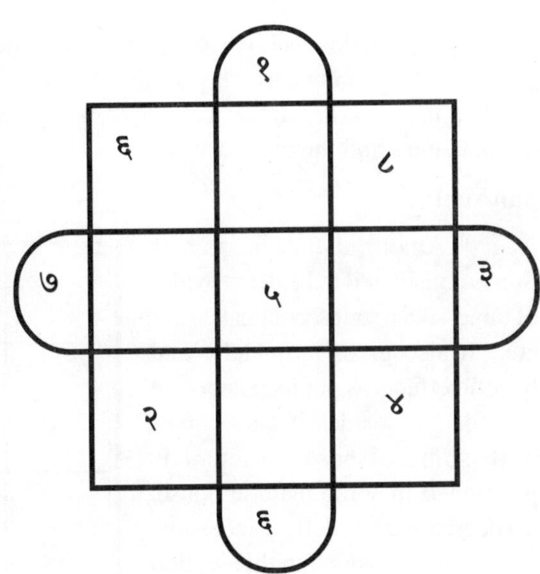

Triangle Pandhriya Yantra

For wealth if the following triangle yantra is drawn by writing the following figures in 2-7-1-2-4-8-5-6-9 order he would certainly get laxmi. The devotee has to draw fifteen thousand yantras and wrap them in wheat flour. Offer them to fish as food. This causes siddhi of the yantra.

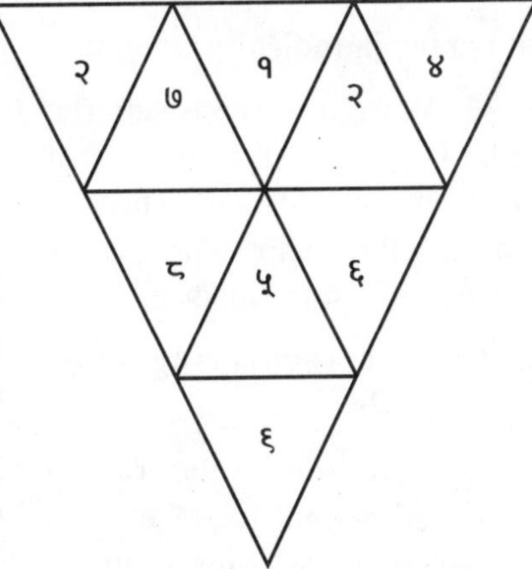

Besides these yantra there are lot of yantras which could be made on the basis of numbers discussed in the beginning of the chapter.

Astrological yantras

Now in this section we would discuss the numerical astrological yantras. This yantras are very similar to Beesa and Pandhriya yantras but their usage is for astrological purposes only. Every yantra is followed by its mantra and the usage for it.

Sun Yantra

Among all the nine planets Sun is considered to be the provider of fame, social status, political power etc. It also gives its malefic and benefic effects as per its position in the chart. Besides it also curses with some diseases when it is positioned in some malefic house. To decrease its malefic effect some yantras are provided in this section which helps the native to keep healthy in the malefic condition of Sun.

६	१	८
७	५	३
२	९	४

Yantra for jaundice

When a person is suffering from Jaundice then *surya* yantra is used. This yantra is to be written on *Bhojpatra* on *Ravi-Pushya yoga* with the ink of *Asthgandh.* This yantra if drawn in the manner as discussed before it will certainly help the native in recovering from jaundice.

Yantra for recovering from tuberculosis

८२	८३	२	७
६	३	५६	५५
५८	६३	८	१
४	५	८४	५७

Following yantra is considered helpful for recovering from tuberculosis. This yantra is drawn on any Ravi-pushya *yog* or any Sunday falling on Ravi pushya yoga. The yantra is written with the stylus of pomegranate and asthgandh ink. After drawing the yantra *panchoopchar* pooja is done. This yantra is tied on the right hand with a pink coloured string or cover the yantra with a copper amulet.

Moon yantra

७	२	९
८	६	४
३	१०	५

In Astrology Moon is considered the heart of the chart. Moon gives its malefic effect in house nos. 5, 9, 12, 1, 4 and 8. It is considered benefic in houses no. 3, 6, 7, 10, and 11. To increase the benefic effect and decrease the malefic effect Moon Yantra is used. Like Sun yantra there are different yantras for Moon which checks the diseases caused due to transit of Moon. Due to malefic effect of Moon the native become lazy, asthmatic and develops diseases related to water. In women it is the factor for decreasing the calcium and develops the calcium related diseases. The menstruation cycle among the women is governed by the transit of Moon. The other problems which are governed by Moon are Urinal track infection, Stone, mental tension, cough and cold. In these circumstances different type of yantras are discovered by the saints and scholars of tantras.

Moon Yantra gives relief from the diseases mentioned above. During cough this Moon yantra is drawn *on Ravi –Pushya yog* or any Monday when *Rohini Nakshatra* is transiting that day. This Moon yantra is drawn with the stylus of *Tulsi* or *chandan* with the ink of sandal mixed camphor. It is written on *Bhojpatra* or in some circumstances it is written on silver plate. This yantra is to be worn on Monday during the Moon's *Hora*. The *Bhojpatra* should be wrapped in the amulet of silver which should be tied with white string on right hand. During the menstruation cycle disorder, women should gaze the yantra daily and worship it in letter and sprit. During Rohini *Nakshatra* if this yantra is tied on the stomach of the women then she will not face any disorder.

Mars Yantra

८	३	१०
९	७	५
४	११	६

In Astrology Mars is considered the significator of power, zeal, enthusiasm, patriotism, anger, hatred etc. Conspiracy, earthquake, explosion, tricks etc., are predicted through this planet. Mars is not considered good as far as maritial life is considered. Sometimes it leads to divorce or separation. Stomach, head, nose, ear, lungs, and blood are significator of Mars in our body. When Mars is malefic in the chart diseases like chicken pox, fever, blood related problems, Hernia, plague, and VD take place.

For rectification of these diseases Mars Yantra is recommended. This yantra is carved or drawn on Tuesday on copper plate or *Bhojpatra* with the stylus of pomegranate and ink of red sandal. The yantra is placed on a pedestal covered with red cloth. The yantra pooja is done with *panchopchar* or *dasupchar*. After completion of pooja, articles of mars are too donated. This yantra is worshipped with the Mars mantra.

Mercury Yantra

९	४	११
१०	८	६
५	१२	७

Mercury is a female planet. Mercury is effective in enhancing the qualities such as singing, dancing, publishing, writing, business etc. When we take note of maternal uncle, uncle, nephew, painting, humour, mathematical calculations, scented oil, medical all these are significator of mercury. Diseases like headache, Asthma, Tuberculoses, blood pressure, cardiac related diseases, and migraine are related to Mercury.

For rectification of mercury related diseases worship of Mercury yantra is recommended. The Yantra is to be drawn on *bhojpatra* with the ink of Asthgandh or white sandal with the stylus of pomegranate. It is also carved on copper plate or bell metal plate.

Writing of the yantra is started during the *hora* of Mercury on Wednesday or during the period of *Ashlesha Nakshatr*a falling on Wednesday. After writing or carving the yantra wash it in the urine of cow or sacred water (Ganges water). The yantra is to be placed on the pedestal covered with green cloth and the mantra of Mercury is recited. The yantra worship is done while facing east direction. If the yantra is placed where it could be seen daily or could be worshipped it will wash off all the malefic effects of Mercury. The articles related to mercury are donated within four hours of sun rise.

३९	४६	२	७
६	३	४३	४२
४५	४०	८	१
४	५	४१	४४

Mercury yantra for migraine

If someone is suffering from migraine then on an auspicious Wednesday the yantra is drawn during the *hora* of Mercury on *bhojpatra* and tied on the forehead of the effected person. The person will get relief through it.

Jupiter Yantra

१०	५	१२
११	९	७
६	१३	८

If Jupiter is posited in benefic houses and is not aspected through any evil planet then the native would be intelligent, studious belonging to a well respected family. Subjects such as money, leisure in life, property, son, children, and ancestral work is deciphered through Jupiter. If Jupiter is malefic in the chart then the native would face problems such as nose, ear, throat, typhoid, goitre, piles etc.

The Jupiter yantra is drawn on Thursday during the *hora* of Jupiter with the stylus of pomegranate with the ink of Asthgandh. This yantra is considered most effective during the *Guru pushya* hora. After writing the yantra it is washed in Ganges water or cow milk. The yantra is to be placed on a pedestal of metal having yellow colour covering with yellow cloth. If the native is suffering from the throat disease then he has to use it in a copper amulet and tie it around the neck.

Jupiter yantra for piles

For those who are suffering from piles following yantra is recommended. The yantra is drawn during the hora of Jupiter with Asthgandh or during *punarvasu* nakshatra on Thursday with the stylus of pomegranate. The yantra is to be tied on the navel of the native for rectification of piles.

१२	३५	३८	५
३७	६	११	३६
७	४०	३३	१०
३४	९	८	३९

Venus Yantra

In astrology Venus is considered the significator of sex, luxuries, etc. If the Venus is strong in the native's chart then he would certainly be attracted towards opposite sex. Profession which are related to luxuries and worldly comforts come in the ambit of Venus. If Venus is malefic in the chart then the native is likely to have problems such as tetanus, diabetes, hysteria etc.

The yantra for Venus is drawn on Friday during auspicious hora of Venus with the stylus of pomegranate and ink of white *chandan* on *bhojpatra*. The

११	६	१३
१२	१०	८
७	१४	९

yantra is carved on gold, silver copper also. After drawing the yantra place the yantra on a pedestal covered with white cloth. Person suffering from tetanus if ties it around the neck he is likely to get relief from the disease during medical supervision.

Saturn Yantra

१२	७	१४
१३	११	९
८	१५	१०

Saturn is considered the significator of iron, buffalo, oil, sesame, salt, sapphire, cremation ground, black colour etc. Disease such as sciatica, skin related, Asthma, leprosy, etc. are due to malefic condition of Saturn in the native's chart.

The yantra is carved during the auspicious hora of Saturn during the Pushya, Ashlesha, *uttar-bhadrapad*, nakshtra on Saturday. It is drawn on *bhojpatra* with Asthgandh and the stylus is of pomegranate.

If the native is suffering from leprosy the yantra is to be tied on the right arm of the native with blue string in a silver amulet.

Rahu Yantra

Rahu is generally known as dragon's head. It is considered as giver. It enhances the effect of the house where it is posited. When Rahu is malefic in the chart the person is likely to have diseases back ache, skin, Hernia, piles etc. Rahu yantra is recommended for healing these diseases. The Rahu yantra is drawn of Saturday during night time. The yantra is drawn on copper plate or *bhojpatra*. The yantra pooja is done with the Rahu

१३	८	१५
१४	१२	१०
९	१६	११

mantra while placing it on a pedestal covered with black cloth.

Ketu Yantra

Ketu is opposite of Rahu i.e., taker. The pooja of the Ketu is done same as of Rahu

१४	९	१६
१५	१३	११
१०	१७	१२

Zodiac Yantras

Aeries

This yantra is of Aries whose lord is Mars. Person having Aries ascendant or Moon Sign Aries should worship this yantra. The mantra for recital is :

ॐ धीं श्रीं श्रीलक्ष्मीनारायाणाय नमः॥

Om Dhim Shrim Laxmi narayana Namah ॥

The yantra is to carved on copper plate or on *bhojpatra* with Asthgand. This mantra is to recited daily in the morning

६	७	२
१	५	९
८	३	४

Taurus

This yantra is of Taurus whose lord is Venus. Person having Taurus ascendant or Moon Sign Taurus should worship this yantra. The mantra for recital is :

४	९	२
३	५	७
८	१	६

ॐ गोपालाय उत्तरध्वजाय नमः।

Om Gopalay uttardvajaya namah ॥

The yantra is to carved on copper plate or on *bhojpatar* with *Asthgand.* This mantra is to recited daily in the morning

Gemini

This yantra is of Gemini whose lord is Mercury. Person having Gemini ascendant or Moon sign Gemini should worship this yantra. The mantra for recital is :

२	७	६
९	५	१
४	३	८

ॐ क्लीं कृष्णाय नमः।

Om Klim Krishnai namah ॥

The yantra is to carved on copper plate or on *bhojpatra* with *Asthgand.* This mantra is to recited daily in the morning

Cancer

This yantra is of Cancer whose lord is Moon. Person having Cancer ascendant or Moon Sign Cancer should worship this yantra. The mantra for recital is :

८	१	६
३	५	७
४	९	२

ॐ ह्रीं हिरण्यगर्भाय अव्यक्तरूपिणे नमः।

Om Hrim Hringarbhaya Avyaktrupine Namah ॥

The yantra is to carved on silver plate or on *bhojpatra* with *Asthgand.* This mantra is to recited daily in the morning

Leo

This yantra is of Leo whose lord is Sun. Person having Leo ascendant or Moon sign Leo should worship this yantra. The mantra for recital is :

ॐ क्लीं ब्रह्मणे जगदाधाराय नमः।

Om Klim Brahamane Jagadadaharaya namah ॥

The yantra is to carved on copper plate or on bhojpatra with Asthgand. This mantra is to recited daily in the morning

६	७	२
१	५	९
८	३	४

Virgo

This yantra is of Virgo whose lord is Mercury. Person having Virgo ascendant or Moon Sign Virgo should worship this yantra. The mantra for recital is :

ॐ पीं पीताम्बराय नमः।

Om Pim Pitambaraya namah ॥

The yantra is to carved on copper plate or on bhojpatra with Asthgand. This mantra is to recited daily in the morning

८	१	६
३	५	७
४	९	२

Libra

This yantra is of Libra whose lord is Venus. Person having Libra ascendant or Moon Sign Libra should worship this yantra. The mantra for recital is :

२	७	६
९	५	१
४	३	८

ॐ तत्त्वनिरंजनाय तारक रामाय नमः।

Om Tatavniranjanaya tarak ramaya namah ॥

The yantra is to carved on copper plate or on bhojpatra with Asthgand. This mantra is to recited daily in the morning.

Scorpio

This yantra is of Scorpio whose lord is Mars. Person having Scorpio ascendant or Moon Sign Scorpio should worship this yantra. The mantra for recital is :

४	९	२
३	५	७
८	१	६

ॐ नारायणाय सूरसिंहाय नमः।

Om Narayana Suryasinghaya namah ॥

The yantra is to carved on copper plate or on bhojpatra with Asthgand. This mantra is to recited daily in the morning.

Sagittarius

This yantra is of Sagittarius whose lord is Jupiter. Person having Sagittarius ascendant or Moon Sign Sagittarius should worship this yantra. The mantra for recital is :

६	७	२
१	५	९
८	३	४

ॐ श्रीं देवकृष्णाय ऊर्ध्वजाय नमः।

Om Shrim Devkrishanaya Udarjaya namah ॥

The yantra is to carved on copper plate or on bhojpatra with Asthgand. This mantra is to recited daily in the morning.

Capricorn

This yantra is of Capricorn whose lord is Saturn. Person having Capricorn ascendant or Moon Sign Capricorn should worship this yantra. The mantra for recital is :

८	१	६
३	५	७
४	९	२

ॐ श्रीं वत्सलाय नमः॥

Om Shrim Vatsalaya namah ॥

The yantra is to carved on copper plate or on bhojpatra with Asthgand. This mantrta is to recited daily in the monrning.

Aquarius

This yantra is for Aquarius whose lord is Saturn. Person having Aquarius ascendant or Moon Sign Aquarius should worship this yantra. The mantra for recital is :

२	७	६
९	५	१
४	३	८

ॐ श्रीं उपेन्द्राय अच्युताय नमः।

Om Shri Upendaraya acchutaya namah ॥

The yantra is to carved on copper plate or on bhojpatra with Asthgand. This mantra is to recited daily in the morning.

Pisces

This yantra is of Pisces whose lord is Jupiter. Person having Pisces ascendant or Moon Sign Pisces should worship this yantra. The mantra for recital is :

४	९	२
३	५	७
८	१	६

ॐ क्लीं उद्धृताय उद्धारिणे नमः।

Om Klim uddhritaya uddharine namah ॥

The yantra is to carved on copper plate, gold or on bhojpatra with Asthgand. This mantra is to recited daily in the morning.

Numerical yantra for different purposes

Yantra for rescue from enemy

On any Saturday night draw this yantra on *bhojpatra* with the juice of thorn apple and stylus of iron. After drawing recite the following mantra for eleven hundred times. Keep this yantra in person and also to others. Till this yantra is in possession of the devotee he will never be scared of enemy.

७६	८६	२	८
७	३	८३	८२
८५	८०	६	१
४	६	०	४८

ॐ नमो भगवते रूद्राय नमः ॥

Om Namo Bhagwate Rudrayee namah ॥

Yantra for disturbing the enemy

This yantra is carved on the fourteenth of black half on a piece of earthen pot with the juice of thorn apple. In this yantra the stylus of iron is used. The earthen pot is put in the fire. Till the piece is in the earthen pot recite the following mantra for 101 times.

३६	४३	२	७
६	३	४	३६
४२	३१	३८	१
४	५	३८	४

ॐ मम् शत्रूणां हन हन स्वाहा ॥

Om Mam shatrunam han han swaha ॥

Yantra for good married life

२५	२०	२७
२६	२४	२२
२१	२८	२३

Draw this yantra on *Bhojpatra* during some auspicious *hora* with the stylus of pomegranate with the ink of Asthgandh and burn the same in the fire lit through camphor. Put the ashes in the roots of any tree. This will lead towards a better and happy married life.

Pisach (ill spirits) peeda Hara Yantra

॥	७	२	७ ॥
४	५ ॥	२ ॥	५
६ ॥	१	८	१ ॥
६	३ ॥	४ ॥	३

This yantra helps the wearer/ keeper to protect himself from the troubles being caused by the demons, ghosts or *Daakinee-Shakinee* (evil goddess always trying to obstruct the progress of human beings). Sit on a wooden platform painted with red or black or dark blue or covered with a cloth having any one of these colours. The yantra may be ties with seven coloured thread and wrapped in a piece of paper. Write the name of the person to whom the yantra is made below the yantra. Also write the name of the evil spirit i.e., *Daakinee/Shaakinee* or the ghosts. In case the trouble is created by human being, the name of such person creating the trouble may be written in place of *Amukh.* For both purposes ink to be used is *yaksha Kardam*.

CHAPTER 14

SAUNDRIYA LAHRI YANTRAS

In Saundriya Lahari by Adi Guru Shankrya Achraya the mantras are considered as a remedy for all diseases, evils, or difficulties for all human ills and also bestows desired objects. In addition Saundriya lahari, has dealt with all aspects of *Devi* as the consort of *Shiva* is also looked upon as a collection of mantras possessed of considerable sanctity and merit. Each stanza has a yantra with *Bijaksara*, prescribed courses of worship, *japa* and distinctive aim to be achieved by the practise of the mantra.

As the Yantras are themselves considered to be possessed of *Caitanya* they are generally inscribed on gold plates. The worship in the case of each yantra is to last for a prescribed number of days and the formalities prescribed for each yantra should be scrupulously adhered to, on each of the days of worship. Such worship is credited with the bestowal of specific fruits. In case, one who is a successful adept in the practice of any other mantra, the fruit of worship of the *Maha Tripursundari* with the reciting of these verses is easily accomplished.

The following general remarks may be offered regarding the worship of the Devi with the Yantra and the *Bijaskara* of the respective verses and the prayer of the Devi with reciting of the respective verses sitting before the Yantra, attended with the *pancopacara* and other observances as detailed below.

Rules of observance for the mantras.

ऋष्यादि- अस्य श्रीसौन्दर्यलहरीस्तोत्रमहामन्त्रस्य गोविन्द ऋषिः अनुष्टुपछन्दः श्रीमहात्रिपुरसुन्दरी देवता, शिवः शक्तया युक्तः इति बीजम, सुधा सिन्धोर्मध्ये इति शक्तिः जपो जल्पः शिल्पम इति कीलकम। श्रीललितामहात्रिपुरसुन्दरीप्रीत्यर्थे पारायणे जपे विनियोगः ।

Rsyaadi: Asya Shri Saundriya Lahri stotra mahamantraasya Govind Rishi anustup chanda Shri Tripursundari Devta, Shiv shaktya yukta iti bijam, sudha sindhormadhya iti shakti, japo jalpa shilpam iti kilkam Shri Lalita Tirpur Sundari pritarrthe parayane jape viniyog.

करन्यासः- हां अंङ्गुष्ठसभ्यां नमः; ह्री तर्जनीभ्यां स्वाह; हूं मध्यमाभ्यां वषट; हैं अनामिकाभ्यां हुं; हौं कनिष्ठिकाभ्यां वौषट; हः करतलकरपृष्ठाभ्यां फट ।

Karanyaasa: Hraam angusthabhayam namah; Hrim to tarjanibhayam svaahaa; Hruum madhaya vasat; Hraim anamikabhayam Hum; Hraum, kanishkabhayam Vausat; Hrah, kartal kar prishthbhayam phat and the backs of the hands Phat.

अंङ्गन्यासः- हां हृदाय नमः; ह्री शिरसे स्वाह; हूं शिखायै वषट; हैं कवचाय हुं; हौं नेत्रत्रयाय वौषट; हः अस्राय फट । भूर्भुवःसुवरोमिति दिग्बन्धः।

Anga Nyaasa: Hram hridaya Namah, Hrim sirshe swah; hrum shikhaya vast hraim kavachaye hum; hrum nettraye vasut; hra astraye phat bhur bhuvya suvartomiti digbandha ।

Dhyana verse

लौहित्यनिर्जिततजपाकुसुमानुरागां पाशाङ्कुशौ धनुरिषूनपि धारयन्तीम ।
ताम्रेक्षणामरूणमाल्यविशेभूषां ताम्बूपूरितमुखीं त्रिपुरां नमामि ॥

Lohitya nirjittajpakusummanuragam
pashangsho dhanurishunapi dharyantim ।
Tamreshanamarunmalayavishebhusham

tambupuritmukhim tripuram namami ॥

पञ्चोपचारः-लं पृथिव्यात्मिकायै गन्धं कल्पयामि; हं आकाशात्मिकायै पुष्पं कल्पयामि ; यं वाय्वात्मिकायै धूपं कल्पयामि; रं वह्नयात्मिकायै दीपं कल्पयामि; वं जलात्मिकायै नैवेद्यं कल्पयामि । सं सर्वात्मिकायै सर्वोपचारम कल्पयामि ॥

Pancopacaara: Lam prithvivayatmikayee gandham kalpayami; ham akashaatmikayee pusham kalpayami; yam vayvatmikayee dhupam kalpayami; ram vahanyatmikayee dipam kalpayamee; vam jalatmikayee nevadayam kalpayami । Sam sarvaatmikayee sarvopacharpan kalpayami ॥

6. Japa The *Shalokas* be recited for the requisite number of times.

7. Naivedya (The food for offerings): Every Yantra has its offerings which is told as and where required.

1. Yantra for all round prosperity

This Yantra is meant for all round prosperity, granting of cherished purposes and solution of intricate problems. The Yantra be inscribed carved or written on gold plate. The mantra is recited for twelve days, one thousand times daily facing east direction. The worship of the yantra is done with *Lalita Sahasarnama* and red flowers are offered during the *Archana*. The foods for offering are cooked rice, scrappings of coconut kernel mixed with powered jaggery and ghee.

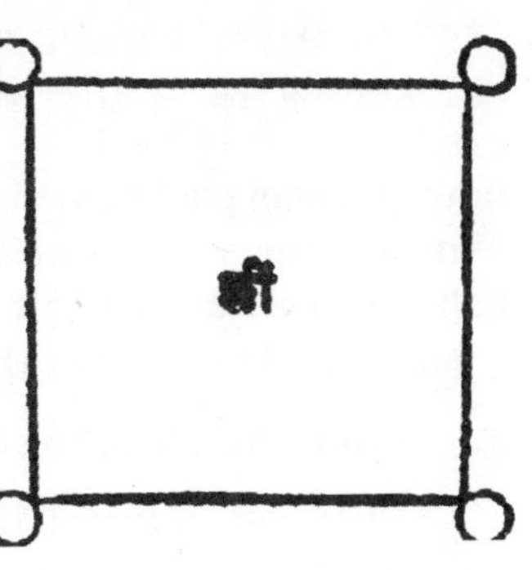

The mantra for recital is:-

शिवः शक्त्या युक्तो यदि भवति शक्तः प्रभवितुं
न चेदेवं देवो न खलु कुशलः स्पन्दितुमपि ।
अतस्त्वामाराध्यां हरिहरविरिञ्चादिभिरपि
प्रणन्तुं स्तोतुं वा कथमकृतपुण्यः प्रभवति ॥ १ ॥

shivaH shaktyaa yukto yadi bhavati shaktaH prabhavitun
na cedevan devo na khalu kushalaH spanditumapi ।
atastvaamaaraadhyaaM hariharavirincaadibhirapi
praNantuM stotuM vaa kathamakR^itapuNyaH prabhavati ॥

2. Yantra for influence

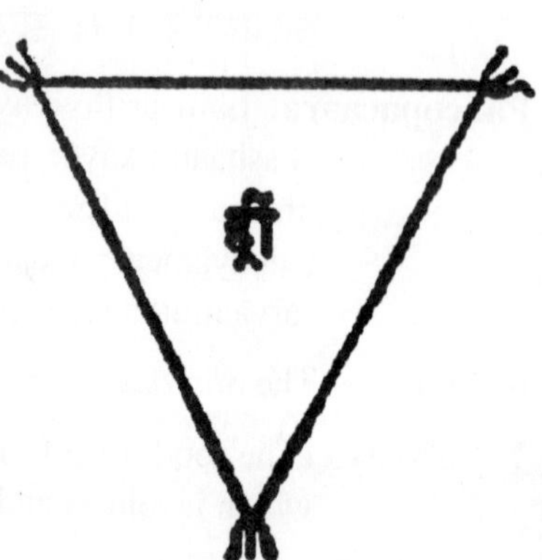

This Yantra is meant for getting vast influence over others and fascination of those around. The Yantra be inscribed carved or written on Gold plate. The mantra is recited for fourty five days, one thousand times daily facing north direction. The worship of the yantra is done with Lalita *thrisahthi* with vermillion. The foods for offering are sweet milk gruel, coconuts and fruits. The mantra for recital is:-

तनीयांसं पांसुं तव चरणपङ्केरुहभवं
विरिञ्चिस्सञ्चिन्वन् विरचयति लोकानविकलम् ।
बहत्येनं शौरिः कथमपि सहस्रेण शिरसां
हरस्संक्षुद्यैनं भजति भसितोद्धूलनविधिम् ॥ २ ॥

taniiyaaMsan paaMsun tava caraNapaNkeruhabhavan
virincissancinvanh viracayati lokaanavikalamh ।
bahatyenaM shauriH kathamapi sahasreNa shirasaaM
harassaMkShudyainaM bhajati hasitoddhuulanavidhimh ॥

3. Yantra for obtaining knowledge

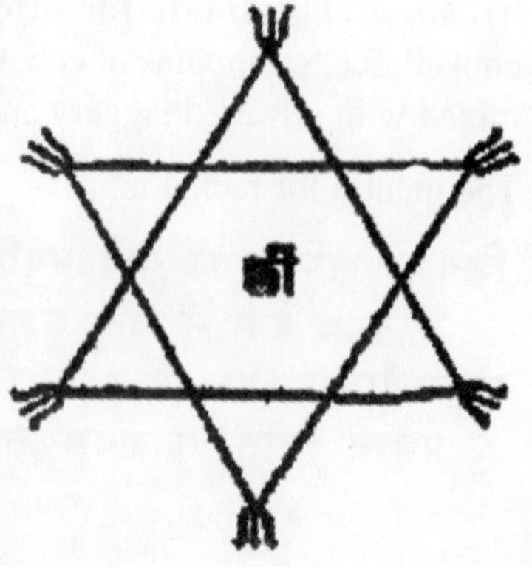

This Yantra is meant for obtaining versatile knowledge in the field of *Vedas*, religion and associated field. The yantra be inscribed carved or written on Gold plate. The mantra is recited for fourty five days, two thousand times daily facing north-east direction. The worship of the yantra is done with Lalita thrisahthi with white flowers such as jasmine, *mallika*, etc. The foods for offering are cooked rice, cakes of black grams, pulse, honey, and betel with slice of areca nut. The mantra for recital is:-

अविद्यानामन्त स्तिमिर मिहिरद्वीपनगरी
जडानां चैतन्य स्तबक मकरन्द स्रुतिझरी ।
दरिद्राणां चिन्तामणिगुणनिका जन्मजलधौ
निमग्नानां दंष्ट्रा मुररिपु वराहस्य भवती ॥ ३ ॥

avidyaanaamanta stimira mihiradviipanagarii
jaDaanaan caitanya stabaka makaranda srutijharii ।
daridraaNaan cintaamaNiguNanikaa janmajaladhau
nimagnaanaan daMShTraa muraripu varaahasya bhavatii ॥

4. Yantra for curing diseases

This Yantra cures diseases, brings out from the uncalled for fear and poverty and helps in possession of vast estates. The yantra be inscribed or carved or written either on gold or silver plate. The mantra is recited for 36 days, (for Gold plated) three thousand times daily facing north-east direction. (Some learned scholars consider east direction as equally good.) and for silver plated the number of days for worshipping the yantra is sixteen, for one thousand times. The worship of the yantra is done with *Lalita Sahasarnama* with vermillion. The foods for offering are cooked rice with green gram pulse, cooked rice with juice of lemons, bits of sugar cane and milk. The mantra for recital is:-

त्वदन्यः पाणिभ्यामभयवरदो दैवतगणः
त्वमेका नैवासि प्रकटितवराभीत्यभिनया ।
भयात् त्रातुं दातुं फलमपि च वाञ्छासमधिकं
शरण्ये लोकानां तव हि चरणावेव निपुणौ ॥ ४ ॥

tvadanyaH paaNibhyaamabhayavarado daivatagaNaH
tvamekaa naivaasi prakaTitavaraabhiityabhinayaa ।
bhayaath traatun daatun phalamapi ca vaanchaasamadhikaM

sharaNye lokaanaan tava hi caraNaaveva nipuNau ॥

5. Yantra for fascinating people

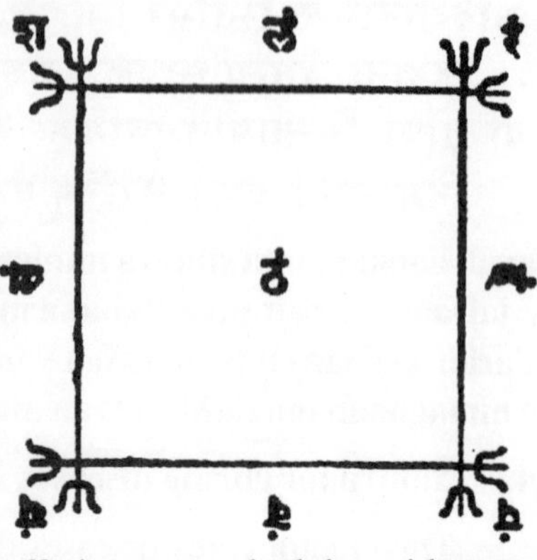

This Yantra gives power to fascinate men and women, enticing people. The yantra be inscribed carved or written either on copper or on nice turmeric powder. The mantra is recited for eight days, two thousand times daily facing east direction. (Some suggest having yantra on head is considered good.) The worship of the yantra is done with Lalita *Ashtothara* and *Durga* Ashtothara with red flowers and vermillion. The foods for offering are cooked rice with green gram pulse, gruel made of green gram pulse and jaggery, honey and coconuts. The mantra for recital is:

हरिस्त्वामाराध्य प्रणतजनसौभाग्यजननीं
पुरा नारी भूत्वा पुररिपुमपि क्षोभमनयत् ।
स्मरोऽपि त्वां नत्वा रतिनयनलेह्येन वपुषा
मुनीनामप्यन्तः प्रभवति हि मोहाय महताम् ॥ ५ ॥

haristvaamaaraadhya praNatajanasaubhaagyajananiin
puraa naarii bhuutvaa puraripumapi kShobhamanayath ।
smaroapi tvaan natvaa ratinayanalehyena vapuShaa
muniinaamapyantaH prabhavati hi mohaaya mahataamh ॥

6. Yantra for cure from impotency

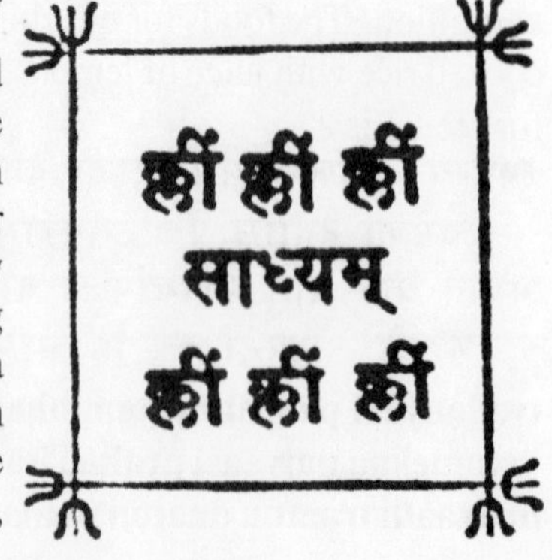

This Yantra cures impotency and bestows children. The yantra be inscribed carved or written either on gold plate or milk placed in a silver vessel. The mantra is recited for twenty one days, five hundred times daily facing east direction. The worship of the yantra is done with Lalita thrisahthi with Jasmine or *Champaka* flowers. The foods for offering are bits of sugar cane, milk gruel, betel, and slices of arica nut with spices.

The mantra for recital is:

धनुः पौष्पं मौर्वी मधुकरमयी पञ्च विशिखाः
वसन्तः सामन्तो मलयमरुदायोधनरथः ।
तथाप्येकः सर्वं हिमगिरिसुते कामपि कृपाम्
अपाङ्गात्ते लब्ध्वा जगदिद-मनङ्गो विजयते ॥ ६ ॥

dhanuH pauShpan maurvii madhukaramayii panca vishikhaaH
vasantaH saamanto malayamarudaayodhanarathaH ।
tathaapyekaH sarvaM himagirisute kaamapi kRipaamh
apaaNgaatte labdhvaa jagadidamanaNgo vijayate ॥

7. Yantra for winning over enemies

This Yantra is helpful in enthralling even royal personages and overcoming the enemies. The yantra be inscribed carved or written either on gold plate or holy ashes (*bhasma*) levelled on a copper plate. The mantra is recited for fourty five days, one thousand times daily facing north-east direction. The worship of the yantra is done with Durga Sahasarnama with Vermillion. The foods for offering are cooked rice, curd, fruit juice and sweet milk-gruel. Some of the scholars are of the view that the yantra be worn on crest.

The mantra for recital is:

क्वणत्काञ्चीदामा करिकलभकुम्भस्तननता
परिक्षीणा मध्ये परिणतशरच्चन्द्रवदना ।
धनुर्बाणान् पाशं सृणिमपि दधाना करतलैः
पुरस्तादास्तां नः पुरमथितुराहोपुरुषिका ॥ ७ ॥

kvaNatkaanciidaamaa karikalabhakumbhastananataa
parikShiiNaa madhye pariNatasharaccandravadanaa ।
dhanurbaaNaanh paashaM sRiNimapi dadhaanaa karatalaiH
purastaadaastaaM naH puramathituraahopuruShikaa ॥

8. Yantra for releasing from prison

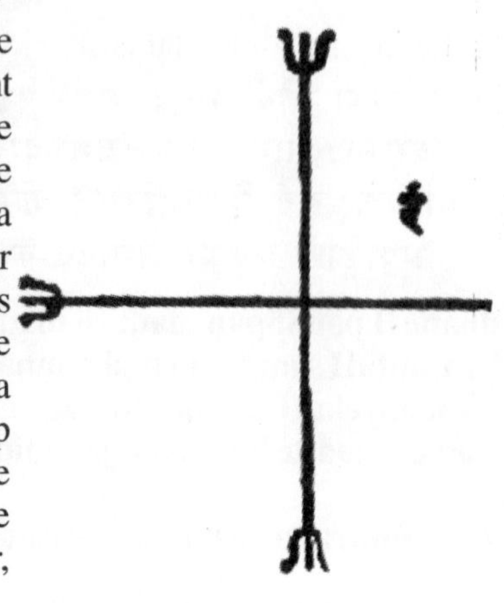

This Yantra is helpful in release from all kinds of bondage, imprisonment and debts and fulfils all desires. The yantra be inscribed on thick sandal paste mixed with saffron powder, placed in a silver plate. The mantra is recited for 16 days, one thousand and eight times daily facing north direction. The worship of the yantra is done with Durga Ashtothara with red flowers and a lamp lit with gingelly oil to burn before yantra. The foods for offering are cooked rice mixed with powdered paper, jaggery, gruel and coconut.

The mantra for recital is:

सुधासिन्धोर्मध्ये सुरविटपिवाटीपरिवृते
मणिद्वीपे नीपोपवनवति चिन्तामणिगृहे ।
शिवाकारे मञ्चे परमशिवपर्यङ्कनिलयां
भजन्ति त्वां धन्याः कतिचन चिदानन्दलहरीम् ॥ ८॥

sudhaasindhormadhye suraviTapivaaTiiparivRite
maNidviipe niipopavanavati cintaamaNigRihe ।
shivaakaare mance paramashivaparyaNkanilayaan
bhajanti tvaan dhanyaaH katicana cidaanandalahariimh ॥

9. Yantra for return of relations from foreign country

This Yantra is helpful in return of persons who are long absent and master of fundamentals. The yantra be inscribed on gold plate or draw it with paste of musk. The mantra is recited for fourty five days, one thousand and eight times daily facing north-east direction. The worship

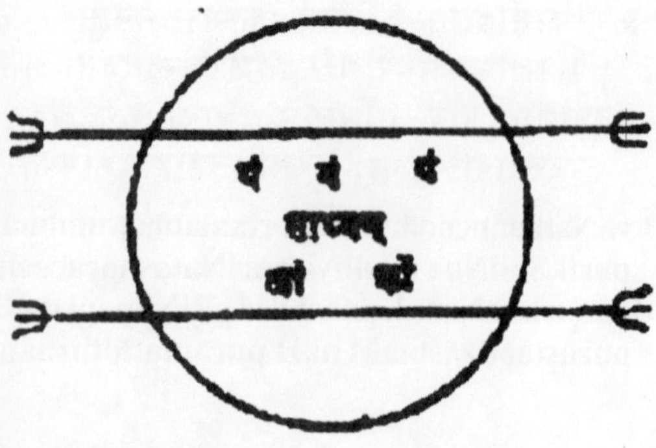

of the yantra is done with Lalita *thrisathi* with white flowers. The foods for offering are cooked rice sweet milk gruel, coconuts and honey.

The mantra for recital is:

महीं मूलाधारे कमपि मणिपूरे हुतवहं
स्थितं स्वाधिष्ठाने हृदि मरुतमाकाशमुपरि ।
मनोऽपि भ्रूमध्ये सकलमपि भित्वा कुलपथं
सहस्रारे पद्मे सह रहसि पत्या विहरसे ॥९॥

mahiin muulaadhaare kamapi maNipuure hutavahaM
sthitaM svaadhiShThaane hRidi marutamaakaashamupari ।
manoapi bhruumadhye sakalamapi bhitvaa kulapathaM
sahasraare padme saha rahasi patyaa viharase ॥

10. Yantra for proper functioning of body.

This Yantra is helpful in purification of bodily frame cures watery diseases, develops breasts and proper menstruation in the case of females. The yantra be inscribed on gold plate. The mantra is recited for six days, one thousand times daily facing east direction. The worship of the yantra is done with Durga Sahasarnama with Vermillion. The foods for offering are cooked rice, plantains and juicy fruits.

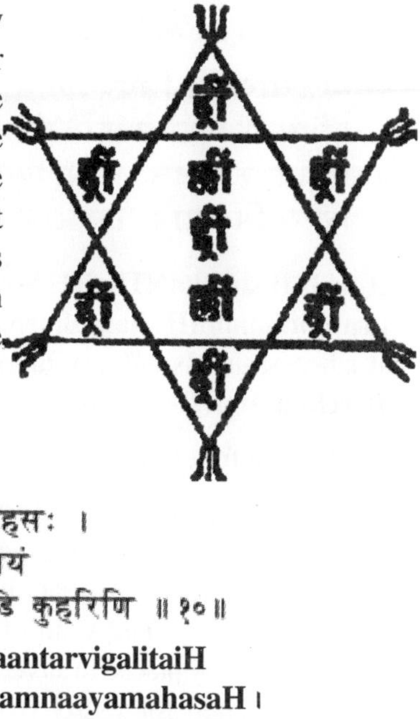

The mantra for recital is:

सुधाधारासारैश्चरणयुगलान्तर्विगलितैः
प्रपञ्चं सिञ्चन्ती पुनरपि रसाम्नायमहसः ।
अवाप्य स्वां भूमिं भुजगनिभमध्युष्टवलयं
स्वमात्मानं कृत्वा स्वपिषि कुलकुण्डे कुहरिणि ॥१०॥

sudhaadhaaraasaaraishcaraNayugalaantarvigalitaiH
prapancaM sincantii punarapi rasaamnaayamahasaH ।
avaapya svaan bhuumin bhujaganibhamadhyuShTavalayaM
svamaatmaanan kRitvaa svapiShi kulakuNDe kuhariNi ॥

11. Yantra for progeny

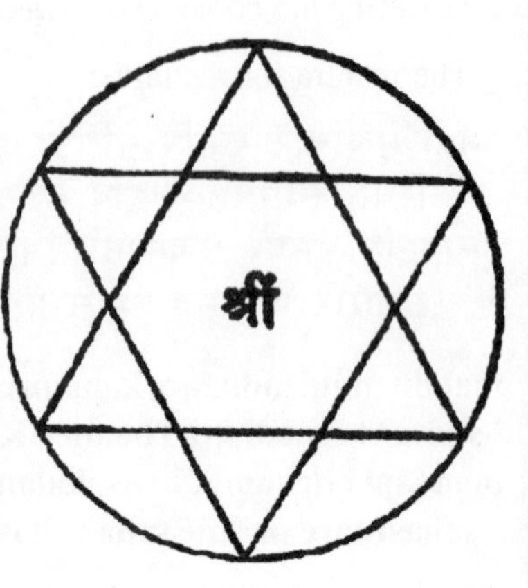

This Yantra is helpful in getting issues. A barren woman is blessed with a child if this yantra is practised in letter and spirit. The yantra be inscribed on gold plate or butter. The yantra on butter is to be consumed daily by the lady herself. The mantra is recited for eighteen days, one thousand times daily facing north direction. The worship of the yantra is done with Lalita Sahasarnama with Vermillion. The foods for offering are cooked rice, cooked rice mixed with turmeric, powder and ghee, jaggery cum green-gram pulse and fruits.

The mantra for recital is:

चतुर्भिः श्रीकण्ठैः शिवयुवतिभिः पञ्चभिरपि
प्रभिन्नाभिः शम्भोर्नवभिरपि मूलप्रकृतिभिः ।
चतुश्चत्वारिंशद्वसुदलकलाश्रत्रिवलय
त्रिरेखाभिः सार्धं तव शरणकोणाः परिणताः ॥ ११ ॥

caturbhiH shriikaNThaiH shivayuvatibhiH pancabhirapi
prabhinnaabhiH shambhornavabhirapi muulaprakRitibhiH ।
catushcatvaariMshadvasudalakalaashratrivalaya
trirekhaabhiH saardhan tava sharaNakoNaaH pariNataaH ॥

12. Yantra for speech power

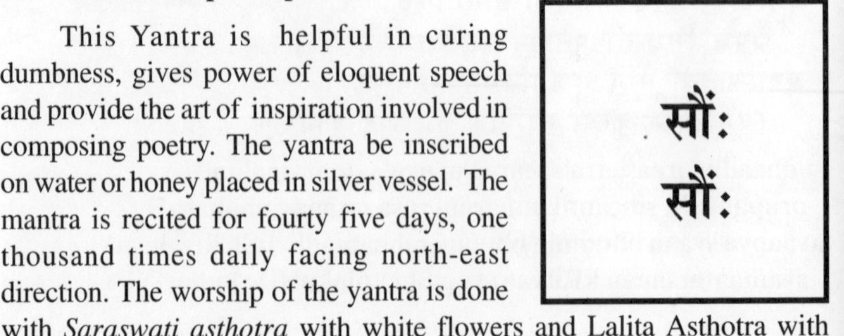

This Yantra is helpful in curing dumbness, gives power of eloquent speech and provide the art of inspiration involved in composing poetry. The yantra be inscribed on water or honey placed in silver vessel. The mantra is recited for fourty five days, one thousand times daily facing north-east direction. The worship of the yantra is done with *Saraswati asthotra* with white flowers and Lalita Asthotra with jasmine flowers. The foods for offering are cooked rice, pomegranates and honey. The mantra for recital is:

त्वदीयं सौन्दर्यं तुहिनगिरिकन्ये तुलयितुं
  कवीन्द्राः कल्पन्ते कथमपि विरिञ्चिप्रभृतयः ।
यदालोकौत्सुक्यादमरललना यान्ति मनसा
  तपोभिर्दुष्प्रापामपि गिरिशसायुज्यपदवीम् ॥ १२ ॥

tvadiiyam saundaryan tuhinagirikanye tulayitun
kaviindraaH kalpante kathamapi virinciprabhRitayaH ।
yadaalokautsukyaadamaralalanaa yaanti manasaa
tapobhirduShpraapaamapi girishasaayujyapadaviimh ॥

13. Yantra for eradicating impotency.

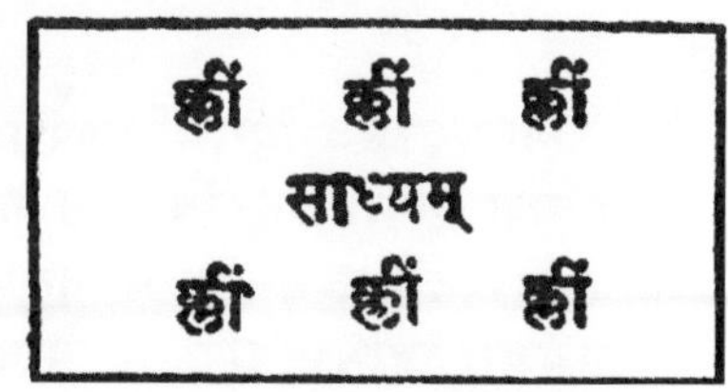

This Yantra is helpful in eradicating the impotency and enhance the power of attracting the women. The yantra be inscribed on gold plate or lead plate. The mantra is recited for 6 days, one thousand and eight times daily facing east direction. The worship of the yantra is done with Lalita thrisathi with Vermillion. The foods for offering are cooked rice, scrapping of coconut kernel mixed with powdered jaggery and milk.

The mantra for recital is:

नरं वर्षीयांसं नयनविरसं नर्मसु जडं
  तवापाङ्गालोके पतितमनुधावन्ति शतशः ।
गलद्वेणीबन्धाः कुचकलशविस्रस्तसिचया
  हठात त्रुट्यत्काञ्च्यो विगलितदुकूला युवतयः ॥ १३ ॥

naraM varShiiyaaMsaM nayanavirasan narmasu jaDan
tavaapaaNgaaloke patitamanudhaavanti shatashaH ।
galadveNiibandhaaH kucakalashavisrastasicayaa
haThaat truTyatkaancyo vigalitadukuulaa yuvatayaH ॥

14. Yantra for removing poverty.

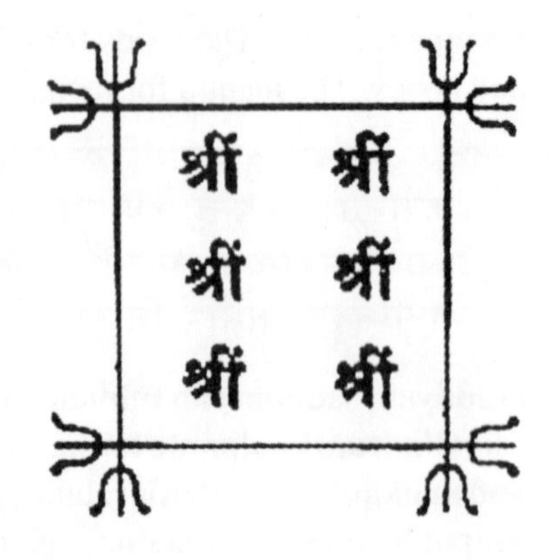

This Yantra is helpful in removing poverty of an individual practitioner and in case of nation it gives freedom from famine, drought etc. The yantra be inscribed on gold plate. The mantra is recited for fourty four days, one thousand and eight times daily facing north direction. The worship of the yantra is done with Lalita Sahasarnama with red flowers and Vermillion. The foods for offering are cooked rice, black gram cakes, milk gruel and betel with slices of nuts. The mantra for recital is:

क्षितौ षट्पञ्चाशद द्विसमधिकपञ्चाशदुदके
हुताशे द्वाषष्टिश्चतुरधिकपञ्चाशदनिले ।
दिवि द्विष्षट्त्रिंशन्मनसि च चतुष्षष्टिरिति ये
मयूखास्तेषामप्युपरि तव पादाम्बुजयुगम् ॥१४॥

kShitau ShaTpancaashad dvisamadhikapancaashadudake hutaashe dvaaShaShTishcaturadhikapancaashadanile.divi ।
dviShShaThtriMshanmanasi ca catuShShaShTiriti ye
mayuukhaasteShaamapyupari tava paadaambujayugamh ॥

15. Yantra for getting poetry imagination.

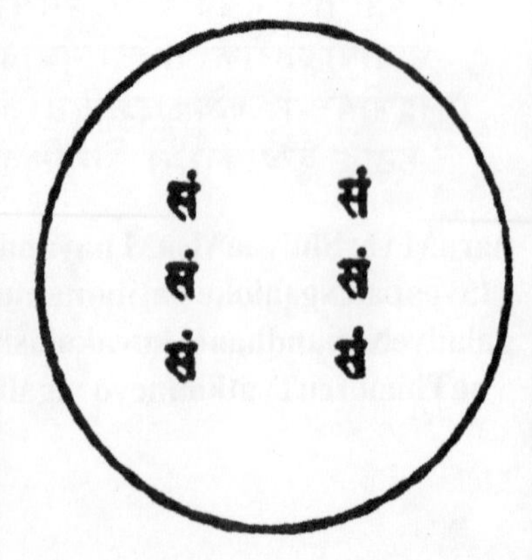

This Yantra is helpful in getting poetic imagination and enlightenment. The yantra be inscribed on gold plate or in water placed in silver vessel. The mantra is recited for fourty five days, one thousand times daily, facing east direction. The worship of the yantra is done with Saraswati Asthotra with white flowers and Lalita Asthotra with red flowers. The foods for offering are cooked rice, honey, brown sugar and fruits.The mantra for recital is:

शरज्ज्योत्स्नाशुद्धां शशियुतजटाजूटमुकुटां
वरत्रासत्राणस्फटिकघुटिकापुस्तककराम् ।
सकृन्नत्वां नत्वा कथमिव सतां संन्निदधते
मधुक्षीरद्राक्षामधुरिमधुरीणाः कणितयः ॥ १५ ॥

sharajjyotsnaashuddhaaM shashiyutajaTaajuuTamukuTaaM varatraasatraaNasphaTikaghuTikaapustakakaraamh । sakRinnatvaan natvaa kathamiva sataaM saMnnidadhate madhukShiiradraakShaamadhurimadhuriiNaaH kaNitayaH ॥

16. Yantra for immunity from evil spirits.

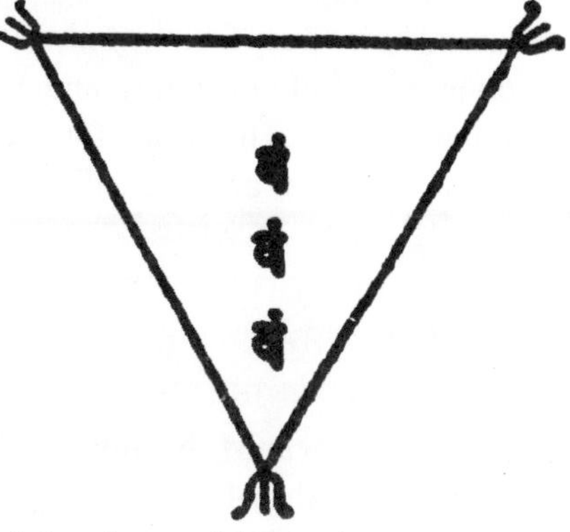

This Yantra gives education, knowledge of Vedas/ *Shastras* knowledge of different languages and immunity from evil effects of spirits. The yantra be inscribed on gold or copper plate. The mantra is recited for fourty four days, one thousand and eight times daily facing north-east direction. The worship of the yantra is done with Lalita thrisathi and *Saraswati Ashtothara* with jasmine or *Mullica* flowers. The foods for offering are cooked rice mixed with curd, milk, fruits and honey. The mantra for recital is:

कवीन्द्राणां चेतःकमलवनबालातपरुचिं
भजन्ते ये सन्तः कतिचिदरुणामेव भवतीम् ।
विरिञ्चिप्रेयस्यास्तरुणतरशृङ्गारलहरी
गभीराभिर्वाग्भिर्विदधति सतांरञ्जनममी ॥ १६ ॥

kaviindraaNaan cetaHkamalavanabaalaataparucin bhajante ye santaH katicidaruNaameva bhavatiimh । virincipreyasyaastaruNatarashRiNgaaralaharii gabhiiraabhirvaagbhirvidadhati sataaMranjanamamii ॥

17. Yantra for good bridegroom.

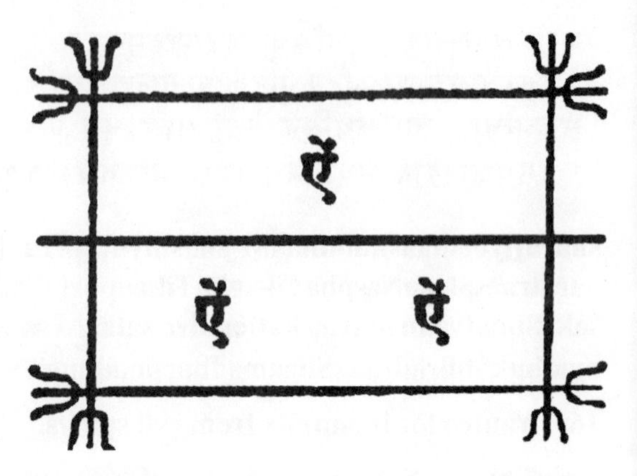

This Yantra could be worshipped for having deep knowledge in science and Shastras, for getting good bride groom and blessings of great men. The yantra be inscribed on gold or copper plate. The mantra is recited for fourty five days, one thousand times daily facing north-east direction. The worship of the yantra is done with Lalita asthotra and Saraswati Asthotra with *champak* or jasmine flowers. The foods for offering are milk, honey bits of sugar cane, brown sugar and cooked rice. The mantra for recital is:

सवित्रीभिर्वाचां शशिमणिशिलाभङ्गरुचिभिः
वशिन्याद्याभिस्त्वां सह जननि संचिन्तयति यः ।
स कर्ता काव्यानां भवति महतां भङ्गिरुचिभिः
वचोभिर्वाग्देवीवदनकमलामोदमधुरैः ॥ १७ ॥

savitriibhirvaacaaM shashimaNishilaabhaNgarucibhiH
vashinyaadyaabhistvaaM saha janani saMcintayati yaH ।
sa kartaa kaavyaanaan bhavati mahataan bhaNgirucibhiH
vacobhirvaagdeviivadanakamalaamodamadhuraiH ॥

18. Yantra for achieving mastery in different trades

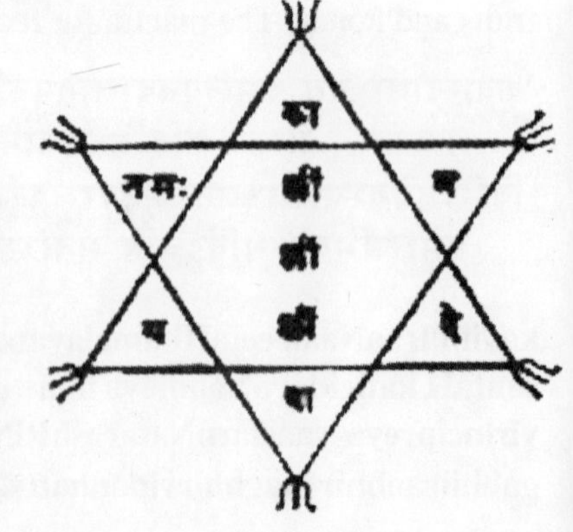

This Yantra is helpful in mastering painting, sculpture, drawing etc., attracting women and children, control over animals and spirits and attaining power of spoken words becoming true. The yantra be inscribed on gold plate or thick sandal paste, vermillion, or nice turmeric powder (levelled on a silver plate or plantain leaf). The mantra is recited for fourty four days, one thousand and eight times daily facing east direction. The worship of the yantra is done with Lalita Sahasarnama with red lotus petals. The foods for offering are cooked rice, mixed with turmeric powder and a little ghee, sweet milk gruel, boiled milk fruits and betel with slices or arica nut.

The mantra for recital is:

तनुच्छायाभिस्ते तरुणतरणिश्रीसरणिभिः
दिवं सर्वामुर्वीमरुणिमनिमग्नां स्मरति यः ।
भवन्त्यस्य त्रस्यद्वनहरिणशालीननयनाः
सहोर्वश्या वश्याः कति कति न गीर्वाणगणिकाः ॥ १८ ॥

tanucchaayaabhiste taruNataraNishriisaraNibhiH divaM sarvaamurviimaruNimanimagnaaM smarati yaH । bhavantyasya trasyadvanahariNashaaliinanayanaaH sahorvashyaa vashyaaH kati kati na giirvaaNagaNikaaH ॥

19. Yantra for attraction.

This Yantra is helpful in attracting young woman, gaining influence in royal courts and government and control over wild animals. The yantra be inscribed on gold plate or thick sandal paste or holy ashes, or vermillion (placed in a silver or copper plate). The mantra is recited for twenty five days, one thousand times daily facing north direction. The worship of the yantra is done with Durga Asthotra and Lalita Sahasarnama with Vermillion or washed rice grains mixed with vermillion. The foods for offering are cooked rice mixed with boiled milk, fruits and honey.

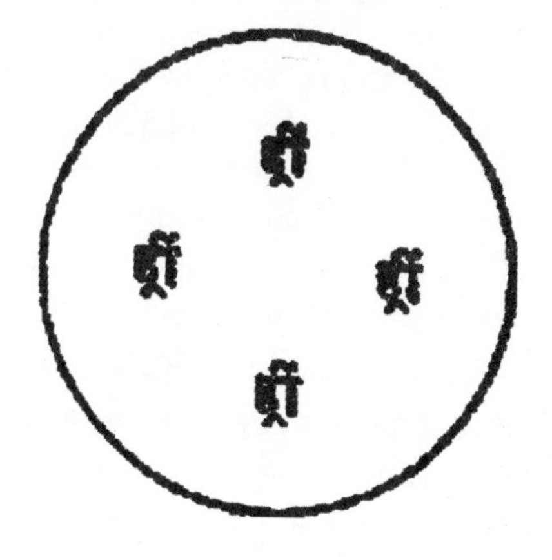

The mantra for recital is:

मुखं बिन्दुं कृत्वा कुचयुगमधस्तस्य तदधो
हरार्ध ध्यायेद्योहरमहिषि ते मन्मथकलाम् ।
स सद्यः संक्षोभं नयति वनिता इत्यतिलघु
त्रिलोकीमप्याशु भ्रमयति रवीन्दुस्तनयुगाम् ॥ १९ ॥

mukhan bindun kRitvaa kucayugamadhastasya tadadho
haraardhan dhyaayedyoharamahiShi te manmathakalaamh ।
sa sadyaH saMkShobhan nayati vanitaa ityatilaghu
trilokiimapyaashu bhramayati raviindustanayugaamh ॥

20. Yantra for curing from poison.

This Yantra helps in curing poisonous fevers, remedy against poison, cures effects of evil eyes and confers power to charm snakes and other poisonous reptiles. The yantra be inscribed on holy Ashes or water kept in a copper plate. The mantra is recited for twenty five days, one thousand times daily facing north direction. The worship of the yantra is done through Durga Ashtothara with *bilva* leaves or leaves of *Vibhuti* plant. The foods for offering are cooked rice mixed with powder of gingelly seeds, milk gruel coconuts and fruits.

The mantra for recital is:

किरन्तीमङ्गेभ्यः किरणनिकुरम्बामृतरसं
हृदि त्वामाधत्ते हिमकरशिलामूर्तिमिव यः ।
स सर्पाणां दर्पं शमयति शकुन्ताधिप इव
ज्वरप्लुष्टान दृष्ट्या सुखयति सुधासारसिरया ॥ २० ॥

kirantiimaNgebhyaH kiraNanikurambaamRitarasaM
hRidi tvaamaadhatte himakarashilaamuurtimiva yaH ।
sa sarpaaNaan darpaM shamayati shakuntaadhipa iva
jvarapluShTaan dR^iShTyaa sukhayati sudhaasaarasirayaa ॥

21. Yantra for gaining physical and military strength

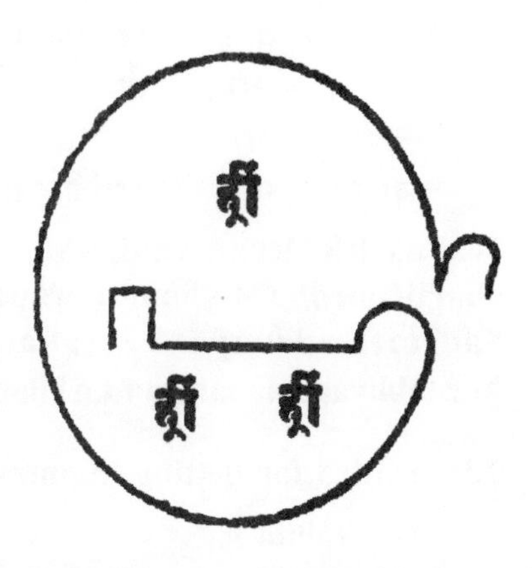

This yantra helps in subduing enemies, freedom from unpopularity, gaining of physical and military strength. The Yantra be inscribed on gold or silver or copper plate. The mantra is recited for one thousand times for eleven days facing west direction. The worship of the yantra be done through Lalita *Asthotri* with vermillion. The foods for offerings are cooked rice, fruits, honey and brown sugar. The mantra for recital is:

तटिल्लेखातन्वीं तपनशशिवैश्वानरमयीं
निषण्णां षण्णामप्युपरि कमलानां तव कलाम् ।
महापद्माटव्यां मृदितमलमायेन मनसा
महान्तः पश्यन्तो दधति परमाह्लादलहरीम् ॥ २१ ॥

taTillekhaatanviin tapanashashivaishvaanaramayiin
niShaNNaaM ShaNNaamapyupari kamalaanaan tava kalaamh ।
mahaapadmaaTavyaan mRiditamalamaayena manasaa
mahaantaH pashyanto dadhati paramaahlaadalahariimh ॥

22. Yantra for getting relief from debts.

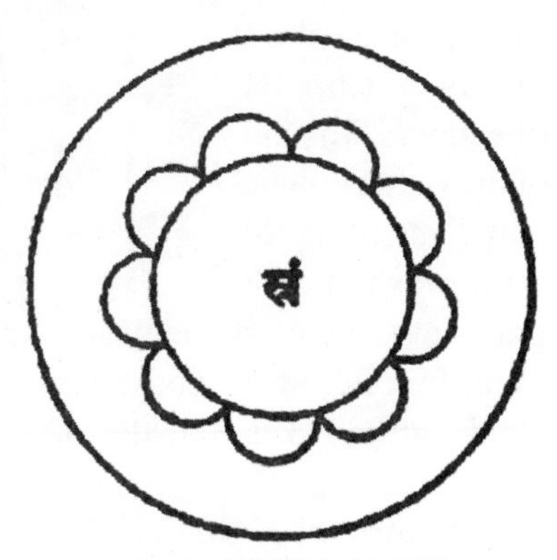

The Yantra is useful in getting attainment of vast, wealth and relief from debts, getting a vehicle, freedom from danger. Yantra be inscribed on gold plate. The mantra be recited for one thousand times, for fourty five days, inside the house, preferably in a place fit for worship, facing north direction. The yantra be worshipped with Lakshmi - Sahasarnama with red-lotus petals. Food for offerings are sweet milk-gruel, black-gram cake, cooked rice, fruits and betel with slices of arica nuts. The mantra for recital is:

त्वया हृत्वा वामं वपुरपरितृप्तेन मनसा
  शरीरार्धं शम्भोरपरमपि शङ्के हृतमभूत ।
यदेतत्त्वद्रूपं सकलमरुणाभं त्रिनयनं
  कुचाभ्यामानम्रं कुटिलशशिचूडालमुकुटम् ॥

tvayaa hR^itvaa vaamaM vapuraparitRiptena manasaa
shariiraardhaM shambhoraparamapi shaNke hRitamabhuut।
yadetattvadruupaM sakalamaruNaabhaM trinayanaM
kucaabhyaamaanamran kuTilashashicuuDaalamukuTamh ॥

23. Yantra for getting immunity curses of deceased ancestors

The Yantra is useful in getting immunity from evil spirits, demon, curses of deceased ancestors and incurable diseases. Yantra be inscribed on gold plate. The mantra should be recital for one thousand and eight times, for 32 days facing north-east direction. Worship of the yantra is done with *Rudra* thrisathi with washed rice grains mixed with sternum and Durga-Ashtothara with bilva leaves. The foods for offering are cooked rice mixed with pepper powder, and ghee, black -gram cakes, powder of sesame mixed with brown sugar and coconuts.

The mantra for recital is:

जगत्सूते धाता हरिरवति रुद्रः क्षपयते
तिरस्कुर्वन्नेतत्स्वमपि वपुरीशस्तिरयति ।
सदापूर्वः सर्वं तदिदमनुगृह्णाति च शिव
स्तवाज्ञामालम्ब्य क्षनचलितयोर्भ्रूलतिकयोः ॥

jagatsuute dhaataa hariravati rudraH kShapayate
tiraskurvannetatsvamapi vapuriishastirayati ।
sadaapuurvaH sarvan tadidamanugRihNaati ca shiva
stavaajnaamaalambya kShanacalitayorbhruulatikayoH ॥

24. Yantra for increase in income

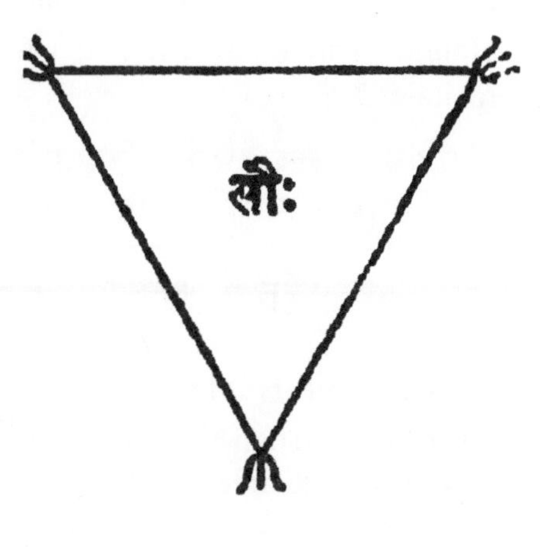

The Yantra is useful in increase of income, over lordship, honour and influence. Yantra be inscribed on gold or copper plate. The mantra be recited for one thousand and eight times, for fourty four days facing east direction. During worship Lalita thrisathi be orated with vermillion. Foods for offerings are cooked rice, honey mixed with milk, brown sugar and fruits. The mantra for recital is:

त्रयाणां देवानां त्रिगुणजनितानान्तव शिवे
भवेत पूजा पूजा तव चरणयोर्या विरचिता ।
तथा हि त्वत्पादोद्वहनमणिपीठस्य निकटे
स्थिता ह्येते शश्वन मुकुलितकरोत्तंसमकुटाः ॥

trayaaNaan devaanaan triguNajanitaanaantava shive
bhavet puujaa puujaa tava caraNayoryaa viracitaa ।
tathaa hi tvatpaadodvahanamaNipiiThasya nikaTe
sthitaa hyete shashvan mukulitakarottaMsamakuTaaH ॥

25. Yantra for destroying enemies

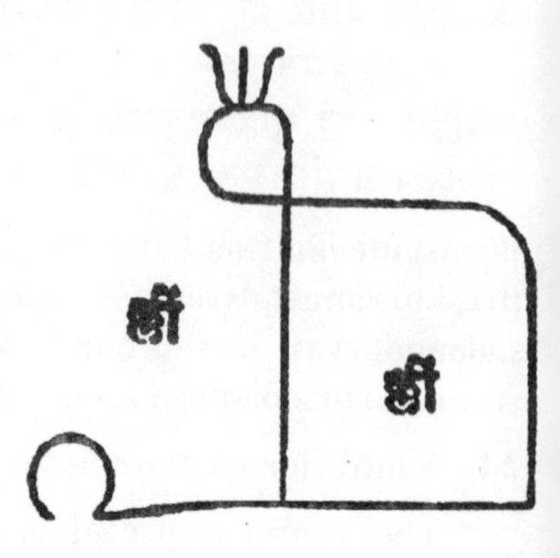

The Yantra is destroyer of enemies and all round success. Yantra be inscribed on gold or lead sheet. The mantra be recited for one thousand times on 6 new-Moon days facing north direction. The worshipping is done through Lalita-thrisathi with vermillion, offerings. The foods for offering are rice cooked with green gram pulse and jaggery, coconuts plantain fruits.The mantra for recital is:

विरिञ्चिः पञ्चत्वं व्रजति हरिराप्नोति विरतिं
विनाशं कीनाशो भजति धनदो याति निधनम् ।
वितन्द्री माहेन्द्री विततिरपि संमीलति दृशां
महासंहारेऽस्मिन विहरति सति त्वत्पतिरसौ ॥ :

virinciH pancatvaM vrajati hariraapnoti
viratiM vinaashan kiinaasho bhajati dhanado yaati nidhanamh ।
vitandrii maahendrii vitatirapi saMmiilati dRishaan
mahaasaMhaare.asmin viharati sati tvatpatirasau ॥

26. Yantra for attainment of knowledge

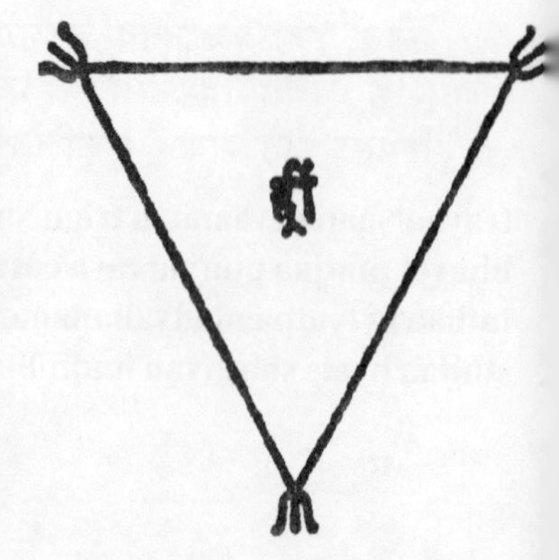

The Yantra is useful in attainment of knowledge of self (*atmagyana*) and misery of spells. Yantra be inscribed on gold or copper plate. The mantra for recital is one thousand times, for fourty five days, facing north east direction. The yantra be worshipped through *Lalita thrisathi* with Champaka flowers or washed rice grams mixed with vermillion. Food for offerings are sweet gruel- cooked lies and milk.

The mantra for recital is:

जपो जल्पः शिल्पं सकलमपि मुद्राविरचना
गतिः प्रादक्षिण्यक्रमणमशनाद्याहुतिविधिः ।
प्रणामस्संवेशस्सुखमखिलमात्मार्पणदृशा
सपर्यापर्यायस्तव भवतु यन्मे विलसितम् ॥

**japo jalpaH shilpaM sakalamapi mudraaviracanaa gatiH praadakShiNyakramaNamashanaadyaahutividhiH ।
praNaamassaMveshassukhamakhilamaatmaarpaNadRishaa
saparyaaparyaayastava bhavatu yanme vilasitamh ॥**

27. Yantra for immunity from accidents

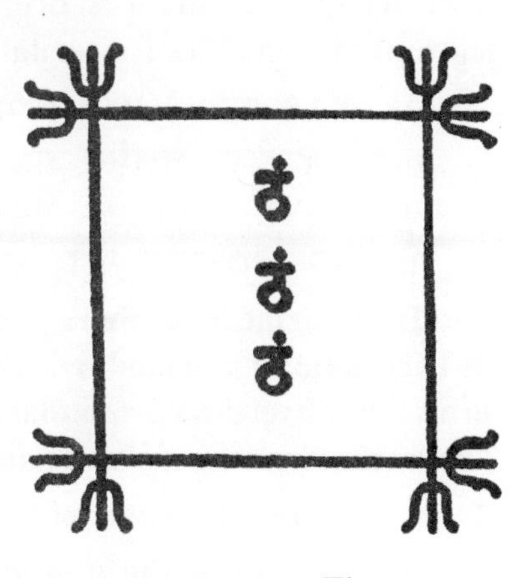

The yantra is effective in immunity from accidents, unnatural and untimely death and attainment of all defies. The Yantra be inscribed on plate of gold or of alloy of five metals. The mantra should be recited for one thousand times for fourty five days facing south-east direction. The yantra be worshipped through Durga Ashtothara with red flowers. Foods for offering are cooked food, sesame powder mixed with brown sugar, black-gram cakes, milk-gruel, betel and slices of arnica nut. The mantra for recital is:

सुधामप्यास्वाद्य प्रतिभयजरामृत्युहरिणीं
विपद्यन्ते विश्वे विधिशतमखाद्या दिविषदः ।
कराळं यत्क्ष्वेळं कबलितवतः कालकलना
न शम्भोस्तन्मूलं तव जननि ताटङ्कमहिमा ॥

**sudhaamapyaasvaadya pratibhayajaraamRityuhariNiiM
vipadyante vishve vidhishatamakhaadyaa diviShadaH ।
karaaLaM yatkShveLan kabalitavataH kaalakalanaa na
shambhostanmuulan tava janani taaTaNkamahimaa ॥**

28. Yantra for bringing bad characters to righteous path

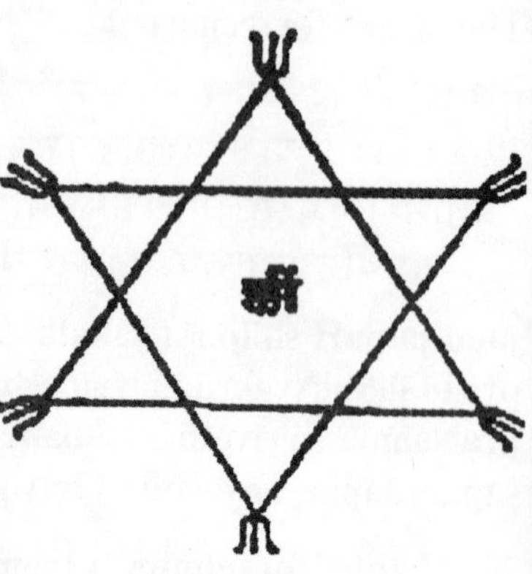

This yantra is for taming wild animals, bringing bad characters to righteous path, quick and easy delivery in case of pregnant. This Yantra is inscribed on gold or copper plate The mantra is recited for one thousand and one times for forty eight days, facing east direction. The worship is done through *Durga Ashtothara* with vermillion. The foods for offerings are cooked rice mixed with curd and pieces of ginger, black-gram cakes, rice, cooked with jaggery and ghee, honey and milk. The mantra for recital is:

किरीटं वैरिञ्चं परिहर पुरः कैटभभिदः
कठोरे कोटीरे स्खलसि जहि जम्भारिमुकुटम्
प्रणम्रेष्वेतेषु प्रसभमुपयातस्य भवनं
भवस्याभ्युत्थाने तव परिजनोक्तिर्विजयते ॥ २

kiriiTaM vairincan parihara puraH kaiTabhabhidaH kaThore koTiire skhalasi jahi jambhaarimukuTamh ।
praNamreShveteShu prasabhamupayaatasya bhavanan bhavasyaabhyutthaane tava parijanoktirvijayate ॥

29. Yantra for power of transmigration into other bodies.

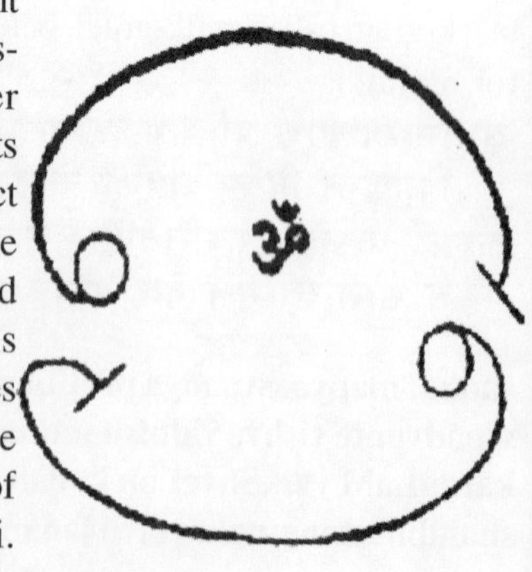

This Yantra is fruitful in attainment of psychic powers, control of senses- power of transmigration into other bodies. Yantra on gold plate (some texts give design of the yantra as a perfect circle with a diameter of 1½ ' and the *bijakshsra* as '6m' in the centre and '*Kleem*', under '*om*'). The mantra is recited for one thousand and one times for ninty six day. The worship is done with white flowers or bilva leaves of *Rudral trisarhi* and Lalita-thrisathi.

Food for offerings are honey, scraps of coconut kernel mixed with ghee and sugar, boiled milk, fruit and cooked rice mixed with curd and spices and fruits. (The yantra is to be borne on the head during recital).

The mantra for recital is:

स्वदेहोद्भूताभिर्घृणिभिरणमाद्याभिरभितो
निषेव्ये नित्ये त्वामिति सदा भावयति यः ।
किमाश्चर्यं तस्य त्रिनयनसमृद्धिं तृणयतो
महासंवर्ताग्निर्विरचयति निराजनविधिम् ॥

svadehodbhuutaabhirghRiNibhiraNmaadyaabhirabhito niShevye nitye tvaamiti sadaa bhaavayati yaH ।
kimaashcaryan tasya trinayanasamRiddhin tRiNayato mahaasaMvartaagnirviracayati niraajanavidhimh ॥

30. Yantra for getting government favours.

The Yantra is used for getting royal and governmental favours, winning popularity and fulfilment of desires. The Yantra is inscribed on plate of gold or alloy of five metals, (some texts prescribe, lm, 'Kleem,' 'Hreem' and 'Sreem' on the four sides inside the square). The mantra is recited for one thousand and eight times for fourty four days facing east direction. The yantra be worshipped with Lalita Sahasarnama with vermillion. Foods for offering are cooked rice, sweet milk-gruel, black-gram cakes, coconuts, grapes and plantains. (Yantra to be held in right palm spread over with a bit of red silk)

The mantra for recital is:

चतुष्षष्ट्या तन्त्रैः सकलमतिसंधाय भुवनं
स्थितस तत्तत्सिद्धिप्रसवपरतन्त्रैः पशुपतिः ।
पुनस्त्वन्निर्बन्धादखिलपुरुषार्थैकघटना
स्वतन्त्रं ते तन्त्रं क्षितितलमवातीतरदिदम् ॥

catuShShaShTyaa tantraiH sakalamatisaMdhaaya bhuvanaM
sthitas tattatsiddhiprasavaparatantraiH pashupatiH ।
punastvannirbandhaadakhilapuruShaarthaikaghaTanaa
svatantraM te tantraM kShititalamavaatiitaradidamh ॥

31. Yantra for getting success in business.

The yantra is effective in getting the powers of alchemy and to attract, and success in business. This yantra is to be fixed at the place of business for getting full benefit from the yantra. For business purposes sweet *pongal* is recommended by the *Agama Shastris*.The Yantra is drawn on gold or copper sheet. (In some texts the yantra is drawn as a circle with two horns at the top and two horns at bottom.) The yantra is energised by reciting the mantra one thousand times for fourty five days facing north direction. Worship of yantra is done with Lalita-thrisathi with vermillion. Foods for offering are cooked rice mixed with curd, black gram cakes and fruits. The mantra for recital is:

शिवः शक्तिः कामः क्षितिरथ रविः शीतकिरणः
स्मरो हंसः शक्रस्तदनु च परामारहरयः ।
अमी हृल्लेखाभिस्तिसृभिरवसानेषु घटिता
भजन्ते वर्णास्ते तव जननि नामावयवताम् ॥

shivaH shaktiH kaamaH kShitiratha raviH shiitakiraNaH
smaro haMsaH shakrastadanu ca paraamaaraharayaH ।
amii hRillekhaabhistisRibhiravasaaneShu ghaTitaa
bhajante varNaaste tava janani naamaavayavataamh ॥

32. Yantra for acquisition of wealth.

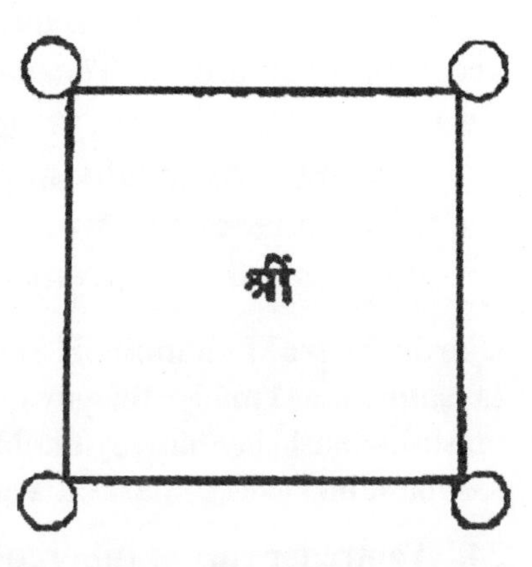

This yantra is effective in amassing of much wealth. The Yantra is inscribed on Gold plate (in some texts *bijakshara* inside yantra is '*Hreem*' and *Kleem*). The mantra is recited for one thousand times for fourty five days facing north direction. The worshipping is done with Lakshmi Sahasarnama with lotus petals. Foods for offering are rice cooked with green gram pulse, jaggery and ghee-coconuts, plantains betel and arica-nut slices. (Coins of the local currency may be kept in closed right hand during recital of mantra, after daily worship the yantra and coin be placed in box made of horn of antelope).The mantra for recital is:

स्मरं योनिं लक्ष्मीं त्रितयमिदमादौ तव मनो
निंधायैके नित्ये निरवधिमहाभोगरसिका: ।
भजन्ति त्वां चिन्तामणिगुननिबद्धाक्षवलया:
शिवाग्नौ जुह्वन्त: सुरभिघृतधाराहुतिशतै: ॥

smaraM yoniM lakShmiiM tritayamidamaadau tava mano
rnidhaayaike nitye niravadhimahaabhogarasikaaH ।
bhajanti tvaaM cintaamaNigunanibaddhaakShavalayaaH
shivaagnau juhvantaH surabhighRitadhaaraahutishataiH ॥

33. Yantra for cure for rheumatism of the joints.

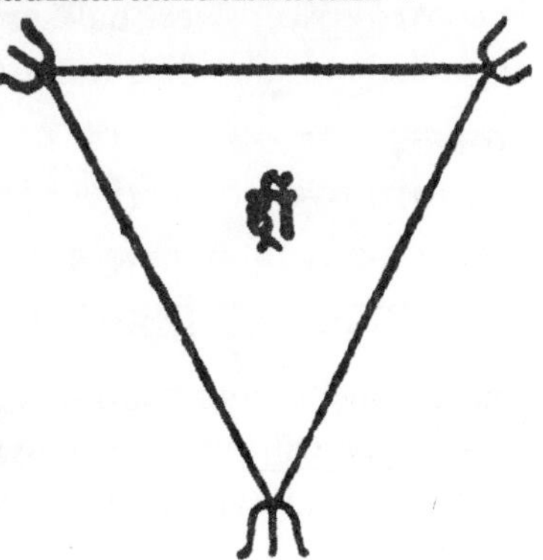

The Yantra is very much useful in clearance of doubts, getting powers of a genius, cure of itches, diabetes, pleurisy and rheumatism. The Yantra is inscribed on Gold or copper plate. The mantra is recited for one thousand and eight times fourty four days, facing east direction. The yantra is worshipped with Lalita thrisathi with vermillion. Foods for offerings are cooked rice mixed with powdered pepper and ghee, honey and coconuts. The mantra for recital is:

शरीरं त्वं शम्भोः शशिमिहिरवक्षोरुहयुगं
तवात्मानं मन्ये भगवति नवात्मानमनघम् ।
अतश्शेषश्शेषीइत्ययमुभयसाधारणतया
स्थितः संबन्धो वां समरसपरानन्दपरयोः ॥

shariiraM tvaM shambhoH shashimihiravakShoruhayugaM
tavaatmaanaM manye bhagavati navaatmaanamanaghamh ।
atashsheShashsheShiiityayamubhayasaadhaaraNatayaa sthitaH
saMbandho vaaM samarasaparaanandaparayoH ॥

34. Yantra for cure of tuberculosis

The yantra is very useful in curing of asthma, tuberculosis and other incurables. One may also get vision of Shiva and Devi in dreams. The Yantra be inscribed on Gold plate and worn as a talisman. The mantra be recited for one thousand times, for fourty five days facing north-east direction. The yantra be worshipped with Rudra-thrisathi with washed sesame on left of yantra and Lalita Thrisathi with vermillion on right. The Food for offering is cooked rice, sweet milk gruel, gingely, powder mixed with brown sugar and plantains.The mantra for recital is:

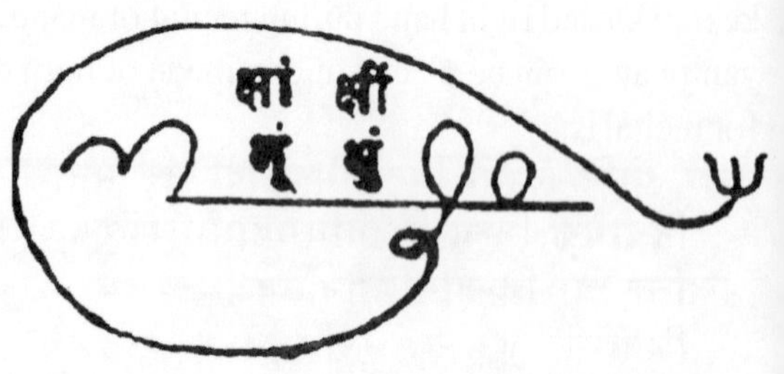

मनस्त्वं व्योम त्वं मरुदसि मरुत्सारथिरसि
त्वमापस्त्वं भूमिस्त्वयि परिणतायां न हि परम् ।
त्वमेव स्वात्मानं परिणमयितुं विश्ववपुषा
चिदानन्दाकारं शिवयुवति भावेन बिभृषे ॥

manastvaM vyoma tvaM marudasi marutsaarathirasi
tvamaapastvaM bhuumistvayi pariNataayaaM na hi paramh ।
tvameva svaatmaanaM pariNamayituM vishvavapuShaa

cidaanandaakaaraM shivayuvati bhaavena bibhR^iShe ॥

35. Yantra for Cure of Incurable diseases.

The yantra cures the chronic diseases and lost eyesight is restored. The Yantra is drawn on gold plate or saffron mixed water kept in silver plate. (Water in which yantra may be inscribed to be drunk by the devotee). The mantra is recited for one thousand times for fourty five days, facing east direction. The Yantra is worshipped with Lalita Sahasarnama with vermillion. Foods for offerings are cooked rice mixed with pepper powder and ghee, black-gram cakes, milk, honey and curd. The mantra for recital is:

तवाज्ञाचक्रस्थं तपनशशिकोटिद्युतिधरं
परं शम्भुं वन्दे परिमिलितपार्श्वं परचिता ।
यमाराध्यन् भक्त्या रविशशिशुचीनामविषये
निरालोकेऽलोके निवसति हि भालोकभवने ॥

tavaajnaacakrasthaM tapanashashikoTidyutidharaM paraM shambhuM vande parimilitapaarshvaM paracitaa । yamaaraadhyanh bhaktyaa ravishashishuciinaamaviShaye niraaloke.aloke nivasati hi bhaalokabhavane ॥

36. Yantra for release from the effects of possession by brahmaraksasa.

This yantra is effective in immunity from devils and spirits, cure of diseases caused by heat, release from the effects of possession by *brahmaraksasa*. The Yantra may be inscribed on water in gold plate or silver or copper cup (to be removed daily). The mantra is recited for one thousand times for fourty five days facing south-east direction. The yantra be worshipped with Durga-Sahasarnama with vermillion. Food for offerings are cooked rice mixed with curd, black-gram cakes, boiled milk, jaggery gruel, coconuts, betels and arica nut slices.The mantra for recital is:

विशुद्धौ ते शुद्धस्फटिकविशदं व्योमजनकं
शिवं सेवे देवीमपि शिवसमानव्यवसिताम् ।
ययोः कान्त्या यान्त्या शशिकिरणसारूप्यसरणिं
विधूतान्तर्ध्वान्ताविलसति चकोरीव जगती ॥

vishuddhau te shuddhasphaTikavishadaM vyomajanakaM
shivaM seve deviimapi shivasamaanavyavasitaamh ।
yayoH kaantyaa yaantyaa shashikiraNasaaruupyasaraNiM
vidhuutaantardhvaantaavilasati cakoriiva jagatii ॥

37. Yantra for cure from infantile disease.

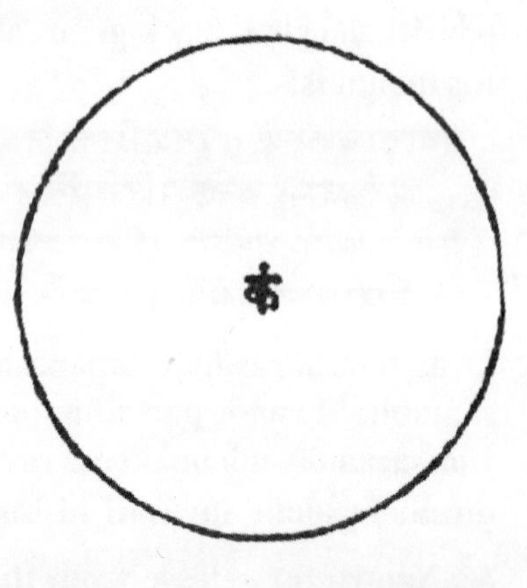

The yantra cures infantile paralysis, other dangerous child diseases and protects from accidents. The Yantra is inscribed on water in a silver dish (The dish is to be renewed every day). The mantra is recited for five thousand times for fourty four days facing east direction (lamp with gingely oil to burn). The yantra is worshipped with Lalita thrisathi with red flowers and Durga-Ashtothara with vermillion. The foods for offerings are cooked nee, black-gram cakes, coconuts and fruits. (Apply yantra drawn on disease affected parts and also drink it).The mantra for recital is:

समुन्मीलत संवित कमलमकरन्दैकरसिकं
भजे हंसद्वन्द्वं किमपि महतां मानसचरम् ।
यदालापादष्टादशगुणितविद्यापरिणति
र्यद आदत्ते दोषाद गुणमखिलमद्भ्यः पय इव ॥

samunmiilat saMvit kamalamakarandaikarasikaM bhaje haMsadvandvaM kimapi mahataaM maanasacaramh । yadaalaapaadaShTaadashaguNitavidyaapariNati ryad aadatte doShaad guNamakhilamadbhyaH paya iva ॥

38. Yantra for avoidance of bad dreams.

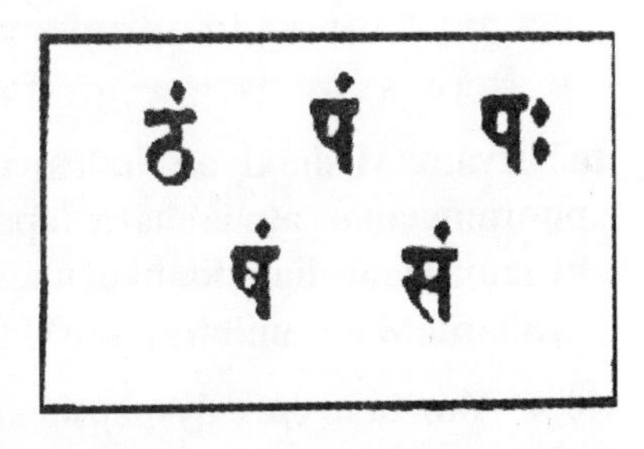

The yantra frees person from bad and fearful dreams, relieved of doubts and suspecting nature. The Yantra is inscribed on gold or copper plate or on holy ashes in a silver plate. The mantra is recited for one hundred and eight times for twelve days facing east direction. Worship is done with Lalita Ashtothara with vermillion at centre of yantra. Foods for offerings are rice cooked with green-gram pulse and some pepper, milk-gruel and fruits.The mantra for recital is:

तव स्वाधिष्ठाने हुतवहमधिष्ठाय निरतं
तमीडे संवर्तं जननि महतीं तां च समयाम् ।
यदालोके लोकान दहति महति क्रोधकलिते
दयार्द्रा यद्दृष्टिः शिशिरमुपचारं रचयति ॥ ३९ ॥

tava svaadhiShThaane hutavahamadhiShThaaya nirataM tamiiDe saMvartaM janani mahatiiM taaM ca samayaamh । yadaaloke lokaan dahati mahati krodhakalite dayaardraa yaddR^iShTiH shishiramupacaaraM racayati ॥

39. Yantra for foreseeing the future through dreams.

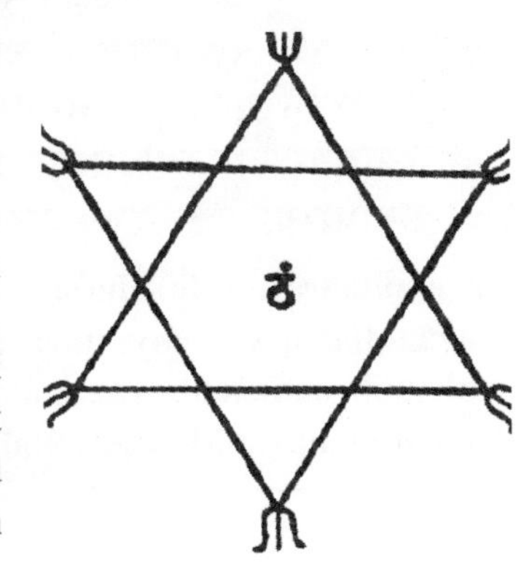

The yantra gives farsightedness in future events and freedom from ignorance. The Yantra is drawn on gold sheet or on powdered salt, levelled on a silver plate. The mantra is recited for four thousand times for forty five days facing north-east direction. The yantra is worshipped through Lalita Sahasarnama with vermillion. The foods for offerings are cooked rice mixed with curd, milk-gruel, fruits betels and arica nut slices. (The yantra is to be placed under a pillow before going to bed). The mantra for recital is:

तटित्त्वन्तं शक्त्या तिमिरपरिपन्थिफुरणया
स्फुरन्नानारत्नाभरणपरिणद्धेन्द्रधनुषम् ।
तव श्यामं मेघं कमपि मणिपूरैकशरणं
निषेवे वर्षन्तं हरमिहिरतप्तं त्रिभुवनम् ॥

taTittvantaM shaktyaa timiraparipanthiphuraNayaa sphurannaanaaratnaabharaNapariNaddhendradhanuShamh । tava shyaamaM meghaM kamapi maNipuuraikasharaNaM niSheve varShantaM haramihirataptaM tribhuvanamh ॥

40. Yantra to cure dyspepsia and other stomach diseases.

This Yantra is good in curing stomach ulcer and intestinal disorders. It may be inscribed on gold sheet or on powdered salt, levelled on a silver plate. The mantra is recited for four thousand times for thirty days, facing east direction. This yantra is worshipped by Shiva Ashtothara with bilva and Lalita thrisathi with vermillion. Foods for offering are rice cooked with green - gram pulse, pepper and ghee, honey and plantains. Mantra for recital is:-

तवाधारे मूले सह समयया लास्यपरया
नवात्मानं मन्ये नवरसमहाताण्डवनटम् ।
उभाभ्यामेताभ्यामुदयविधिमुद्दिश्य दयया
सनाथाभ्यां जज्ञे जनकजननीमज्जगदिदम् ॥

tavaadhaare muule saha samayayaa laasyaparayaa navaatmaanaM manye navarasamahaataaNDavanaTamh । ubhaabhyaametaabhyaamudayavidhimuddishyadayayaa sanaathaabhyaaM jajne janakajananiimajjagadidamh ॥

41. Yantra for cure of dropsy.

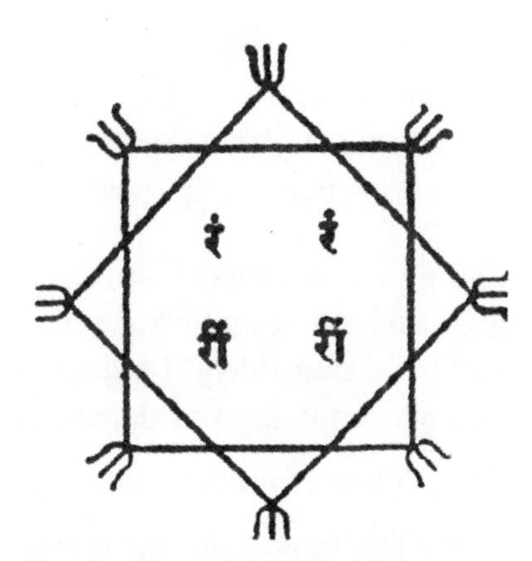

This yantra is used in curing dropsy, urinal diseases, gives power to attract others. The yantra be drawn on gold plate or on rice flour mixed with *omam* or sesame powder (This powder is to be removed daily). The mantra is recited for one thousand times, for fourty four days, facing north direction. The yantra is to be worshipped daily with Lalita Sahasarnama with red flowers. The foods for offerings are cocked rice, milk, fruits and brown sugar. (Rice flour of yantra may be taken as medicine).Mantra for recital is:-

गतैर्माणिक्यत्वं गगनमणिभिः सान्द्रघटितं
किरीटं ते हैमं हिमगिरिसुते कीर्तयति यः ।
स नीडेयच्छायाच्छुरणशबलं चन्द्रशकलं
धनुः शौनासीरं किमिति न निबध्नाति धिषणाम् ॥

gatairmaaNikyatvaM gaganamaNibhiH saandraghaTitaM
kiriiTaM te haimaM himagirisute kiirtayati yaH ।
sa niiDeyacchaayaacchuraNashabalaM candrashakalaM
dhanuH shaunaasiiraM kimiti na nibadhnaati dhiShaNaamh ॥

42. Yantra for fascination of all.

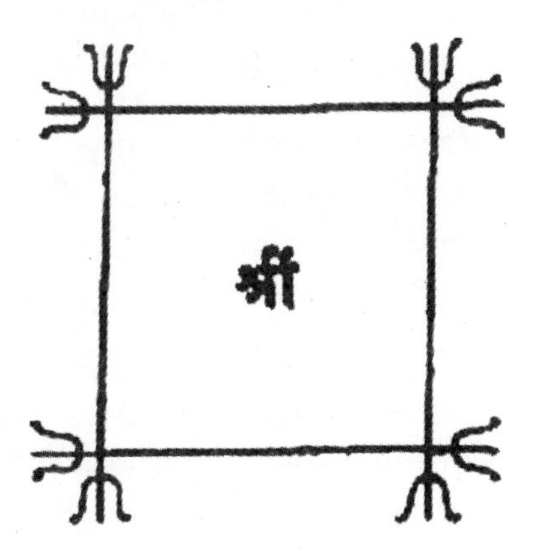

This yantra is a cure of ordinary diseases, and gives success in all endeavours. Yantra is to be inscribed on gold sheet. The mantra is recited for one thousand and one times for fourty eight days facing east direction. The yantra is worshipped through Lalita-thrisathi with red-lotus petals offerings cooked rice boiled pulse, milk-gruel and honey.

Mantra for recital is:-

धुनोतु ध्वान्तं नस्तुलितदलितेन्दीवरवनं
घनस्निग्धश्लक्ष्णं चिकुरनिकुरम्बं तव शिवे ।
यदीयं सौरभ्यं सहजमुपलब्धुं सुमनसो
वसन्त्यस्मिन मन्ये वलमथनवाटीविटपिनाम् ॥

dhunotu dhvaantaM nastulitadalitendiivaravanaM
ghanasnigdhashlakShNaM cikuranikurambaM tava shive ।
yadiiyaM saurabhyaM sahajamupalabdhuM sumanaso
vasantyasmin manye valamathanavaaTiiviTapinaamh ॥

43. Yantra for alleviation of suffering and hysteria.

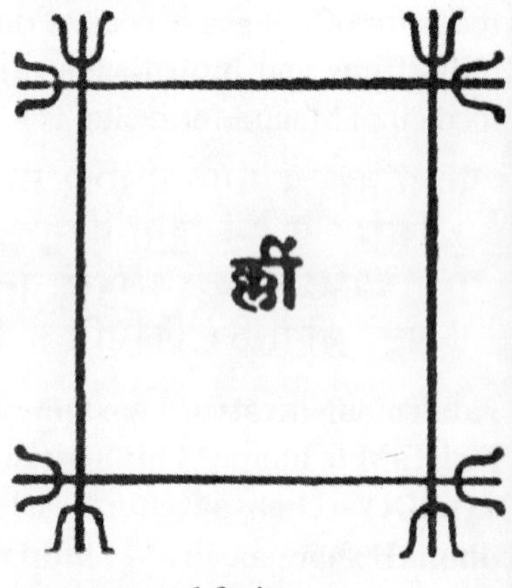

This yantra is helpful in curing hysteria, other diseases and sufferings, gains and mastery over others. This Yantra is effective when carved on nice turmeric powder, or powder of saffron placed in silver plate. The mantra is recited for one thousand and eight times for twelve days, facing south-east direction. The worship is done by Lalita-Sahasarnama with red flowers or vermillion. Foods for offerings are milk boiled with a little saffron honey coconuts and fruits.

Mantra for recital is:-

तनोतु क्षेमं नस्तव वदनसौन्दर्यलहरी
परीवाहस्रोतःसरणिरिव सीमन्तसरणिः ।
वहन्ती सुन्दूरं प्रबलकबरीभारतिमिर
द्विषां बृन्दैर्बन्दीकृतमिव नवीनार्ककिरणम् ॥

tanotu kShemaM nastava vadanasaundaryalaharii
pariivaahasrotaHsaraNiriva siimantasaraNiH ।
vahantii sunduuraM prabalakabariibhaaratimira
dviShaaM bRindairbandiikRitamiva naviinaarkakiraNamh ॥

44. Yantra for fortune telling.

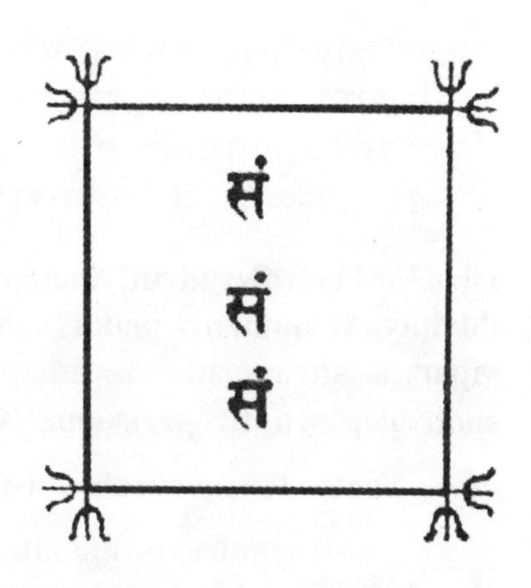

This yantra also gives power of expressiveness, foretelling the future, blessing of eight goddesses of wealth. The yantra is inscribed on gold plate and the mantra is recited for one thousand times for fourty five days, facing east direction. The yantra is worshipped by Lalita-thrisathi with vermillion. Foods for offering are cooked rice scrappings of coconuts kernel mixed with ghee and brown sugar, sugar cane, honey and fruits. Mantra for recital is:-

अरालैः स्वाभाव्यादलिकलभसश्रीभिरलकैः
परीतं ते वक्त्रं परिहसति पङ्केरुहरुचिम् ।
दरस्मेरे यस्मिन् दशनरुचिकिञ्जल्करुचिरे
सुगन्धौ माद्यन्ति स्मरदहनचक्षुर्मधुलिहः ॥

araalaiH svaabhaavyaadalikalabhasashriibhiralakaiH
pariitaM te vaktraM parihasati paNkeruharucimh ।
darasmere yasminh dashanarucikinjalkarucire
sugandhau maadyanti smaradahanacakShurmadhulihaH ॥

45. Yantra for return of husband.

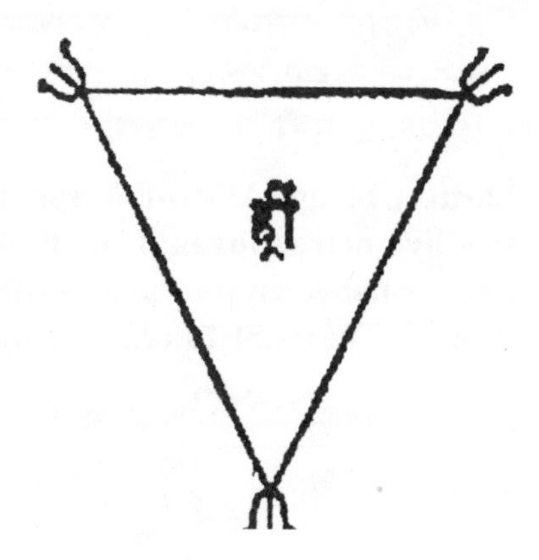

This yantra helps in getting male issue, return of husband or wife after long absence and attaining desired objects. This yantra is inscribed on gold plate or levelled paddy grains and the mantra is recited for one thousand times for fourty five days facing east direction. It is worshipped with Lalita Sahasarnama with vermillion. Foods for offerings are cooked rice, sweet milk-gruel and honey. Mantra for recital is:-

ललाटं लावण्यद्युतिविमलमाभाति तव य
दिद्वतीयं तन्मन्ये मकुटघटितं चन्द्रशकलम् ।
विपर्यासन्यासादुभयमपि संभूय च मिथः
सुधालेपस्यूतिः परिणमति राकाहिमकरः ॥

lalaaTaM laavaNyadyutivimalamaabhaati tava ya
ddvitiiyaM tanmanye makuTaghaTitaM candrashakalamh ।
viparyaasanyaasaadubhayamapi saMbhuuya ca mithaH
sudhaalepasyuutiH pariNamati raakaahimakaraH ॥

46. Yantra for favourable disposition of deities.

This yantra is meant for obtaining grace of gods and all round success. The Yantra be inscribed on gold plate or holy ashes. The mantra is recited for one thousand times for twenty five days, facing east direction. The worship is done by Lalita thrisathi with red flowers. Foods for offering are cooked rice, coconuts, honey and fruits.

Mantra for recital is:-

भ्रुवौ भुग्ने किंचिद्भुवनभयभङ्गव्यसनिनि
त्वदीये नेत्राभ्यां मधुकररुचिभ्यां धृतगुणम्
धनुर्मन्ये सव्येतरकरगृहीतं रतिपतेः
प्रकोष्ठे मुष्टौ च स्थगयति निगूढान्तरमुमे ॥

bhruvau bhugne kiMcidbhuvanabhayabhaNgavyasanini
tvadiiye netraabhyaaM madhukararucibhyaaM dhRitaguNamh ।
dhanurmanye savyetarakaragRihiitaM ratipateH
prakoShThe muShTau ca sthagayati niguuDhaantaramume ॥

47. Yantra for counteracting adverse planetary influence.

बु	शु	च
गु	र	कु
रा	श	के

This yantra is effective in averting evil effects of planets, success in efforts, attaining all desires. This Yantra is to be inscribed on gold or copper plate. The mantra is recited one thousand times for fourty five days, facing east direction.

In this yantra the nine small squares with the respective letters represent the nine planets. The numbers of the nine squares with the letters and the planets they represent are as follows:-

(1) 'Bu' (बु) = Mercury, (2) 'Su' (शु) = Venus, (3) Cha'- (च)Moon, (4) 'Gu'- (गु) Jupiter, (5) 'Ra.' (र) (at centre) = Sun, (6) 'Ku = (कु) Mars,(7) 'Raa'- (रा) Rahu (Dragon's head) , (8) 'Sa' = (श) Saturn, (9) 'Ke'- Ketu (के) (Dragon's tail).

This yantra is worshipped with the Ashtothara of the respective planets with flowers etc., to be used for worship, the respective offerings to be made and also the order in which the planets are to be worshipped are given as under :-

1. **Sun-** with japakusuma or red lotus flowers, offerings of sweet wheat gruel, and cooked rice mixed with fried strap pings of coconuts kernel
2. **Venus-**with red flowers or washed rice grains mixed with vermillion, offering of rice cooked with green-gram pulse jaggery and ghee.
3. **Mars-**with red flowers offerings of cooked rice mixed with tamarind, soup.
4. **Jupiter-** with bilva leaves or scent-giving white flowers offering of cooked rice mixed with curd.
5. **Moon-**with scent-giving white flowers or washed unbroken rice grains, offerings of cooked rice mixed with boiled milk.
6. **Mercury-**with leaves of *Tulsi* plant, offering of rice cooked with green-gram pulse and fried pepper.

7. **Rahu-**with red flowers or vermillion-mixed rice grains, offering of cooked rice mixed with powder of fried black - gram pulse.

8. **Saturn -**with leaves of Vahni tree or washed gingely seeds, offering of cooked rice with powdered sesame.

9. **Ketu-**with white flowers, offering of plain cooked rice.

After worship of the nine planets (in this manner} Lalita Ashtothara worship with vermillion on the left, in the space outside yantra is prescribed. Then general offerings of coined rice, sweet gruel, coconuts, plantains and betel with slices of arnica nut, are to be made.

Mantra for recital is:-

विशाला कल्याणी स्फुटरुचिरयोध्या कुवलयैः
कृपाधाराधारा किमपि मधुरा भोगवतिका ।
अवन्ती दृष्टिस्ते बहुनगरविस्तारविजया
ध्रुवं तत्तन्नामव्यवहरणयोग्या विजयते ॥ ४९ ॥

vishaalaa kalyaaNii sphuTarucirayodhyaa kuvalayaiH
kRipaadhaaraadhaaraa kimapi madhuraa bhogavatikaa ।
avantii dRiShTiste bahunagaravistaaravijayaa
dhruvaM tattannaamavyavaharaNayogyaa vijayate ॥

48. Yantra for discovery of treasure trove.

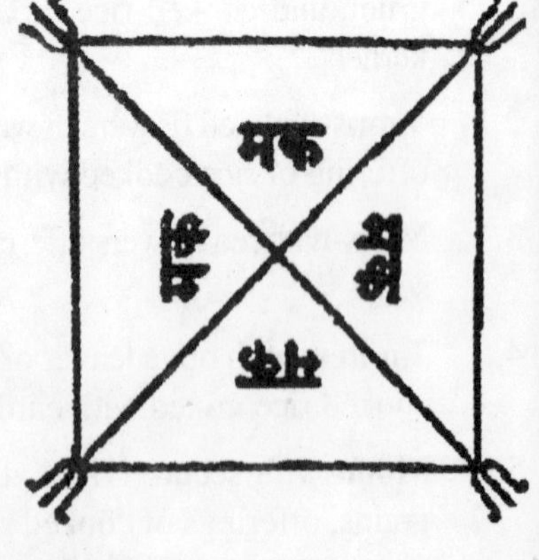

This yantra is helpful in discovering hidden treasure, gaining of lost property, cure of eye-diseases. This yantra is drawn on nice turmeric powder (or charred turmeric). The mantra is recited for one thousand times for ten days, facing north direction. The worship is done through Lalita Sahasarnama at centre of yantra with vermillion and Laxmi Ashtothara at top triangle with petals of red lotus. Foods for offerings are cooked rice, cooked rice mixed with milk, honey, betels and slices of arnica nut. {(Some texts prescribe using the yantra drawn on turmeric-after chairing it as a collyrium (A medicinal lotion applied to the eye) after mixing it with gingely oil after recital every day)}. Mantra for recital is:-

अहः सूते सव्यं तव नयनमर्कात्मकतया
त्रियामां वामं ते सृजति रजनीनायकतया ।
तृतीया ते दृष्टिर्दरदलितहेमाम्बुजरुचिः
समाधत्ते संध्यां दिवसनिशयोरन्तरचरीम् ॥

ahaH suute savyaM tava nayanamarkaatmakatayaa
triyaamaaM vaamaM te sRijati rajaniinaayakatayaa ।
tRitiiyaa te dRiShtirdaradalitahemaambujaruciH samaadhatte
saMdhyaaM divasanishayorantaracariimh ॥

49. Yantra for immunity from small-pox.

The yantra is effective in prevention from and quick cure of small -pox, chicken pox and dysentery. Yantra is drawn on gold plate or water or butter (renewed daily). The mantra is recited for one thousand times for 7 days facing east direction. The worship is done by Lalita-thrisathi with red rose or red arali flowers. Foods for offerings are sweet milk gruel, sugar cane bits, and brown sugar coconuts and fruits. (The water or butter on which yantra is inscribed is to be consumed daily).

Mantra for recital is:-

कवीनां संदर्भस्तबकमकरन्दैकरसिकं
कटक्षव्याक्षेपभ्रमरकलभौ कर्णयुगलम् ।
अमुञ्चन्तौ दृष्ट्वा तव नवरसास्वादतरला
वसूयासंसर्गादलिकनयनं किंचिदरुणम् ॥

kaviinaaMsaMdarbhastabakamakarandaikarasikaM
kaTakShavyaakShepabhramarakalabhau karNayugalamh ।
amuncantau dRiShTvaa tava navarasaasvaadataralaa
vasuuyaasaMsargaadalikanayanaM kiMcidaruNamh ॥

50. Yantra for bestowal of all desires.

Yantra on thick sandal paste kept in silver plate or on gold sheet. The mantra is to be recited for one thousand and eight times for 32 days facing east direction. The yantra is to be worshiped with Lalita thrisathi with vermilion. Foods for offerings are cooked rice, black-gram cakes, boiled milk and honey. This yantra is useful in enticing people, getting of Devi's grace, and high influence. Mantra for recital is:-

क्लीं
क्लीं
क्लीं

शिवे शृङ्गारार्द्रा तदितरजने कुत्सनपरा
सरोषा गङ्गायां गिरिशचरिते विस्मयवती ।
हराहिभ्यो भीता सरसिरुहसौभाग्यजयिनी
सखीषु स्मेरा ते मयि जननि दृष्टिः सकरुणा ॥

shive shRiNgaaraardraa taditarajane kutsanaparaa
saroShaa gaNgaayaaM girishacarite vismayavatii ।
haraahibhyo bhiitaa sarasiruhasaubhaagyajayinii
sakhiiShu smeraa te mayi janani dRiShTiH sakaruNaa ॥

51. Yantra for curing all eye and ear diseases.

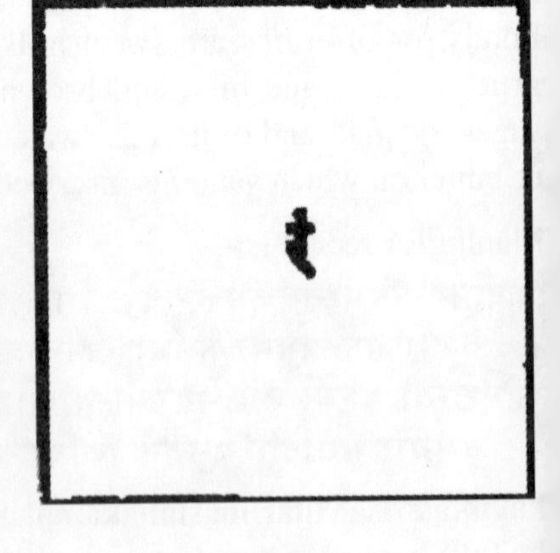

The yantra is effective in curing all ear and eye diseases. This Yantra is inscribed on gold plate or holy ashes. The mantra is recited for one thousand one times for fourty five days facing north-east direction. The worship is done by Rudra thrisathi with bilva on right side of yantra and Lalita thrisathi with red flowers on left side. Foods for offerings are cooked rice mixed with sesame powder, milk-gruel coconuts and plantains.

Mantra for recital is:-

गते कर्णाभ्यर्णं गरुत इव पक्ष्माणि दधती
पुरां भेत्तुश्चित्तप्रशमरसविद्रावणफले ।
इमे नेत्रे गोत्राधरपतिकुलोत्तंसकलिके
तवाकर्णाकृष्टस्मरशरविलासं कलयतः ॥

gate karNaabhyarNaM garuta iva pakShmaaNi dadhatii
puraaM bhettushcittaprashamarasavidraavaNaphale ।
ime netre gotraadharapatikulottaMsakalike
tavaakarNaakRiShTasmarasharavilaasaM kalayataH ॥

52. Yantra for foreseeing future

This yantra gives vision of Devi and power to foresee future. This Yantra is drawn on gold plate or rice flour spread on a plantain leaf. The mantra is recited for one thousand times for fourty five days facing east direction by sitting near a ghee-lit lamp, placed to the right of the yantra. The yantra is worshipped through Lalita Sahasarnama with vermilion. Foods for offerings are cooked rice, sweet cakes and milk-gruel. (Lamp burning bright is considered as a good omen)

Mantra for recital is:-

विभक्तत्रैवर्ण्यं व्यतिकरितलीलाञ्जनतया
विभाति त्वन्नेत्रत्रितयमिदमीशानदयिते ।
पुनः स्रष्टुं देवान द्रुहिणहरिरुद्रानुपरतान
रजः सत्त्वं बिभ्रत तम इति गुणानां त्रयमिव ॥

vibhaktatraivarNyaM vyatikaritaliilaanjanatayaa
vibhaati tvannetratritayamidamiishaanadayite ।
punaH sraShTuM devaan druhiNaharirudraanuparataan
rajaH sattvaM bibhrat tama iti guNaanaaM trayamiva ॥

53. Yantra for curing venereal diseases.

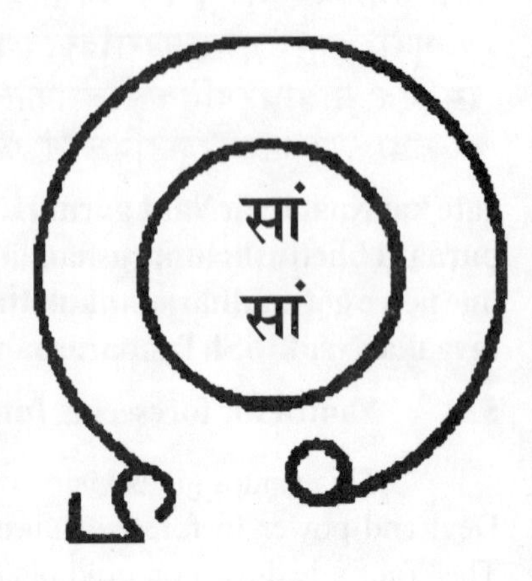

This yantra cures venereal and kidney diseases and gives scientific knowledge. This yantra is drawn on gold plate or in pure water mixed with musk, and saffron, placed in silver dish. The mantra for recital is one thousand times for fourty five days facing north direction. The worship is done through Durga-Ashtothara with red flowers at opening in the ring, and Lalita-Ashtothara with vermilion at centre of yantra. Foods for offerings are cooked rice mixed with curd, jaggery gruel. (In some texts Bija letters are given as 'Sauh, 'Sauh and in some as 'bamla, samla. The given version is the right version which should be followed). Mantra for recital is:-

पवित्रीकर्तुं नः पशुपतिपराधीनहृदये
दयामित्रैर्नेत्रैररुणधवलश्यामरुचिभिः ।
नदः शोणो गङ्गा तपनतनयेति ध्रुवममुं
त्रयाणां तीर्थानामुपनयसि संभेदमनघम् ॥

pavitriikartuM naH pashupatiparaadhiinahRidaye
dayaamitrairnetrairaruNadhavalashyaamarucibhiH ।
nadaH shoNo gaNgaa tapanatanayeti dhruvamamuM
trayaaNaaM tiirthaanaamupanayasi saMbhedamanaghamh ॥

54. Yantra for curing hydrocele

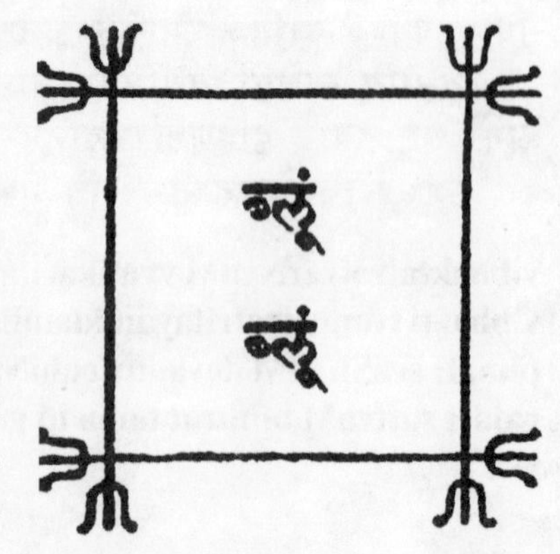

This yantra is effective in curing hydrocele and elephantiasis, causes death or subduing of enemies. This Yantra is inscribed on gold plate. The mantra is recited for 2500 times for fourty five days, facing south-east direction. The worship is done through Lalita-Sahasarnama with washed sesame and rice grains mixed with vermilion. Foods for offerings are cooked rice mixed with boiled milk, milk gruel, brown sugar, coconuts and betels with arnica nut slices. Mantra for recital is:-

निमेषोन्मेषाभ्यां प्रलयमुदयं याति जगती
तवेत्याहुः सन्तो धरणिधरराजन्यतनये ।
त्वदुन्मेषाज्जातं जगदिदमशेषं प्रलयतः
परित्रातुं शङ्के परिहृतनिमेषास्तव दृशः ॥

nimeShonmeShaabhyaaM pralayamudayaM yaati jagatii
tavetyaahuH santo dharaNidhararaajanyatanaye ।
tvadunmeShaajjaataM jagadidamasheShaM pralayataH
paritraatuM shaNke parihRitanimeShaastava dRishaH ॥

55. Yantra for freedom from imprisonment.

It is effective in freedom from imprisonment and from fetters (physical or mental) and effect of evil eyes, causes rain. The Yantra is inscribed on gold plate, ivory piece (bone of big fish). The mantra is recited for two thousand times for fourty eight days facing north-east direction and worship is done through Lalita-thrisathi with red flowers. Foods for offerings are cooked rice honey and fruits. Mantra for recital is:-

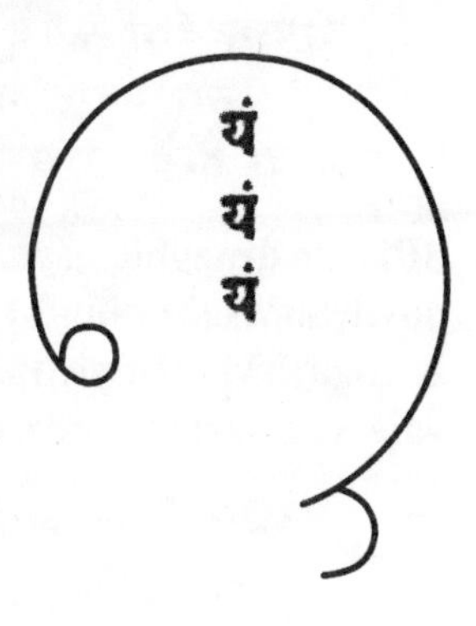

तवापर्णे कर्णेजपनयनपैशुन्यचकिता
निलीयन्ते तोये नियतमनिमेषाः शफरिकाः ।
इयं च श्रीर्बद्धच्छदपुटकवाटं कुवलयम
जहाति प्रत्यूषे निशि च विघटय्य प्रविशति ॥

tavaaparNe karNejapanayanapaishunyacakitaa
niliiyante toye niyatamanimeShaaH shapharikaaH ।
iyaM ca shriirbaddhacchadapuTakavaaTaM kuvalayam
jahaati pratyuuShe nishi ca vighaTayya pravishati ॥

56. Yantra for attaining all prosperity.

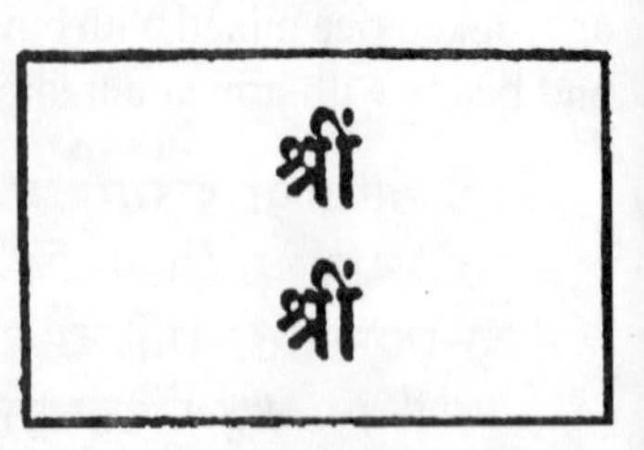

This yantra helps in getting wealth, fame, progeny and prosperity. It should be drawn on gold plate, and the mantra be recited for one thousand times for fourty five days facing east direction. The yantra worshiped with Lalita-thrisathi with red flowers at upper centre of yantra and Laxmi Ashtothara with red lotus petals at bottom centre of yantra. Foods for offerings are milk gruel, honey, cooked rice mixed with curd and betels with arnica nut slices.

Mantra for recital is:-

दृशा द्राघीयस्या दरदलितनीलोत्पलरुचा
दवीयांसं दीनं स्नपय कृपया मामपि शिवे ।
अनेनायं धन्यो भवति न च ते हानिरियता
वने वा हर्म्ये वा समकरनिपातो हिमकरः ॥

dRishaa draaghiiyasyaa daradalitaniilotpalarucaa
daviiyaaMsaM diinaM snapaya kRipayaa maamapi shive ।
anenaayaM dhanyo bhavati na ca te haaniriyataa
vane vaa harmye vaa samakaranipaato himakaraH ॥

57. Yantra for getting royal favours.

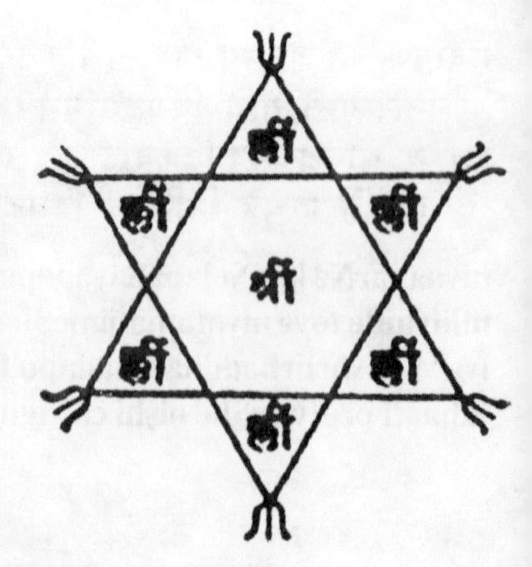

It shows its effect in command over others and cures diseases. Yantra is inscribed on gold plate or vermilion and the mantra is recited for one thousand times for fourty five days. The yantra is worshipped by Lalita -Sahasarnama with vermilion. Food for offerings are cooked rice mixed with lemon juice, honey placed in gold or silver vessel and fruits.

Mantra for recital is:-

अरालं ते पालीयुगलमगराजन्यतनये
न केषामाधत्ते कुसुमशरकोदण्डकुतुकम् ।
तिरश्चीनो यत्र श्रवणपथमुल्लङ्घ्य विलस
न्नपाङ्गव्यासङ्गो दिशति शरसंधानधिषणाम् ॥

araalaM te paaliiyugalamagaraajanyatanaye
na keShaamaadhatte kusumasharakodaNDakutukamh ।
tirashciino yatra shravaNapathamullaN^ghya vilasa
mnapaaNgavyaasaNgo dishati sharasaMdhaanadhiShaNaamh ॥

58. Yantra for fascination.

It shows its effects in gaining mastery over all and fascination of women. The Yantra be inscribed on gold plate or nice turmeric powder. The mantra is recited for twenty five thousand times for 6 days facing east direction. It is worshipped through Lalita Ashtothara with red flowers at centre 'Aim', Durga-asthotra with white flowers at centre Sauh'. Foods for offerings are rice cooked with green-gram pulse and jaggery, honey, and milk.

Mantra for recital is:-

स्फुरद्गण्डाभोगप्रतिफलितताटङ्कयुगलं
चतुश्चक्रं मन्ये तव मुखमिदं मन्मथरथम् ।
यमारुह्य द्रुह्यत्यवनिरथम अर्केन्दुचरणं
महावीरो मारः प्रमथपतये सज्जितवते ॥

sphuradgaNDaabhogapratiphalitataaTaN^kayugalaM
catushcakraM manye tava mukhamidaM manmatharathamh ।
yamaaruhya druhyatyavaniratham arkenducaraNaM
mahaaviiro maaraH pramathapataye sajjitavate ॥

59. Yantra for acquisition of learning.

It provides great knowledge, skill in fine arts and eloquence attained, removes dumbness and makes foretelling effective. It is inscribed on gold plate and the mantra is recited for one thousand and eight times for fourty eight days. It is worshipped through Lalita-Sahasarnama with white flowers. Foods for offerings are cooked rice mixed with milk, sweet gruel, coconuts and honey. Mantra for recital is:-

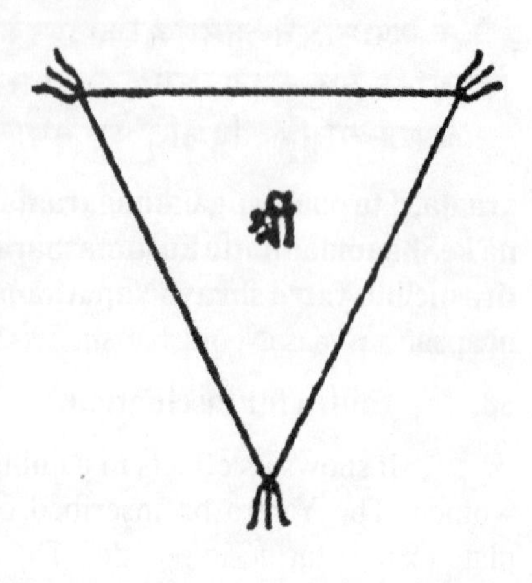

सरस्वत्याः सूक्तीरमृतलहरीकौशलहरीः
पिबन्त्याः शर्वाणि श्रवणचुलुकाभ्यामविरलम् ।
चमत्कारश्लाघाचलितशिरसः कुण्डलगणो
झणत्कारैस्तारैः प्रतिवचनमाचष्ट इव ते ॥ ६० ॥

**sarasvatyaaH suuktiiramRitalahariikaushalahariiH pibantyaaH sharvaaNi shravaNaculukaabhyaamaviralamh ।
camatkaarashlaaghaacalitashirasaH kuNDalagaNo jhaNatkaaraistaaraiH prativacanamaacaShTa iva te ॥**

60. Yantra for gratification of desires.

It is effective in success in all endeavours in trade, speculations etc., power to fascinate men and conquer minds. The Yantra is inscribed on gold plate and the manta is recited for twelve thousand times for 8 days, facing east direction. It is worshipped through Lalita Sahasarnama with vermilion Foods for offerings are rice (cooked with green-gram pulse, pepper and ghee),

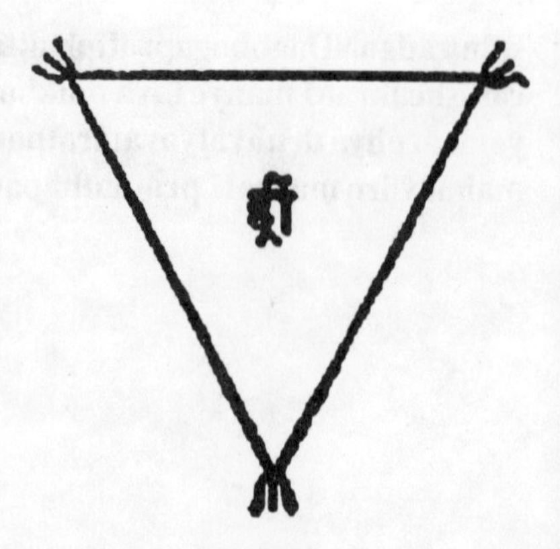

coconuts, fruits, honey and milk. Mantra for recital is:-

असौ नासावंशस्तुहिनगिरिवंशध्वजपटि
त्वदीयो नेदीयः फलतु फलमस्माकमुचितम् ।
वहन्नन्तर्मुक्ताः शिशिरतरनिश्वासगलितं
समृद्ध्या यस्तासां बहिरपि च मुक्तामणिधरः ॥

asau naasaavaMshastuhinagirivaMshadhvajapaTi
tvadiiyo nediiyaH phalatu phalamasmaakamucitamh ।
vahannantarmuktaaH shishirataranishvaasagalitaM
samRiddhyaa yastaasaaM bahirapi ca muktaamaNidharaH ॥

61. Yantra for profound sleep.

मं
मं
मं

It is effective insomnia, robust personaloty and power of enticing. It is inscribed on gold plate and the mantra is recited for one thousand times for eight days facing north-east direction. The worship is done through Lalita-thrisathi with jasmine flowers. Foods for offerings are Cooked Rice (mixed with powder of buck-gram), honey and pure water. Mantra for recital is:-

प्रकृत्यारक्तायास्तव सुदति दन्तच्छदरुचेः
प्रवक्ष्ये सादृश्यं जनयतु फलं विद्रुमलता ।
न विम्बं त्वद्बिम्बप्रतिफलनरागाद अरुणितं
तुलामध्यारोढुं कथमिव न लज्जेत कलया ॥

prakRityaaraktaayaastava sudati dantacchadaruceH
pravakShye saadRishyaM janayatu phalaM vidrumalataa ।
na bimbaM tvadbimbapratiphalanaraagaad aruNitaM
tulaamadhyaaroDhuM kathamiva na lajjeta kalayaa ॥

62. Yantra for ready obedience.

It shows its effects in ready obedience from those around and gives salvation. The Yantra is inscribed on gold plate and the entire versa to be inscribed in 4 lines inside Yantra. The mantra is recited for three thousand times, for 32 days, facing east direction. The yantra is worshipped through Lalita

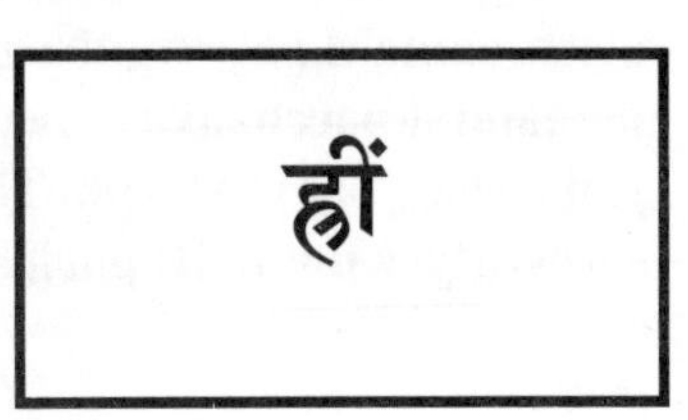

Ashtothara with durva grass. Foods for offerings are cooked rice (mixed with curd), coconuts, fruits, honey and milk. Mantra for recital is:-

स्मितज्योत्स्नाजालं तव वदनचन्द्रस्य पिबतां
चकोराणामासीदतिरसतया चञ्चुजडिमा ।
अतस्ते शीतांशोरमृतलहरीमम्लरुचयः
पिबन्ति स्वच्छन्दं निशि निशि भृशं काञ्जिकधिया ॥

smitajyotsnaajaalaM tava vadanacandrasya pibataaM
cakoraaNaamaasiidatirasatayaa cancujaDimaa ।
ataste shiitaaMshoramRitalahariimamlarucayaH
pibanti svacchandaM nishi nishi bhRishaM kaanjikadhiyaa ॥

63. Yantra for curing venereal diseases.

It shows its effects especially for women, curing diseases, attraction of men and in pacifying of angry husband. The Yantra is inscribed on gold plate set with rubies at four corners or on vermilion and the manta is recited for ten thousand times, for eighteen days, facing north-east direction. The worship is done through Lalita Sahasarnama with vermilion. Foods for offerings are cooked rice, jaggery-gruel, fruits, and betels with nuts and spices. Mantra for recital is:-

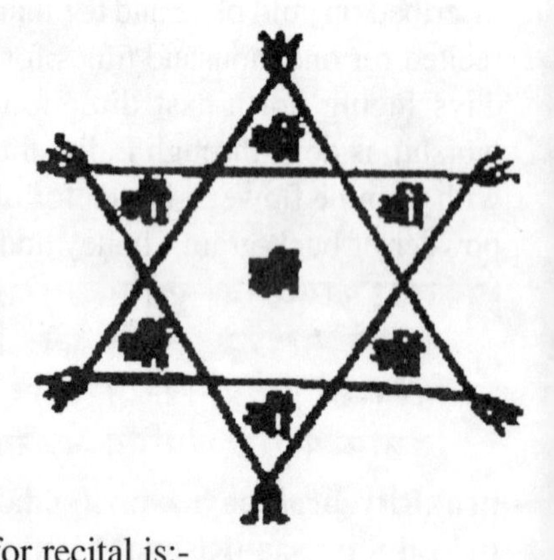

अविश्रान्तं पत्युर्गुणगणकथाम्रेडनजपा
जपापुष्पच्छाया तव जननि जिह्वा जयति सा ।
यदग्रासीनायाः स्फटिकदृषदच्छच्छविमयी
सरस्वत्या मूर्तिः परिणमति माणिक्यवपुषा ॥

avishraantaM patyurguNagaNakathaamreDanajapaa
japaapuShpacchaayaa tava janani jihvaa jayati saa ।
yadagraasiinaayaaH sphaTikadRiShadacchacchavimayii
sarasvatyaa muurtiH pariNamati maaNikyavapuShaa ॥

64. Yantra for fascination of people.

It is effective in blessing success in life and promotes intelligence. The Yantra is inscribed on gold plate and the mantra is recited for one thousand times for fourty five days, facing east direction. Sri-Chakra is to be worshipped along with the yantra with Lalita-Sahasarnama with vermilion. Foods for offerings are cooked rice (mixed with turmeric powder and ghee), fruits, honey and boiled milk. Mantra for recital is:-

रणे जित्वा दैत्यानपहृतशिरस्त्रैः कवचिभिर
निवृत्तैश्चण्डांशत्रिपुरहरनिर्माल्यविमुखैः ।
विशाखेन्द्रोपेन्द्रैः शशिविशदकर्पूरशकला
विलीयन्ते मातस्तव वदनताम्बूलकबलाः ॥

raNe jitvaa daityaanapahRitashirastraiH kavacibhir
nivRittaishcaNDaaMshatripuraharanirmaalyavimukhaiH ।
vishaakhendropendraiH shashivishadakarpuurashakalaa
viliiyante maatastava vadanataambuulakabalaaH ॥

65. Yantra for accomplishment in different musical instruments.

This yantra shows its effects in curing minor ailments, gets skill in vocal and instrumental music. It is inscribed on gold plate or on holy ashes and the mantra is recited for five thousand and one times for 3 days facing east direction. It is worshipped through Lalita-thrisathi with bilva leaves. Foods for offerings are rice cooked with jaggery and ghee, milk and

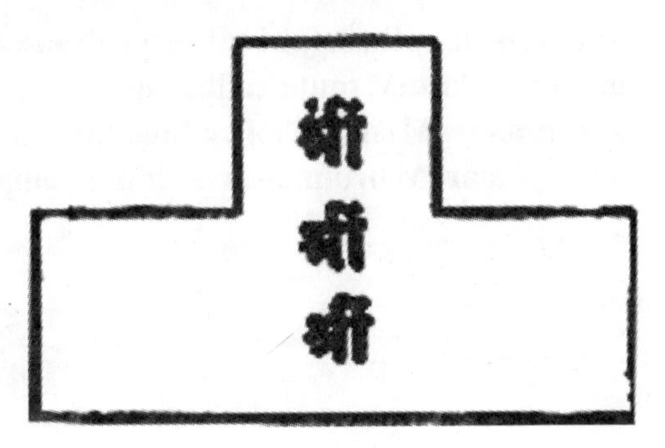

honey. Mantra for recital is:-

विपञ्च्या गायन्ती विविधमपदानं पशुपते:
त्वयारब्धे वक्तुं चलितशिरसा साधुवचने ।
तदीयैर्माधुर्यैरपलपिततन्त्रीकलरवां
निजां वीणां वाणी निचुलयति चोलेन निभृतम् ॥

vipancyaa gaayantii vividhamapadaanaM pashupateH
tvayaarabdhe vaktuM calitashirasaa saadhuvacane ।
tadiiyairmaadhuryairapalapitatantriikalaravaaM
nijaaM viiNaaM vaaNii niculayati colena nibhR^itamh ॥

66. Yantra to visualise Devi .

It gives its effects in royal and governmental favours, power to visualise Devi and success of plans. Yantra is inscribed on gold plate and the mantra is recited for one thousand times, for fourty five days, facing east direction (with wife as mentioned in some of the texts). It is worshipped by Lalita-Sahasarnama with red flowers. Foods for offerings are sweet rice gruel (with milk), honey and betel with slices of arnica nut.

Mantra for recital is:-

कराग्रेण स्पृष्टं तुहिनगिरिणा वत्सलतया
गिरीशेनोदस्तं मुहुरधरपानाकुलतया ।
करग्राह्यं शम्भोर्मुखमुकुरवृन्तं गिरिसुते
कथङ्कारं ब्रूमस्तव चिबुकमौपम्यरहितम् ॥

karaagreNa spRiShTaM tuhinagiriNaa vatsalatayaa
giriishenodastaM muhuradharapaanaakulatayaa ।
karagraahyaM shambhormukhamukuravRintaM girisute
kathaNkaaraM bruumastava cibukamaupamyarahitamh ॥

67. Yantra for royal favours.

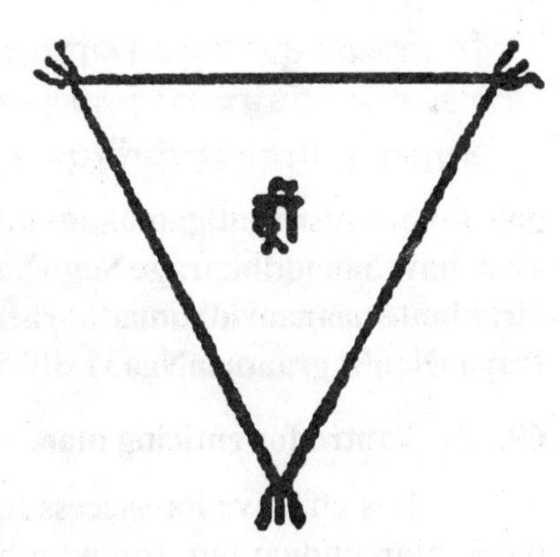

This yantra is used in getting favours of kings and government and influence on others. The Yantra is drawn on vermilion levelled in a silver plate and the mantra is recited for one thousand times for fourty five days facing east direction. Worship is done through Lalita-Sahasarnama with, scent-giving flowers. Foods for offerings are cooked rice, fruits, honey and betel leaves with nut slices. It may be noted here that usage of this verse is said to be learnt only from a preceptor, however, some texts give details of it practical usage which may be referred to. Mantra for recital is:-

भुजाश्लेषान नित्यं पुरदमयितुः कण्टकवती
तव ग्रीवा धत्ते मुखकमलनालश्रियमियम् ।
स्वतः श्वेता कालागरुबहुलजम्बालमलिना
मृणालीलालित्यम वहति यदधो हारलतिका ॥

bhujaashleShaan nityaM puradamayituH kaNTakavatii
tava griivaa dhatte mukhakamalanaalashriyamiyamh ।
svataH shvetaa kaalaagarubahulajambaalamalinaa
mRiNaaliilaalityam vahati yadadho haaralatikaa ॥

68. Yantra for longevity of husband.

It is good for success in all endeavours, in case of women longevity of husbands and skill in music. The Yantra is inscribed on gold sheet and the mantra is recited for one thousand times for fourty five days, facing south-east direction (with wife by the side). The yantra be worshipped by Lalita thrisathi with vermilion. Foods for offerings are cooked rice honey, coconuts fruits and betels with slices of nut.Mantra for recital is:-

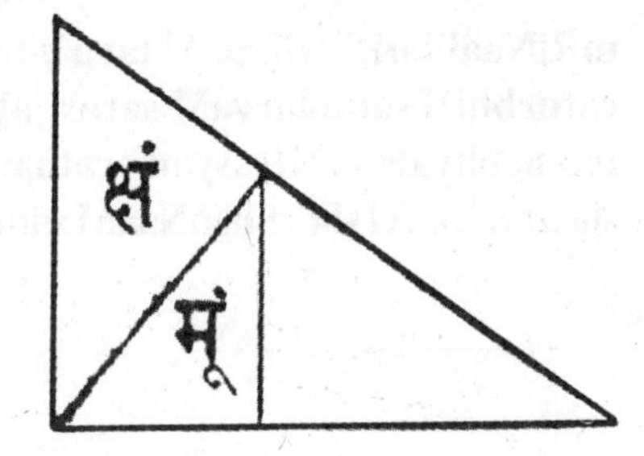

गले रेखास्तिस्रो गतिगमकगीतैकनिपुणे
विवाहव्यानद्धप्रगुणगुणसंख्याप्रतिभुवः ।
विराजन्ते नानाविधमधुररागाकरभुवां
त्रयाणां ग्रामाणां स्थितिनियमसीमान इव ते ॥

gale rekhaastisro gatigamakagiitaikanipuNe
vivaahavyaanaddhapraguNaguNasaMkhyaapratibhuvaH ।
viraajante naanaavidhamadhuraraagaakarabhuvaaM
trayaaNaaM graamaaNaaM sthitiniyamasiimaana iva te ॥

69. Yantra for enticing man.

It is effective for success in particular endeavour for which meditation is intended, freedom from Siva apachara and relief from fear. Yantra is drawn on gold plate and the mantra is recited for one thousand and eight times for fourty eight days, facing east direction. It is worshipped through Lalita-Sahasarnama with vermilion. Foods for offerings are cooked rice (mixed with turmeric powder), coconuts, honey and betels with nut slices. Mantra for recital is:-

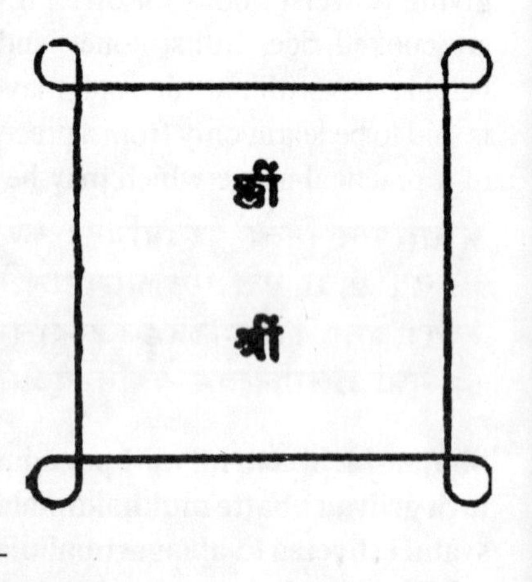

मृणालीमृद्वीनां तव भुजलतानां चतसृणां
चतुर्भिः सौन्दर्यं सरसिजभवः स्तौति वदनैः
नखेभ्यः संत्रस्यन प्रथममथनादन्धकरिपो
श्चतुर्णां शीर्षाणां सममभयहस्तार्पणधिया ॥ १

mRiNaaliimRidviinaaM tava bhujalataanaaM catasRiNaaM
caturbhiH saundaryaM sarasijabhavaH stauti vadanaiH ।
nakhebhyaH saMtrasyan prathamamathanaadandhakaripo
shcaturNaaM shiirShaaNaaM samamabhayahastaarpaNadhiyaa ॥

70. Yantra for command over fairies.

It is useful in relief from all fears, purity of life and control over *yakshinis* (fairies). The Yantra is inscribed on gold plate, and the mantra is recited for two thousand times for fourty five days, facing south-east direction sitting under banyan tree. It is worshipped through Lalita-thrisathi with red flower. Foods for offerings are cooked rice and honey. Mantra for recital is:-

नखानामुद्द्योतैर्नवनलिनरागं विहसतां
कराणां ते कान्तिं कथय कथयामः कथमुमे
कयाचिद्वा साम्यं भजतु कलया हन्त कमलं
यदि क्रीडल्लक्ष्मीचरणतललाक्षारुणदलम् ॥

nakhaanaamuddyotairnavanalinaraagaM vihasataaM
karaaNaaM te kaantiM kathaya kathayaamaH kathamume ।
kayaacidvaa saamyaM bhajatu kalayaa hanta kamalaM
yadi kriiDallakShmiicaraNatalalaakShaaruNadalamh ॥

71. Yantra for night travel without fear.

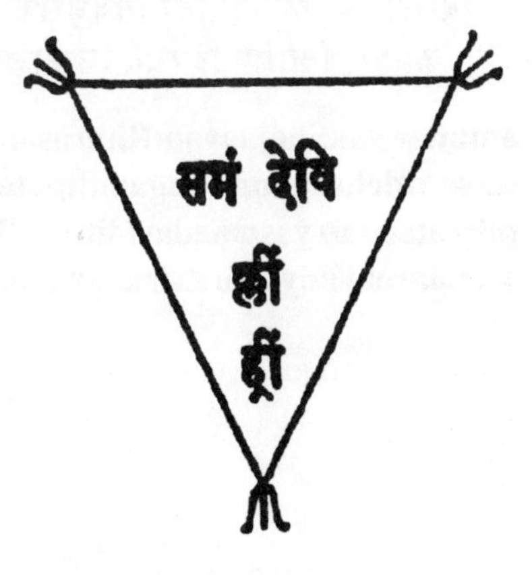

The yantra gives freedom from all fears, safe travel and gets strength of mind. The Yantra is drawn on gold plate or mango plank and the mantra is recited for one thousand times for fourty five days, facing north-east direction. The yantra is worshipped with Durga-Ashtothara with bilva Foods for offerings are cooked rice (mixed with milk), black-gram cakes and fruits. Mantra for recital is:-

समं देवि स्कन्दद्विपवदनपीतं स्तनयुगं
तवेदं नः खेदं हरतु सततं प्रस्नुतमुखम् ।
यदालोक्याशङ्काकुलितहृदयो हासजनकः
स्वकुम्भौ हेरम्बः परिमृशति हस्तेन झटिति ॥

samaM devi skandadvipavadanapiitaM stanayugaM
tavedaM naH khedaM haratu satataM prasnutamukhamh ।
yadaalokyaashaNkaakulitahRidayo haasajanakaH
svakumbhau herambaH parimRishati hastena jhaTiti ॥

72. Yantra for increase flow of milk in women .

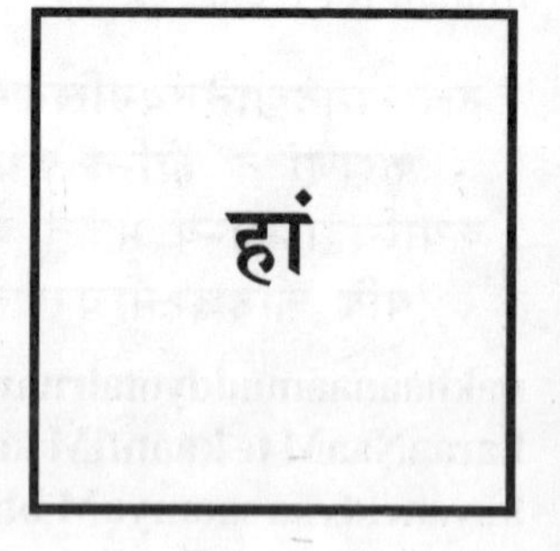

The yantra increases flow of milk in females and in cows, power to realise Brahman. The Yantra is drawn on gold plate or water and the mantra is recited for one thousand times for eight days, facing east direction. It is worshipped through Laxmi Ashtothara with lotus petals. Foods for offerings are cooked rice (mixed with milk), fruits and honey. Mantra for recital is:-

अमू ते वक्षोजावमृतरसमाणिक्यकुतुपौ
न संदेहस्पन्दो नगपतिपताके मनसि नः
पिबन्तौ तौ यस्मादविदितवधूसङ्गरसिकौ
कुमारावद्यापि द्विरदवदनक्रौञ्चदलनौ ॥

amuu te vakShojaavamRitarasamaaNikyakutupau
na saMdehaspando nagapatipataake manasi naH ।
pibantau tau yasmaadaviditavadhuusaNgarasikau
kumaaraavadyaapi dviradavadanakrauncadalanau ॥

73. Yantra for enhanced reputation.

This yantra helps in attainment of fame, eroding and honour. Yantra is carved on gold plate and the mantra is recited for one thousand and eight times, facing north direction. The place for recitation of mantra is before or in Devi shrine or ghee-lit lamp for three days. The yantra be worshipped by Shiva Ashtotharasat namavali (Shiva's one hundred and eight names) with bilva at top of Yantra and Lalita's Ashtotharasat namavali (Lalita's one hundred and eight names) at centre 'kleem'. Foods for offerings are cooked rice (mixed with pepper powder), milk gruel, and honey. Mantra for recital is:-

वहत्यम्ब स्तम्बेरमदनुजकुम्भप्रकृतिभिः
समारब्धां मुक्तामणिभिरमलां हारलतिकाम् ।
कुचाभोगो बिम्बाधररुचिभिरन्तः शबलितां
प्रतापव्यामिश्रां पुरदमयितुः कीर्तिमिव ते ॥

vahatyamba stamberamadanujakumbhaprakRitibhiH
samaarabdhaaM muktaamaNibhiramalaaM haaralatikaamh ।
kucaabhogo bimbaadhararucibhirantaH shabalitaaM
prataapavyaamishraaM puradamayituH kiirtimiva te ॥

74. Yantra for poetry.

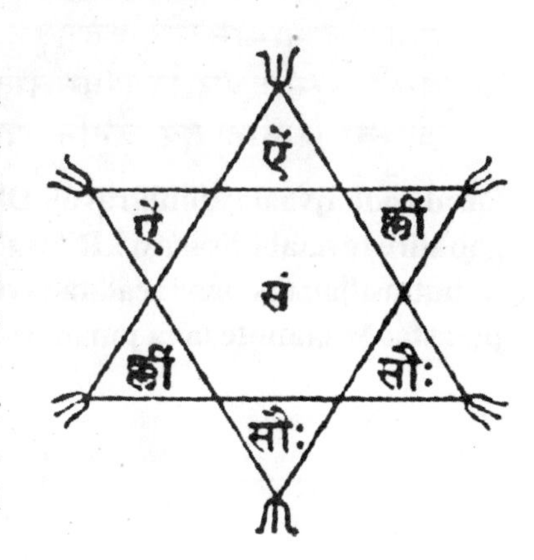

This yantra is used for good memory and attention, fame and gift of poetry. The Yantra is inscribed on gold plate and the mantra is recited for twelve thousand times, for 3 days, facing north-east direction. The yantra is worshiped through Lalita-thrisathi with vermilion. Foods for offerings are rice cooked with green-gram pulse and pepper, fruits and

तव स्तन्यं मन्ये धरणिधरकन्ये हृदयतः
पयःपारावारः परिवहति सारस्वत इव ।
दयावत्या दत्तं द्रविडशिशुरास्वाद्य तव यत
कवीनां प्रौढानामजनि कमनियः कवयिता ॥

tava stanyaM manye dharaNidharakanye hRidayataH
payaHpaaraavaaraH parivahati saarasvata iva ।
dayaavatyaa dattaM draviDashishuraasvaadya tava yat
kaviinaaM prauDhaanaamajani kamaniyaH kavayitaa ॥

75. Yantra for acquisition of all powers.

The yantra is effective in providing success in financial and legal affairs, and knowledge of self if so intended. Yantra is inscribed on gold plate and the mantra is recited for one thousand times, for 10 days, facing north-east direction. The worship is done by Lalita-thrisathi with vermilion. Foods for offerings are cooked rice (mixed with curd) sweet gruel, coconuts and fruits. Mantra for recital is:-

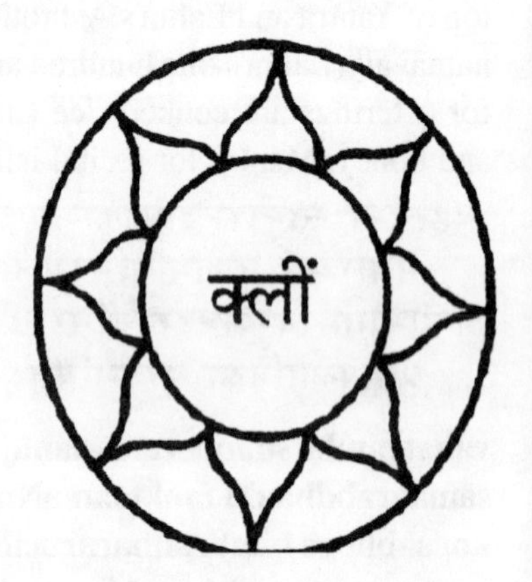

हरक्रोधज्वालवलिभिरवलीढेन वपुषा
गभीरे ते नाभीसरसि कृतसङ्गो मनसिजः ।
समुत्तस्थौ तस्मादचलतनये धूमलतिका
जनस्तां जानीते तव जननि रोमावलिरिति ॥

harakrodhajvaalavalibhiravaliiDhena vapuShaa
gabhiire te naabhiisarasi kRitasaNgo manasijaH ।
samuttasthau tasmaadacalatanaye dhuumalatikaa
janastaaM jaaniite tava janani romaavaliriti ॥

76. Yantra for domination over others.

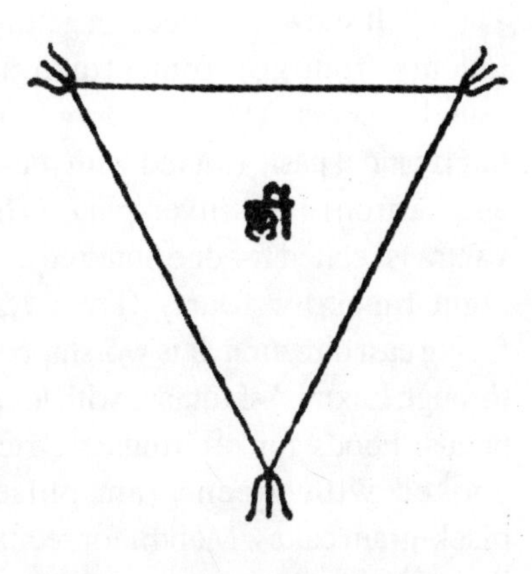

Through this yantra one can start dominating over others and increase his power of deep insight. Yantra is drawn on the paste of burnt red lotus petals mixed with cow's ghee. The whole of mantra is to be inscribed inside the yantra - first and second line at the top and third and fourth along the sides. To energise he mantra is recited for two thousand times, for 15 days, facing east direction. The worship is done through one hundred and eight names of Lalita, with red flowers. Foods for offerings are cooked rice, sweet gruel, honey and fruits. Mantra for recital is:-

यदेतत कालिन्दीतनुतरतरङ्गाकृति शिवे
कृशे मध्ये किंचिज्जननि तव तद्भाति सुधियाम्
विमर्दादन्योऽन्यं कुचकलशयोरन्तरगतं
तनूभूतं व्योम प्रविशदिव नाभिं कुहरिणीम् ॥ ७

yadetat kaalindiitanutarataraNgaakRiti shive
kRishe madhye kiMcijjanani tava tadbhaati sudhiyaamh ।
vimardaadanyo anyaM kucakalashayorantaragataM
tanuubhuutaM vyoma pravishadiva naabhiM kuhariNiimh ॥

77. Yantra for success in all endeavours.

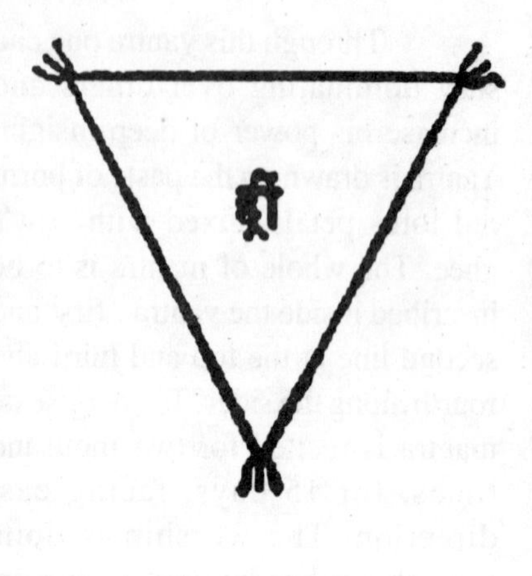

It shows its effects in getting favours from government and all round success. Yantra is drawn on thick sandal paste (mixed with musk and saffron) in a silver plate. The yantra is recited for one hundred and eight times for fourty five days, facing east direction. It is worshipped through Laxmi Ashtothara with lotus petals. Foods for offerings are rice cooked with green-gram pulse, black-gram cakes. Mantra for recital is:-

स्थिरो गङ्गावर्तः स्तनमुकुलरोमावलिलता
निजावालं कुण्डं कुसुमशरतेजोहुतभुजः ।
रतेर्लीलागारं किमपि तव नाभिर्गिरिसुते
बिलद्वारं सिद्धेर्गिरिशनयनानां विजयते ॥

sthiro gaNgaavartaH stanamukularomaavalilataa
nijaavaalaM kuNDaM kusumasharatejohutabhujaH ।
raterliilaagaaraM kimapi tava naabhirgirisute
biladvaaraM siddhergirishanayanaanaaM vijayate ॥

78. Yantra for legerdemain.

The yantra gives power to entice and of jugglery and mesmerism. Yantra is inscribed on gold or copper plate and the mantra is recited for one thousand times, for fourty five days, facing north-east direction. The yantra is worshiped through Lalita Sahasarnama with vermilion. Foods for offerings are cooked rice, milk-gruel, coconuts, honey and fruits. Mantra for recital is:-

निसर्गक्षीणस्य स्तनतटभरेण क्लमजुषो
नमन्मूर्तेर्नारीतिलक शनैस्त्रुट्यत इव ।
चिरं ते मध्यस्य त्रुटिततटिनीतीरतरुणा
समावस्थास्थेम्नो भवतु कुशलं शैलतनये ॥

nisargakShiiNasya stanataTabhareNa klamajuSho
namanmuurternaariitilaka shanaistruTyata iva ।
ciraM te madhyasya truTitataTiniitiirataruNaa
samaavasthaasthemno bhavatu kushalaM shailatanaye ॥

79. Yantra for success in betting.

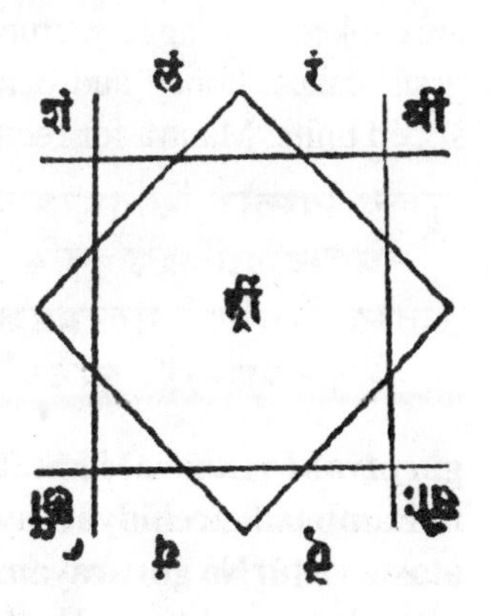

The yantra helps in attainment of magical powers, success in betting and developing handsome personality. Yantra is inscribed on gold plate or new piece of red silk (with stripes made of turmeric solution). The mantra is recited for one thousand times for fourty five days. It is worshipped through Lalita's three hundred names with red flowers. Foods for offerings are cooked rice (mixed with curd), honey and fruits. Mantra for recital is:-

कुचौ सद्यःस्विद्यत्तटघटितकूर्पासभिदुरौ
कषन्तौ दोर्मूले कनककलशाभौ कलयता ।
तव त्रातुं भङ्गादलमिति वलग्नं तनुभुवा
त्रिधा नद्धं देवि त्रिवलि लवलीवल्लिभिरिव ॥

kucau sadyaHsvidyattaTaghaTitakuurpaasabhidurau
kaShantau dormuule kanakakalashaabhau kalayataa ।
tava traatuM bhaNgaadalamiti valagnaM tanubhuvaa
tridhaa naddhaM devi trivali lavaliivallibhiriva ॥

80. Yantra for floating on fire.

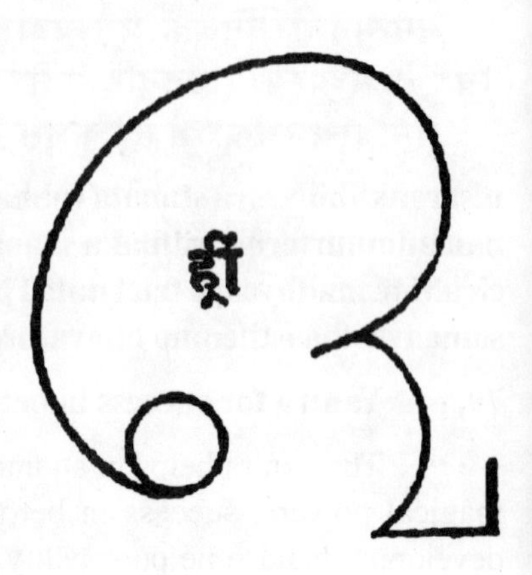

This yantra gives power to float on fire and freedom from fire accidents. The Yantra is inscribed on gold plate and the mantra is recited one thousand and eight times for fourty five days facing east direction. The yantra is worshipped through one hundred and eight names of Lalita with vermilion. Foods for offerings are cooked rice, jaggery, gruel, black-gram cakes, honey and betels with sliced units. Mantra for recital is:-

गुरुत्वं विस्तारं क्षितिधरपतिः पार्वति निजा
न्नितम्बादाच्छिद्य त्वयि हरणरूपेण निदधे ।
अतस्ते विस्तीर्णो गुरुरयमशेषां वसुमतीं
नितम्बप्राग्भारः स्थगयति लघुत्वं नयति च ॥

gurutvaM vistaaraM kShitidharapatiH paarvati nijaa
nnitambaadaacchidya tvayi haraNaruupeNa nidadhe ।
ataste vistiirNo gururayamasheShaaM vasumatiiM
nitambapraagbhaaraH sthagayati laghutvaM nayati ca ॥

81. Yantra for floating on water.

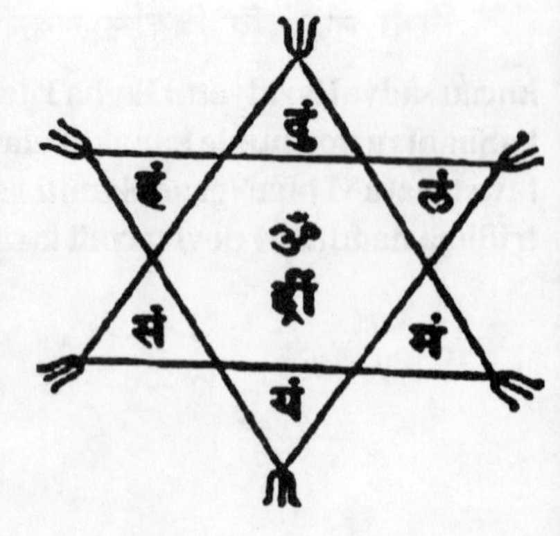

The yantra provides skill to float on water, to be under water, ownership of mines and vast wealth. Yantra is drawn on 'asvikarna' or sandal plank. The mantra is recited for one thousand times for 43 days, facing east direction. The mantra is worshipped through Lalita- thrisathi with vermilion. Foods for offerings are cooked rice (with curd), coconuts, grapes and honey. Mantra for recital is:-

करीन्द्राणां शुण्डाः कनककदलीकाण्डपटलीम
उभाभ्यामूरुभ्यामुभयमपि निर्जित्य भवती ।
सुवृत्ताभ्यां पत्युः प्रणतिकठिनाभ्यां गिरिसुते
विजिग्ये जानुभ्यां विबुधकरिकुम्भद्वयमसि ॥

kariindraaNaaM shuNDaaH kanakakadaliikaaNDapaTaliim
ubhaabhyaamuurubhyaamubhayamapi nirjitya bhavatii ।
suvRittaabhyaaM patyuH praNatikaThinaabhyaaM girisute
vijigye jaanubhyaaM vibudhakarikumbhadvayamasi ॥

82. Yantra for keeping at bay an entire army.

It gives its effects in case of a nation power to rout out enemy's army, in case of individuals power to subdue enemies and getting high posts. The Yantra is inscribed on gold plate. Mantra for recital is one thousand times for twelve days facing east direction. Worship of the yantra is done through Lalita Sahasarnama with red flowers. Foods for offerings are sweet gruel, coconut, fruits and honey. Mantra for recital is:-

पराजेतुं रुद्रं द्विगुणशरगर्भौ गिरिसुते
निषङ्गौ जङ्घे ते विषमविशिखो बाढमकृत ।
यदग्रे दृश्यन्ते दश शरफलाः पादयुगली
नखाग्रच्छद्मानः सुरमुकुटशाणैकनिशिताः ॥

paraajetuM rudraM dviguNasharagarbhau girisute
niShaNgau jaNghe te viShamavishikho baaDhamakRita ।
yadagre dRishyante dasha sharaphalaaH paadayugalii
nakhaagracchadmaanaH suramukuTashaaNaikanishitaaH ॥

83. Yantra for entering other bodies.

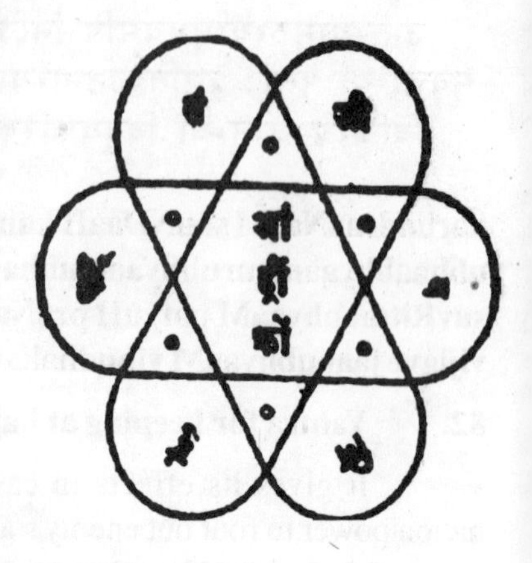

It gives power of mesmerism and transmigration into other bodies ability to cure others, ills and siddhies. The Yantra is inscribed on gold sheet and the mantra is recited for one thousand times for one full year, facing east direction. For daily worship of the yantra Lalita Sahasarnama is orated with vermilion. Foods for offerings are cooked rice, milk-gruel honey and betels with arnica nut slices.Mantra for recital is:-

श्रुतीनां मूर्धानो दधति तव यौ शेखरतया
ममाप्येतौ मातः शिरसि दयया धेहि चरणौ ।
ययोः पाद्यं पाथः पशुपतिजटाजूटतटिनी
ययोर्लाक्षालक्ष्मीररुणहरिचूडामणिरुचिः ॥८४॥

shrutiinaaM muurdhaano dadhati tava yau shekharatayaa
mamaapyetau maataH shirasi dayayaa dhehi caraNau ।
yayoH paadyaM paathaH pashupatijaTaajuuTataTinii
yayorlaakShaalakShmiiraruNaharicuuDaamaNiruciH ॥

84. Yantra for warding off evil spirits.

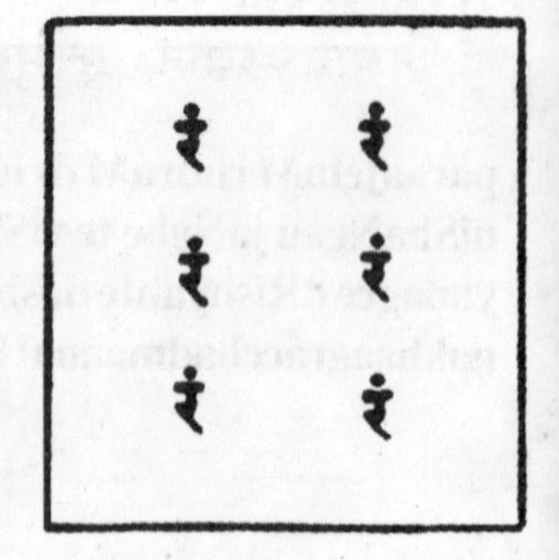

This yantra liberates from hold of evil spirits and helps in attainment of devotion to Devi. The Yantra is inscribed on gold plate or holy ashes. The mantra is recited for one thousand times for twelve days, facing south east direction. The yantra is worshipped by Durga-Sahasarnama with flowers of eight kinds. Foods for offerings are cooked rice (mixed with soup of vegetables), honey, milk and sweet gruel. Mantra for recital is:-

नमोवाकं ब्रूमो नयनरमणीयाय पदयो
स्तवास्मै द्वन्द्वाय स्फुटरुचिरसालक्तकवते ।
असूयत्यत्यन्तं यदभिहननाय स्पृहयते
पशूनामीशानः प्रमदवनकङ्केलितरवे ॥ ८५ ॥

namovaakaM bruumo nayanaramaNiiyaaya padayo
stavaasmai dvandvaaya sphuTarucirasaalaktakavate ।
asuuyatyatyantaM yadabhihananaaya spRihayate
pashuunaamiishaanaH pramadavanakaNkelitarave ॥

85. Yantra for subduing enemies.

यं
यं
यं

This yantra helps in subduing enemies, warding off evil spirits, power and strength. The Yantra is inscribed on gold plate or water. The mantra is recited for one thousand and one times for twenty one days, facing east direction. It is worshiped through Durga Ashtothara and Lalita Ashtothara with vermilion. Foods for offerings are milk gruel, honey, coconut, mangoes and pomegranates.Mantra for recital is:-

मृषा कृत्वा गोत्रस्खलनमथ वैलक्ष्यनमितं
ललाटे भर्तारं चरणकमले ताडयति ते ।
चिरादन्तःशल्यं दहनकृतमुन्मूलितवता
तुलाकोटिक्वाणैः किलिकिलितमीशानरिपुणा ॥

mRiShaa kRitvaa gotraskhalanamatha vailakShyanamitaM
lalaaTe bhartaaraM caraNakamale taaDayati te ।
ciraadantaHshalyaM dahanakRitamunmuulitavataa
tulaakoTikvaaNaiH kilikilitamiishaanaripuNaa ॥

86. Yantra for foreseeing things.

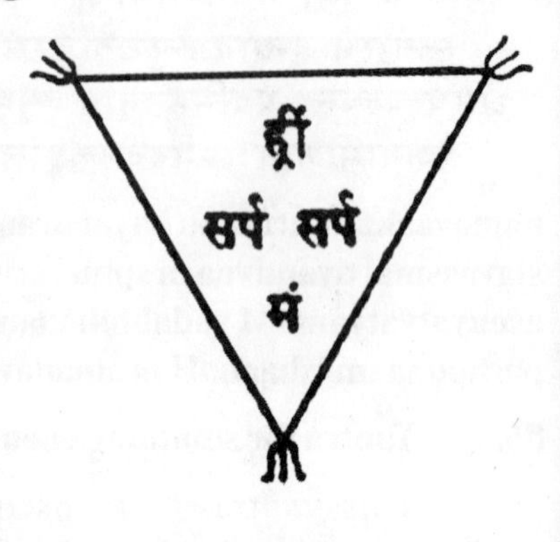

It enhances power to plan, to fore see things, and getting vast. Yantra is inscribed on gold plate, or sandal paste or holy ashes. The mantra for recital is one thousand times for 10 days, facing east direction. The worship is done through Lalita-thrisathi with lotus petals. Foods for offerings are milk-gruel, honey, coconut and fruits. Mantra for recital is:-

हिमानीहन्तव्यं हिमगिरिनिवासैकचतुरौ
निशायां निद्राणां निशि च परभागे च विशदौ ।
परं लक्ष्मीपात्रं श्रियमतिसृजन्तौ समयिनां
सरोजं त्वत्पादौ जननि जयतश्चित्रमिह किम् ॥ ८७ ॥

himaaniihantavyaM himagirinivaasaikacaturau
nishaayaaM nidraaNaaM nishi ca parabhaage ca vishadau ।
paraM lakShmiipaatraM shriyamatisRijantau samayinaaM
sarojaM tvatpaadau janani jayatashcitramiha kimh ॥

87. Yantra for calling off animals.

This yantra holds the power of controlling wild animals, freedom from troubles, and bestows prosperity. Yantra is inscribed on gold or silver plate. Mantra for recital is one thousand and eight times for one hundred eighty two days facing south-east. The yantra is worshipped through Lalita-Sahasarnama with fried paddy grains. Foods for offerings are cooked rice, jaggery gruel, brown sugar and plantains. Mantra for recital is:-

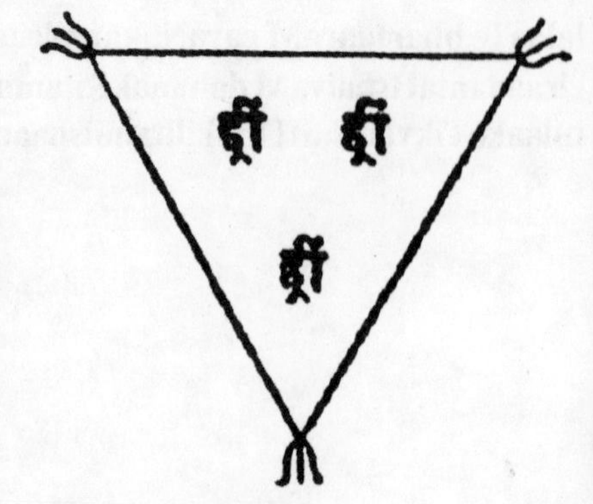

पदं ते कीर्तीनां प्रपदमपदं देवि विपदां
कथं नीतं सद्भिः कठिनकमठीकर्परतुलाम् ।
कथं वा बाहुभ्यामुपयमनकाले पुरभिदा
यदादाय न्यस्तं दृषदि दयमानेन मनसा ॥

padaM te kiirtiinaaM prapadamapadaM devi vipadaaM
kathaM niitaM sadbhiH kaThinakamaThiikarparatulaamh ।
kathaM vaa baahubhyaamupayamanakaale purabhidaa
yadaadaaya nyastaM dRiShadi dayamaanena manasaa ॥

88. Yantra for alleviation of disease.

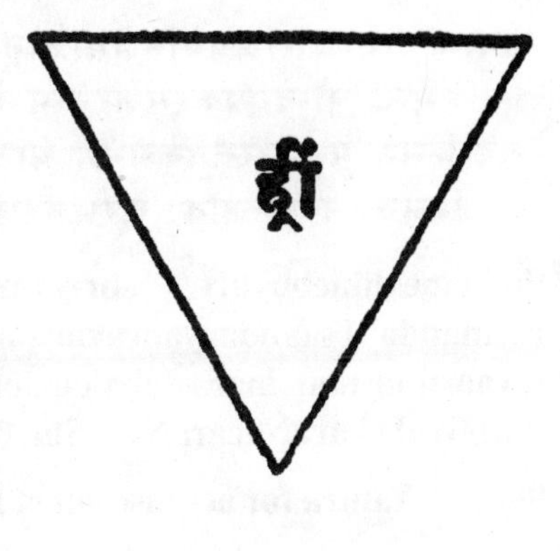

It helps in cure of all diseases, physical strength. Yantra is inscribed on gold plate or holy ashes. Mantra for recital is one thousand and eight times for thirty days, facing east direction. The yantra is worshipped through Lalita Ashtothara with red flowers. Foods for offerings are cooked rice (mixed with curd), sweet-gruel, honey and water. Mantra for recital is:-

नखैर्नाकस्त्रीणां करकमलसंकोचशशिभि
स्तरूणां दिव्यानां हसत इव ते चण्डि चरणौ ।
फलानि स्वःस्थेभ्यः किसलयकराग्रेण ददतां
दरिद्रेभ्यो भद्रां श्रियमनिशमह्नाय ददतौ ॥८९॥

nakhairnaakastriiNaaM karakamalasaMkocashashibhi
staruuNaaM divyaanaaM hasata iva te caNDi caraNau ।
phalaani svaHsthebhyaH kisalayakaraagreNa dadataaM
daridrebhyo bhadraaM shriyamanishamahnaaya dadatau ॥

89. Yantra for counteracting the influence of witchcraft.

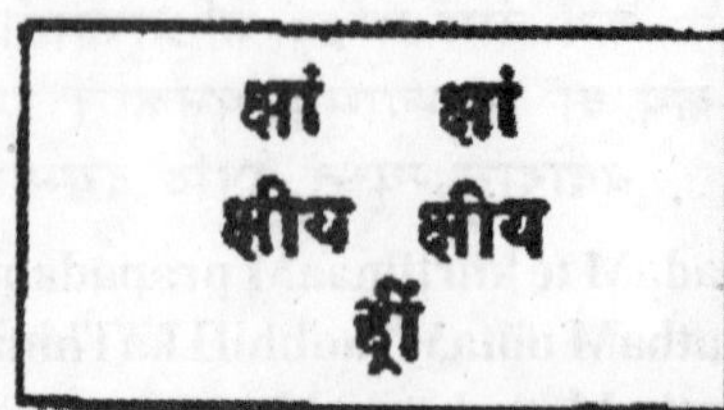

Yantra on Copper plate or holy ashes, Recital one thousand times for thirty days, facing south - east, The yantra is worshipped with Durga Ashtothara with red flowers. Foods for offerings are cooked rice (mixed with tamarind soup), sweet gruel, honey and fruits. It is effective in removal of charms and enchantment by enemies and dispels poverty. Mantra for recital is:-

ददाने दीनेभ्यः श्रियमनिशमाशानुसदृशी
ममन्दं सौन्दर्यप्रकरमकरन्दम विकिरति ।
तवास्मिन मन्दारस्तबकसुभगे यातु चरणे
मिनज्जन मज्जीवः करणचरणः षट्चरणताम् ॥

dadaane diinebhyaH shriyamanishamaashaanusadRishii mamandaM saundaryaprakaramakarandam vikirati । tavaasmin mandaarastabakasubhage yaatu caraNe minajjan majjiivaH karaNacaraNaH ShaTcaraNataamh ॥

90. Yantra for acquisition of land and wealth.

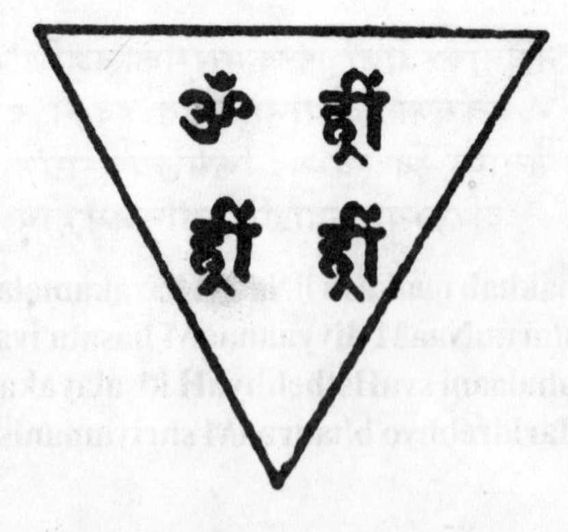

Yantra is inscribed on gold plate. The mantra for recital is two thousand times, for fourty five days. The worship is done with Lalita-Sahasarnama with vermilion before recitation and Laxmi Sahasarnama with red lotus petals at end. Foods for offerings are cooked rice (mixed with boiled milk), milk-gruel, coconut, fruits and betels with nut slices. The yantra is effective during buying of lands and betting of richest contact with great men and scholars. Mantra for recital is:-

पदन्यासक्रीडापरिचयमिवारब्धुमनसः
स्खलन्तस्ते खेलं भवनकलहंसा न जहति ।
स्वविक्षेपे शिक्षां सुभगमणिमञ्जीररणित
च्छलादाचक्षाणं चरणकमलं चारुचरिते ॥९१॥

padanyaasakriiDaaparicayamivaarabdhumanasaH
skhalantaste khelaM bhavanakalahaMsaa na jahati ।
svavikShepe shikShaaM subhagamaNimanjiiraraNita
cchalaadaacakShaaNaM caraNakamalaM caarucarite ॥

91. Yantra for bestowal of kingdom.

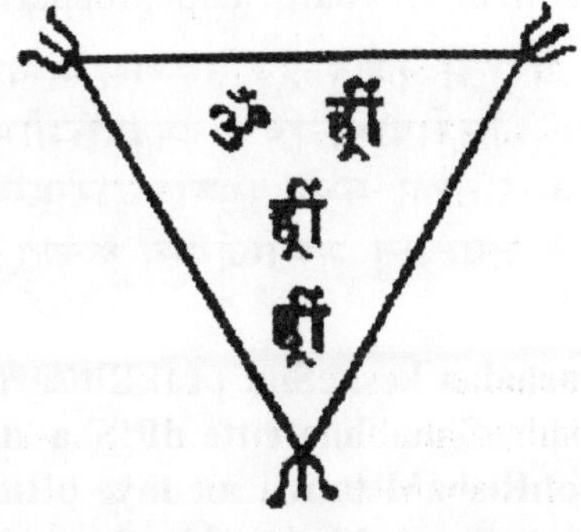

This yantra helps in recovery of lost property, getting large estates and vast knowledge. The Yantra is inscribed on plate of either gold or alloy of five metals. The mantra for recital is four thousand times for 15 days facing east direction. This yantra is worshipped through Lalita-thrisathi with vermilion. Foods for offerings are cooked rice (mixed with milk, with dhal, with curd, and pepper powder of four different kinds) milk gruel and betels with nut slices. Mantra for recital is:-

गतास्ते मञ्चत्वं द्रुहिणहरिरुद्रेश्वरभृतः
शिवः स्वच्छच्छायाघटितकपटप्रच्छदपटः ।
त्वदीयानां भासां प्रतिफलनरागारुणतया
शरीरी शृङ्गारो रस इव दृशां दोग्धि कुतुकम् ॥

gataaste mancatvaM druhiNaharirudreshvarabhRitaH
shivaH svacchacchaayaaghaTitakapaTa pracchadapaTaH ।
tvadiiyaanaaM bhaasaaM pratiphalanaraagaaruNatayaa
shariirii shrNgaaro rasa iva dRishaaM dogdhi kutukamh ॥

92. Yantra for accomplishment of desires.

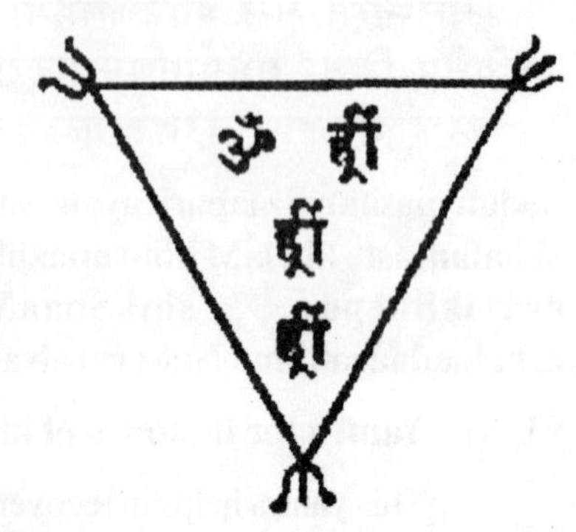

The Yantra is drawn on nice turmeric powder. The mantra of recital is two thousand times for thirty days facing north-east direction. It is worshipped with Lalita Ashtothara and Laxmi -Ashtothara with lotus petals. Foods for offerings are cooked rice, milk, honey, fruits. Through this yantra all desires are fulfilled, wealth and prosperity.

अराला केशेषु प्रकृतिसरला मन्दहसिते
शिरीषाभा चित्ते दृषदुपलशोभा कुचतटे ।
भृशं तन्वी मध्ये पृथुरसिजारोहविषये
जगत्त्रातुं शम्भोर्जयति करुणा काचिदरुणा ॥

araalaa kesheShu prakRitisaralaa mandahasite
shiriiShaabhaa citte dRiShadupalashobhaa kucataTe ।
bhRishaM tanvii madhye pRithurasijaarohaviShaye
jagattraatuM shambhorjayati karuNaa kaacidaruNaa ॥

93. Yantra for getting great renowned moksha.

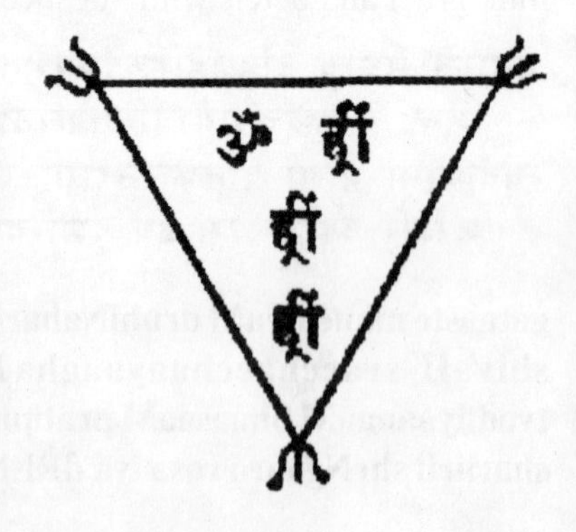

The yantra bestows moksha and a shining face. Yantra is inscribed on gold plate or sandal paste and the mantra for recital is one hundred and eight times for fourty five days in Devi temple or before Yantra and lamp lit with ghee, facing east direction. The yantra is worshipped by Lalita Sahasarnama with red flowers. Foods for offerings are rice cooked with green - gram pulse milk-gruel, mangoes and honey. Mantra for recital is:-

कलङ्कः कस्तूरी रजनिकरबिम्बं जलमयं
कलाभिः कर्पूरैर्मरकतकरण्डं निबिडितम् ।
अतस्त्वद्भोगेन प्रतिदिनमिदं रिक्तकुहरं
विधिर्भूयो भूयो निबिडयति नूनं तव कृते ॥

kalaNkaH kastuurii rajanikarabimbaM jalamayaM
kalaabhiH karpuurairmarakatakaraNDaM nibiDitamh ।
atastvadbhogena pratidinamidaM riktakuharaM
vidhirbhuuyo bhuuyo nibiDayati nuunaM tava kRite ॥

94. Yantra for gratification of desires.

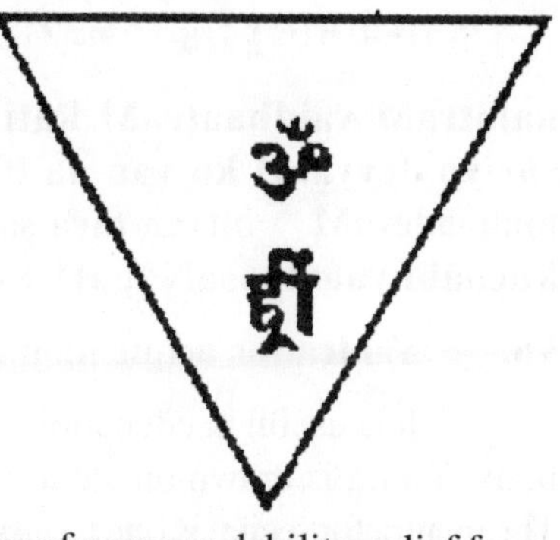

Yantra is inscribed on gold plate, and the mantra for recital is one thousand times for fourty five days facing north-east direction. The worship is done through Shiva Asthotrsata namavali at top triangle with bilva leaves and Lalita-Ashtothara with vermilion at bottom triangle in Yantra. Foods for offerings are cooked rice, brown sugar, honey and plantains. This yantra is helps in cure of nervous debility, relief from debts, and sins gift of poesy. Mantra for recital is:-

पुरारातेरन्तःपुरमसि ततस्त्वच्चरणयोः
सपर्यामर्यादा तरलकरणानामसुलभा ।
तथा ह्येते नीताः शतमखमुखाः सिद्धिमतुलां
तव द्वारोपान्तस्थितिभिरणिमाद्याभिरमराः ॥

puraaraateranta Hpuramasi tatastvaccara NayoH
saparyaamaryaadaa taralakaraNaanaamasulabhaa ।
tathaa hyete niitaaH shatamakhamukhaaH siddhimatulaaM tava
dvaaropaantasthitibhiraNimaadyaabhiramaraaH ॥

95. Yantra for healing of wounds.

Yantra is carved on gold plate or drawn in gingely oil (in a small pan). The mantra is recited for twelve thousand times for eight days facing east direction, Lalita-Sahasarnama with vermilion is used in

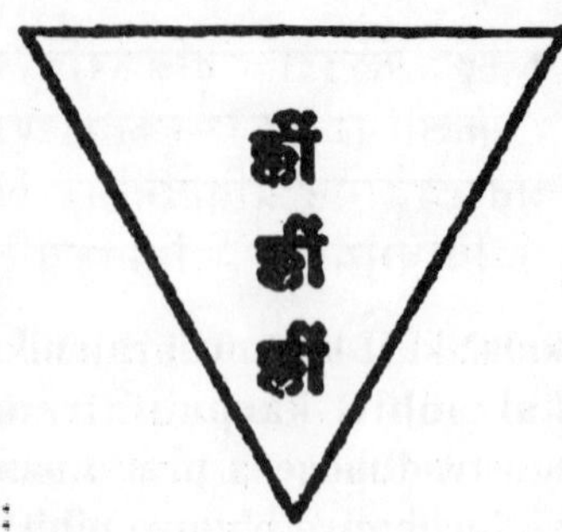

worshiping the yantra. Foods for offerings are cooked rice (mixed with curd) sesame, jaggery, Coconut, honey and plantains. The yantra is effective in healing of long-standing wounds, place of mind, and influence over others. Mantra for recital is:-

कलत्रं वैधात्रं कति कति भजन्ते न कवयः
श्रियो देव्याः को वा न भवति पतिः कैरपि धनैः ।
महादेवं हित्वा तव सति सतीनामचरमे
कुचाभ्यामासङ्गः कुरवकतरोरप्यसुलभः ॥९६॥

kalatraM vaidhaatraM kati kati bhajante na kavayaH
shriyo devyaaH ko vaa na bhavati patiH kairapi dhanaiH ।
mahaadevaM hitvaa tava sati satiinaamacarame
kucaabhyaamaasaN^gaH kuravakatarorapyasulabhaH ॥

96. Yantra for acquisition of learning.

It is useful in education, youthful energy and appearance, robust body. Yantra is drawn on stout white 'arka' stem or white sandal plank. The mantra for recital is one thousand times for eight days facing east direction. Ashtotharasat namavali of Saraswati is used in worship of this yantra with white flowers. Foods for offerings are cooked rice, milk-gruel, honey and fruits. Mantra for recital is:-

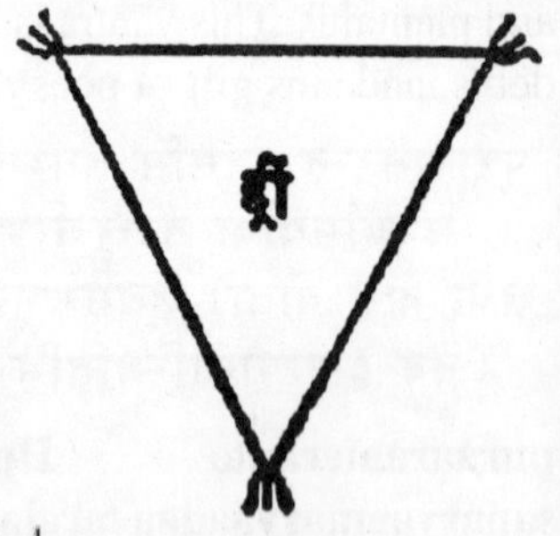

गिरामाहुर्देवीं द्रुहिणगृहिणीमागमविदो
हरेः पत्नीं पद्मां हरसहचारीमद्रितनयाम् ।
तुरीया कापि त्वं दुरधिगमनिःसीममहिमा
महामाया विश्वं भ्रमयसि परब्रह्ममहिषि ॥

giraamaahurdeviiM druhiNagR^ihiNiimaagamavido
hareH patniiM padmaaM harasahacaariimadritanayaamh ।
turiiyaa kaapi tvaM duradhigamaniHsiimamahimaa
mahaamaayaa vishvaM bhramayasi parabrahmamahiShi ॥

97. Yantra for physical strength and virility.

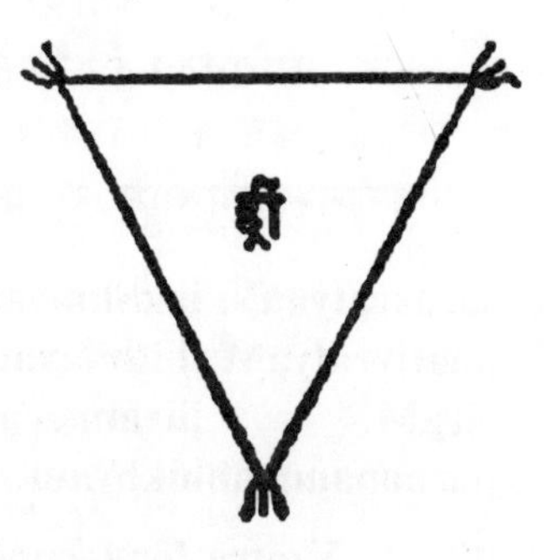

The yantra makes woman pregnant, men get virility and divine knowledge. The Yantra is inscribed on gold or copper plate. The mantra for recital is one thousand times for thirty days facing north-east direction. Lalita-Sahasarnama with red flowers is used for worshiping of this yantra. Foods for offerings are cooked rich honey and fruits. Mantra for recital is:-

कदा काले मातः कथय कलितालक्तकरसं
पिबेयं विद्यार्थी तव चरणनिर्णेजनजलम् ।
प्रकृत्या मूकानामपि च कविताकारणतया
यदाधत्ते वाणीमुखकमलताम्बूलरसताम् ॥

kadaa kaale maataH kathaya kalitaalaktakarasan
pibeyaM vidyaarthii tava caraNanirNejanajalamh ।
prakR^ityaa muukaanaamapi ca kavitaakaaraNatayaa
yadaadhatte vaaNiimukhakamalataambuularasataamh ॥

98. Yantra for getting god's grace.

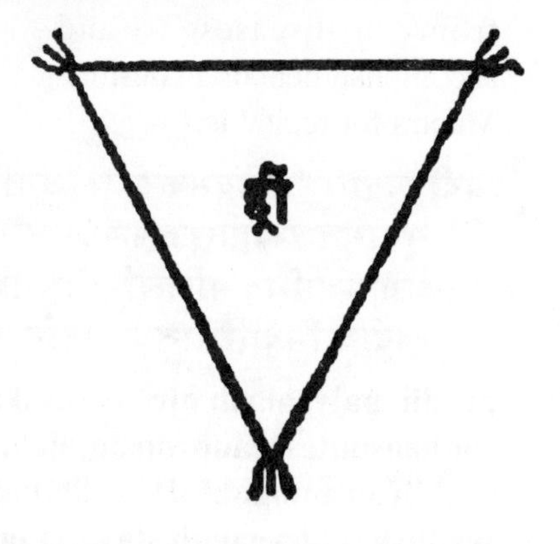

This yantra shows its effects in getting valour, happiness and god's grace. The Yantra is inscribed on gold plate. The mantra for recital is one thousand times for 16 days, facing east direction. Lalita thrisathi with vermilion are used in worship of the yantra. Foods for offerings are cooked rice brown sugar honey and plantains. Mantra for recital is:-

सरस्वत्या लक्ष्म्या विधिहरिसपत्नो विहरते
रतेः पातिव्रत्यं शिथिलयति रम्येण वपुषा ।
चिरं जीवन्नेव क्षपितपशुपाशव्यतिकरः
परानन्दाभिख्यम रसयति रसं त्वद्भजनवान ॥

sarasvatyaa lakShmyaa vidhiharisapatno viharate rateH paativratyaM shithilayati ramyeNa vapuShaa । ciraM jiivanneva kShapitapashupaashavyatikaraH paraanandaabhikhyam rasayati rasaM tvadbhajanavaan ॥

99. Yantra for fecundity after riddance of disease.

Yantra is inscribed on gold sheet. The mantra for recital is one thousand times for 16 days facing east direction. Worship is done with different kinds of flowers and Lalita Sahasarnama. Foods for offerings are cooked rice, sweet gruel, honey, fruits and betels with nut slices. The yantra is effective in providing all round success, freedom from diseases and accomplishment of all desires. Mantra for recital is:-

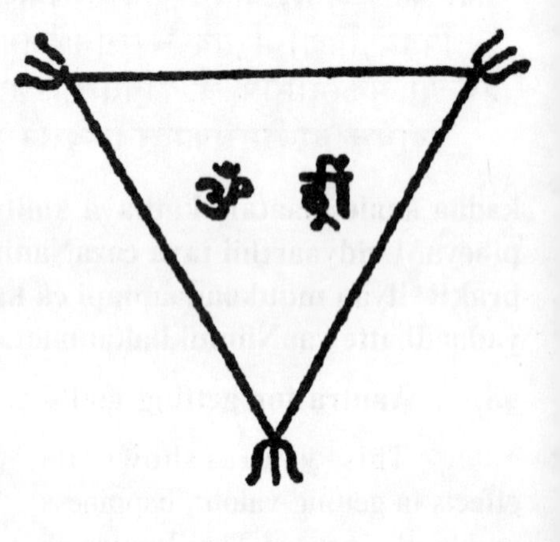

प्रदीपज्वालाभिर्दिवसकरनीराजनविधिः
सुधासूतेश्चन्द्रोपलजललवैरर्घ्यरचना ।
स्वकीयैरम्भोभिः सलिलनिधिसौहित्यकरणं
त्वदीयाभिर्वाग्भिस्तव जननि वाचां स्तुतिरियम् ॥

pradii pajvaalaab hir divasakaranii raajana vidhiH sudhaasuuteshcandropalajalalavairarghyaracanaa । svakiiyairambhobhiH salilanidhisauhityakaraNaM tvadiiyaabhirvaagbhistava janani vaacaaM stutiriyamh ॥

CHAPTER 15

BHAIRON YANTRA

In *Shiva Purana Bhairon* has been termed as incarnation of Lord *Shiva. Bhairon* can be appeased easily through worship and the famous worship is known as *Bhootak Bhairon Sadhana.* According to *Vishnu Purana,* Bhairon has been described as part of *Lord Vishnu*. In *Durga Saptsati upasana* of Bhairon in the beginning and at the end of *Durga japa* has been termed essential. This worship is particularly done in *Kalyuga*. The public at large is fearful about Bhairon but we may clear that this *sadhana* is easy and more fruitful. It gives comforts, *siddhi of mantras,* Yantras etc.

Some points to be remembered during Bhairon Sadhana

1. Bhairon worship has to be performed during night only.
2. This sadhana is to be performed for a specific purpose or for with a desire of future reward.
3. As per *Rudrayamal tantra* there are eleven types of *Nyasa* without which one cannot attain *siddhi* of this yantra. These are *prêt bija, narshing* bija, *kwan* bija, *satya* bija, *shree* bija, *pran* bija, *ghanta* bija, *khyati* bija, *mul* bija, *brahamari* bija and the last one with *matrika* nyasa.
4. Bhairon is worshipped in three characters i.e., *satwik* (pious), rajas (dictator), *tamas* (destructive). The *dhyana* of these characters is different for each *character*. If the devotee wants

to worship *Bhairon* for destructive purpose then he has to do *tamas* dhyana, if he wants to worship Bhairon for good works then he should worship Bhairon in *satwik* manner and for six rites Bhairon is worshipped in *rajas* manner. The *dhayana shalokas* for these three characters are as under:-

Tamas dhyana verse

ॐ त्रिनेत्रं रक्तवर्णं च
वरदाभयहस्तकम् ।
सव्ये त्रिशूलमभयं कपालं
वरमेव च ॥१॥
रक्तवस्त्रपरीधानं रक्तमाल्यानुलेपनम् ।
नीलग्रीवं च सौमयं च
सर्वाभरणभूज़ितम् ॥२॥

Om Trinetram raktvarn cha
vardabhayahastkam ।
savye trishulambhayam kapalam
varmev cha ॥ १॥
Raktvastrparidhanam
raktmalyanupleplam ।
nilgrivam cha saumayam cha
sarvabharan bhushitam ॥ २॥

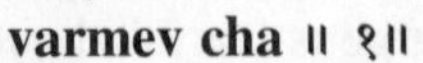

Rajas dhyana verse

तुज़ारकणिकाभासं
मायारूपमनन्तकम् ।
मूर्ध्नि खण्डेन्दुशकलं त्रिनेत्रं
शान्तिलोचनम् ॥१॥
सर्वकारणकर्तारं द्विभुजं रत्नभूज़ितम् ।
कपालं वामहस्ते च सूक्ष्मदण्डं च
दक्षिणे ॥२॥

पादनूपुरसंयुक्तंछिन्नष्शीर्ज़्विभूज़्तम् ।
सर्पमालासमायुक्तं हस्तोरुस्थूलजानुज़ु ॥ ३॥
आन्त्रमालासमायुक्तं सर्वाभरणभूज़्तम् ।

Tusharkanikabhasham mayarupamnantkam ।
Murdhin khandendushakalam trinetram shantilochanam ॥ १॥
Sawarankarankartaram dwibhujam ratanbhushitam ।
Kapalam vamhaste cha sukshamdandam cha dakshine ॥ २॥
Padnupursanyuktn chinnshirsh vibhushitam ।
Sarpmala samayuktam hastorusthulajanushu ॥ ३ ॥
Aantarmalasamayuktam sarvabharanbhushitam ।

Satwik dhyana verse

श्वेतवर्णं चतुर्बाहुं जटामुकुटधारिणम् ।
भुजङ्गपाशहस्तं च हस्तेदण्डकमण्डलुम् ॥१॥
शुक्लयज्ञोपवीतं च शुक्लकौपीन वाससम् ।
शुक्लवस्त्रपरीधानं श्वेतमालानुलेपनम् ॥२॥
त्रिनेत्रं नीलकण्ठं च मुक्ताभरणभूज़्तम् ।

Shwetvaran chaturbhahum jatamukutdharinam ।
Bhujangpashastam cha haste dand kamandalum ॥ १ ॥
Shukalyagopavitam cha shukalkopin vassam ।
Shukal vastra paridhanam shewat mala nulepnam ॥ २ ॥
Trinetram nilkantham cha muktabharanbhushitam ।

5. Before starting Bhairon *sadhana* the devotee should take bath during night. After getting fresh he should take permission before doing yantra worship.

6. The lamp should have cotton wicks made of *madar* in the equal

number of consonants of the mantra.

Aapdudharak Batuk Bhairon puja yantra

First we will discuss Aapdudharak batuk Bhairon yantra which is used for many purposes. The yantra could be drawn on *bhojpatra* with the stylus of pomegranate and ink of *Asthgandh* or could be carved on copper or gold. The mantra is as follows:-

ॐ ह्रीं बटुकाय आपदुराणायकुरुकुरुबटुकायह्रीम् ॥

Om Hrim Batukaya apdoidasanay kuru kuru Batukaye hareeng॥

The sage of the mantra is *Brahadiranya Rishi*, *Anustup* meter, deity Batuk Bhairon, Hrim *Bijam*, Om *Kilkam*. The yantra consists of eight petal lotus (*asthmatrkamaya)*, then a triangle, enveloped by one hexagon, circle, then eight petal lotus covering them all then a beautiful *bhupura*. Outside the bhupura four circles in each direction and three circles in south west direction. The mantra is recited for twenty one thousand times (according to ***Rudrayamla*** the mantra is to be recited for one hundred thousand times). The *homa* is done with the sesame seed mixed with pure ghee and honey.

Dhyana Verse

ॐ शुद्धस्फटिकसङ्काशं सहस्रादित्यवर्चसम् ।
नीलजीमूतसङ्काशं नीलाञ्जनसमप्रभम् ॥१॥
अष्टवाहुं त्रिनयनं चतूर्बाहुं द्विबाहुकम् ।
दंष्ट्राकरावलवदनं नूपुरारावसंकुलम् ॥२॥
भुजङ्गमेखलं देवमग्निवर्णं शिरोरुहम् ।

दिगम्बरं कुमारेशं बटुकाख्यं महाबलम् ॥३॥
खष्ट्वाङ्गमसिपाशं च शूलं दक्षिणभागतः ।
डमरुं च कपालं च वरदं भुजङ्गं तथा ।
अग्निवर्णसमोपेतं सारमेयसमन्वितम् ॥ ४ ॥

Om Sudh saftik sankasam sahasaradatiya varchsam
Niljimutsankasam nilanjamsamprabham
Asthvahum trinayanam chaturbahaum dvibahukam
Danstrakaravalvadnam nupuriravasankulam
Bhujangmekhlam devmaganivarnam shiroruham
Digambaram kumaresham batukakhayam mahabalam
Khsathvangmasipasham cha shulam dakshinbhagata
Damrum cha kapalam cha bhujangam thatha
Agnivarnsamopatam sarmeyasmanvitam

After realising the yantra the devotee can do the usages as under:-

1. On *dwitya* of *Shukla paksh* when it is Friday recite the mantra for three thousand times after placing powder of *adha pal vacha,* mixed with pure ghee in the same ratio by placing it on one plate of leaves. Eat those articles and recite the mantra once again for one hundred thousand times. The person who worships the yantra in this manner is bestowed with a sweet voice, ability to write scholarly, and to listen the sound from a far off place.

2. If the devotee does the homa with grains mixed in honey, pure ghee, flowers or turmeric mixed with red flowers milk and ghee he can attract any one.

3. If the devotee does the homa with the flowers of *palash* then he attains the *siddhi* of voice.

4. If he does homa with camphor and *gugal* mixed with *aguru* then he gets the spiritual knowledge.

5. For long life do homa with *durva* grass smeared in milk.

6. A devotee who treats a barren woman, if he worships Bhairon like son in child form, the lady will be blessed with a beautiful son, long life beauty etc. The devotee has to take ¼ grams of turmeric powder

of Vacha. Both have to be mixed in the urine of cow and make small balls of the paste. The same is to be placed in the plate in front of Bhairon. He has to do *japa* of Bhairon for one thousand times.

7. On Thursday morning at the time of Sun rise on a river bank or in a jungle the mantra is recited for ten thousand times to put any body under control.

8. On the midnight of Tuesday, recite the mantra for ten thousand times sitting at a four cross roads points. Perform the homa of one thousand mantra with ghee, rice boiled with milk *(kheer),* and red sandal. Say the name of the intended person for the purpose of *maran*.

Aapdudharak Batuk Bhairon dharan yantra

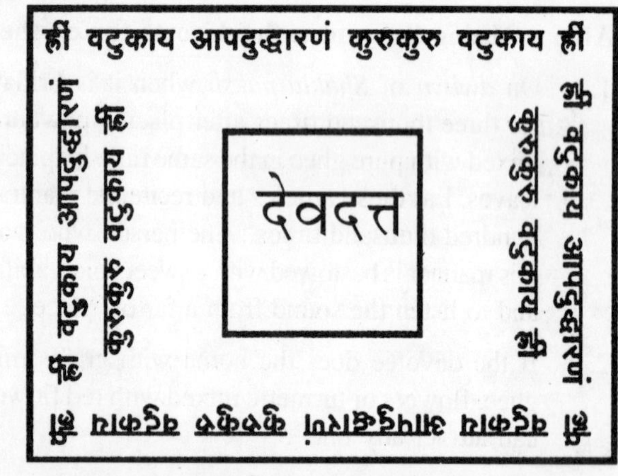

This yantra is written on bhojpatra and worn as an amulet covered in gold, silver or copper. The yantra is tied on right hand or worn in the neck. This yantra bestows all wishes in life. In place of *Devdatta* write the intended purpose or the name of the intended person.

Svarnakarsana Bhairva Yantra

If the devotee wants the effectiveness of all the Yantras mentioned so far he has to worship Matrika goddess or the *Bhutlapi* or at the time of writing any yantra, Svarnakarsana Bhairva. The mantra for recital is:-

ऐं ह्रींश्रींऐंश्रींआपादुद्धारणायह्रां ह्रीं ह्रूं
अजामलबद्धायलोकेश्वरायस्वर्णाकर्षण
भैरवायममदारिद्र्यविद्वेषणायममहाभैरवाय नमः श्रीं ह्रीं ऐं ॥

Aem hrim shirm aem shrim apdudharanaya hram hrim hrum ajamalbadhaay lokeshawaray swaranakarshanay bhairavaye mam daridraya vidweswanayee mahabhairava Namah Shrim Hrim Aem ॥

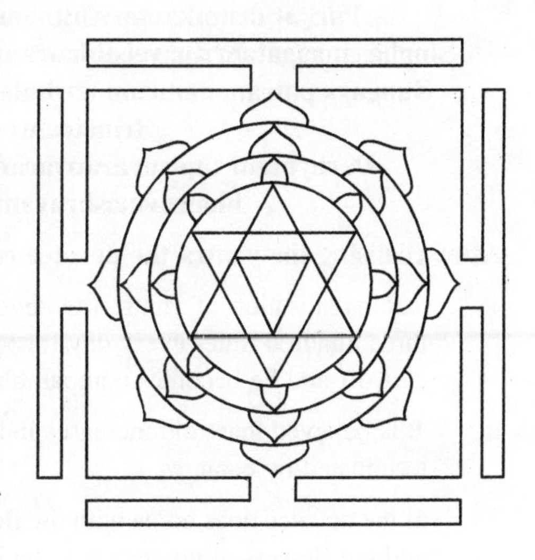

The sage of the mantra is *Brahma*, metre is *pankti* and the deity is Svarnakarsana Bhairva Hrim is *bija* and hrim is *shakti*. The mantra is recited for one hundred thousand times and perform ten thousand homa with milk pudding. The yantra consists of a down facing triangle, a hexagon, covered by three eight petal lotus then all enveloped by a bhupura. The mantra ॐ ह्रीं श्री एं श्री आपादुद्धारणाय be written in the triangle.

Dhyana Verse

पीतवर्णं चतुर्बाहुं त्रिनेत्रं पीतवाससम् ।
अक्षयस्वर्णमाणिक्यं तडित्पूरितपात्रकम् ॥१॥
अभिलषितं महाशूलं तोमरं चामरद्वयम् ।
सर्वाभरणसम्पन्नं मुक्ताहारोपशोभितम् ॥२॥
मदोन्मत्तं सुखासीनं भक्तानां च वरप्रदम् ।
सन्ततं चिन्तयेद्वश्यं भैरवं सर्वसिद्धिम् ॥३॥
पारिजातद्रुमकान्तारस्थितं मणिमण्डपे ।
सिंहासनागतं ध्यायेद्भैरवं स्वर्णदायकम् ॥४॥

गाङ्ग्यपात्रं डमरुं त्रिशूलं वरं करैः सन्दधतं त्रिनेत्रम् ।
देव्यायुतं तप्तसुवर्णवर्ण स्वर्णाकृतिं भैरवमाश्रयामि ॥ ५ ॥

Peet varn chaturbaahum trinetram peetvassam ।
Akshaya swaran manikayam taditpurit patrkam ॥ १॥
Abhilashitam mahashulam tomaram chamarduyam ।
Sarvabharansampanam muktaharopashobhitam ॥ २॥
Madonmattam sukhanisam bhaktanam cha varpardam ।
Santtam chintyedyasham bhairvam sarvasiddham ॥ ३ ॥
Parijat drumkantarsthitham manimandpee ।
Singhasanaagatam dhayeedbhairam swarandayakam ॥ ४ ॥
Gangaya patram damrum trishulam varam sanddatham trinetram।
Devayutam taptsuvaranvaran swaranakritiam bhairavmashrayami ॥ ५ ॥

After realising the yantra the devotee can do the usages as under:-

1. After realisation of yantra the devotee should recite the mantra three hundred times every day for forty nine days. His poverty is cast off and he becomes comparable with Lord Kubera.

2. It is believed that gold increases in the house and it will never be terminated by enemies.

3. If the devotee does homa with the flowers of *karavir*, *jati*, adhool, and red flowers of pomegranate he is blessed with good luck.

4. Homa with twigs of sandal blesses the devotee with siddhi of yantra and mantra.

5. During the night while facing west, lit lamp of mustard oil and recite this mantra for ten thousand times. This will remove poverty from the house.

CHAPTER 16

VASTU YANTRA

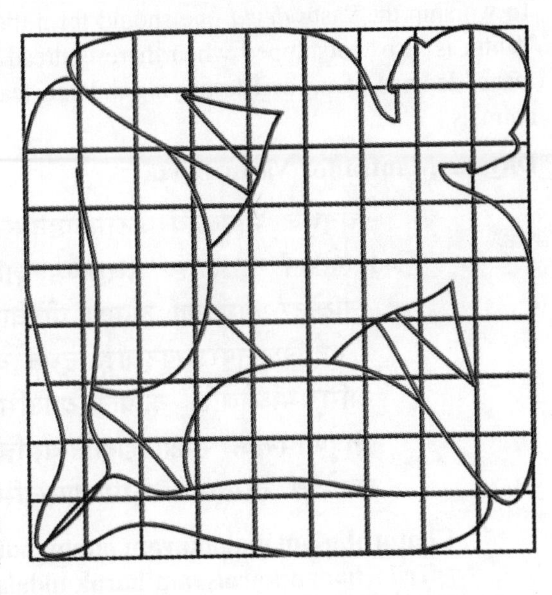

Now a days people are very much concerned with the Vastu of their houses, offices, business establishments etc. Even while consecrating a tank, temple, garden, a bridge, a tree or an idol, *vastu* God is worshipped. To rectify the *Vastu Doshas Vastu Shastris* recommends the physical changes in the building structure which are especially important because these changes most directly effect the overall energy situation. Secondly, the vastu shastris uses mirrors, the different elements, precious stones, herbs, and other means in order to influence the quality of the energies. This also yields a sustaining effect and a noticeable improvement of the well being of the people living in the building. However, another deep level of Vastu is the *karmic* plane, focusing on the combination and interaction of planetary influences inside the house. Such subtle means of correction are effective because Vastu qualities mainly effect the subtle plane, and therefore one can also find counteractive means on this plane. Yantras have been used in Vastu for thousands of years in order to balance defects on the energetic and karmic plane.

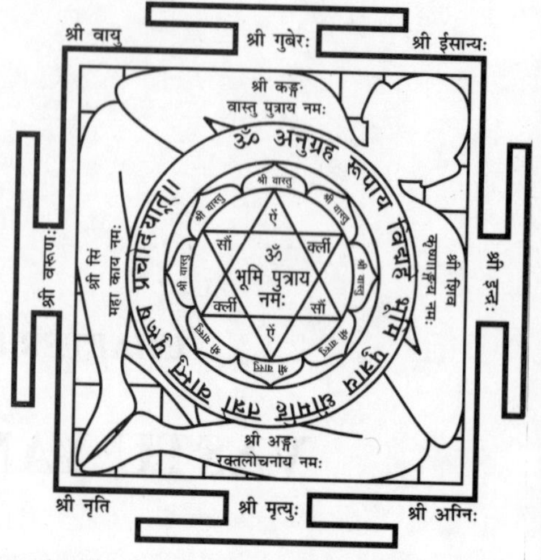

To worship the vastu *devta* one should form the Vastu *Mandala*. Vastu Yantra is also worshipped when there is dread of plague or a disease, fear of demons, of any evil destroying children, fear of accidents, voracious animals.

Dhyana Mantra for Vastu Devta

चतुर्भुजं महाकायं जटामण्डितमस्तकम् ।
त्रिलोचनं करालास्यं हारकुण्डलशेभितम् ॥
लम्बोदरं दीर्घकर्णं लोमशं पीतवाससम् ।
गदात्रिशूलपरशुखट्वाङ्गं दधतं करै ॥
असिचर्म्मधरैर्वीरैः कपिलास्यादिभिर्वृतम् ।
शत्रूणामन्तकं साक्षादुद्यदादित्यसन्निभम् ॥
ध्यायेद्देवं वास्तुपतिं कूर्म्मपद्मासनस्थितम् ॥

Chaturbhujam mahakayam jatamanditamastakam ।
Trilochanan karalsyam harakundalasobhitam ॥
Lambodaram dirghakarnam lo,asam pitavasasam ।
Gadatrisulaparasukhatvangam dadhatam karaih ॥
Asicharmmadharairviraih kapi8lsayadibhirvrtam ।
Satrunamantakam saksadudyadadityasannibham ॥
Dhyayeddevam vastupatim kurmmdpadmasanasthitam ॥

The Vastu Mantra:

क्षां क्षीं क्षं क्षैं क्षौं क्षृं: ।

Ksram Ksrim Ksram Ksraim Ksraum Ksrrumh ॥

Vastu Gayatri

ॐ वास्तुपुरुषाय विद्महे भूमिपुत्राय धीमहि तन्नो वास्तु प्रचोदयात् ।

Om vastu purushayee vidhmahe bhumiputraaye dhimahi tanno vastu parchodayat ॥

If a person performs *Homa* with sesame seed, clarified butter and pudding all his fears are pacified. When *Vastudevta* is worshipped, nine planets, ten guardians deities of the quarters, *Brahama*, *Vishnu*, *Rudra*, *Saraswati*, *Lakshmi*, *Parvati*, *Ganesha* as well all god and goddess are also worshipped.

If one finds a Vastu defect in the house or on the plot, he should find out first which planet is effected by this. Once he identified one or more planets, he should place a yantra to rectify the spot effected. In most cases one fixes the yantra on the wall; the height of the yantra depends on the yantra selected. The following chart provides an overview for the height of each yantra. The details given in the right column refer to the body of the person most effected.

Planet	Height
Sun	Heart/4th *chakra*
Venus	Solar plexus/3rd chakra
Mars	Spleen/2 nd chakra
Rahu	Coccyx/1st chakra
Saturn	Spleen/2 nd chakra
Moon	Throat / 5 th chakra
Mercury	Eyes/6 th chakra
Ketu	Crown of head/7 th chakra
Jupiter	Crown of head/7 th charka

Another possibility is to apply the *yantras* directly on the ceiling. In this case, it is important to position the yantra in such a way that its head (the side opposite the yantra, the upper side) is directed towards the east.

Vastu and nine planets

According to Vastu all forces and influences of the universe which have an effect on people can also be found inside the house. Utilizing the effective and simple system of the nine planets of our solar system, Jupiter, Venus, Mars, Saturn, Mercury, Rahu, Ketu, the Sun, and the Moon — as described in Astrology — we can understand these influences. By referring to these nine planets the astrological all over the world describe very precisely the forces on people which influence their fate like invisible threads. All areas of a person's life are represented by the nine planets and their interaction, so that their position can be seen as a reflection of the life situation of a person, home, or other building. Just as the various areas of life are dominated by individual planets, each direction, each function of a room, each building material, and every detail of a house is under the influence of a certain planet. Inside the house there is a lively exchange between these things and therefore also between the nine planets by which the inhabitants of the house will be effected. A house or apartment acts just like a lens which focuses the influences of the nine planets on its inhabitants and makes them feel their interactions. For instance, if a person is in a room located in the north of the house, he is automatically under the influence of Mercury, the ruler of the north. If the person sets up an office there, in which he intends to administer his financial dealings, the influence of Mercury is very beneficial for this endeavour as Mercury fosters financial affairs in general. In this case one must see to it that the north sector is designed according to Vastu principles. An office in the south dominated by planet Mars is under other influences. The planet Mars tends to foster more pragmatic aspects of life connected to work, research, or technology. The following table assigns the dominating planets to each direction:

Direction	Dominating planet
East	Sun
Southeast	Venus
South	Mars
Southwest	Rahu
West	Saturn
Northwest	Moon

North	Mercury
Northeast	Jupiter/Ketu

Vastu pursha

Vastu *purusha* always sleep on his left, but he goes on changing his head. No construction should be undertaken during the months when the construction ground is covered with his head, legs hand and back. This will cause harm to father, wife and children respectively. It also causes loss of money, theft and many other problems. As discussed, the directions must be propitiated with their yantras which have been provided in the previous chapters of this book. The mantras as per Vastu *Shastra* are given below :

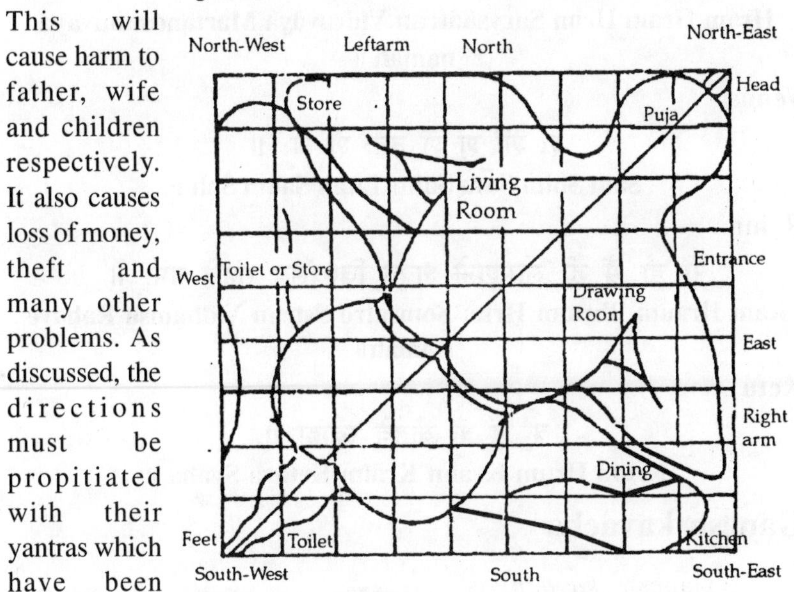

Sun

ॐ ह्रीं तिग्मरशमे आरोग्यदाय स्वाहा।।

Om Hrim Tigmarasme Arogyadaya Svaha ॥

Moon

क्लीं ह्रीं ऐम् अमृतकराऽमृतमं प्लावाय स्वाहा।।

Klim Hrim Aim Amrtakara Amrtam Plavaya plavaya Svaha॥

Mars

ऐं ह्रां ह्रीं सर्व्वदुष्टान्नपशाय नाशाय स्वाहा।।

Aem Hrim Hram Sarvadustannpashaya nashaya Svaha ॥

Jupiter

ॐ ऐं ॐ सुरगुरो अभीष्टं यच्छ यच्छ स्वाहा॥

Om Aem Om Surguro Abhistam yach yach swah ॥

Saturn

ह्रां ह्रां ह्रीं सर्व्वशत्रुन् विद्रावय मार्त्तण्डसूनुवे नमः ॥

Hram Hram Hrim Sarvshatrun Vidravaya Martandsunuvaya namah ॥

Venus

शं शीं शूं शैं ततः शैं शः ॥

Sam Shim Sum Saim Tatah Saum Sah ॥

Rahu

रां ह्रौ भ्रैं ह्रीं सोमशत्रो शत्रून् विध्वंसय राहवे नमः ॥

Ram Hraum Bhraim Hrim Somsatro Sstrun Vidhamsa Rahave Namah ॥

Ketu

क्रूं ह्रूं क्रैं केतवे स्वाहा ॥

Krum Hrum Kraim Kraim Ketava Svaha ॥

Ganesh kavacha

Ganesh *kavach* is prepared for rectifying most of the vastu doshas where modification is not possible in the house. It is prepared in Gold as under on *Guru pushya* day or any other most auspicious day and time and kept in the office of the Chief executive of the company or safe of the owner of the house or in the *pooja* room.

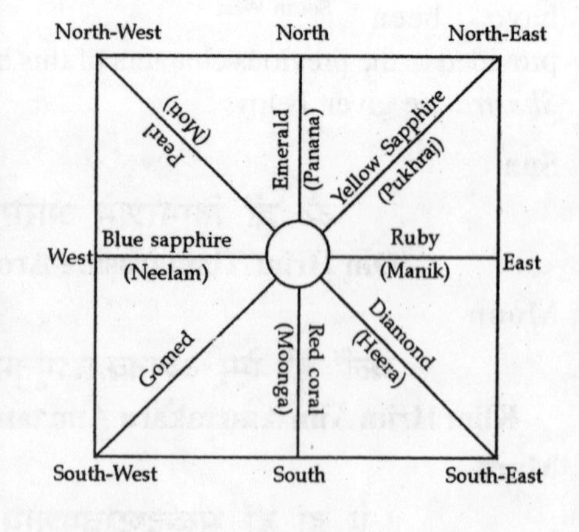

Vastu Digdosh Nashak yantra

This yantra is applied on all places where there are defects of directions, according to Vastu guidelines. It has a complex structure in which geometric elements, symbols, colours, and mantras are combined. Vastu-Purusha, the symbol of the life space, is in the centre of the Yantra. His head is directed towards the northeast, his feet to the southwest, and his joints are located in the two dynamic directions, the northwest and the southeast. If the yantra is mounted horizontally, the head of the Vastu Purusha should be pointed towards the northeast. The head should point towards the left side, if the yantra is affixed vertically on a wall. Around the Vastu Purusha there is a geometrical structure made of three circles, in which the thirty two directions of the sky are named and numbered. This structure has the effect of an antenna and at the same time of a mechanism which balances wrong placements of rooms or objects. In the outer environment of this geometry are the respective mantras of the demigods ruling over the particular directions. According to *Vedic* understanding, the demigods are powerful entities who are connected to the cosmic laws. The mantra for recital for worshipping this yantra is:-

ॐ महा भगवताय: वास्तुपुरुषाय: स्वाहा ॥

Om Mahabhagwataya vastu purashayee swaha ॥

This mantra is to be recited for hundred and eight times daily after the process of energising the yantra for better results.

CHAPTER 17

SIX RITES YANTRAS

There are six categories which are used by devotees for different purposes. By proper application they all bestow great powers and fulfilment of desires. They are as under:-

1. **Shanti karan: -** The literal meaning of *shanti* is peace but in this context the *shanti* word refers to destruction of sickness, cure of diseases and warding off the malefic influence of planets.

2. **Vashikaran: -** *Vashikaran* means under the influence and control but in this context this rite is undertook by the devotee for making a person do as was bidden by perceptor. In other words it could be said that one can control any woman, man, officer, minister, *devta*, soul animal etc., and can gain according to his wishes.

3. **Stambhan: -** *Stambhan* is a rite for stunning or it is intended to prevent some activity of some one in view or check persons as mentioned above to stop acting him.

4. **Vidveshan: -** *Vidveshan* is hatred. The purpose of this yantra is to bring split and mutual ill well between two friends.

5. **Ucchatan: -** The literal meaning of *Ucchatan* is driving away. It is used to dislodge some one from his state. The yantras deals with the distraction of mind of enemy and other persons so that they may remain away from their country, birth place, residence, home and family members etc. It also deals with when the Devotee

requires one to remain at war with others.

6. **Maaran: -** Maaran means killing. These are death persuading yantras through which any body can be killed.

To practice these rites there are some rituals which need to be understood before undergoing them. Without performing those, these yantras would not give their fruits. They are as under:-

1. **Deity: -** *Rati*, *Vaani*, *Rama*, *Jyestha*, *Durga* and *Kali* are the deities which are to be worshipped respectively in these rites.

2. **Colour of the deities: -** Their respective colours are white, pink, yellow, variegated, dark, coloured and grey. The deities are to be worshipped with the flowers of their respective colours.

3. **Seasons: -** There are six seasons described in the classics. They are spring, chilled winter, summer, rainy, autumn and winter. Each of these is represented in a day and lasts four hours starting with Sunrise. These are to be taken into account when performing the above rites.

4. **Directions: -** The directions of these rites are northeast, north, east, southwest, northwest and southeast. The devotee should face the respective quarter and repeat the mantra.

5. **Days:-**

   a) *Shantikaran* rites are performed on the *dwitya, tirtya, panchmi,* and *saptmi tithi* of *shukla paksha* of the lunar month coinciding with Wednesday or Thursday.

   b) *Vashikaran* rites are performed on the *chaturdashi, sashti, navmi, and triodashi* of *shukla paksha* of the lunar month coinciding with Monday or Thursday.

   c) *Vidveshan* rites are to be performed on the *ashtmi, navmi, dashmi,*and *ekadashi* of *shukla paksha* of the lunar month coinciding with a Saturday.

   d) *Ucchatan* rites are performed on the *ashtimi,* and *chaturdashi* of *krishna paksha* coinciding with a Saturday.

   e) The *Stambhan* and *Maaran* rites are to be performed on

the *ashtmi, chaturdashi,* of *krishan paksh* on the *poornima* day and on the *partipada* in the *Shukla paksha* coinciding with Sunday, Saturday or Tuesday.

Yantra for Shantikaran

1. For the purpose of subduing all calamities, quarrels and evil spirits the devotee should use this yantra. The yantra is written with *gorochana*, *musk*, *kapur*, and *kessar* on *bhojpatra* on an auspicious day with stylus of *jati*. Draw eight parallel lines horizontally and vertically constituting forty nine squares. The alphabets from *a* (अ) to *ja* (ज) with ma (म) are written in the outer squares. In the next inner squares sixteen letters from *jha* (झ) to *bha* (भ) (with *ma*) are written. The eight letters from *ma* (म) to *sa* (सः) (with *ma*) are written in the next inner squares and ha (ह) in the inner most square. Make thirty two tridents like marks at the extremities of the parallel lines. Above and below, in the spaces between the tridents *Hrim* (ह्रीं) is written (seven below and seven above).

The devotee should worship this yantra for three days by reciting *Durga Saptsati*. After that he should feed *Brahmins*. During these three days he has to lie on the bare ground at night. The yantra is to be covered in a metal box made of gold, copper or silver and worn on the arm or round the neck as an amulet.

2. This *shanti* yantra is used for checking the evil effect of spirits like *sakini*, goblins, vampires and evil planets posited in the natal chart. The devotee should write this yantra with *gorochana*, milk, *kapur*, and *kessar* on a *bhojpatra* with the stylus of *jati*. After drawing an eight petal lotus the name of the intended person is written in the middle replacing *devdatta* (देवदत्त) and *sah* (सः) in every one of he eight petals. This yantra is also worshipped with the *Durga Saptsati*. This yantra is tied around the neck or arm of the person as an amulet.

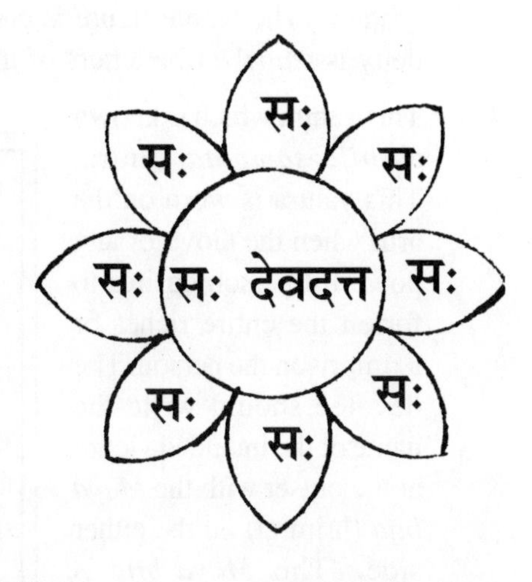

Yantra for Vashikaran

3. This yantra causes attraction and accord perfect achievement. The yantra is drawn on a brass vessel clean through ash of cow dung. It could also be drawn on gold, silver or copper metal. The yantra is worshipped for seven days. The devotee should draw eight petal lotus with the stylus of *jati* twig and *gorochana, kessar* as ink. The name of the intended person is to written in the pericarp in place of *devdatta* (देवदत्त) and in the petals the eight groups of letters are to written

encircled by a sixteen petal lotus in which sixteen vowels are written. The whole figure is encircled by three circles. Here the deity is *matrika* (the letters of the alphabet).

4. This yantra which is known as *bija samputa* yantra. This yantra is worn on the arm when the Govt. or any powerful person desires to forfeit the entire riches or to imprison the person. The devotee should write the name of the intended victim at the outset with the *Maya bija* (hrim ह्रीं) on the either side. This *Maya bija* is written above and below four times each. Surround this figure with *bhupura* with two parallel lines drawn in the figure. The yantra is written on *bhojpatra* with *gorochana,* sandal paste and *kessar* mixed with the blood taken out of the ring finger. It is duly worshipped. It is considered to be effecyive in attraction. The devotee shall feed virgins, women and religious students and offer oblation of red flowers, cooked rice and meat in order to perfect the rite of attraction.

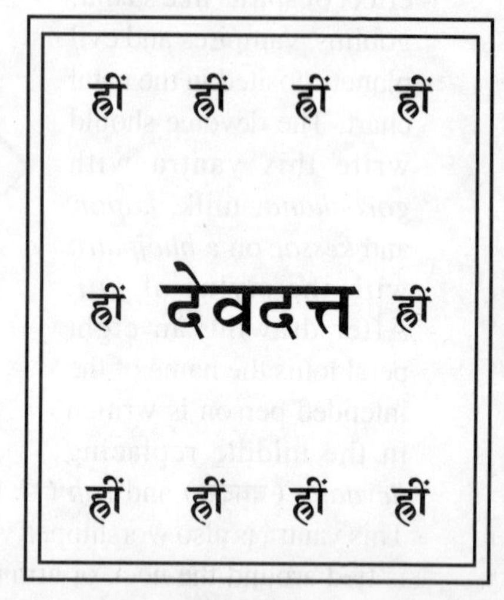

5. This yantra is known as *Raj Mohan* yantra which wards off the Govt.'s wrath when it is worn by drawing on a *bhojpatra* with the ink of *gorochana* and *kessar*. The yantra consists of an eight petal lotus. The name of the intended person is written

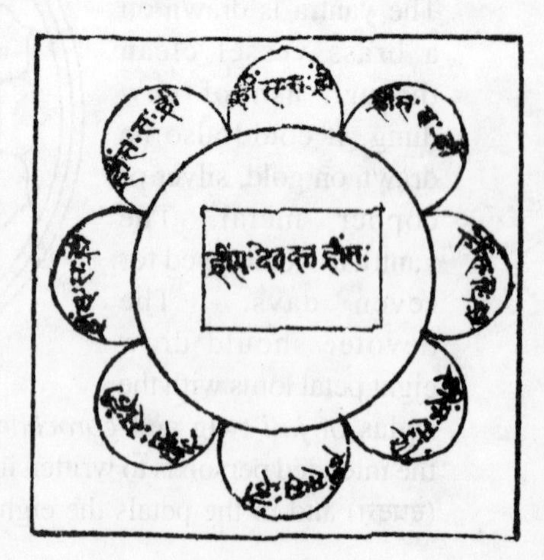

with *Maya bija* (hrim ह्रीं) suffixing sah (सः) and *sah hrim* (सःह्रीं). It is also written in all the petals. The whole figure is covered with a *bhupura.* It is put in two trays and worshipped for seven days by repeating the *Maya* bija (ह्रीं).

6. This yantra is used for fascinating people. This is drawn on a *bhojpatra* with *gorochana kapur*, *kessar* and *agar* four petal louts with the name of the intended person and also write the letter in the pericarp. Write *Om namoh* (ॐ नमो) in the entire petal and in the south and north petals write *ajite Om namoh* (अजिते ॐ नमों). Worship this yantra for three days and on the fourth day feed a *Brahmin* and wear this yantra as an amulet.

Stambhan Yantra

7. This yantra is known as *divya* Stambhan yantra. The devotee should write the name of the intended person in the middle of the hexagonal on a *bhojpatra* with the ink of *Gorochana* and *Kessar*. The *Maya Bija* spaces between triangles (sixteen in all) and place the yantra in a tray for worship. *Hrim* (ह्रीं) is repeated in front of it. Thereafter the devotee takes it out of the tray and ties to his head. In the course of the *Divya* ordeals with fire water etc., the devotee remains

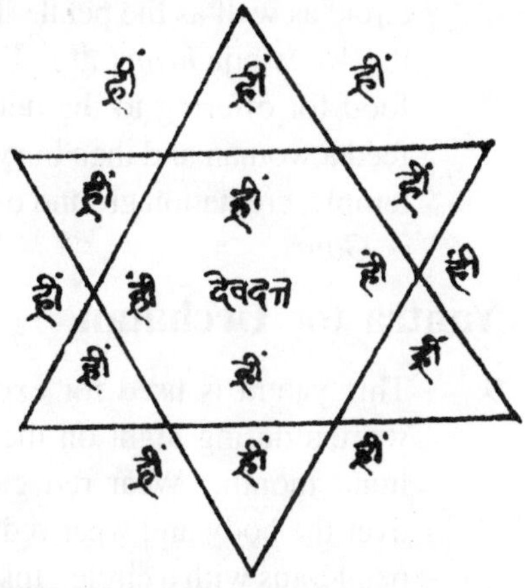

unscathed without being burned or otherwise affected. He performs the ordeals at night and he will get success.

Yantra for Vidveshwan

8. The *Vidveshan* yantra is used to bring the mutual enmity of the two enemies of the devotee for a long time. For writing this yantra feather of a crow is used as stylus and the blood of the enemy as ink. The devotee writes the name of the activity (ह्रीं यं ह्रीं देवदत्त स्पजगदत्तयोर्विद्वेषं कुरु कुरु) of the intended person as well as *Hrim yam Hrim* (ह्रीं यं ह्रीं) in a four petal lotus both in the circle as well as the petal. The yantra is worshipped at night with the *Maya* bija *hrim* (ह्रीं). Cooked rice mixed with goat's blood is food for offering to the deity. To complete the ritual one should feed a woman and then bury the yantra underground in an isolated temple, cremation ground or *Shiva* temple. The deity of this yantra is *Gauri*.

Yantra for Ucchatan

9. This yantra is used for exorcising of the enemy. The yantra is written during night on the *chaturdasi* of *krishna paksha* during lunar month. Wear red garments and applies red sandal paste over the body and wear red garlands. The yantra consists of four petal lotus with a circle. Ink used for writing the yantra is blood of an owl and a crow. The yantra is written on *bhojpatra*. The

name of the intended person is written inside the circle and letter *yah* (यः) in each of the four petals. In the centre write *devadatta ucchattanam kuru kuru* (देवदत्त उच्चाटनं कुरु कुरु). The yantra is worshipped with red flowers and sandal paste with the *vayu bija ya* (य). One virgin is fed everyday and given monetary gifts for twenty days. On the twenty first day the yantra is split into pieces and encased into stale food which should be given to crows. The deity of this yantra is *Gauri*.

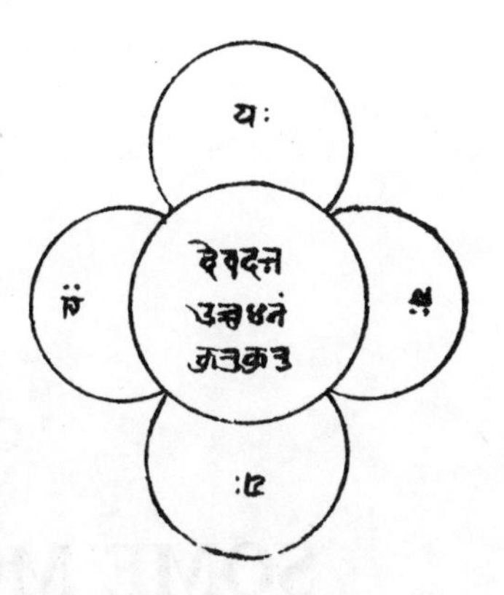

Yantra for Maaran

10. The *Maaran* yantra is used for death of enemy. The yantra is written on human skull with the feather of a crow as stylus and coal from funeral pyre. The ink is made of eight types of poison and sheep's blood by mixing together as material. The yantra consists of an eight petal lotus, name of the intended person with *Hum phat* (हूं फट) is written on either side. Write *Hum phat devadatta phat hu* (हूं फट् देवदत्त फट् हूं) in the petals of east, south, west and north write *hum* (हूं) and in the other petals *phat* (फट्) is written. The whole yantra is surrounded by *Hums* (हूं). This yantra is worshipped with *Astra Bija*, *phat* (फट्) . The yantra should be covered with ashes and partially burned everyday until on the twentieth day it is completely burned. The deity of this yantra is *Astram*.

CHAPTER 18

SOME MORE YANTRAS

Kuber yantra

In our classics if our sages emphasized upon *Lakshmi sadhna*, they haven't ignored the *Kubera*. The logic behind would be that the devotee has to increase the very effect of Lakshmi and then he has to please lord Kubera for maintaining her blessings over the devotee. The reason behind this concept is as water, fire, air, etc., are governed by different gods, likewise wealth is governed by Kubera.

Kubera is lord of *nav nidhis, padam, mahapadam, sankh, kachap, ukund, kund, makar, nil, and varchasav. Yaksha, kinner* (the musicians) , and other prosperity giving deities are governed by Kubera. All this is blessed by Lord *Brahma* on the wishes of Lord *Shiva*. If Kubera is worshipped, Lord Shiva and Lord *Shukra* (Venus) automatically bestows their blessings. The Kubera *sadhan* is done on the day of *Dhan Tirodhashi* (two days before deepawali). It could also be worshipped on *tirodhasi* of every month during *shukla paksha.* The yantra is to be carved on gold or copper plate. The devote could draw it on *Bhojpatra* with *asthgandh.*

Following is the Mantra of Kubera that bestows all types of prosperity. The Mantra of Kubera is as follows:

यक्षाय कुबेराय वैश्रवणाय धनधान्याधिपतये धनधान्यसमृद्धिं मे देहि दापय स्वाहा ॥

Yaksaya Kuberaya Vaisravanaya Dhanyadhipatye Dhana Dhanya Samrddhim Me Dehi Dapaya Svah ıı

The sage of this Mantra is *Visrava*, the meter is *Brhati* and the deity is the lord of wealth, the friend of *Shiva*.

The *sadanga Nyasa* is to be performed with the syllable of the Mantra split at 3, 4, 5, and 7 syllables. The devotee then meditates on *Dhanada* (Kubera) the resident of *Alkapuri*.

Dhyana Verse

मनुजवाहयविमानवरस्थितं गरूडरत्ननिभं निधिनायकम् ।
शिवसखं मुकुटादिविभूषितं वरगदे दधतं भज तुन्दिलम् ॥

Manujvahavviman var sitham garudratan nibham nidhinayakamı
Shiv sakham mukutaadivibhusitham vargade dadadhatam bhaj tundilam ıı

The devotee shall repeat the Mantra a hundred thousand times and perform ten thousand *Homas* with gingelly seeds. He shall worship in the pedestal with *Dharma* etc. The *Angas,* the guardians of the quarters and their weapons should be worshipped.

For the increase of wealth the devotee should repeat the Mantra ten thousand times in a Shiva temple. The Mantra is to be repeated a hundred thousand times while seated at the foot of *Bilva* tree This will bestow increase in wealth. Another Mantra of Kubera is destructive of all types of poverty. It is as follows:

ॐ श्री ह्रीं श्रीं ह्रीं क्लीं श्रीं क्लीं वित्तेश्वराय नमः ॥

Om Srim Om Hrim Srim Hrim Klim Srim Klim Vittesvaraya Namah ॥

The *sadanga* Nyasa is to be performed with the syllables of the Mantra split as follows - 3, 2, 2, 2, 5 and 2. The process of meditation, worship etc., as told earlier.

Good luck- *vijay* Yantra

This Yantra can be used by the ladies for infatuation of men and by men to infatuate the ladies. This Yantra is written with sweet water and *gorochan* on *bhooj patra.* The pooja of this Yantra is performed with scent, flowers *dhoop* etc.

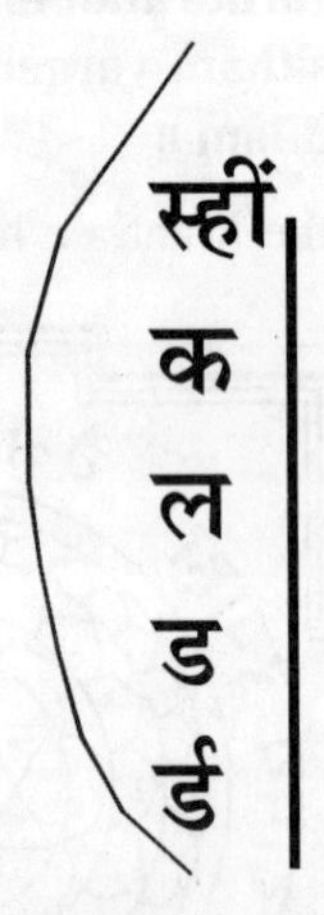

The Yantra be wrapped in gold talisman and be worn by man on his right arm. The woman should wear it in neck. In addition this Yantra is useful for good luck and all desires are fulfilled.

Yantra for epilepsy

The Yantra is written with *Ashatgand* on *Bhoojpatra* and is used in neck or kept on person. The yantra can also be embossed or engraved on copper or stainless steel plate.

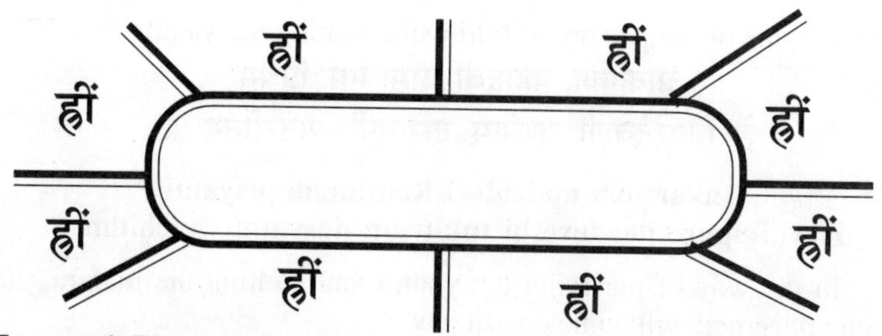

Kamraj Yantra

This yantra is known for attraction of a woman. Write this yantra on the palm of left hand with the blood of third finger of right hand. Write the name of Lady in place of word " *Devdatta* " as shown in the yantra. It should be purified with *Asth gand*, flowers, etc., and the lady who is to be infatuated be thought in mind. The lady will come at her own accord within six hours. Following mantra is recited for one hundred and eight times daily.

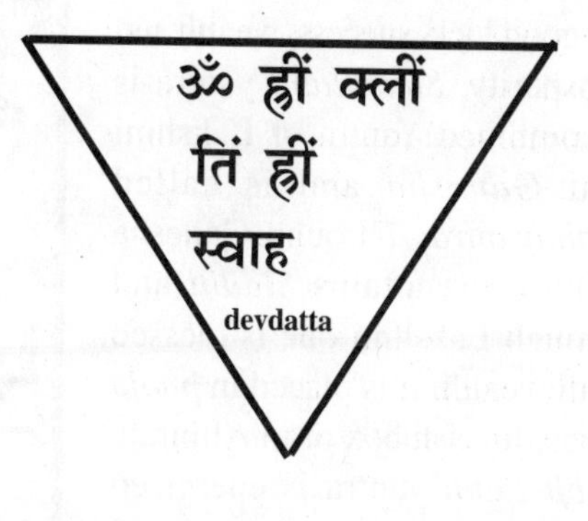

ॐ ह्रीं क्लीं तिं ह्रीं स्वाहा ॥

Om Hrim Klim tim hrim swah ॥

For attraction of any body

This yantra is used for attraction of anybody. Write this yantra on *Bhooj patra* with water mixed with Gorochan. Replace the word "*Devdatta*" with the name of intended person.

Purify the yantra with Gand, flowers etc. Put yantra in *ghee* and recite the following mantra for hundred and eight times. In the mantra replace the word "*Devdatta*"

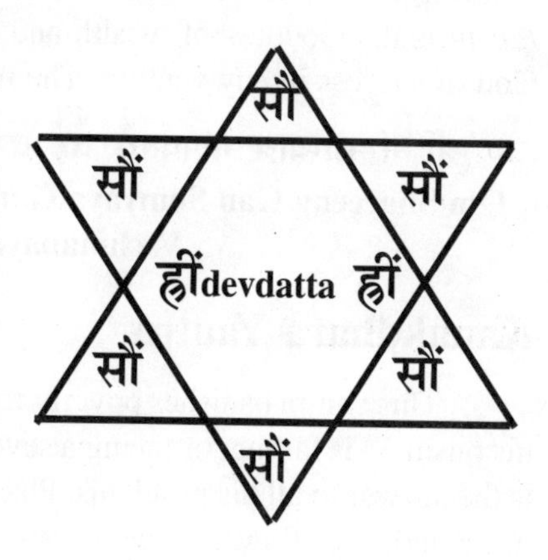

with the name of the person as told while writing the yantra.

आकर्षण महादेवी राम मम प्रियम
हे त्रिपुरदेवेशी तुभ्याम दसयामी यानचीतम् ॥

Aakarshan mahadevi Ram mam priyam
Hey Tripure devdeveshi tubhyam dasyami yanchitam

In the way of purifying the yantra and reciting the mantra, the person concerned will come on 7th day.

Subhlabh or Vyapar vridhi Yantra

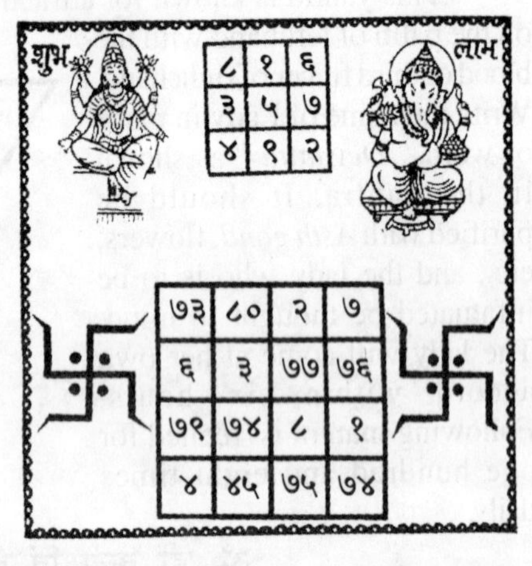

This Yantra is considered for good luck, success, wealth and prosperity. *Shubhlabh* yantra is a combined Yantra of Lakshmi and *Ganesha* and is called *Mahayantra*. Through Ganesha Yantra one attains *Siddhi* and through Lakshmi one is blessed with wealth. It is placed in *pooja* place, in cash box or in Almirah. *Subh Labh* yantra is energised by reciting its *Bij* mantra 1008 times and also the *homa* is performed with 108 mantras. It is very auspicious and is a combined Yantra for worship of Goddess Lakshmi and Lord Ganesha. Goddess *Laxmi* is the Goddess of wealth and prosperity and Lord Ganesha, the God of success in any venture. The mantra for recital is :-

ॐ श्रीं गं सौम्याय गणपतये वर वरद सर्वजनं मे वशमानय स्वाहा ॥
Om Shareeng Gan Somyaya Ganpataye var varad Sarvjan me Vashmanaya Svaha ॥

Kanakdhara Yantra

This yantra banishes poverty from life. If one is heavily in debt, or his business is failing, or facing a severe financial crisis, then this Yantra is the answer to all his problems. Place it on a wednesday in the worship place and offer flowers, rice, grains, light and incense, then chant only twenty one times the following mantra. One should do this for eleven consecutive wednesdays and then place the Yantra in safe or where the valuables or cash is kept in the home. Besides the following mantra, the yantra is worshipped through the Kanakdhara *stotra* by Adi Guru Shankra Acharya.

The mantra for recital is:-

ॐ ह्रीं सहस्त्रवदने कनकेश्वरी शीघ्रं अवतार आगच्छः ॐ फट् स्वाहा ॥

Om Hreem Sahastravadane Kanakeshwari Sheeghram Avatar Aagachh Om Phat Swaahaa ॥

Dhanda Yantra

This yantra is very effective for eradicating and removal of poverty and the wearer owns a vast wealth. According to *tantra kalpadrum* if the devotee can perform hundred thousand *japa* with beads of jewels he can achieve success in this mantra. By performing eighty thousand japa every night for seven consecutive days a devotee can have every thing he desires. The foods for offering are rice cooked with milk and sugar either before or after taking food. If he utters Dhanda mantra, given below, ten times whether pure or impure in body and mind he has not to suffer a pinch of poverty.

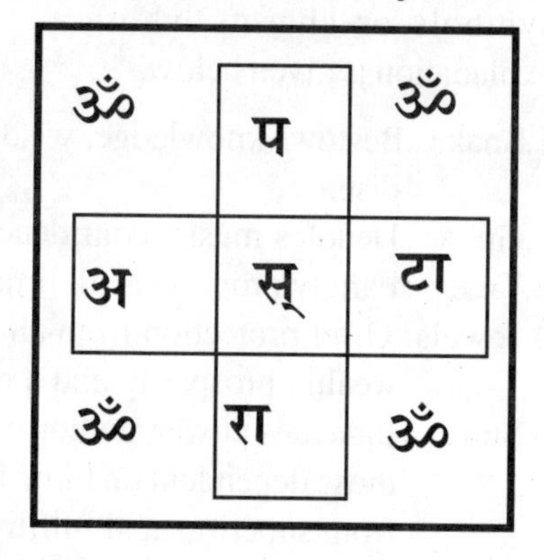

Its *purascharan* becomes effective if one thousand japa and one hundred homas with ghee, honey and sugar are performed daily for a week. By doing so, poverty is removed. If the goddess is worshipped inside the circle drawn inside a copper pot by applying sandal paste, poverty can never afflict the devotee who thus becomes owner of vast wealth. The mantra for recital is:-

ॐ नमः विष्णवे सुरपतये महावलाय स्वाहा ॥

Om namah Vishnave Surpataye mahavilaye savah ॥

This Yantra is to be carved on cooper plate or *bhojpatra*. Only worshipping of this yantra makes the person rich. This yantra is to be kept in *pooja* room. This yantra gives its benefit if worshipped on the day of *deepawali*.

Karya siddhi yantra

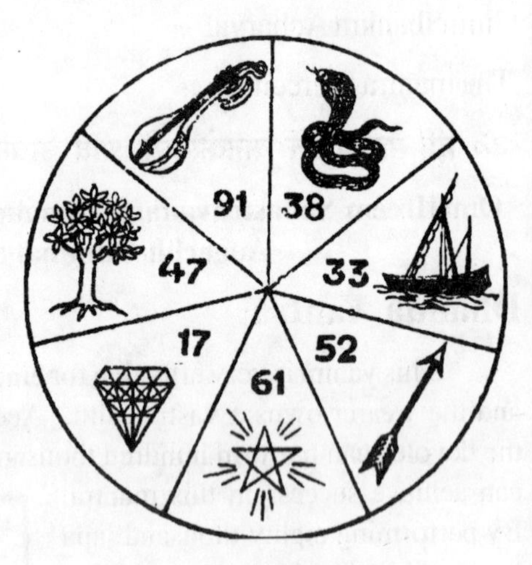

This yantra is very effective in ensuring the individual's well-being and success in almost every aspect of life. The Yantra is composed of a circle, divided into seven equal segments which have a digit of its significance having sum total of 339. The symbols shown in the yantra are lucky symbols or charms whose explanation is given below.

1. Snake : Bestows knowledge, wisdom and means of healing from disease.
2. Guitar : Denotes music, confidence and happiness
3. Tree : Family progress at all times including in the future.
4. Jewels: Offer protection from all troubles and stands from health, wealth, prosperity and a comfortable and happy home.
5. Sun : Indicates power, authority and finances of the individual and those dependent on him. It indicates success in politics, favour from superiors and fulfilment of desires.
6. Arrow: Denotes protection against evil eye and other dangers to both the individual and his family.
7. Ship : A unique mark as it indicates courage for the individual against any odds and ensures his success in all activities.

These symbols are used by people as lucky charms. This yantra bestows the individual's well being and success in life. After performing *pooja,* it is hung in house. It is carved on copper, stainless steel plate etc.]

Vahan Durghatna Yantra

(Protection from Accidents/ Mishaps)

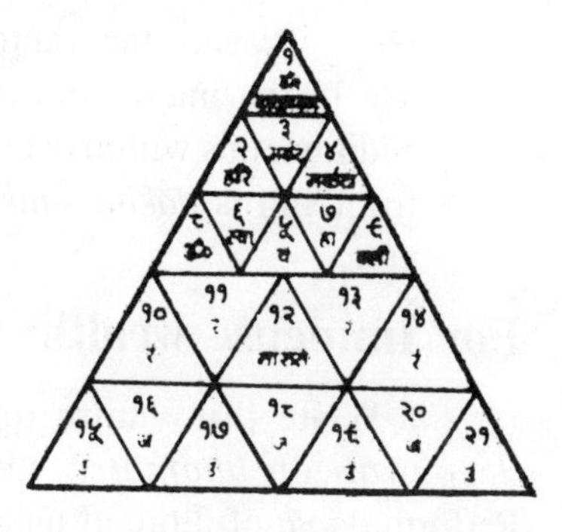

Vaahan' is vehicle and *'Durghatna'* is accident. As the name denotes, this Yantra ensures protection from accidents, injury, or other mishaps, especially which are related to motor vehicles. It acts as a shield to protect and save the devotee from any such misfortunes and ensures family's and his belonging's safety during journeys.

Child dosh nashak yantra

These are two types of yantras. The first yantra have eight petal lotus having hrim as *bija* mantra. The other yantra is written with *sah*, the bija written in it.

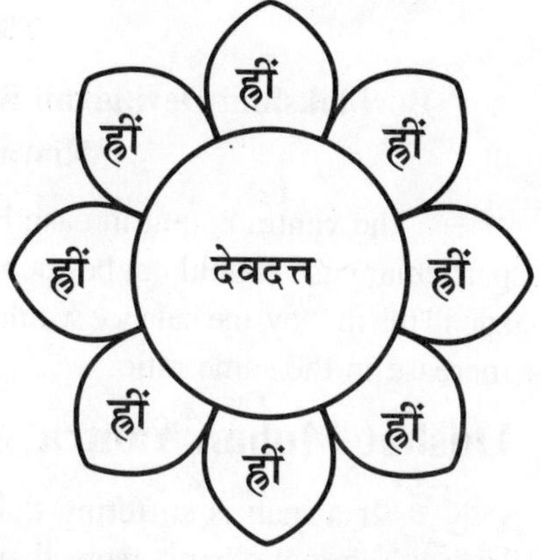

a) Children are afflicted easily by evil spirits. If any patient is suffering from epilepsy or a child remains with afflicted health, this yantra is to be used. The yantra is written on *bhojpatra* with *kasturi*, red vermillion and camphor with the stylus of jasmine. The *pooja* of yantra is to be performed with flowers, incense, lamp, *gandh* etc. After this exercise the yantra be closed in the metal talisman. This talisman can be put in the neck of child or be worn by a person in neck. Write the name of child or patient in the centre of the yantra replacing *devdatta* (देवदत्त). Actually this yantra is used for a child from early age for safety.

b) Repeat the yantra by writing above. Replace the word *hrim* (ह्री) with *sah* (*स:*). Prepare the yantra as above and use in the matter indicated above. In addition, this will save the person or child from spirits *dakini shakini* and *balgrah* etc.

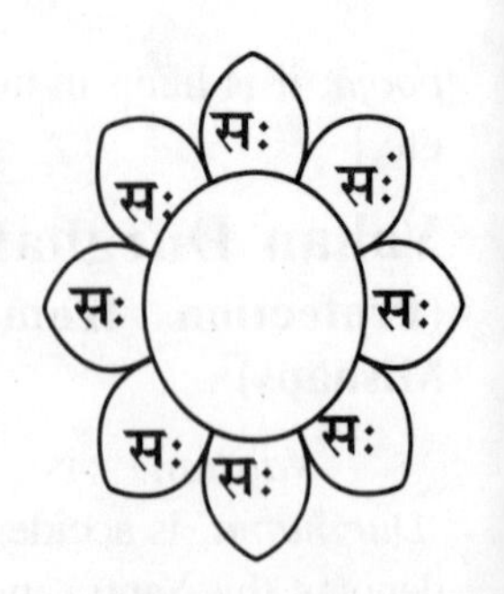

For Immense wealth

Write this yantra on the night of *deepawali* on *bhojpatra* with *Asthgandh*. Perform *pooja* of Lord of monkeys Hanuman with dhoop lamp etc. After that yantra be placed before the photograph of hanumanji and recite the following mantra for one hundred and twenty five times. The mantra for recital is:-

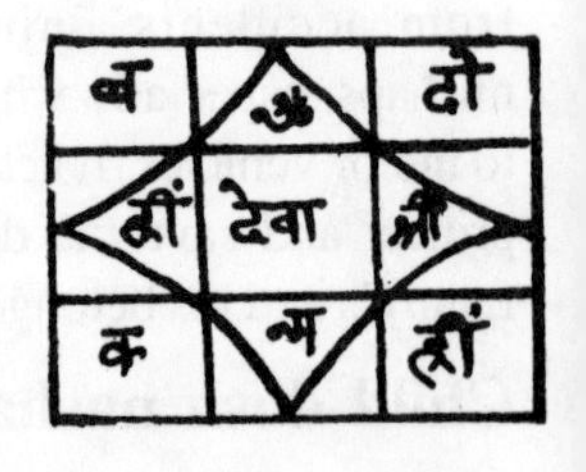

बोरी लक्ष्मी देवी लक्ष्मी दे सिद्धकारणी मम भण्डारपुरी क्रियं स्वाहा ॥

Bori lakshmi Devi laxmi Siddhikarini mam Bhanmdarpuri Kriyam Svaha॥

The yantra be put in cash box or safe where money is kept. The particular cash should not be spent for nine days. After nine days as you spend the money, the balance would increase in the same ratio.

Dushat Mohan Yantra

If a man is suffering due to backbiting of other persons then in order to infatuate them use this yantra. It destroys the enemies. The devotee should write this yantra on Bhojpatra with his blood. Write the name of other person instead of word '*devdatta*'. Then

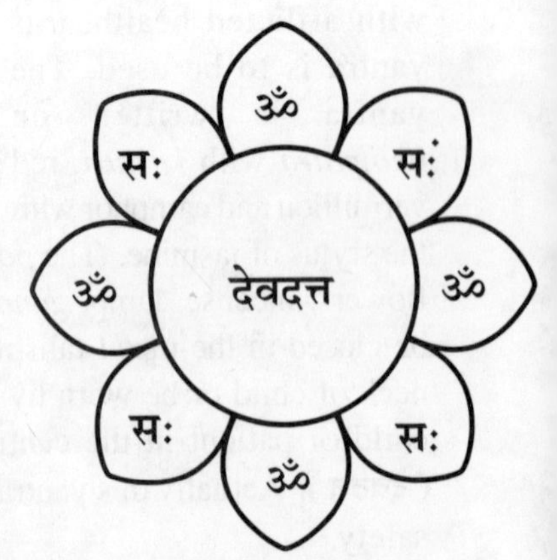

pooja be performed of yantra as per standard directions. After Pooja, the yantra is kept in milk for twenty one days, the enemy or the persons back biting against devotee will be infatuated and would stop their actions.

Shri Jagdishvar Yantra

This yantra is used authentically for *Vashikaran* of all. This yantra is to be written on *Bhojpatra* with stylus of *chameli* and *kessar, kasturi*, red sandal and *Gorochan* are to used for the purpose of ink. Pooja of yantra is performed with incense, flowers etc. for three days. After that yantra be enclosed in three metals talisman and be worn on the arm. All the intended persons will be in your favour and infatuated. The *pooja* of this yantra is performed daily to maintain its strength.

ॐ	वं	जे	ह्रीं	डं
ढैं	बुं	ह्रीं	ॐ	डं
वं	डं	जगत बं	ॐ	ह्रीं

Kamakasha Yantra

This is used to put the ladies of royal families under control or those connected with higher status etc. Write this yantra on *Bhojpatra* with *Gorochan, kumkum*, and *kapur* with *chameli* stylus and write the name of lady instead of word "*Devi*". While writing the yantra, the writer should wear white clothes and perform *pooja* of yantra with full confidence with flowers, dhoop etc., during night, keeping in view the

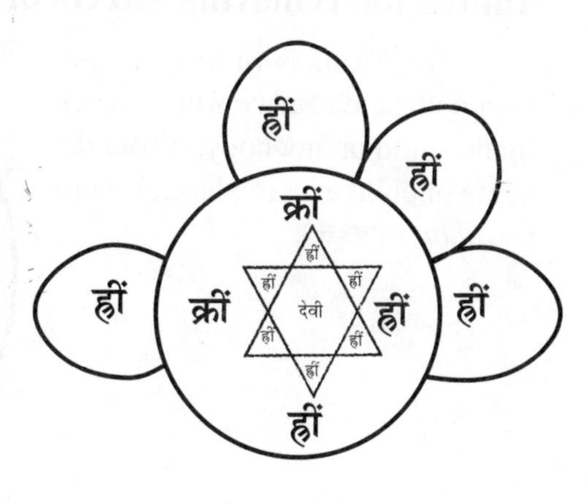

figure of the intended Lady. This *pooja* should remain continued for seven days and after that lunch be offered to female Brahmins and give donation. The mantra for recital is:-

ॐ नमः कामाख्यायै सर्वसिद्धिदायै अमुककर्म कुरु कुरु स्वाहा ॥

Om Namah kamakhyaee sarvsiddhidayee amukkaram kuru kuru swaha ॥

The sage of the mantra is *vahinik*, metre *jagti*, deity *kamakshya pranav shakti*, *avyaktam kilkam*. The mantra is to recited for ten thousand times.

Dhyana verse

ॐ योनिमात्रशरीर या कंगुवासिनि कामदा ।
रजस्वला महातेजा कामाक्षी दयायातम् सदा ॥

Om yonimatra sharir ya kanguvasini kamada ।
rajasvala mahateja kamakshi dyayatam sada ॥

Recite the words, *(Kamakshee Priyatam,)* and enclose the yantra in three metals talisman, which be worn on right hand arm. This yantra is very powerful, what to talk of ordinary ladies, the ladies of royal families are automatically infatuated.

Yantra for removing effects of Evil eyes

This Yantra is written on paper with Asthgandh and be worn in neck by the child or any body. Write the name of child etc., in place of word *Devdatta* (देवदत्त).

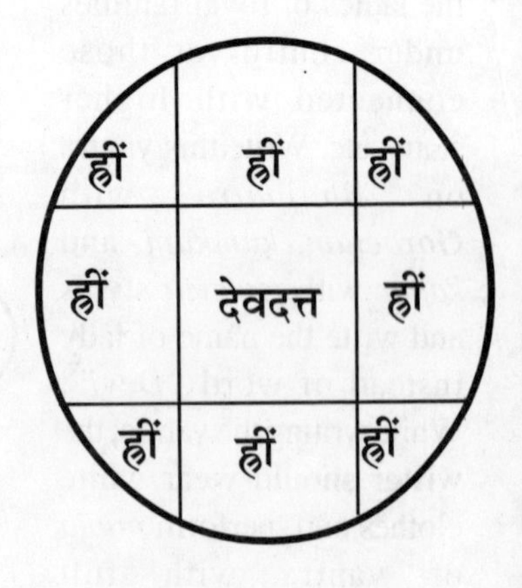

Yantra for cure from windy complaints

Write this yantra with saffron on a *bhojpatra.* Wash it on Sunday before sunrise. The water, after washing the yantra is taken by the patient. He will be cured of windy complaints. Write the name of patient in place of word *Devdatta* (देवदत्त).

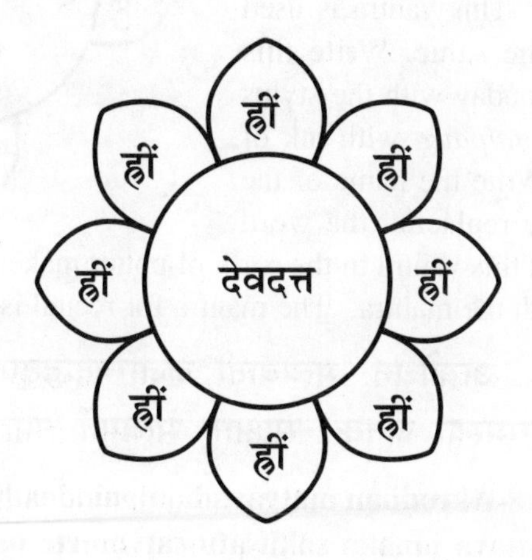

Yantra for barren woman

This yantra is quite useful for women who do not conceive. By the use of this yantra, they will become pregnant. Write this yantra on bhojpatra or *talpatra* (birch of palmyra palm) with *Asthgandh*. Perform *pooja* of *Rudra* or *Rudra kali* and wear this yantra on left arm or waist or in the neck. She will become pregnant.

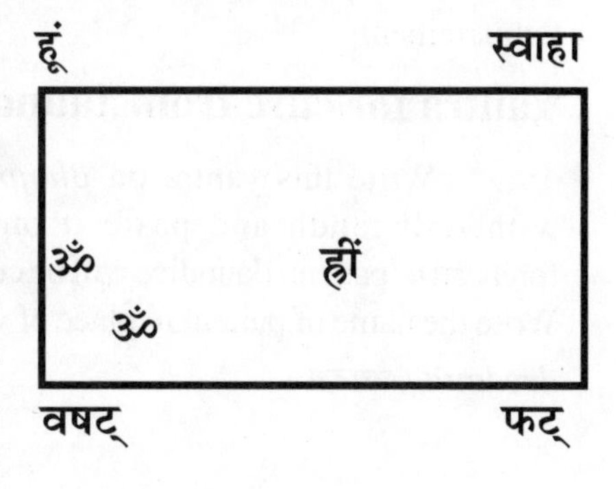

Jamdagney Yantra

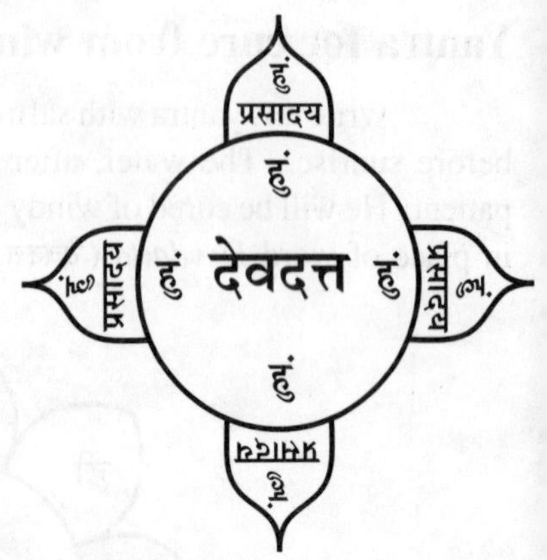

This yantra is used when either husband or wife or a friend, or an officer etc., is of continuous trouble to the other due to rash temperament. This yantra is used to control the same. Write this yantra on Monday with the stylus of iron on a *talpatra* with ink of *gorochan*. Write the name of the person while replacing the word *Devdata.* Put this yantra in the earth of potter maker and perform *pooja* of yantra with the mantra. The mantra for recital is:-

अक्रोधनः मत्यवादी जजग्निद्द्धदप्रत ।
रामस्या जनकः साक्षातु सत्वमूर्ते नमोस्तुते ॥

Akrodhan matyavadi jajgniddaadprat
Ramsaya janaka sakhsatu satvmurte namostute ॥

Recite the mantra for seven days for eleven hundred times daily. The devotee should take only curd and rice during worship of yantra. The person will leave the habit of rashness and have a calm temperament.

Yantra for cure from Jaundice

Write this yantra on *Bhojpatra* with Asthgandh and paste it on the forehead of patient. Jaundice will be cured. Write the name of patient in place of word *devdatta* (देवदत्त).

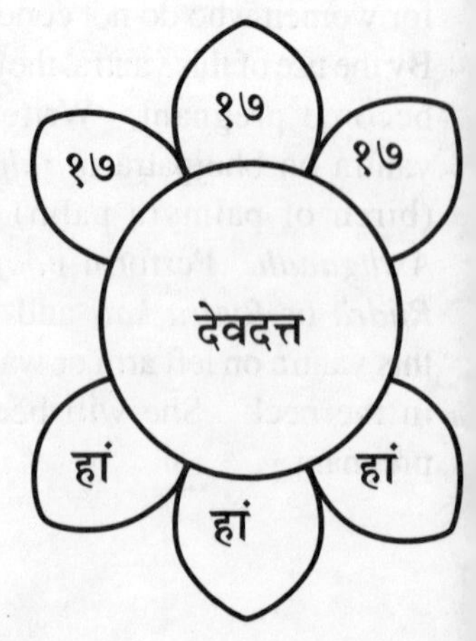

Vypar vridhi yantra (Yantra for boosting business and career)

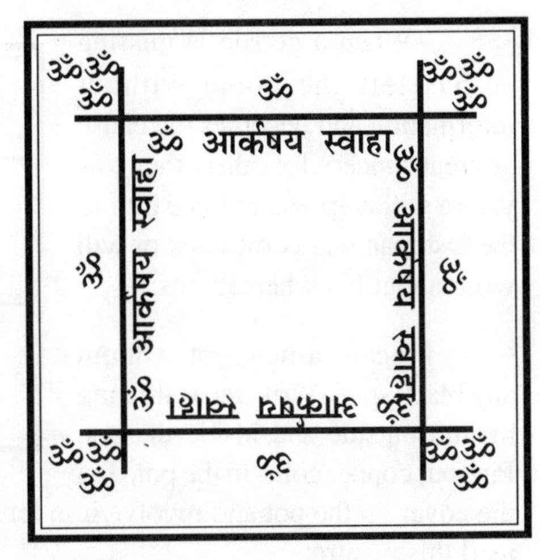

This is most effective yantra. The yantra be written on *bhojpatra* or inscribed or carved on a copper or silver plate and be hung on the shop in a beautiful frame or be kept in person to get the described results. The yantra has been used and found successful. The mantra is recited for one hundred and twenty five thousand times and after that *pooja* be performed. People who are out of employment or want upgrading on their service or increase in the business must use this yantra. The mantra for recital is:-

ॐ आर्कषय स्वाहा ॥

Om akarshaye swaha

Mahasaubhagaya Janan Yantra

This yantra is written with water mixed with *Gorochan* and *pooja* of yantra is performed with *gandh,* flowers etc., and wrapped in a talisman of Gold worn on the right arm by man and on the left by a woman for good luck, removing poverty and such like miseries. The person who wears this yantra is always loved by the opposite sex and likewise is the case with ladies.

Yantra for finding missing person

When a person is missing or has left the home without information and becomes the cause of great concern for others then this yantra will help you to trace him or the lost man will come back or will write about his whereabouts.

ऐं	ह्रीं	क्लीं
डा	मुं	चा
यै	बि	च्चै

Procure a new pot without any black spot. Write the following mantra outside and inside the pot. Put four copper coins in the pot. Put the cover on the pot and revolve it in left direction (anti-clockwise) and read this mantra: -

ॐ ऐं ह्रीं क्लीं चमुण्डा हई विजय ॥

Om Aeeng Hareeng Kaleeng Chamunda Hae Vijay ॥

Revolve the pot for seven times and keep it aside. Repeat the process for seven days, the man will either come back or write a letter. Alternatively write this yantra on white paper and revolve in reverse direction after mounting it on spinning wheel.

Annapurna Yantra

Goddess Annapurna is worshipped for getting all desires fulfilled. By worshipping this yantra the person become honoured by the people and he shall be at par with Kubera by means of his riches. It is said that Lord Kubera by worshipping Devi Annapurna became the Lord of treasures and he got friendship with Lord Shiva.

The yantra consists of a Triangle, four petal lotus, eight petal lotus, sixteen petal lotus surrounded by a beautiful *bhupura*. The yantra could be made on gold, silver copper or *bhojpatra* with the stylus of pomegranate with ink of *Asthgandh*. The mantra for recital is:-

ॐ ह्रीं श्रीं क्लीं नमो भगवते माहेश्वरि अन्नपूर्णे स्वाहा ॥

Om Hrim Srim Klim Namo Bhagwati Mahesvari Annapurne Svaha ॥

Dhyana Verse

तप्तस्वर्णनिभा शशाङ्कमुकुटा रत्नप्रभासुरा
नानावस्त्रविराजिता त्रिनयना भूमिरमाभ्यां युता।
दर्वीं हाटकभाजनं च दधती रम्ययोचच्यीनस्तनी
नित्यं शिवमाकलय मुदिता ध्येयान्नपूर्णेश्वरि ॥

Taptsawarnnibha shasankmukuta ratanprabha sura
nanavastvirajata trinayana bhumiramabhayam yuta ।
darvi hatkabhajanam cha dadhati ramyyochcpinastani
nityam shivmakalya mudita dhayyannpurneshwari ॥

The sage of the mantra is *Druhina*, the metre is *Krti* and the deity is *Annapurnesi*. During the worship of *Annapurna, Shiva Varha* and *Madhava* are worshipped with their respective mantras. The mantra has to be repeated a hundred thousand times and the *homa* is to performed ten thousand times with *caru* smeared with ghee.

To Prevent Abortion

When a lady faces abortions one after another this yantra prevent it. Write this yantra on *Bhojpatra* with excreta of elephant or be embossed or carved on copper plate. After *pooja* of yantra with flowers etc. this yantra is worn in neck of lady putting in

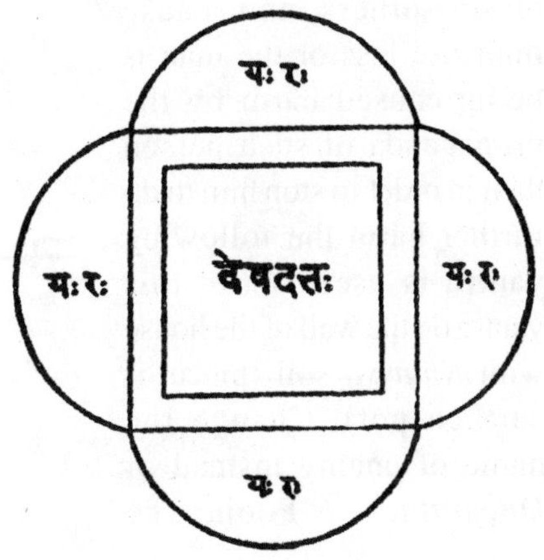

silver talisman or pendent. All recurring or threatened abortions will stop and she will be saved from such trouble.

Uchattan yantra for tenant

When one is teased by a man or enemy and want to stop him or in case of dispute with a tenant, this yantra is very useful for this purpose. When this yantra is used tenant will leave the place and go else where and the devotee is saved. Write this yantra on *Bhojpatra* with stylus of crow feather using the ink of juice of *neem* tree leaves. Write the name of enemy etc. in the centre of the yantra after replacing *devdatta*.

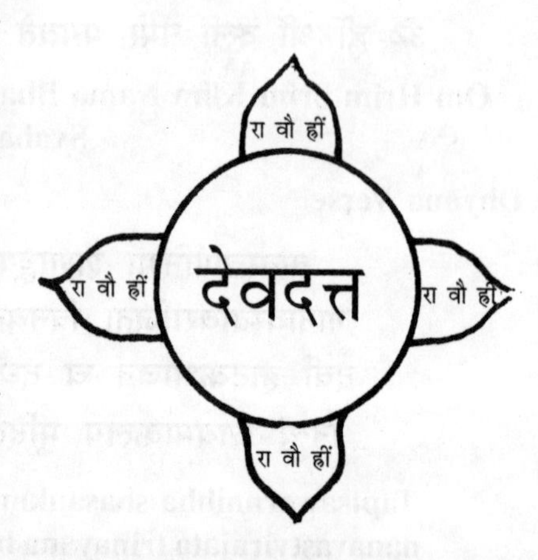

After performing *pooja* as per rituals, bury the yantra in ground in reverse direction. Write the name of the intended person in place of *devdatta*. The devotee is advised to keep this whole process as a guarded secret which should only be known to him.

To stop person to harm

When any body teases others and cause immense loss or the man is being caused harm by the propaganda of such person then in order to stop him to do further harm the following yantra is used. Write this yantra on the wall of the house with *Khariya* soil (piece of earthen pot). Change the name of enemy instead of *Devdatta*. Pooja be

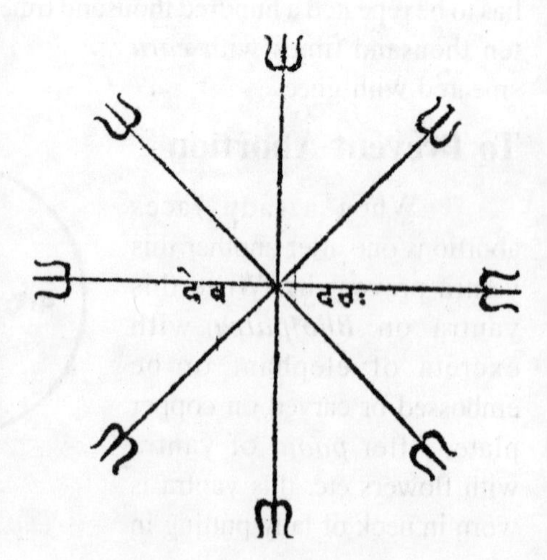

performed of yantra with white flowers fruits essence, white clothes etc. Invite one *Brahmin* for lunch. After that recite the following mantra for eleven thousand times. The enemy will stop doing against the person and keep his mouth shut. The mantra is recited for thousand and eight times.

श्री शिव प्रियताम् ॥
Shri Shiv Priyatam ॥

Yantra for stopping a person to talk against you

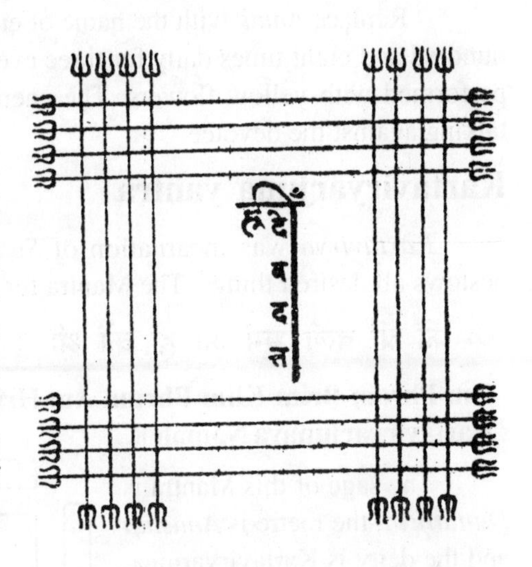

When a person is continuously talking against you or you have either been harmed or you fear harm from him, use this yantra to stop him talking against you. Write this yantra with *Khariya* soil (piece of earthen pot) on a stone stab, perform *pooja* of yantra with flowers etc. After that invite a *brahmin* for lunch and after that recite the mantra **श्री विद्या प्रियताम् ॥** (**Shri Vidya Priyatam ॥**). Use the name of enemy instead of *Devdutt.* Enemy will stop talking against you.

To stop enemy doing evils

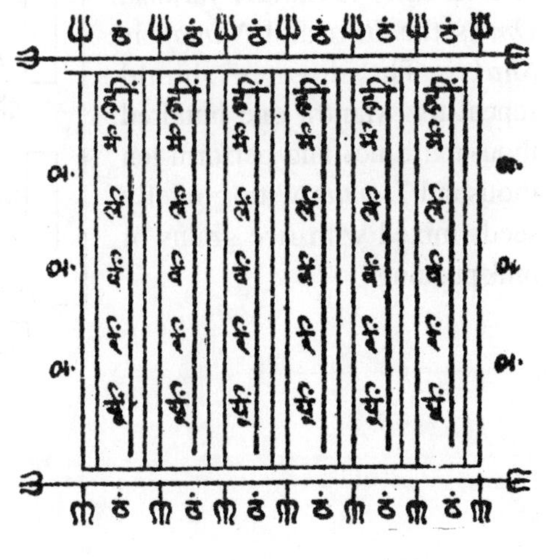

When an enemy is constantly troubling you and does not stop doing evils and in addition talks too much against you. Put a stop to him through this effective yantra. Write this yantra on with *Gorochan*, perform pooja of yantra with flowers. The mantra for recital is:-

ॐ हृदल्लयूं ल ल ल ल अमुकस्य मुखं स्तंभय ठः ठः ठः ठः ठः स्वाहा ॥

Om hardllyum la la la la Amukassaya mukham stambhaya tha tha tha tha tha swaha ॥

Replace *Amuk* with the name of enemy. Recite this mantra one hundred and eight times daily for three evenings and *pooja* of yantra be performed with yellow flowers. The enemy will stop doing evils and talking against the devotee.

Kartaviryarjuna yantra

Kartavirya was incarnation of *Sudarsana* discus. This yantra bestows all desired things. The Mantra for recital is:-

ॐ फ्रों ब्रीं क्लीं भ्रुमं आं ह्रीं क्रों श्रीं हुं फट् कार्तवीर्यार्जुनाय नमः ॥

Om Phrom Brim Klim Bhrum Am Hrim Krom Srim Hum Phat Kartaviryarjunaya Namah ॥

The sage of this Mantra is *Dattatreya*, the metre is *Anustup* and the deity is Kartaviryarjuna. *Om* is the *Bija* and *Namah* is *Shakti*. The devotee should repeat the Mantra one hundred thousand times and perform ten thousand *Homas* with gingelly seeds mixed with rice grains or milk pudding.

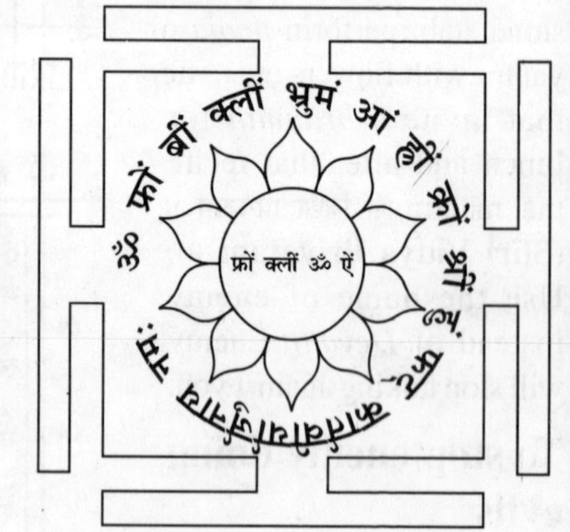

Dhyana verse

उद्यत्सूर्यसहस्त्रकान्तिरखिलक्षेणीधवैर्वन्दितो हस्तानां
शतपञ्चकेन च दधच्चापानिषूंस्तावतः।
कण्ठे हाटकमालया परिवृतह्रींश्चक्रावतारो हरेः
पायात्स्यंदनगोऽरुणाभवसनः श्री कार्तवीर्यो नृपः ॥

Udyatsurya sahasar kantirkhilksaani dhavivarandito hastaanam
Satpanchken cha dadhchchaapanishustawat ।
kante haatkamalaye parivarthrimschakraavtaro hare
payatasayandangoarunabhavsana shri kartiviro narpa ॥

Design of the yantra

The deity is to be worshipped in the *Vaisnava* pedestal in the Yantra. The yantra consists of ten petal lotus. In the circle write *Phrom* (फ्रों) `*Klim* (क्लीं) *Om* (ॐ) *Aim* (ऐं). The ten *Bijas* beginning with *Om* and ending with *Hum* (हुं) should be written in the petals. The other syllables i.e. *Phat Kartaviryarjunaya Namah* (फट् कार्तवीर्यार्जुनाय नमः) should be written in the spaces between petals. All the vowels with *Sasasa* should be written in the filaments. The other letters should be written all rounds. In the four corners of *Bhupura* the *Bhuta* letters (Here Ur, I, A, L) should be written. The yantra is written with *Asthgandh* on the ground.

Usage of the yantra

The ground wherein the yantra is written should be meticulously clean. The water pot should be placed there on. The deity should be invoked therein and worshipped. The Mantra is to be repeated touching the water pot; remain celibate throughout the period. Repeat the mantra a thousand times. For the sake of achieving everything desires, sprinkle holy-water from the pot on every one who is near and dear.

The person sprinkled with the waters of the holy pot is blessed with sons, fame, riddance from ailments, longevity, fluency of speech, overlay women and amicability with his own men. If there is any disturbance from enemies, this Yantra has to be installed for wading off the fear from the enemies.

Bhutyakshni prasanta karak yantra

This yantra is used by those persons who are found of calling spirits. This yantra pleases the spirits and does not harm them. It is also believed that these spirits often come to rescue such persons. The devotee should write this yantra under the Banyan tree for one hundred thousand times on paper with the ink of *Asthgandh*.

तं	तं	तं	तं
पं	पं	पं	पं
इं	इं	इं	इं
लं	लं	लं	लं

Yantra for cure from leprosy and other associated diseases

This yantra is to be written on some auspicious Thursday on copper plate. The yantra is to be energised on the same day. The mantra is to be recited for 108 times daily while applying the mixture of turmeric, *ram bhangra, indra varuni, bavchi*, and blue of blue flower on the spot where the devotee is suffering from leprosy. If water is sanitised through the mantra and given to the patient the medicine starts giving early results. The mantra for recital is:

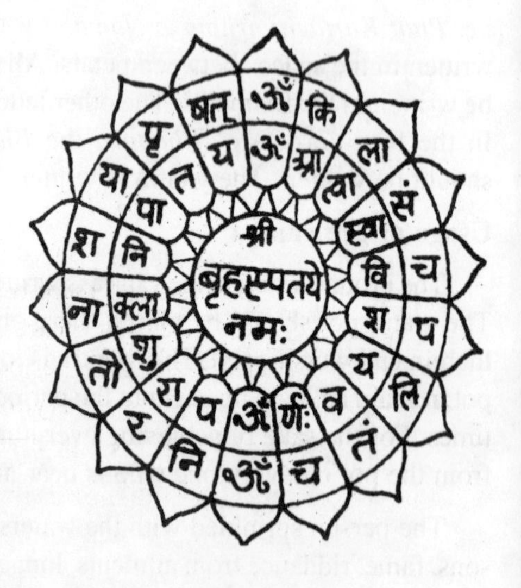

ॐ किलासं च पलितं च निरतो नाशया पृषत् ।
आत्वा स्वा विशय वर्णः परा शुक्लानि पातय ॥

Om Kilasam cha palitam cha nitro nashya parsht ।
Atva swa vushwa varna para shukalani patya ॥

Vaibhavaayurdata yantra (Yantra for longivity and comforts)

This yantra is considered for longivity, children and enhancement of business. First of all recite the following mantra for twenty one thousand times for realisation.

ॐ संमा सिञ्चन्तवादित्याः संमा सिञ्चन्त्वग्न्यः। इन्द्रः समस्यान् सिञ्चतु प्रजया च धनेन च । दीर्घमायुः कृणोत मे ॥

Om Sanma Sinchant vaditya sanma sinchantvagnaya । indra samasyana sinchtoo pargaya cha dhanen cha । dirgham ayu karnot me ॥

Now write the yantra on a copper plate and energise it. Worship the yantra through following mantra. The mantra is recited for twenty one thousand times.

ॐ संमा सिञ्चन्तु मरुतः सं पूषा सं बृहस्पतिः। समा यमाग्निः संचन्तु प्रजया च धनेन च । दीर्घमायुः कृणोतु में ॥

Om Sanma Sinchantu Maruta sam pusha sam brashapti । sama yamaagni sanchtu pargaya cha dhanan cha । dirgham ayu karnot me ॥

If the devotee worships this yantra he would lead a better and comfortable life. If some one wanted to use this yantra to check premature death, then start the process on Thursday, Monday or Wednesday. The devotee should sit on a seat made of wood or wool and do three thousand japa daily with the rosary of *rudraksh*. On the seventh day do homa with twenty one hundred mantras with pure ghee and *Asthgandh*. If he does this religiously then he will not

face premature death. For all other desires same process is adopted.

Sarvakarya siddhi karak yantra

This yantra is provided by Lord Shiva to his consort *Parvati*. Write this yantra on *bhojpatra* with *Asthgandh.* Make an amulet of this yantra by tying either in gold, silver or copper. Perform *pooja* of the yantra with dhoop, lamp, and sweets. Tie the yantra on right hand or wear it in the neck.

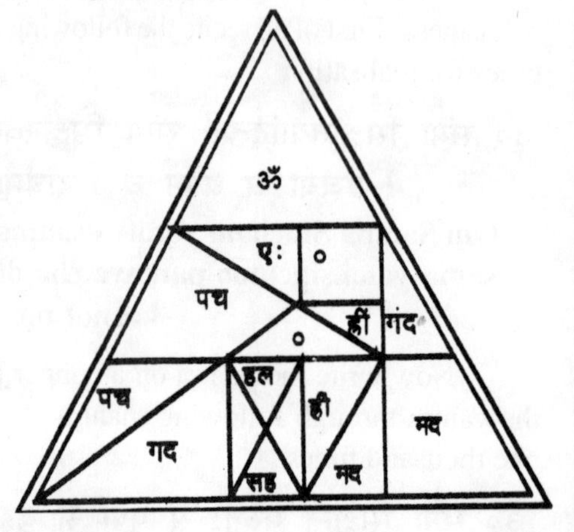

Dust swapan nashak yantra

If some one dreams bad during night then he should write this yantra with *Asthgandh* on *bhojpatra* and give smoke of *Googal*. The yantra is worn as an amulet and the same is tied in the neck. The person will not dream bad during night time.

गं	छं	जं	चं
छं	नं	जं	ठं
ठं	जं	ठं	चं
नं	छं	जं	टं

Vridhi yantra

This yantra is written on the day of Deepawali and kept in the safe or any place where the devotee feels that the desired increase is lacking.

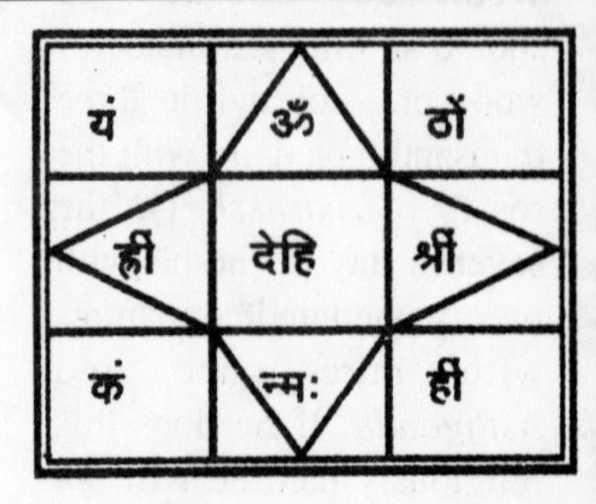

Swapan Varahi pooja yantra

This yantra is used for realisation of all desires connected with love and wealth. The mantra for recital is:-

ॐ ह्रीं नमो वाराहि घोरे स्वप्नं
ठः ठः स्वाहा ।

Om Hrim namo Varahi Ghore Svapanam Thah Thah Swaha ।

The sage of the mantra is *Isvara*, metre is *jagati* and the deity is *Svapnavarahi*. *Om* is the *Bija* and *Hrim* is *Shakti*, *Thah thah* is the *kilkam*. The mantra is repeated for a hundred thousand times and *homa* is performed with blue lotuses and good gingelly seeds. For realisation of all cherished dreams the devotee should apply the mantra by performing *tarpan* with the coconut or holy water.

Dhyana verse

ॐ मेघश्यामरुचिं मनोहरकुचां नेत्रयोद्भासितां कोलास्यां
शशिशेखरामचलया दंष्ट्रातले शोभिताम् ।
बिभ्राणां स्वकराम्बुजैरसिलतां चर्मापि पाशं सृणिं
वाराहीमनुचिन्तयेद्धयवरारूढां शुभालंकृतिम् ॥

Om Megshyam ruchim manoharkucham netryodbhsitam kolasyam
Shashi shekra machlaya danstratale shobhitam ।
bhibranam savkarambujeerasiltam charmapi pasham sarnim
varahi manuchintyedhyvararudam subhalankritim ।।

For the purpose of *Vashikaran* the devotee should keep fast on *ashtami* or *chaturdashi* of the lunar fortnight and bring clay from the cross roads, river banks or the hut of the potter and mix in the *dhatura* juice. Make an image of the intended person and inspire it. The yantra is written on the shroud of dead body with the blood of a man, crow and goat. The blood is mixed with the ash of funeral pyre. The yantra consists of a triangle, a hexagon, and the bhupura. Following mantra is written inside the bhupura as shown in the picture on page no. 310.

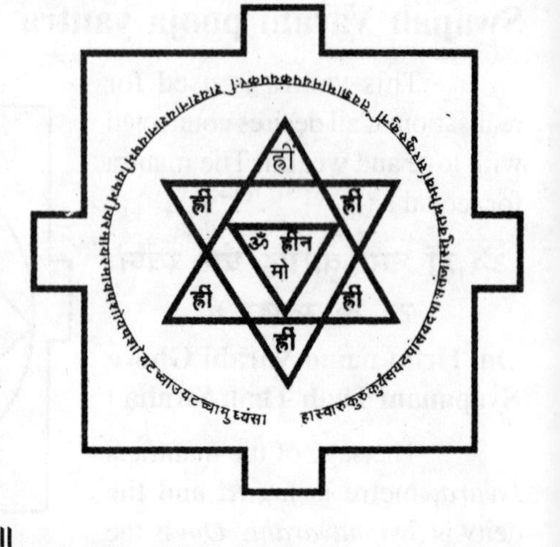

साध्यम् उच्चाटय
उच्चाटय शोषय मारय मारय
भीषय भीषय नाशाय
नाशाय शिरः कम्पाय कम्पाय
ममज्ञावर्तिनं कुरु कुरु
सर्वाभिमतवस्तुजातं सम्पदाय
सम्पदाय सर्व कुरु कुरु स्वाहा ॥

Sadhyam ucchataya ucchataya shoshya maraya maraya bhishaya bhishaya nashaya shiraa kampaya kampaya mamgavartinam kuru kuru sarvabhimatvastujatam sampaday sampaday sarv kuru kuru swaha ॥

Swapaneshwari pooja yantra

After realisation of the yantra it is used at night. During night the devotee should repeat the mantra in front of the yantra. The bed to be used should be of deer skin scattered over *kusa* grass on the ground. The mantra for recital is:-

ॐ श्रीं स्वपनेश्वरी कार्यं मे वद स्वाहा ॥

Om Srim Svapaneswari karyam me vada swaaha ॥

Dhyan Verse

ॐ वराभये पद्मयुगं दधानां करैश्चतुर्भिः कनकासनस्थनम् ।
सिताम्बरां शारदचन्द्रकान्ति स्वप्नेश्वरीं नौमि विभूषणाठयाम् ॥

**Om Varabhaye padamyugam dadhanam karayeeshchaturbhikanakasanamsthanam ।
Sitambram sharadchanderkanti swapanshawari naumi Vibhusanathayam ॥**

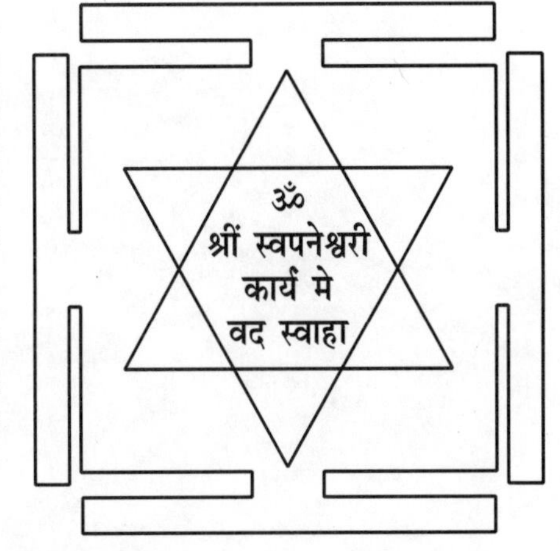

The sage of the mantra is *Upmanyu*, metre *brahati* and the deity is Svapaneswari. The mantra is repeated for a hundred thousand times and ten thousand homa are performed with *bilva* leaves.

When devi comes to the devotee in the dream, he should tell his cherished desires to the goddess.

सर्वे भवन्तु सुखिनः सर्वे सन्तु निरामया ।
सर्वे भद्राणि पश्यन्तु मा कश्चिद् दुःखभाग्भवेत् ॥

ॐ द्यौ शान्तिरतरिक्षं शान्तिः पृथ्वी शन्तिरापः
शान्ति रोषधयः शान्ति वनस्पतयः शान्तिर्विश्वे
देवाः शान्तिब्रह्मा शान्तिः सर्वशान्ति शान्तिरेव
शान्ति सामा शान्तिरेधि ॥ ॐ शान्तिः शान्तिः
शान्तिः ॐ ॥

ॐ श्री हनुमते नमः॥